AF840279

"*The Dearest Birth Right of the People of England*"

The Jury in the History of the Common Law

"The Dearest Birth Right of the People of England"

The Jury in the History of the Common Law

Edited by

JOHN W CAIRNS
and
GRANT McLEOD

·HART·
PUBLISHING

OXFORD – PORTLAND OREGON
2002

Hart Publishing
Oxford and Portland, Oregon

Published in North America (US and Canada) by
Hart Publishing
c/o International Specialized Book Services
5804 NE Hassalo Street
Portland, Oregon
97213-3644
USA

Distributed in Netherlands, Belgium and Luxembourg by
Intersentia, Churchillaan 108
B2900 Schoten
Antwerpen
Belgium

© The editors and contributors severally, 2002

The editors and contributors have asserted their rights under the
Copyright, Designs and Patents Act 1988, to be identified as
the authors of this work.

Hart Publishing is a specialist legal publisher based in Oxford, England.
To order further copies of this book or to request a list of other
publications please write to:

Hart Publishing, Salters Boatyard, Folly Bridge, Abingdon Rd,
Oxford, OX1 4LB
Telephone: +44 (0)1865 245533 Fax: +44 (0) 1865 794882
email: mail@hartpub.co.uk
WEBSITE: http//:www.hartpub.co.uk

British Library Cataloguing in Publication Data
Data Available

ISBN 1-84113-325-6 (hardback)

Typeset by John Saunders Design & Production. Reading UK
Printed and bound in Great Britain by
Biddles Ltd www.biddles.co.uk

Preface

This book on the jury in the common law arose out of the Fourteenth British Legal History Conference on the theme of "Parliaments, Juries, and the Law" held in Edinburgh in July, 1999, in the suitably grand surroundings of the Old College of the University of Edinburgh, on the invitation of the Centre for Legal History and the Faculty of Law of the University of Edinburgh. Some 120 individuals attended. The Conference saw a rich mix of papers on these two main related themes, only a small number of which are to be found in this volume. A full list of all the papers given (other than those revised as chapters here) will be found below, as will an account of past conferences and published proceedings.

One highlight of the proceedings was the illustrated lecture on the history of Parliament House in Edinburgh, given by Lord Cullen, which opened the Conference.[1] This fascinating building, constructed by the Town Council of Edinburgh in the 1630s for the Scottish Parliament and the Court of Session, has grown into a complex series of historic and modern structures running between the High Kirk of St Giles and the Cowgate. Among other illustrations were those of the sitting of the historic Court of Session. The slides displayed by Lord Cullen provoked a question from an English barrister: where had the jury sat? This revealed the fact that Scottish civil courts had managed without juries until the nineteenth century! The introduction of juries led to necessary rebuilding of the civil courts. There had always been juries in Scottish criminal trials; the recent introduction of them in civil matters is a topic not yet thoroughly researched, but indicating the interesting nature of the Scottish civil procedure and law. In the first chapter of this volume, the first-named editor explores some of the complex issues raised by this transplant of an English institution into Scottish soil and sets a programme for further research, while also indicating the breadth and rage of the themes raised by the topic of the jury.[2]

The jury has long been a staple of English legal history. In recent years one need only point to Professor Cornish's important book of 1968 as indicating its significance for research.[3] Major interest has tended to focus on the jury in criminal trials, because of its implications for social and political history as well as legal history narrowly conceived. The recent outstanding

[1] See also The Hon. Lord Cullen, *Parliament House: A Short History and Guide* (Edinburgh, Scottish Courts Administration, 1992).

[2] See N T Phillipson, *The Scottish Whigs and the Reform of the Court of Session 1785-1830*, Stair Soc., vol. 37 (Edinburgh, 1990); see also I D Willock, *The Origins and Development of the Jury in Scotland*, Stair Soc. vol. 23 (Edinburgh, 1966).

[3] W R Cornish, *The Jury* (London, Allen Lane, 1968).

work of Professors Cockburn and Green can be picked out in particular.[4] Related work, not specifically focusing on the jury but still of primary importance here, is that by Professor Langbein.[5] The last has also been strongly concerned with developing an understanding of the appropriate comparative context and the issues of proof with which much of the discussion of the jury is often connected.[6] Indeed, there has been much fruitful interdisciplinary work on such matters.[7] The linkage between the criminal jury and the development of certain rules of evidence, however, can easily be overstated. This indeed is the lesson of the chapter here by Professor Friedman on the jury and the hearsay rule. Of course, the criminal jury is full of political resonance in England: a political resonance transplanted to North America, where, thanks to certain constitutional provisions in the United States, it perhaps sounds even louder than in England. Here Professor Pole's chapter on the Anglo-American jury and, especially, the colonial Grand Jury, indicates just how the Grand Jury could be used to articulate political and social claims in the eighteenth century.

Professor Groot's chapter shows how early the jury started to make findings of fact in a way that allowed them to manipulate the result of the trial. Jury lenity or equity is a standard theme, almost a cliché of legal history. The chapter by Dr Handler *infra* shows, however, that it was not a simple issue. Old Bailey juries were unwilling to convict forgers, not because of sympathy towards them, but rather out of distrust of the Bank of England. The jurors were made up of men from the class who suffered most because the Bank's notes were easy to forge. Moreover, the acquittals resulted from a particular and complex series of events and initiated interesting developments of their own, ultimately feeding into the debates over reform of criminal procedure. This was almost the swan song of the activist jury. Handler's study should alert us to the importance of not making overly broad claims about the actions of juries from a few examples.

For an institution absolutely central to the common law, there has been surprisingly little recent work on the civil jury, in comparison with the level

[4] See T A Green, *Verdict According to Conscience: Perspectives on the English Criminal Trial Jury 1200-1800* (Chicago, University of Chicago Press, 1985); J S Cockburn, *A History of English Assizes, 1558-1714* (Cambridge, University Press, 1972). Cockburn has also edited collections of assize records. The two edited an important collection of essays: J S Cockburn and T A Green, *Twelve Good Men and True: The Criminal Jury in England, 1200-1800* (Princeton, University Press, 1988).

[5] J H Langbein, "The Criminal Law Before the Lawyers", (1978) 45 *University of Chicago LR*, 263; idem, "Shaping the Eighteenth-Century Criminal Trial: A View from the Ryder Sources", (1983) 50 *University of Chicago LR*, 1.

[6] J H Langbein, *Prosecuting Crime in the Renaissance: England, Germany, France* (Cambridge, Harvard University Press, 1974); idem, *Torture and the Law of Proof: Europe and England in the Ancien Régime* (Chicago, University of Chicago Press, 1977).

[7] See, e.g., B Shapiro, *"Beyond Reasonable Doubt" and "Probable Cause": Historical Perspectives on the Anglo-American Law of Evidence* (Berkeley, University of California Press, 1991).

of interest displayed in the criminal. Perhaps this is because it is seen as dealing with more technical issues of legal rules and procedure; perhaps also, the criminal jury raises interesting interpretative issues that range far beyond the interests of legal historians. This volume should go some way in showing the new research being carried out on the jury.[8] This said, there have been some studies of the first significance, as well, of course, as the important discussions in standard textbooks such as that of Professor Baker.[9] One can point to a few as of special significance. Of the first importance has been the work of Professor Oldham, who has devoted a series of studies to research on the jury. Amongst his most important work has been a series of articles on the special jury.[10] Special juries have achieved almost mythical significance as the institutions by which, for example, Lord Mansfield created, supposedly almost single-handedly, a modern English commercial law. One can see, of course, that this is a fit topic for the editor of Mansfield's notebooks.[11] Oldham's chapter *infra* supplements his fundamental research on the special jury. His work also includes a study of the jury of matrons, who had the task of determining whether a litigant or convicted individual was pregnant.[12] Again Oldham's chapter extends our existing knowledge of this institution. The issue of special juries also has a particular contemporary relevance in the United States, where the Seventh Amendment to the constitution protects the right to a jury trial in suits where more than twenty dollars is at issue. This has given rise to considerable and indeed also historical discussion.[13] The obvious issue is: what right to a jury trial is protected? The test is a historical one, being the right to a trial by jury as it existed in English law in 1791. Professor Oldham has recently addressed this problem and follows up that study *infra*.[14]

[8] And indeed the other conference papers listed below.

[9] J H Baker, *An Introduction to English Legal History*, 3rd edn (London, Butterworths, 1990).

[10] J Oldham, "The Origins of the Special Jury", (1983) 50 *University of Chicago LR* 137; idem, "Special Juries in England: Nineteenth Century Usage and Reform," (1987) 8 *JLH* 148; idem, "The History of the Special (Struck) Jury in the United States and Its Relation To Voir Dire Practices, the Reasonable Cross-Section Requirement, and Peremptory Challenges", (1998) 6 *William and Mary Bill of Rights Journal* 623.

[11] J Oldham, *The Mansfield Manuscripts and the Growth of English Law in the Eighteenth Century* (Chapel Hill and London, University of North Carolina Press, 1992).

[12] J Oldham, "On Pleading the Belly: A History of the Jury of Matrons", (1985) 6 *Criminal Justice History* 1

[13] P Devlin, "Jury Trial of Complex Cases: English Practice at the Time of the Seventh Amendment", (1980) 80 *Columbia LR* 43; idem, "Equity, Due Process and the Seventh Amendment: A Commentary on the *Zenith* Case", (1983) 81 *Michigan LR* 1571; M Arnold, "A Historical Inquiry into the Right to Trial by Jury in Complex Civil Litigation", (1980) 128 *Pennsylvania LR* 829.

[14] J Oldham, "The Seventh Amendment Right to Jury Trial: Late-Eighteenth-Century Practice Reconsidered", in K O'Donovan and G R Rubin (eds), *Human Rights and Legal History* (Oxford, University Press, 2000), 225.

The work of Oldham and others has exposed much about the eighteenth-century jury. As we move into the twenty-first century, the nineteenth century is in danger of becoming one of the new dark ages of legal history. So much of the agenda of English legal history in particular was set in that century by Maitland, that it is still difficult for historians of law to see the nineteenth century as an object of historical study; this effect is compounded by the fact that many of that century's cases are still taught as setting out the pre-eminent doctrines of the common law. There have been particular studies, of course, notably the classic study of the Victorian jury by Jackson.[15] This very obvious gap in studies of the jury is here remedied by two important chapters, one by Dr Lobban, the other by Dr Getzler. Both chapters reveal a more complex story behind the decline of the civil jury in the Victorian period than the research of Jackson allowed; also, both strongly reinforce the critique of the thesis associated with Morton Horwitz and Patrick Atiyah that the judges squeezed out the jury in favour of efficient market principles.[16] Of course, not everyone favoured restriction of the role of the jury and the circumscribing of its actions by increasing bodies of substantive and adjectival law. Getzler shows this clearly with his study in particular of the litigation in *Lister* v. *Perryman*.[17] His chapter clearly demonstrates the complexity of the issues, especially in torts. Lobban's magisterial chapter marshals a considerable body of evidence, statistical and drawn from a wide range of sources, such as periodicals and correspondence, to present a more nuanced picture of the decline of the jury in the Victorian period, challenging the general views found in standard texts. Lobban argues that the jury remained an important part of the English legal scene, well into the twentieth century. Lobban's work presents an important challenge to received orthodoxies.

In the introduction to *Twelve Good Men and True* in 1987, Professors Cockburn and Green regretted that their study was limited to that of the criminal jury and that it has generally been studied separately from that of the civil jury. They hoped for a similar set of essays to be produced on the civil jury.[18] This set of essays goes some way to filling the gap they identified. It also has a comparative aspect, considering the transplant of the civil jury to Scotland, while also paying some attention to the jury in the United States. The volume is not limited, however, merely to the civil jury. Some of the essays expressly concern the criminal jury, while others explore territory

[15] R M Jackson, "The Incidence of Jury Trial during the Past Century", (1937) 1 *Modern LR* 132.

[16] M J Horwitz, *The Transformation of American Law 1780-1860* (Cambridge, Harvard University Press, 1977); P S Atiyah, *The Rise and Fall of Freedom of Contract* (Oxford, University Press, 1979). See, above all, A W B Simpson, "The Horwitz Thesis and the History of Contracts", in idem, *Legal Theory and Legal History. Essays on the Common Law* (London, Hambledon Press, 1987), 203.

[17] (1870) LR 4 HL 535.

[18] Cockburn and Green (eds.), *supra* n. 4, xv-xvi.

that involves both. Here one can point to Maureen Mulholland's discussion of the jury in manorial courts, raising questions about the links between these courts and the common law, and David Seipp's fascinating account of the travails and miseries of the late mediaeval jury: this chapter also provides important insights into how juries acquired the information they needed to decide the causes before them. Of course, in the long perspective, juries are relatively modern. The legal systems of the British Isles have had other methods of fact-finding, methods that have attracted increasing interest. From a comparative point of view one can point to Professor Bartlett's study of the ordeal.[19] As the jury was increasing in importance in the English Common Law, in Scotland the central civil court adopted—and adapted—the Romano-canonical procedures of the church courts. Professor Jenkins, however, shows us another tradition, that of Wales, which rejected battle and the ordeal, but developed its own complex set of rules of proof by oaths.

If this volume does not exactly meet the challenge thrown down by Cockburn and Green, it nonetheless goes a considerable part of the way and, even more importantly, shows the way (or ways) forward for further research. It demonstrates how the jury should be studied comparatively, ignoring questions of whether jurisdiction is criminal or civil. It shows how there should always be sensitivity to the relationship between rules relating to proof and the jury and an awareness of how received traditions may be challenged. Moreover, the ideological justifications of the jury are shown to have a significant impact on legal practice. Finally, the volume opens up the topic of the jury in the nineteenth century for further research.

[19] R Bartlett, *Trial by Fire and Water: The Medieval Judicial Ordeal* (Oxford, Clarendon Press, 1986).

Contents

List of Contributors

John W Cairns
Professor of Legal History, University of Edinburgh

Richard D Friedman
Ralph W Aigler Professor of Law, University of Michigan

Joshua Getzler
Fellow of St. Hugh's College, Oxford

Roger D Groot
Alumni Professor of Law, Washington and Lee University

Philip Handler
Lecturer in Law, University of Leicester

Dafydd Jenkins
Professor of Legal History and Welsh Law Emeritus, University of Wales Aberystwyth

Michael Lobban
Reader in Law, Queen Mary, University of London

Grant McLeod
Sometime Lecturer in Law, University of Edinburgh

Maureen Mulholland
Lecturer in Law, University of Manchester

James Oldham
St Thomas More Professor of Law and Legal History, Georgetown University

J R Pole
Rhodes Professor of American History Emeritus, University of Oxford

David J Seipp
Professor of Law, Boston University

List of Abbreviations

AJLH	*American Journal of Legal History*
BL	British Library
CP 40	Public Record Office, Plea Rolls, Court of Common Pleas
EETS	Early English Text Society (London, 1864)
ER	English Reports
f.	folio(s)
Hil.	Hilary
How. St. Tr.	T B Howell, *Complete Collection of State Trials and Proceedings for High Treason and other Crimes and Misdemeanours from the Earliest Period*, 33 vols (London, 1809-26)
JLH	*Journal of Legal History*
JUST 1	Public Record Office, Plea Rolls, Justices in Eyre
LHR	*Law and History Review*
LJ	*Law Journal*
LQ	*Law Quarterly*
LQR	*Law Quarterly Review*
LR	*Law Review*
Mich.	Michaelmas
Pasch.	Paschal
pl.	plea
Pollock and Maitland	F Pollock and F W Maitland, *History of English Law before the Time of Edward I*, 2nd edn (Cambridge, University Press, 1898; repr. 1968)
PP	Parliamentary Papers
PRO	Public Record Office (London)
Rot. Parl.	*Rotuli Parliamentorum* (London, 1783)
RS	Rolls Series: *Rerum Britannicarum Medii Aevi Scriptores* (London, 1858-97)
Seld. Soc.	Selden Society Publications (London, 1887-)
ser.	series

Soc.	Society
Trin.	Trinity
UCL	University College, University of London
YB	Yearbook; references are given by term, regnal year, placitum, and folio

Acknowledgements

The main organiser of the Conference was the first of the editors of this volume, although he gratefully acknowledges the assistance he was given by Ms Andrea Loux and, especially, by Professor Hector L MacQueen, both of the Faculty of Law, University of Edinburgh. Much administrative help was also given by Mr Hamish MacAndrew and Mrs Frances Wright of Edinburgh Research and Innovation and also by Mrs Elaine Yuill, sometime Secretary in the former Department of Private Law, University of Edinburgh. Thanks for sponsorship and support are also due to The Stair Society, the Centre for Legal History and the Department of Private Law, both in the University of Edinburgh, the *Journal of Legal History*, Cambridge University Press, Oxford University Press, the Hambledon Press, and W. Green, the Scottish Law Publisher. The cartoon from *Punch* on p. 208 is reproduced by permission.

Conference Papers not Included in the Present Volume

Lord Cullen (Lord Justice-General of Scotland), "Parliament House"

Mike Macnair (St Hugh's College, Oxford), "Jurors as Witnesses to Local Reputation: Possible Antecedents and Implications"

Mark Godfrey, "Parliament, the King's Council and Jurisdiction over Land in Scotland, 1425-1559"

Thomas E Carney, "The English Parliament, the Scottish Estates, and the Parliament of Great Britain: Religion, Law, and the Politics of Union"

Paul T Riggs, "Parliament and Criminal Justice in Scotland in the 18th and 19th Centuries"

Rose Melikan, "Queen Caroline and the House of Lords, 1820"

Dan Klerman, "Judges, Jurors and Female Appellants: Private Prosecution by Thirteenth-Century Women"

Sue Sheridan Walker, "The Civil Jury and the Resolution of Pleas of Dower in Thirteenth- and Fourteenth-Century England"

Anthony Musson, "The Legal Voice in the English Parliament, 1299-1399"

Andrew Lewis, "Breton Assizes and the Entail"

Richard W Ireland, "Putting Oneself on Whose Country? Carmarthenshire Juries in the Mid-Nineteenth Century"

Lynette M Costello, "The Stannary Parliaments: Celtic Heritage or Miners' Gala?"

A W B Simpson, "Victorian Substantive Law: Controlling the Jury"

Michael L Nash, "'Leaven in the Lump': Bishops in the House of Lords"

Julian Goodare, "The Admission of Lairds to the Scottish Parliament"

Gwen Seabourne, "The Coroner's Jury and its Place in the Proud History of Jury Perversity"

Charles Donahue, "Jurors, Suitors, Suit, and Witnesses in Lex Mercatoria (c. 1285)"

David Millon, "Parliamentary Legislation and Jury Discretion"

John Finlay "Inordinate and Erroneous Proceedings: The King's Advocate and Inquest Juries in Early-Sixteenth-Century Scotland"

Penny Tucker, "The Triumph of the Jury: Chance, Judgment or Politics?"

H Narsinghen, "The Incorporation, Adaptation and Evolution of the Westminster Model of Parliament in Mauritius"

M J Burr, "The Royal Scot: Ecclesiastical Taxation in Anglo-Saxon England"

Joseph Biancalana, "The Writing Requirement in Covenant"

Lorie Charlesworth, "The Legal Settlement of Arthur Clennan and Little Dorrit: A Poor Law History"

Christopher Fritsch, "A Most Ancient and Republican Process? Examining the Social and Economic Background of Jurors in Germanic Regions in Pennsylvania"

W M Gordon, "Balfour's Practicks: The Registrum"

C H van Rhee, "Romano-Canonical Influences: Civil Procedure and the Judicature Acts (1873-1875)"

The British Legal History Conference

The first British Legal History Conference was held in 1972 in Aberystwyth on the initiative of Professor Dafydd Jenkins. Since then there have been meetings at London/Cambridge (1974 and 1975), Edinburgh (1977), Birmingham (1979), Bristol (1981), Norwich (1983), Canterbury (1985), Cardiff (1987), Glasgow (1989), Oxford (1991), Exeter (1993), Durham (1995), Cambridge (1997), and Edinburgh (1999).

Proceedings of the Conference have been published as follows:

Legal History Studies 1972, ed. by D Jenkins (Cardiff, University of Wales Press, 1975)

Legal Records and the Historian, ed. by J H Baker (London, Royal Historical Society, 1978)

Law-Making and Law-Makers in British History, ed. by A Harding (London, Royal Historical Society, 1980)

Law, Litigants and the Legal Profession, ed. by W Ives and A H Manchester (London, Royal Historical Society, 1983)

Law and Social Change in British History, ed. by J A Guy and H G Beale (London, Royal Historical Society, 1984)

Customs, Courts and Counsel, ed. by A Kiralfy, M Slatter and R Virgoe, in *Journal of Legal History*, 5 (1984), and as a separate volume (London, Frank Cass, 1985)

The Political Context of Law, ed. by R Eales and D Sullivan (London, The Hambledon Press, 1987)

Legal Record and Historical Reality, ed. by T G Watkin (London, The Hambledon Press, 1989)

Legal History in the Making, ed. by W M Gordon and T D Fergus (London, The Hambledon Press, 1991)

The Life of the Law, ed. by P Birks (London, The Hambledon Press, 1993)

Law Reporting in Britain, ed. by C Stebbings (London, The Hambledon Press, 1995)

Community and Courts in Britain, 1150-1900, ed. by C W Brooks and M Lobban (London, The Hambledon Press, 1997)

Learning the Law: Teaching and the Transmission of English Law, 1150-1900, ed. by J A Bush and A Wijffels (London, The Hambledon Press, 1999)

1

"The Dearest Birth Right of the People of England": The Civil Jury in Modern Scottish Legal History

JOHN W CAIRNS (EDINBURGH)*

The main title of this book is taken from a motion put to the Society of Writers to His Majesty's Signet in 1815. The context was the introduction into Scots legal practice of trial by jury in civil causes. Two Whig members of this august body of Edinburgh lawyers disapproved of a Bill currently in Parliament to establish a separate Jury Court, since it did not make civil trial by jury compulsory in certain classes of case, but only at the discretion of the Court of Session. The Court was to be empowered to send specific issues of fact to be tried by a jury, on the model of the use of the jury in procedure in Chancery in England.[1] The legislation introducing the Jury Court in Scotland ultimately did allow for general issues to be put to a jury. Indeed, the scope for use of jury trial in Scotland was widened significantly in the 1820s, until the jurisdiction of the Jury Court was finally merged into that of the Court of Session in 1830.[2]

The terms of the Whig lawyers' motion indicates the extent to which jury trial had come to be seen not only as a defining characteristic of the (English) common law but also as having significant political impact as a mark of liberty and freedom. It indicated a society whose inhabitants were privileged and sufficiently educated to be able to decide the fate of the life and property of their fellow subjects (or citizens). This ideological role of the jury not only still has a significant resonance but perhaps remains central to popular

* The author is grateful to Mr D Jardine and Professor H L MacQueen for comments on the draft of this paper. The permission of the British Library Board is gratefully acknowledged for quotations from a manuscript under its care.

[1] See N T Phillipson, *The Scottish Whigs and the Reform of the Court of Session 1785–1830*, Stair Soc., vol. 37 (Edinburgh, 1990), 130–1.

[2] Jury Trial (Scotland) Act 1815 (55 Geo. III c. 42); see Phillipson, *supra* n. 1, 127–64; J W Cairns, "Historical Introduction", in K Reid and R Zimmermann (eds), *A History of Private Law in Scotland. Volume 1: Introduction and Property* (Oxford, University Press, 2000), 14 at 152–4.

understandings of the institution, as demonstrated by the heated contemporary debate over the abolition of the right (in England) for offenders to opt for jury trial, or controversies such as that over the level of jury awards—and decisions—in libel cases. The jury is, however, a complex phenomenon that carries multiple meanings and values. For example, for many in early-nineteenth-century Scotland, introduction of the civil jury was seen as a means, not only perhaps of promoting more efficient trial of certain civil matters, but also of carrying a significant message about the Union with England. With a variety of other measures at the beginning of the nineteenth century, it marked a departure from the Romano-canonical procedure of early modern Scots private law: the Union was being made more complete.[3] Moreover, by taking in some way power away from the judges of the Court of Session, it was also democratising Scotland and marking a transition from the "old corruption" that Whigs, such as Lord Cockburn, in his myth-making *Memorials of his Time*, were to see as marking eighteenth-century Scotland, and especially its courts.[4]

The Whig ideologues were able to argue that what was happening was the *revival* of civil jury trial, suggesting that, by adopting Romano-canonical procedure, Scots law had somehow gone on a strange detour from a natural progression of development. Medieval Scots law was seen as having been much the same as medieval English law, but as having subsequently gone a-whoring after the strange Gods of the *ius commune*. Scots law—and the Union—could therefore be perfected by the reintroduction of the jury.[5] Of course, the history was nonsense—as the perceptive and subtle historical sense of Walter Scott pointed out—but with a tempting and dangerous kernel of truth.[6] Process on brieve in medieval Scotland had indeed generally involved decisions by an inquest or jury of some type;[7] indeed, residual notions of an inquest had survived for the few very specialised brieves that had endured into the modern period, such as those of idiotry, succession, and tutory.[8] But what the Scottish Whigs of course favoured was the

[3] Cairns, *supra* n. 2, 142–6, 151–5, 166–8. For a general explanation of the Romano-canonical nature of Scottish civil procedure, see R C van Caenegem, "History of European Civil Procedure", in *International Encyclopaedia of Comparative Law* (Tübingen, J C B Mohr, 1971–), vol. XVI.ii, 76–77 § 58.

[4] H Cockburn, *Memorials of his Time* (Edinburgh, Adam and Charles Black, 1856).

[5] Cairns, *supra* n. 2, 163–5.

[6] W Scott, "View of the Changes Proposed and Adopted in the Administration of Justice in Scotland", (1810) 1, pt. 2 *The Edinburgh Annual Register for 1808*, 342, reprinted in *Sir Walter Scott's Annual Register*, ed. by K Curry (Knoxville, University of Tennessee Press, 1977), 170 at 200–1

[7] See now, above all, H L MacQueen, *Common Law and Feudal Society in Medieval Scotland* (Edinburgh, University Press,1993), 50 and *passim*; Cairns, *supra* n. 2, 26–7.

[8] See, e.g., J Dalrymple, Viscount Stair, *Institutions of the Law of Scotland Deduced from its Originals, and Collated with the Civil, Canon and Feudal Laws, and with the Customs of Neighbouring Nations*, 2nd edn (Edinburgh, Heir of Andrew Anderson 1693; Edinburgh, University Press, 1981), 816–7 (IV.iii.5–7).

eighteenth-century English jury, with its strong implications and myths of political freedom—no Star Chamber—and protection of property rights from arbitrary judicial and governmental action. The jury symbolised the legal culmination of a history redolent with great events in the rise of freedom: Magna Carta, the Commons' resistance to Charles I, the Glorious Revolution. This was indeed the mythic English history that Scots themselves helped propound. John Dalrymple wrote in his *Memoirs of Great Britain*: "The history of England is the history of liberty."[9] Many of the Whig reformers had been former pupils or admirers of John Millar, Professor of Civil Law in the University of Glasgow, and author of *An Historical View of the English Government from the Settlement of the Saxons* (1783). The focus on the government of England was notable in a discussion that dismissed the significance of the Scottish past.[10]

Of course, there were arguments in favour of the civil jury that were not dependent on such "Whig" history and purely ideological aims. One evident desire was to create a court procedure that would diminish the level of appeals from the Court of Session to the House of Lords. Around 1800, four-fifths of the appeals to the House of Lords came from the Court of Session. In the early years of the nineteenth century, the Lords were at least three years in arrears in their business and it was easy to blame Scottish legal procedure as leading to this state of affairs.[11] Developed eighteenth-century Scottish civil procedure did not at all resemble procedure at English common law, although it was possible to make comparisons with English equity procedure and that in the English ecclesiastical courts. Procedure before the Court of Session was still very obviously derived from Romano-canonical procedure. It gave no scope for trial by jury.[12] To understand this it is necessary to examine the structure of the Court of Session and its workings around 1800. Exploration of the issues revolving around the introduction of the civil jury in Scotland will help illuminate the chapters in this book devoted to the jury in England. It will allow an assessment of the significance of arguments in favour of the jury, whether on the basis of ideology or utility.

[9] J Dalrymple, *Memoirs of Great Britain* (Edinburgh and London, A Kincaid, J Bell & J Balfour and W Strachan & T Caddell, 1771–88), vol. 1, "Review", 1; found quoted in C Kidd, *Subverting Scotland's Past: Scottish Whig Historians and the Creation of an Anglo-British Identity, 1689–c.1830* (Cambridge, University Press, 1993), 210.

[10] See generally on this Kidd, *supra* n. 10.

[11] Phillipson, *supra* n. 1, 85. For an interesting case study of one example of Scottish litigation at this period and how, when it reached the House of Lords, the Scottish procedures and law were not always entirely understood, see A C Loux, "The Great Rabbit Massacre - A 'Comedy of the Commons'? Custom, Community and Rights of Public Access to the Links of St Andrews", (2001) 23 *Liverpool Law Review* 123.

[12] See generally Cairns, *supra* n. 2, 120–2 on the development of procedure in Scotland. See also on the early procedure of the Court: J Finlay, *Men of Law in Pre-Reformation Scotland* (East Linton, Tuckwell Press, 2000), 87–122.

THE COURT OF SESSION AND ROMANO-CANONICAL PROCEDURE

The Court consisted of the President and fourteen Ordinary Lords of Session (or Senators of the College of Justice). It was divided, both physically and procedurally, into an Inner and an Outer House. The President and the Ordinary Lords sat in the Inner House together, nine being a quorum, and decided by vote on an issue before them. The Ordinaries would weekly take it in turn to sit in the Outer House as Lord Ordinary of the Week, Lord Ordinary on the Bills, Lord Ordinary on Oaths and Witnesses, and Lord Ordinary on Concluded Causes. These were separate offices, but the Lord Ordinary of the Week would commonly also act as Lord Ordinary on the Bills (dealing with bills suspending the decrees of lower courts or advocating causes from them to the Session).[13]

The Ordinary of the Week dealt with the ordinary actions enrolled before him for that week on the basis of the pursuer's libel (or summons) and the defender's defences. The parties' counsel would debate the cause before him *viva voce* and he could dispose of the matter by interlocutor if it was unnecessary to take parol evidence. It was common for the Lord Ordinary to require the parties to reduce their arguments to writing in the form of what were called Memorials if he considered there was a legal point of difficulty. He could also report any matters of difficulty to the Inner House for decision: this would generally require the production of written (printed) documents for the Inner House, embodying the parties' arguments, called Informations. The parties could always ask him, any number of times, to review his own interlocutors. Where proof was necessary in a case because facts were in dispute, this would be taken by the Lord Ordinary on Oaths and Witnesses. Such proof could only be taken if the Ordinary of the Week had passed an Act of Litiscontestaion deciding issues of relevancy and which matters of fact required to be proved. The Lord Ordinary of the Week, however, might allow proof to be taken before answering a preliminary plea in law, if issues of fact and law were not easily separated: he would pass an Act before Answer. The Ordinary on Oaths and Witnesses would either examine witnesses himself or order them to be examined on commission. Such evidence would be reduced to written form.[14] (Until 1686, the evidence had been taken by the judge in private and sealed up to be made

[13] See generally Lord Cooper of Culross, "The Central Courts after 1532", in G C H Paton (ed), *An Introduction to Scottish Legal History*, Stair Soc., vol. 20 (Edinburgh, 1958), 341 at 342–4; Phillipson, *supra* n. 1, 43–5. On the historical development, see R K Hannay, *The College of Justice: Essays on the Institution and Development of the Court of Session* (Edinburgh, William Hodge, 1933 [= *The College of Justice: Essays by R K Hannay*, ed. by H L MacQueen, Stair Soc., supplementary vol. 1 (Edinburgh, 1990)]), 91–134.

[14] Phillipson, *supra* n. 1, 43–6.

available to the Court when it advised the cause; after 1686, the parties and their advocates could be present when witnesses were examined and could have access to the written depositions.)[15] If witnesses had been examined, the process would pass to the Lord Ordinary on Concluded Causes. He would prepare an ultimately printed document, setting out the pleadings of the parties and the evidence of the witnesses, generally called a Statement of the Cause. This was the basis on which the Inner House would decide the case. It would also be accompanied by further Informations prepared by the counsel for the parties.[16]

As a case progressed through the Court, one can see that the process (as it is called) would accumulate as a potentially enormous bundle of papers, prepared by the parties with the interlocutors issued by the judges written on them. These were the bundles in the "pokes" that so dismayed Alan Fairford and infused his father with pleasure when they saw the process in the case of *Peebles* v. *Plainstanes* in Scott's *Redgauntlet*.[17]

As noted above, at advising in the Inner House the cause would be decided by the judges on a vote. There was no requirement for them to give reasons for their decisions. Indeed, it was only in 1693 that Parliament required that "all Bills Reports Debates Probations and others relating to processes shall be considered reasoned and advised and voted by the Lords of Session with open doors where parties procurators and all others are hereby allowed to be present".[18] Furthermore, it was not until the 1790s that the first steps were taken to preserve the opinions of the judges in law reports.[19] Such opinions were not entered in the process, which would only preserve the final interlocutor. The reasons individual judges gave for deciding one way or another were occasionally preserved by themselves and others in cases of popular concern and interest, such as the Douglas cause.[20] Many thought that the reason litigants were so willing to appeal was that they were often uncertain as to why a decision against them had been reached.[21]

[15] The Evidence Act, 1686, c. 30; *Acts of the Parliaments of Scotland*, ed. by T Thomson and C Innes (Edinburgh, Record Edition, 1814–1875; hereafter *APS*), vol. 8, 599.

[16] Phillipson, *supra* n. 1, 43–4, 56. For a flavour of the extensive written pleadings (the "Session Papers"), see J A Inglis, "Eighteenth Century Pleading", (1907–8) 19 *Juridical Review* (Old Ser.), 42.

[17] W Scott, *Redgauntlet*, ed. by G A M Wood with D Hewitt, Edinburgh Edition of the Waverley Novels (Edinburgh, University Press, 1997), 117.

[18] Court of Session Act 1693, c. 42, *APS*, supra n. 15, vol. 9, 305.

[19] Cairns, *supra* n. 2, 172–5.

[20] See *A Summary of the Speeches, Arguments, and Determinations of the Right Honourable The Lords of Council and Session in Scotland, upon that Important Cause wherein His Grace the Duke of Hamilton and Others were Plaintiffs, and Archibald Douglas of Douglas Esq.; Defendant. With an Introductory Preface, giving an Impartial and Distinct Account of this Suit* (Edinburgh, printed for and sold by Francis Robertson, 1767).

[21] Philipson, *supra* n. 1, 86.

CRITICISM AND REFORM OF PROCEDURE IN THE SESSION

While there was nothing obviously intrinsically wrong with this form of process, in the later eighteenth century it came under increasing criticism. One of the most important criticisms was that it promoted delay. Whether there was anything inherent in the procedure bringing about the slow progress of cases through the Court is a moot point. It appears that the volume of litigation before the Court more than doubled between 1761 and 1800.[22] Phillipson's somewhat speculative calculations give a picture of a court increasingly clogged up with litigation that its procedures did not allow it to deal with in an expeditious manner.[23] Be that as it may, there certainly was a perception that the Court was slow. Henry Brougham, while scarcely a dispassionate commentator on the Scottish legal scene, told Lord Grey in 1814 that cases before the Session could last three to four years that could have been dealt with "in an hour or less" in England.[24] This may have been an example of Brougham's usual heated and perfervid exaggeration, but it is evident that there was a more widespread assumption that the form of process before the Court of Session was the cause of delay. Phillipson puts forward a convincing case for this, based on correspondence and, above all, on the evidence taken before the Commission appointed in 1823 to investigate procedure before the Session.[25]

The basic defects that were identified were as follows: parties were not forced to determine early and carefully what was in dispute in the litigation; judges too freely allowed amendments to the pleadings changing the nature of the cause; and parties were not forced to ensure their action progressed swiftly and expeditiously through the Court. If these were the problems, the causes were less certain. Were they the result of the very nature of the form of process before the Session or of the way that form of process was executed? Further research is undoubtedly required. Moreover, such research would have to consider the reforms and problems in a comparative European context: this, after all, was the period of reforms in procedure in England and the civil law countries of continental Europe.

Why the question remains to some extent open in Scotland was that Parliamentary Commissions of this era were not yet the dispassionate investigative bodies into which they were to develop. There can be little doubt but that their proceedings were calculated to bring about a specific general result, if not all its particular details. In 1808, the Session was split into two Divisions, the First presided over by the Lord President, the Second by the Lord Justice-Clerk, effective head of the (criminal) Justiciary Court, now

[22] Ibid., 46.
[23] Ibid., 46–7.
[24] Found quoted in ibid., 48.
[25] 4 Geo. IV, c. 85.

given for the first time an official role in the Court of Session. The hope was that two equal courts of co-ordinate jurisdiction would deal with business more expeditiously than one.[26] As well as some procedural reforms, the Act also authorised the appointment of a Commission to "inquire into the Forms of Process in the Court of Session". The aims hoped for are indicated by the Commission being particularly required to consider the introduction of jury trial, the possibility of more pleading *viva voce*, the issue of taking evidence on commission, and the creation of permanent Lords Ordinary.[27] It was clear from what direction the wind of reform was blowing. Lessons were to be learned from English procedure. By 1813, there was a permanent Outer House creating the appearance of a court of first instance and a court of second instance in place of the older collegiate structure.[28]

Given the remit established under the act of 1808, it is no surprise that, in December 1814, a bill was finally introduced into Parliament to create a separate Jury Court in Scotland, the content of the act sparking the criticism that has given a title to this book and chapter. The new court was originally established experimentally for seven years, intended to deal with issues sent by the Court of Session for determination by a jury.[29] In 1819, the Jury Court having been judged to be successful, it was made permanent by a statute that *required* the Lord Ordinary to send to it any case raised in the Outer House that dealt with "injuries to the person, whether real or verbal, as assault or battery, libel or defamation, or on account of any injury to moveables, or to lands, where the title is not in question, or on account of breach of promise of marriage, seduction, or adultery, or any action founded on delinquency or quasi delinquency of any kind, where the conclusion shall be for damages and expences only".[30] In 1825, a further act, reforming the Court of Session and creating the direct ancestor of the current system of procedure, added to the list of causes that *had* to be sent to the Jury Court from the Court of Session or the Admiralty Court:

> "[A]ll actions on the responsibility of shipmasters and owners, carriers by land or water, innkeepers or stablers, for the safe custody and care of goods and commodities, horses, money, clothes, Jewels, and other articles, and in general all articles grounded on the principle of the edict nautae caupones stabularii; all actions brought for nuisance; all actions of reduction on the head of furiosity and idiotry, or on facility and lesion, or on force and fear; all actions on policies of insurance, whether for maritime or fire or life insurance; all actions on charter parties and bills of lading; all actions for freight; all actions on contracts for the carriage of goods by land or water; and actions for the wages of masters and mariners of ships or vessels."[31]

[26] Court of Session Act, 1808, 48 Geo. III, c. 151.
[27] Ibid., s. 22; Phillipson, *supra* n. 1, 113–26.
[28] Cairns, *supra* n. 2, 151–2.
[29] Jury Trials (Scotland) Act, 1815, 55 Geo. III, c. 42.
[30] Jury Trials (Scotland) Act, 1819, 59 Geo. III, c. 35; Cairns, *supra* n. 2, 152.
[31] Court of Session Act, 1825, 6 Geo. IV, c. 120.

No longer an exotic transplant into Scots procedure, civil juries were becoming common in legal process north of the border. In 1830, the separate Jury Court was abolished and its jurisdiction merged with that of the Court of Session, where now jury trials would be held before the Lord Ordinary.[32]

There were other important reforms that need only be noted here: a greater emphasis on oral rather than written pleading; an attempt to ensure that parties narrowed down relatively early the issues of law and fact in dispute between them through the system of open and closed records; the Ordinary could decide the cause or report it to the Inner House; and neither the Ordinaries nor the Divisions of the Inner House could be asked any more to reconsider their decisions.[33] The obvious question, however, is: given the desire to have more expeditious process, what was the advantage of jury trial? This question becomes more pressing since a modern perspective sees jury trial as slower and adding to the expense of the action, so that it should only be sought in exceptional circumstances.

It would certainly be wrong to conclude that, in the search for efficiency of process, jury trial was introduced into Scottish civil procedure for purely ideological reasons, important though they may have been. It was seen as having advantages in making civil proceedings more expeditious. Phillipson has shown how opposition to the proposal by Henry Dundas in 1785 to reduce the number of judges in the Court of Session led to calls for the introduction of civil juries.[34] While many of these revolved around notions of English liberty and greater assimilation to the "sister kingdom", some of those who intervened in these debates also saw the jury as a means to bring about a more speedy civil process. "Thus might that Grievance arising from our voluminous mode of procedure, the *Law's Delay* be redressed", as one memorialist put it.[35]

These claims were not necessarily convincing or well informed. In 1789, however, a judge of the Court of Session, John Swinton of Swinton, in a pamphlet strongly influenced by English practice, proposed various reforms in the Court of Session, including the introduction of jury trial for certain limited purposes.[36] He argued that the advantages would be: the presentation of the evidence directly to those who would decide the cause; and the need for careful preparation and a clear summing up to the jury, which would ensure that all were clear about what was at issue, so that litigants would be discouraged from appealing the decision.[37]

[32] Court of Session Act, 1830, 11 Geo. IV and 1 Will. IV, c. 69.

[33] Court of Session Act, 1825, 6 Geo. IV, c. 120; Cairns, *supra* n. 2, 152–3.

[34] Phillipson, *supra* n. 1, 62–77.

[35] Found quoted ibid., 74.

[36] [J Swinton], *Considerations Concerning a Proposal for Dividing the Court of Session into Classes and Chambers; And for Limiting Litigation in Small Causes; And for the Revival of Jury Trial in Certain Civil Actions* (Edinburgh, printed for Peter Hill, 1789); Phillipson, *supra* n. 1, 79–84.

[37] Phillipson, *supra* n. 1, 80–1.

In 1805, the proposal to introduce jury trial into Scottish civil proceedings was revived by the judges themselves. The main argument in its favour was that it would compel agents and advocates to focus more clearly on the case at an early stage. Judges would need to be firm in forcing parties to communicate clearly and early in the litigation all matters in dispute and counsel would comply to avoid the expense of a second jury trial.[38] Nothing came of this, but in 1807 a set of radical new proposals to restructure completely the Scottish civil courts, evidently modelled on English practice, included the suggestion that all parties be able to opt for jury trial on the model of that provided in the English common law courts.[39] Behind this lay a desire to correct suspected judicial partiality and to help make litigation more precise by ensuring a clear separation of issues of fact and law in deciding cases.[40]

JURIES AND IMPROVING THE LAW

If the reasons why civil juries were introduced into Scotland were evidently complex, relating to ideals of Union, ideologies of liberty, and hopes of practical improvement in the form of process, there also was an ambition that they should bring about an improvement in the substantive law. The argument for this is a straightforward one, though difficult in some respects.

By 1700, Scotland was a country of the *usus modernus Pandectarum* and there had developed what one might call on analogy with the idea of Roman-Dutch law a Roman-Scots law. This had taken place through the blending of Roman law with other sources regarded as "Scottish", such as statutes, medieval law texts, and the decisions of the Lords of Session.[41] This was a legal system where the most important treatise on criminal law for long was that by Matthaeus, commenting on the *libri terribiles* of the *Digest*, and where the texts of Roman law and the commentaries on them guided civil litigation.[42] Sir George Mackenzie gave the most detailed account of the sources of Scots law and the operation of legal argument in the period to 1700 in a late, unpublished, but vitally important,

[38] Ibid., 87–8.

[39] Ibid., 89.

[40] Ibid., 93–4.

[41] See Cairns, *supra* n. 2, 135–9; J W Cairns, "The Civil Law Tradition in Scottish Legal Thought", in D L Carey Miller and R Zimmermann (eds), *The Civilian Tradition and Scots Law: Aberdeen Quincentenary Essays* (Berlin, Duncker and Humblot, 1997), 191 at 211–6; R Zimmermann, *Roman Law, Contemporary Law, European Law: The Civilian Tradition Today* (Oxford, University Press, 2001), 152.

[42] See Cairns, *supra* n. 2, 138–9; J W Cairns, "Hamesucken and the Major Premiss in the Libel 1672–1770: Criminal Law in the Age of Enlightenment", in R Hunter (ed.), *Justice and Crime: Essays in Honour of the Right Honourable the Lord Emslie M.B.E., P.C., L.L.D., F.R.S.E.* (Edinburgh, T and T Clark, 1993), 138 at 156.

manuscript.[43] In 1686, Mackenzie had written that "our Statutes . . . be the chief Pillars of our Law".[44] Of course, pillars may support, but they cannot form the complete edifice. Mackenzie recognised that authority had to be given to decisions of the courts, but he was sceptical about their value. Given that the Lords of Session advised in secret until 1693, and decided causes by voting, he had good cause to be. The reasons behind any decision might well be obscure, contradictory, or even corrupt and ignorant. In Mackenzie's view, it was far better that "our Law [be] directed by the Writings of Learned Lawyers who give their Judgment in abstract Cases wherein none are concern'd ... and who have great Leisure to meditate upon what they transmit to Posterity as Law".[45] For Scots lawyers it was the writings of the great jurists of the *ius commune* and *usus modernus* that were to be drawn on to develop Scots law, which gained its core certainty from its statutes and the texts of Roman law. Indeed, Scots law would hardly have made sense as a system without the texts of the *ius commune* and the *usus modernus*.

In the course of the eighteenth century this attitude started to change.[46] In part, this was due to the impact of the modern natural law movement, which was very influential in Scotland. Roman law started to lose its authority. What was crucial, however, was the development of moral theory in Scotland in the eighteenth century. From Francis Hutcheson onwards, the most influential Scottish thinkers rejected ethical rationalism. Influenced by Lord Shaftesbury, Hutcheson instead propounded the idea of a "moral sense" that allowed us to form moral judgements. Others followed Hutcheson's lead. The most noted lawyer among these was Lord Kames, who refined Hutcheson's views by arguing that justice was derived not from the benevolence of the moral sense but rather from its sense of duty.[47] The

[43] BL, Add. MS 18236.

[44] G Mackenzie, *Observations on the Acts of Parliament, Made by King James the First, King James the Second, King James the Third, King James the Fourth, King James the Fifth, Queen Mary, King James the Sixth, King Charles the First, King Charles the Second. Wherein 1. It is Observ'd, if they be in Desuetude, Abrogated, Limited, or Enlarged. 2. The Decisions relating to these Acts are mention'd. 3. Some new Doubts not yet decided, are hinted at. 4. Parallel Citations from the Civil, Canon, Feudal and Municipal Laws, and the Laws of other Nations, are adduc'd for clearing these Statutes* (Edinburgh, Heir of Andrew Anderson, 1686), sig. A4r. On Mackenzie's thinking in general political and intellectual context, see now, above all, J C L Jackson, "Royalist Politics, Religion and Ideas in Restoration Scotland, 1660–1689" (unpublished Ph.D. thesis, University of Cambridge, 1998), *passim*.

[45] BL, Add. MS 18236, fos. 57v-58r; see ibid., 57, 60v-61v for his criticism of court decisions.

[46] For what follows, see J W Cairns, "Ethics and the Science of Legislation: Legislators, Philosophers, and Courts in Eighteenth-Century Scotland", (2000) 8 *Jahrbuch für Recht und Ethik* 159.

[47] Kames first set out his moral theory in Henry Home, Lord Kames, *Essays on the Principles of Morality and Natural Religion* (Edinburgh, printed by R Fleming for A Kincaid 1751). He further developed it in *Principles of Equity*, 2nd edn (Edinburgh, printed for A Millar, London, and A Kincaid and J Bell, Edinburgh, 1767) and *Sketches of the History of Man* (Edinburgh, printed for W Creech, Edinburgh, and for W Strahan and T Cadell, London 1774). See: I S Ross, *Lord Kames and the Scotland of his Day* (Oxford, Clarendon Press, 1972).

most noted exponent of a version of moral sense theory was David Hume. In his *Treatise of Human Nature* (1739), he mounted a devastating attack on ethical rationalism and natural law. When it came to justice, however, he rejected the approach of Hutcheson or Kames. Justice was not derived from the moral sense, but rather was an "artificial" virtue that originated in social convention, in that rules for allocation of the scarce resources necessary for life developed out of customary practices on the basis of expediency and necessity. He later stressed in the *Enquiry Concerning the Principles of Morals* (1751) that the sole origin of justice was utility.[48]

Though much influenced by Hume, Adam Smith reacted strongly against his friend's reduction of justice to utility. In his treatise, *The Theory of Moral Sentiments* (1759), Smith built up his theory of moral judgement using his ideas of sympathy, propriety, and the impartial spectator.[49] For Smith, justice developed through the historical appearance of differing rights. Rights were recognised by the impartial spectator who made moral judgements of propriety and merit based on a sympathetic response to the observed behaviour of others. Smith argued that legal rights were best recognised, not through legislation, but through the operation of judges and juries. This was because they were more responsive to the moral nuances of particular circumstances than was generally possible in legislation. This put a premium not only on the structure of courts but also on the form of process within them. Both had to be such as to maximise the possibility of the development of the best law.[50]

Smith's thinking on court procedures can be worked out from the lectures he gave on jurisprudence in the University of Glasgow, which have been preserved in two sets of student notes.[51] Elsewhere, I have shown how much in these lectures can be seen as a critique of the existing structure and procedures of the unreformed Court of Session and also the way in which his thinking influenced the debates over reform.[52] If we focus here on what he said about juries, we can reach a deeper understanding of the arguments that influenced the introduction of civil juries into Scottish procedure. Smith evidently saw juries as reacting sympathetically in litigation.[53]

48 See, e.g., K Haakonssen, *The Science of a Legislator: The Natural Jurisprudence of David Hume and Adam Smith* (Cambridge, University Press, 1981), 4–44.

49 A Smith, *The Theory of Moral Sentiments*, ed. by D D Raphael and A L MacFie (Oxford, Clarendon Press, 1976).

50 For a full discussion of this aspect of Smith's legal theory, see J W Cairns, "Adam Smith and the Role of the Courts in Securing Justice and liberty", in R P Malloy and J Evensky (eds), *Adam Smith and the Philosophy of Law and Economics* (Dordrecht, Kluwer, 1994), 31.

51 A Smith, *Lectures on Jurisprudence*, ed. by R L Meek, D D Raphael, and P G Stein (Oxford, Clarendon Press, 1978), (hereafter cited as LJ(A) by volume and page of original MS (report of 1762–1763) and LJ(B) by page of original MS (report of 1766)).

52 Cairns, *supra* n. 50; Cairns, *supra* n. 46.

53 LJ(B), *supra* n. 51, 475.

For Smith, the great danger to the liberty of the subject was the unregulated activity of the judge. In England the judges at common law were controlled, first, by the "ordinary method of proceeding", that is, by the forms of action. Secondly, "[a]nother thing which curbs the power of the judge is that all causes must be try'd with regard to the fact by a jury."[54] This meant that proceedings in England were very "strict"; this related to their historical development. In contrast, the Court of Session was a new court, established when government was strong. Smith commented that "courts at their first institution take great liberties", being "neither tied down by the brieves nor encumbered with a jury". Instead of following existing precedents, they "would rather follow the rules of the civill law". This was evidently the case with the Court of Session.[55]

The lack of control over the activities of judges, such as those in the Session, meant that they were not compelled to act according to justice as defined by the impartial spectator. In contrast, the long continuous history of English common law and the strictness of its procedures meant that it had been created taking account of the demands of justice in particular situations:

> "The English law was ... formed into a system before the discovery of Justinians Pandects; and its courts established, and their method of proceedings pretty much fixed, before the other courts in Europe were instituted, or the civil and cannon law came to be of any great weight. It is for this reason that it borrows less from those laws than the law of any other nation in Europe; and is for that reason more deserving of the attention of a speculative man than any other, as being more formed on the naturall sentiments of mankind."[56]

This was a point that Smith stressed more than once in his lectures.[57] English law had been created in accordance with principles of justice through the mechanisms of the common law. He stressed this in his Lectures on Rhetoric in discussing precedent:

> "This is the case in England. The sentences of former Cases are greatly regarded and form what is called the common law, which is found to be much more equitable than that which is founded on Statute only, for the same reason as what is founded on practise and experience must be better adapted to particular cases than that which is derived from theory only."[58]

Common law and juries not only served justice, but also created a greater and more precise clarity of rules.

[54] LJ(A), *supra* n. 51, v.31–2.
[55] LJ(A), *supra* n. 51, v.42–3.
[56] LJ(A), *supra* n. 51, ii.74–5.
[57] See also LJ(A), *supra* n. 51, v.43.
[58] A Smith, *Lectures on Rhetoric and Belles Lettres*, ed. by J C Bryce (Oxford, Clarendon Press, 1983) (cited by volume and page of the original MS), ii.200.

During the eighteenth century, as Scots law moved away from the *usus modernus* and started to find certainty and justice in court decisions, it came to be realised that it was imperative to find a form of process that would result in clearer precedents and which, in Smithian terms, would allow the mechanisms of sympathy and propriety to function appropriately. A multiplicity of judges deciding causes for differing and perhaps contradictory reasons in a process did not make for certain precedents. As early as 1712, one lawyer had commented:

> *In Cumulo* one of your Lordships is moved by one Reason, and another by another, which Reasons, if they were examined or determined separately, would be repelled by the Plurality, which also is the Case why in most Sovereign Courts, especially in England, the Judges do resolve particular Points, which renders the Reason of the Decisions clear, and makes the Precedent of greater Use in other Cases.[59]

As court decisions became an increasingly important source of law, ultimately really the only source accepted alongside statute (apart from the strange and anomalous position of the "institutional" writers), it was necessary that they should have a clearer meaning as precedents than the traditional Scottish form of process allowed.[60]

One obvious solution was to avoid decisions being made by such large numbers of judges; the division of the Court and the establishment of a permanent Outer House achieved this.[61] Jury trial was also seen as playing an important part in this process. Its alleged advantage was that it compelled parties to separate clearly issues of fact from points of law.[62] Points of law were thus clarified. Indeed the eventual reform introducing the Jury Court was ultimately stimulated by Lord Eldon's complaints that many of the causes that reached the House of Lords from the Court of Session were really disputes about issues of fact rather than issues of law. Indeed, Eldon stated that one case, that of *Smith* v. *McNeill*, was one which would have been settled in a few weeks in England by a jury of merchants, whereas it had been depending in Scotland for twelve years.[63]

The hope for civil juries was therefore that, by forcing a clearer separation of issues of fact and issues of law, they would not only simplify litigation but also make it clear what points of law were at stake. This would inevitably help clarify the law as a system of rules. This was to be a necessary way of thinking about law in a century that was to glorify Parliamentary sovereignty and supremacy in law making. Instead of Scots law being a traditional set of

[59] David Dalrymple in *Millar* v. *Robertson*, found quoted in Inglis, *supra* n. 16, 52.

[60] See Cairns, *supra* n. 2, 168–77.

[61] See ibid., 151–3.

[62] See, e.g. Phillipson, *supra* n. 1, 93, 127–9.

[63] 2 Dow 538–45; see Phillipson, *supra* n. 1, 128.

argumentative practices, drawing on Roman law and its commentators, natural law, statutes, and decisions, negotiated through a complex procedural structure, it was to be conceived of as a system of dynamic precedent and statutes creating national rules that were to be applied in a rational court structure that separated law from fact.[64] Introducing the civil jury was an important part of that major transformation.

CONCLUSIONS

In Scotland, introduction of the civil jury in 1816 was thus a result of multiple causes and it represented many different values: efficiency, liberty, Union with England, better "national" law. The nineteenth century was the era when the jury was exported to many other European countries, with differing results. What was exported was the criminal jury.[65] Scotland was the only country that consciously adopted the civil jury on an English model, although it was successfully exported to the English and later British colonies. How successful this export to Scotland has been it is difficult to say. This is an obvious topic for further detailed research; superficial knowledge suggests that despite a heyday in the mid-Victorian period, in the twentieth century the civil jury had a very mixed history. Its use is now confined to delictual cases, and only a minority of those. While still used in some cases where they no longer would be in England, jury trials are relatively rare, but seem none the less to have a waxing and waning popularity, explicable, at least to the outsider, only on the basis of changing and fickle fashion. There may be more to it than this and the attitude of the Scottish Legal Aid Board may be significant. This said, it is evident that much remains to be explored.

One of the ironies is that the civil jury was introduced in Scotland just shortly before it started to come under attack in England.[66] The very functions and behaviour of the jury that had been argued as needed in Scotland were those that came under attack south of the border. Technicality of law started to win over jury decision-making. Matters of fact increasingly became matters of law. This is another issue that still awaits research in Scotland.[67] The elaboration of rules of law that is found in the weighty volumes of the nineteenth-century reporters such as Rettie and Dunlop is one that could not have taken place by letting juries have wide discretion in deciding matters on general issues. Perhaps it was the very existence of the

[64] See further Cairns, *supra* n. 2, 175–7.

[65] See A Padoa Schioppa, "Introduction", in A Padoa Schioppa (ed.), *The Trial Jury in England, France, Germany 1700–1900* (Berlin, Duncker and Humblot, 1987), 7 at 7.

[66] See Lobban, ch. 10 *infra*; Getzler, ch. 11 *infra*.

[67] For perceptive remarks, see H L MacQueen and W D H Sellar, "Negligence", in K Reid and R Zimmermann (eds), *A History of Private Law in Scotland. Volume 2: Obligations* (Oxford, University Press, 2000), 517 at 530–3.

jury that encouraged in Scotland the elaboration of rules of law to avoid jury decisions. The doctrinal history of Scots law in the nineteenth century would thus be of development by the judges to avoid the new jury. This would be a further wonderful irony.

2

Towards the Jury in Medieval Wales

DAFYDD JENKINS (ABERYSTWYTH)

INTRODUCTION

With the exercise of some ingenuity, it would be possible to write a general history of law around the word which has in English the form "right", for it appears in the juristic vocabulary of so many Indo-European languages—in Scandinavian *rätt*, in German *Recht*, and in the indirectly related French *droit* and corresponding forms in other Romance languages. In all these languages the word has more than one meaning, so that, for instance, in German the sense of English "law" has to be distinguished as *objectives Recht*, and the sense of English "right" as *subjektives Recht*. In English it is "law" which confuses by its two senses, of *objektives Recht* and of what is in German *Gesetz*. It was failure to distinguish the two senses which caused Austin to send English jurisprudence astray for a century; there is some excuse for him in the precedent set by medieval Roman law, which misinterpreted a famous text from the Digest by omitting its explanation. *Quod principi placuit legis habet vigorem* was read as meaning that it was the ruler's command which gave the law its power; the explanation *cum lege, quae de imperio eius lata est, populus ei et in eum omne suum imperium et potestatem concessit* shows that for Ulpian the justification of the legislative power of the *princeps* was the legislative act of the people, who could, in theory, by another legislative act rescind the delegation.[1] If we admit that the people's power over the Roman *princeps* was purely theoretical, that does not acquit the medieval Romanists of a charge of misreading the text.

[1] D. 3.1pr. Austin was groping after a truth about law in a developed society. Where he spoke of the command of a sovereign, one or many, he should have thought of a rule enforced by the state, which is the legal person representing society. Of course, the concepts of enforcement and the state need much fuller analysis than is possible or would be appropriate here. The philosophers' criticism of Austin and of other lawyer-jurists is too often misconceived because the philosopher does not distinguish between moral duty and legal obligation. Lord Hewart, Lord Chief Justice at the time, saw the distinction clearly when he said during the hearing of an application to remove a re-trial from Caernarfon to London, "I seem to remember an eighteenth-century philosopher who said that a rebel might think it a moral duty to rebel, but the State might think it a duty to hang him for it": D Jenkins, *A Nation on Trial*, tr. by A Corkett (Cardiff, Welsh Academic Press, 1998), 104. There may well be a *prima facie* duty to obey the law because there is a presumption in an ordered society that the law is aiming at maintaining the right; but the presumption is certainly rebuttable.

In Irish, *recht* means "law", but the Welsh cognate means neither "right" nor "law", though a compound *cyfraith*[2] ("co-law", as it were), is the still living word for "law", in the *Recht* sense, and often in ordinary usage in the *Gesetz* sense also.[3] *Rhaith* is not a living word in modern Welsh; in the medieval lawbooks it means compurgation or the group of compurgators, and *rheithiwr* ("*rhaith*-man") means "compurgator"; today *rheithiwr* means "juror", and the twentieth century coined *rheithgor* for "jury". The account which here follows will suggest that this development is not an accident; and any reader familiar with English medieval law will recognise parallels and contrasts with that law: most of them can be traced through Pollock and Maitland, so that we can be sparing of references. Before we can begin to trace the development, however, we must look at the sources of our information about medieval Welsh law. Our main source is the manuscript lawbooks in Latin and Welsh, for we have no "native Welsh" court records:[4] it was apparently a principle of Welsh law that the written record of proceedings should be destroyed when the case was concluded, and if any question later arose about the proceedings it would be decided by the testimony of the judges involved.[5]

THE EARLY TEXTS

In medieval Welsh texts, and in modern Welsh-language treatment, Welsh medieval law is *Cyfraith Hywel*, "the law of Hywel", and no one doubts that the Hywel in question was Hywel Dda, "Howel the Good", who died in 949 or 950 as ruler of all Wales except the far south-east. Most of the medieval manuscripts of Welsh law have a preface that tells of a codifying assembly convened by Hywel at "the White House",[6] which is taken to mean Whitland on the Carmarthenshire-Pembrokeshire border.[7] Most students agree that

[2] Here and elsewhere modern Welsh spelling is used for Welsh words, since there is no uniform standard medieval orthography; but quotations will follow the spelling of the quoted texts.

[3] In careful writing and speech, *Gesetz* will be *deddf*, and in the names of statutes, "Act" is translated *Deddf*. In theological writing "Law" (as contrasted with "Grace") is normally *cyfraith*; but *deddf* is also fairly common.

[4] The best general introduction to the sources is T M Charles-Edwards, *The Welsh Laws*, Writers of Wales Series (Cardiff, University of Wales Press, 1989).

[5] "The court priest has three functions in sessions: to delete every case (*dadl*) which has been concluded from the roll; second is to keep in writing until judgment every case until it is concluded; third is to be ready and sober at the king's need to write letters and to read them": *Cyfreithiau Hywel Dda yn ôl Llyfr Blegywryd*, ed. by S J Williams and J E Powell (Cardiff, University of Wales Press, 1942, repr. 1961; hereafter Bleg.) 13.15–20.

[6] More detail, and more improbable detail, is added in manuscripts from the early fourteenth century on.

[7] Whitland Abbey is *Y Tŷ Gwyn*, "the White House" in Welsh, but the abbey was founded some two centuries after Hywel's time; it is argued that Hywel would have had an administrative centre in that district, and one manuscript says that the White House was a white-walled hunting lodge. See also *infra* at n. 85.

Hywel did something for Welsh law; but it is clear, as Maitland said well over a hundred years ago, that much of the material in the Welsh lawbooks is "neither law made by any 'sovereign one or many' ..., nor yet 'judge-made' law, nor yet again a mere record of popular customs. It is lawyer-made law, glossators' law, text-writers' law".[8] Yet there can be no doubt that until 1536, when the law and constitution of Wales were assimilated to those of England, we had in parts of Wales a quite advanced body of law of our own. In these manuscripts, written between the first half of the thirteenth century and the early sixteenth, practitioners or teachers of law recorded old and new material which might be of use in court or classroom: hence they show some survivals from a much earlier age, often in fossilised form, but they also contain some sophisticated statements of principle, as well as effective rules of practice.[9] The picture they present is partly modified by such records as survive, in extents and surveys and court records from the period after 1282, but is on the whole confirmed by them: if medieval Wales had no sovereign law-makers, it certainly had official law-enforcement officers.[10]

The oldest surviving manuscripts of this law are of the thirteenth century; some 40 manuscripts, five in Latin and the rest in Welsh, survive from the period during which Welsh law was of practical importance somewhere in Wales, rather than of merely antiquarian interest. Among all these manuscripts there is only one exception to the rule that they are all at least slightly different,[11] because every compiler, to use a neutral word, took into his book whatever he thought might be useful, so that any Welsh law manuscript is virtually certain to include, on the one hand, obsolete material retained *ex abundanti cautela* or from force of habit, and, on the other, recent innovations and even statements of what the compiler hoped would be accepted as good law.[12] All the manuscripts are made up of tractates,

[8] F W Maitland, "The Laws of Wales—the Kindred and the Blood Feud", in *The Collected Papers of Frederic William Maitland*, ed. by H A L Fisher (Cambridge, University Press, 1911; repr. Professional Books Ltd, Abingdon, 1983), vol. 1, 202. The paper was first published in 1881.

[9] Because an item in a lawbook may be a fossil or a recent innovation, it is unsafe to cite passages from the lawbooks as evidence of conditions in either Hywel's century or that in which the manuscript was written.

[10] See R A Griffiths with the assistance of R S Thomas, *The Principality of Wales in the Later Middle Ages; I: South Wales 1277–1536* (Cardiff, University of Wales Press, 1972).

[11] MS Cardiff 2 is an exact copy of BL Cotton Titus D.IX. On the other hand, Gwilym Wasta (of the New Town of Dinefwr, near Llandeilo in the Tywi Valley), cut out the "Laws of Court" from the three manuscripts which he wrote early in the fourteenth century because they were no longer in use. Gwilym was an "English burgess" of this new borough, though his name, like that of several of his fellow-burgesses, shows that he was Welsh: M E Owen and D Jenkins, "Gwilym Was Da", (1980) 21 *National Library of Wales Journal* 429.

[12] "Every legal treatise, to one degree or another, states law as the author thinks it should be": D J Seipp, "The Mirror of Justices", in J A Bush and A Wijffels (eds), *Learning the Law* (London and Rio Grande, The Hambledon Press, 1999), 85 at 97. This accounts for the many statements in the Mirror which conflict with the law found in the records of its age.

with or without fragments and a "tail".[13] In a few manuscripts the tractates are not arranged in any discernible order, but the manuscripts which have the Hywelian preface show enough order to imply an intention to present a comprehensive statement of the law; and in spite of their differences, the comprehensive Welsh-language manuscripts fall into three groups, which we now label with the personal names "Cyfnerth", "Blegywryd", and "Iorwerth", without thereby implying any particular relation between the lawbook and the person. Most of our attention will be given to the Iorwerth Redaction, with its presentation of the "classical law" of thirteenth-century Gwynedd, and to the "revised edition" (*Llyfr Colan*), which draws on the Iorwerth Redaction and a lost Latin source.[14] All three redactions purport to present their material in three books, the first being "the Laws of Court" and the second "the Laws of the Country"; but whereas these two can be clearly identified, the third book can be so identified only in the Iorwerth Redaction, which is the most tidily organised of the three.

The Cyfnerth and Blegywryd Redactions have a southern bias and Iorwerth was quite certainly put together in Gwynedd early in the thirteenth century. Of the five Latin manuscripts, Redactions B, C and E "probably belong to North Wales",[15] whereas Redactions A and D have a southern bias, and indeed it has been shown that the Blegywryd Redaction is a translation of a lost Latin manuscript from which Latin Redaction D is also derived.[16]

[13] A tractate is a collection of statements on some particular aspect of law. The name was adopted by Sir Goronwy Edwards because "tract" (the word used by specialists in Irish law) "might suggest something which smacks of political or ecclesiastical propaganda": G Edwards, "The Historical Study of the Welsh Lawbooks", (1962) 12 *Transactions of the Royal Historical Society*, 5th series, 144.

[14] The existence of the three groups was first brought before the public in *Ancient Laws and Institutes of Wales*, ed. by A Owen (Public Record Commission, 1841; hereafter AL) in two editions—a two-volume octavo and a one-volume folio. References are to book, chapter and section e.g. VI.vi.6, with the addition e.g. VC, DC or GC for books I-III. Owen called the Iorwerth, Blegywryd, and Cyfnerth Redactions respectively the Venedotian, Dimetian, and Gwentian Codes—names which are now avoided, though the abbreviations are used for any necessary reference to these texts (hereafter VC, DC and GC respectively), using the division into books, chapters, and sections which is the same in octavo and folio editions. The "Codes" are followed (in the second volume) by books numbered IV to XIV, of various dates. Book XIII was suspect for Maitland, *supra* n. 8, vol. 1, 206 and note 1 and, having been doctored about 1800, is not now used by scholars. Charles-Edwards, *supra* n. 4, 17–38 discusses the manuscripts. See also D Jenkins, "The Lawbooks of Medieval Wales", in R Eales and D Sullivan (eds.), *The Political Context of Law* (London and Ronceverte, The Hambledon Press, 1987), 1: this needs revision in the light of later work by other students, and I would no longer venture on a stemma diagram. For a general account of work on Welsh medieval law, see D Jenkins, "A Hundred Years of *Cyfraith Hywel*", (1997) 49/50 *Zeitschrift für celtische Philologie* 349.

[15] Charles-Edwards, *supra* n. 4, 20.

[16] H D Emanuel, "The Book of Blegywryd and Ms. Rawlinson 821", in D Jenkins (ed.), *Celtic Law Papers Introductory to Welsh Medieval Law and Government* (Brussels, Les éditions de la librairie encyclopédique, 1973; hereafter CLP), 163.

There is abundant evidence, in the wholesale copying of fragments and tractates from one redaction to another, for what can be called the dogma that there was one law for all Wales, despite its political fragmentation, so that any lawbook could be used anywhere in Wales. The work of nearly half a century has refined, but in essence confirmed, the view expressed in 1951 by the late Professor T Jones Pierce, "that from the point of view of content the books of *Cyfnerth*, *Blegywryd*, and *Iorwerth* stand in related chronological sequence—and in the order named".[17]

The third book in the Iorwerth Redaction is given the title "Justices' Test Book" (*Llyfr Prawf Ynaid*),[18] and the prologue of some manuscripts to that Book tells us that it

> "was gathered together by Iorwerth ap Madog from the book of Cyfnerth ap Morgenau and the book of Gwair ap Rhufawn and the book of Goronwy ap Moriddig and the old book of the White House, and besides that from the best books that he found also in Gwynedd and Powys and Deheubarth."[19]

The first chapters of this Test Book are a fine illustration of the way in which the lawbooks took the form in which we now have them. At some date at which I will not try to guess, someone, probably a teacher rather than a practitioner, saw the mnemonic value of the ennead form, and cast his learning about abetment into that form, perhaps with a little stretching at some points. He may have dictated it to pupils, who made it the nucleus of their commonplace books, adding to it other statements about the same subjects; the added statements would of course vary from pupil to pupil, and might lead from one subject to a subject related to it: so the treatment of homicide (*galanas*) led to *sarhaed*. Perhaps the principle had already

[17] T Jones Pierce, *Medieval Welsh Society*, ed. by J B Smith (Cardiff, University of Wales Press, 1972), 295. The passage comes from a lecture delivered in 1951 and published in 1952.

[18] The Welsh word translated "judicial office" is the abstract noun *yneidiaeth*: it might be more correct to translate it by "judicial status" or even "juristic status". One of the officers of the court is sometimes called *brawdwr*, which can be analysed as "judgement-man", i.e. "judge": he is sometimes called *ynad*, which is less easily analysed and may imply learning rather than office. The court *ynad* would give advice on law to the court as well as sitting in judgement on occasion.

[19] *The Law of Hywel Dda, Law Texts from Medieval Wales*, ed. and tr. by D Jenkins (Llandysul, Gomer Press, 1986; 2nd edn with minor corrections, 1990; hereafter LTMW), 141.25–31, translating AL, *supra* n. 14, VC III. pr., (vol. 1, 218.7–13). This introduction is not in *Llyfr Iorwerth*, ed. by A R Wiliam (Cardiff, University of Wales Press, 1960; hereafter Ior.). Its main text is taken from manuscript C, which is now thought likely to be the oldest surviving manuscript of the Iorwerth Redaction: see D Huws, "The Manuscripts", in T M Charles-Edwards et al. (eds), *Lawyers and Laymen* (Cardiff, University of Wales Press, 1986), 119: but the mention of the White House book is an addition from a fifteenth-century manuscript. The White House Book is, however, cited as authority in *Llyfr Colan*, ed. by D Jenkins (Cardiff, University of Wales Press, 1963; hereafter Col. cited by numbered sentences) in terms which suggest that it was in Latin: see *infra* at n. 87.

emerged that no-one should be accepted as a lawyer without a knowledge of the Three Columns and the Value of Wild and Tame: this principle is presented in a single sentence in the Cyfnerth Redaction;[20] but in the Blegywryd Redaction and in some Iorwerth manuscripts there is much more detail, including a description of the procedure for formal admission to the status after an examination by the Court Justice.[21] It was then a good teacher (a successful crammer?) who saw the value of a Test Book which would contain those materials of which his pupils had most need. So was created a separate book, in manuscript C, which appears to have existed separately before being attached to the books I and II of the Iorwerth Redaction.

There was good reason for the importance to young lawyers of the Three Columns: the abetments were crimes which were not primarily torts. The Welsh lawbooks certainly support Maine's assertion "that in the infancy of jurisprudence the citizen depends for protection against violence or fraud not on the Law of Crime but on the Law of Tort".[22] We need to remember that private prosecution, the appeal of felony in medieval England, came before any organised public presentation of crime, and in Welsh law it is clear that crime is secondary. The norm may allow the state (that is the ruler, whether he is called king or lord) a penalty as incidental to the compensation paid to the victim: but to allow the ruler to claim a penalty when no claim is made on behalf of the victim was exceptional, as the triad of the "three stays of blood" strikingly illustrates. Bloodshed was an offence against the ruler as well as the victim; the ruler was entitled to the larger penalty, the *dirwy* of twelve kine for this.[23] But there were three degrees,

[20] *Welsh Medieval Law*, ed. by A W Wade-Evans (Oxford, Clarendon Press, 1909; hereafter WML), 16.13–15, in all manuscripts of the chapter on the Court Justice in the Laws of Court.

[21] Bleg., *supra* n. 5, 16.16–17.18, in the chapter on the Court Justice; LTMW, *supra* n.19, 141.1–35, translating AL, *supra* n. 14, vol. 1, 216.23–218.13.

[22] H S Maine, *Ancient Law*, ed. C K Allen, World's Classics (Oxford, University Press, 1931), 309 (chap. X).

[23] *Dirwy* is cognate with Irish *díre*, which is the verbal noun of *diren*, "I pay", and means "compensation". The Welsh word always names a penalty payable to the ruler, and must have been regarded as compensation to him for the indignity done to him: "it is because loss was caused to him that the lord is entitled to the penalty (*cosb*)": *Damweiniau Colan*, ed. by D Jenkins (Aberystwyth, Cymdeithas Lyfrau Ceredigion, 1973; hereafter DwCol), §436. The ruler could mitigate the penalty, taking 3d instead of £3, but he could not reduce or release the payment due to the victim: DwCol, §435. A sentence in the first Column of Law tells us that there is "a dirwy for theft, and a dirwy for violence (*trais*) and a dirwy for fighting; and save for those, every offence which a person commits attracts camlwrw": LTMW, *supra* n. 19, 144.4.-7, translating Ior., *supra* n. 19, §104/18: but the lawbooks give this penalty in other cases. The smaller penalty of three kine seems to be a later device, as the name *camlwrw*, readily understood as "wrong-spoor" suggests: one may compare the contrast between the obscurity of the old name "felony" in English law and its readily-understood new "misdemeanour". The old-fashioned plural "kine" is used here and elsewhere because the corresponding Welsh word is *bu* or *buhyn*, which could cover an ox as well as a cow: the full-grown ox and cow had the same value in Welsh law; Latin texts have *vaccae*.

blood reaching the cheek, blood reaching the breast, and blood reaching the ground, and only if the ground was made bloody was the ruler entitled to prosecute; for the less serious cases, the ruler would get the penalty only if there was a plaint, that is, an action by the victim. The background of this rule can fairly be called pre-forensic or sacral.[24]

As found in all the redactions, both in Welsh and in Latin, the Three Columns differ slightly, but show enough agreement to imply a common ultimate origin, and to authorise the translation of *naw affaith* as "nine abetments", though some of the offenders would be guilty of the principal offence in English law, and others would be accessories before or after the fact. The Welsh word *affaith* is a regular borrowing from the Latin *affectus*, but that word is not to be found in the vocabulary of Roman law and "abetment" may not have been the original meaning of *affaith*. This is deduced from Latin Redaction B, an unusual manuscript which was peculiarly handled in *Ancient Laws*: in that edition, it has two sets of chapters numbered from I to XVII, with duplicated numbers reflecting duplicated content, so that (for instance, and for us the most revealing instance) the Three Columns of Law come at II.I.VI,VIII (corresponding to LTWL, 209.20–32), and again at what we must call II.I'-V'(LTWL, 250.35–251.19). II.V', "*Nau affeith galanas herwyd guyr Gwyned*" is in Welsh and agrees substantially with the Welsh redactions: but II.I'-IV' are defined as "the Three Columns of Law according to the men of Powys" (*tres sunt columpne juris herwid guyr Powys*). As Emanuel said, "might this suggest a Welsh manuscript of Powys usage" as one of the sources of Redaction B?[25] But for us the interest of the Powys version of the *affeithiau* is in the fact that this version has nothing to do with abetment, but sets out nine causes of blood-feud, and likewise the causes of liability for arson and theft.[26] The social conditions reflected in the Powys version are certainly what we have called pre-forensic or sacral. That version changes, and indeed doubles, the linguistic problem, for we now have to explain how this Latin borrowing was applied to the Powysian Columns, and also how it was transferred to those of the other versions; but that double problem can be left to others, while we turn to the jurisprudential interest of the abetments as crimes.

That interest lies in the fact that the abetments were unmixed crimes. Those charged with them must disprove the charge by a properly supported oath, and those guilty of them must pay a penalty:

[24] Cf. Numbers 35.33: "for blood, it defileth the land; and the land cannot be cleansed of the blood that is shed therein, but by the blood of him that shed it."

[25] *Latin Texts of the Welsh Laws*, ed. by H D Emanuel (Cardiff, University of Wales, 1967; hereafter LTWL, cited by page and line), 22.2–3. This gives the Latin Redactions A, D, and E (hereafter Lat A, Lat D and Lat E).

[26] See the discussion by M E Owen in Excursus I to "Shame and Reparation; Women's Place in the Kin", in D Jenkins and M E Owen (eds), *The Welsh Law of Women, Studies Presented to Professor Daniel A Binchy* (Cardiff, University of Wales Press, 1980),40 at 61–5.

> "Some say that the money which we have specified above comes to the kindred. The law says that it goes to the Lord, and that if there is denial, there is no right save to denial (and this is the reason that there is no right: because denial plus payment is not proper, and though it be admitted, the kin are entitled to nothing, for there is no principal offence in it)".[27]

The point could be more clearly made; but it is evident that the victim of theft or arson, or the kin of the homicide victim, took nothing from the abettor, because they were fully compensated by the principal offender and/or his kin. And though we speak of compensation, the Powysian Three Columns will serve to remind us that homicide was originally ground for feud between the kin of the killer and the victim; and though the word *galanas* is in most instances applied to an act of homicide or to the compensation due for the homicide (in English terms *wergeld*), its basic meaning is "blood-feud", and indeed *galanas* is linguistically equal to *gelyniaeth*, the still living word for "enmity".[28] The ruler, the infant state, comes into the picture as soon as he feels important enough to regard the blood-feud as damaging to the prosperity of society or to his own dignity and strong enough to induce the victim's kin to waive the feud in return for a price paid by the homicide and his kin. That price is the price of peace for the homicide's kin, rather than compensation for the loss of a kinsman. If such a distinction seems a little too fine-drawn, we can cite in its support a ruling about the payment of land in discharge of *galanas* liability: if a man gave up all his patrimony in such discharge, his son could not reclaim the land, "since peace was bought with it for the son as for the father".[29] The ruler was concerned to preserve harmony in his realm, but in the basic case he claimed no penalty from the homicide, though he did take a commission of a third of the compensation as the "enforcing third" (*traean cymell*).[30] Only where some special feature of the killing could be regarded as affecting the dignity of the ruler was a penalty payable to him in respect of the principal offence; but it was the ruler alone who claimed payment in respect of the abetments. Those guilty of abetment would often be of kin to the principal offender so that they must contribute to the *galanas*: that would not affect their liability for abetment.

[27] LTMW, *supra* n. 19, 143.23–9, translating Ior., *supra* n. 19, §104/10–12.

[28] The form *gelyniaeth* already existed in the early lawbooks' period: the modern word for "enemy", *gelyn*, has replaced *gal*, (plural *galon*) which seems to have other meanings as well as the undoubted meaning of "enemy". The comments of some language specialists have tended to confuse by concealing the truth that *galanas* means "homicide" and "wergeld" because it means "enmity".

[29] LTMW, *supra* n. 19, 110.16, translating Ior., *supra* n. 19, §87/2.

[30] The *galanas* payment was distributed among the victim's kin in the same way as it was levied from the homicide's kin: thus the victim's brother would take as much as the homicide's brother paid. The homicide himself must pay one-third of the *galanas*, and as the victim was not alive to take that payment, it was conveniently available for the ruler.

MEDIEVAL TEXTS ON PROCEDURE

Material relevant to procedure can appear almost anywhere in a lawbook: thus it is a triad that brings out effectively a principle of procedure:

> "There are three legal replications in law, differing from each other: confession; or denial; or lawful defence *so that the claim is not answered*".[31]

The third replication is what would be called "confession and avoidance" in English law. A simple Welsh example would be that of a defendant charged with theft, who could plead that he acquired the property from a named person—in English terms, "voucher to warranty". We shall return to this point later.

There are, however, some tractates which concentrate on procedure: the Iorwerth Redaction has a detailed account of procedure in land law. But overarching interest attaches to a tractate which is dignified in the manuscripts with the name of "*Llyfr Cynghawsedd*". Aled Wiliam made *Llyfr Cynghawsedd* conveniently available in a paper of that name in 1988.[32] T M Charles-Edwards had broken new ground in his of 1986.[33] Both men followed *Ancient Laws* in translating *cynghawsedd* by "pleadings", but *Llyfr Cynghawsedd* is better understood as "the Book of Procedure" than as "the Book of Pleadings".[34] Charles-Edwards pointed out that it was a sign of the maturity of thirteenth-century Welsh law that it developed a "new genre of legal writing", which created a lasting record of instruction on the presentation of cases to the courts—earlier in the Welsh lawbooks than in the English works published under such modern names as *Novae Narrationes* and *Brevia Placitata*.[35] *Llyfr Cynghawsedd* assumes the existence of the Iorwerth Redaction and is a conscious supplement to it.

[31] AL, *supra* n. 14, XIV.xv.1, correcting in italics the translation of AL.

[32] A Wiliam, "*Llyfr Cynghawsedd*", (1988) 35 *Bulletin of the Board of Celtic Studies* 73. Unlike such modern labels as *Llyfr Iorwerth*, *Llyfr Cynghawsedd/Cynghawsaeth* is used in the medieval manuscripts to identify (not always very clearly) a particular collection of material.

[33] T M Charles-Edwards, "*Cynghawsedd*: Counting and Pleading in Medieval Welsh Law", (1986) 33 *Bulletin of the Board of Celtic Studies* 188. Charles-Edwards has presented much of the thesis of that paper in *The Welsh Laws*, *supra* n. 4.

[34] I have been glad to find that my translation was forestalled by M Owen in *Y Traddodiad Rhyddiaith yn yr Oesau Canol*, ed. by G Bowen (Llandysul, Gomer Press, 1974), 237.

[35] Attention has been drawn before now to passages in Welsh lawbooks which anticipate declarations of principle by English common law judges: see D Jenkins, "The Significance of the Law Of Hywel", (1978) *Transactions of the Honourable Society of Cymmrodorion* 54 at 66. Like some of the names used for Welsh material, the names of these English collections are modern labels.

MEDIEVAL WELSH PROCEDURE

Medieval methods of deciding cases have traditionally been condemned as irrational. The better view about the contrast between those methods and our modern methods is that the former are objective and the latter subjective: that is why it has been appropriate to say that in the medieval context, "we have not to speak of trial, we have to speak of proof".[36] For England, the painfulness of the ordeal and the apparent unfairness of battle excuse the condemnation; but Wales knew neither ordeal nor battle. There is no early Welsh word for "ordeal";[37] and the word *ornest*, found in some late texts for "trial by battle", is a borrowing first clearly evidenced in the fourteenth century.[38] The references in the lawbooks are all late and ambiguous: at the most they may be evidence of a little infiltration of English practice into a marcher or near-marcher community. For medieval Welsh law, the all-important element was the oath: the litigants' oaths in affirmation of their claims or their denials of assertions made against them, and the oaths of testifiers of one kind or another. If we suppose that the operation of those oaths was unconditionally mechanical, so that in the absence of supernatural intervention the final judgment of the court might be directly contrary to

[36] Pollock and Maitland, vol. 2, 594.

[37] The word *diheurbrawf* is found earliest in a dictionary of the early eighteenth century. A poem in the classical form known as the *awdl* is given in the manuscripts the title "Awdl yr Haearn Twymyn", "the *awdl* of the Hot Iron". This was written by a poet who composed for many years on either side of the year 1200, and is an appeal to the saints and to God for help in carrying the hot iron: but there is nothing to show where the ordeal was to be conducted, and it is more than likely that it was somewhere in the Marches where Norman practice ruled: N A Jones, "Prydydd y Moch: Dwy Gerdd 'Wahanol' ", (1992) 18 *Ysgrifau Beirniadol* 71. The only reference to trial by ordeal in the law manuscripts is a triad (AL, *supra* n. 14, XIV.xiii.4) listing the three pains (*tair poen*) according to the law of Dyfnwal, the mythical predecessor of Hywel Dda. These were hot iron, hot water and combat: since Hywel Dda is said to have ruled that these were not right, it is clear that ordeals were not used in indigenous Welsh law. For a persuasive explanation of this striking fact see T G Watkin, "Saints, Seaways and Dispute Settlements" in W M Gordon and T D Fergus (eds), *Legal History in the Making* (London and Rio Grande, The Hambledon Press, 1991), 1. The passage cited as referring to ordeal in T P Ellis, *Welsh Tribal Law and Custom in the Middle Ages* (Oxford, Clarendon Press, 1926), vol. 2, 303 in fact refers to battle (*ornest*). The agreement of 1126 AD recorded in the Book of Llan Dâv, under which ordeals at Cardiff were to be sanctified by the church of Llandaff, is of course concerned with the law of the Norman lordship: J Gwenogvryn Evans and J Rhys (eds), *The Text of the Book of Llan Dâv* (Oxford, issued to subscribers, 1893, repr. Aberystwyth, National Library of Wales, 1979), 28.

[38] According to *Geiriadur Prifysgol Cymru* (Cardiff, University of Wales Press, 1950–; hereafter GPC), s.v. "*ornest*", the borrowing may be from Old English, but this seems improbable. The word is found in some late law texts in Old English, but is not recorded in the dictionaries of Middle English. Like many other borrowed words in Welsh, *ornest* has acquired an initial g; and *gornest* is now used for sporting contests of all kinds, and also figuratively, perhaps most often in politics.

the truth, we have not looked at the lawbooks closely enough. The presentation of oaths in evidence and compurgation is so hedged about by special conditions, with the obvious intention of making it as likely as possible that the truth would emerge, that few swearers can have succeeded in the effort to mislead the court. In England:

> "The concentration of justice at Westminster did much to debase the wager of law by giving employment for a race of professional swearers. In the village courts, on the other hand, it would not be easy for a man of bad repute to produce helpers: his neighbours would be afraid or ashamed to back his negations".[39]

So for Wales, where there was no central concentration of justice, much of the learning about procedure relates to the validity of oaths and to the extent and conditions of the support required for them.

The abnormal word "testifier" has just been used with intent, partly because the word "witness" would carry too much of the aura of twentieth century trials, and partly because of a linguistic difficulty, which arises from an overlap between terms and senses. Like Irish, Welsh has borrowed the Latin *testis*, in the regular form *tyst*, and has formed from it the verb *tystu* and the action-noun *tystiolaeth*, which in turn has given a verb *tystiolaethu*. The basic noun *tyst* is used in two senses: the wide sense of the giver of any kind of evidence, which I have translated as "testifier", and the narrow sense of my "attestor", who is specifically called to witness to something. So when a *tyst* is contrasted with a testifier of another kind, he must be an attestor; and the verb *tystu* is used for actions concerned with attestation, and *tystiolaethu* for the giving of evidence.[40] The other kinds of testifier were the "keeper" or "maintainer" (*ceidwad*) and the "knower" (*gwybyddiad*).[41] The maintainer testified to some state of affairs, the *gwybyddiad* to some event. Testifiers would need certain qualifications and must confirm their testimony in a specified way, but if the objective requirements were fulfilled, the matter was concluded: the court must give its verdict accordingly, though it might hold it up until security had been given for payment of the judges' fees. This means that the judge's function was simpler than in modern Wales, though it

[39] Pollock and Maitland, vol. 2, 636. Cf. ibid. 543: "The church could not keep up the character of the compurgators in her own courts. To say of a man that he was a common swearer before the ordinary was to blast his character." For a twentieth-century parallel, see M Hasluck, *The Unwritten Law in Albania* (Cambridge, University Press, 1954), updated by P Stein, *Legal Institutions* (London, Butterworths, 1984), 22–3.

[40] In modern Welsh another form, *tystio*, is most often used for the giving of evidence; *tystiolaethu* may be written and heard in that sense, but perhaps more naturally in relation to testimony to religious experience.

[41] In some translations "eye-witness" is used, though the *gwybyddiad* is often an ear-witness. "The Irish parallel suggests that *gwybyddiad* is a re-formation from *gwyddiad*, in which the root is *gŵydd*, 'presence' ": (LTMW, *supra* n. 19, 256). But *knower* is kept as the translation here, if only because "presence" does not offer a convenient agent-noun.

was comparable in one respect with that of the judge in a jury trial. The modern judge sums up the evidence, and tells the jury what the law requires from the evidence. Because the jury has to decide what evidence to believe as well as applying the law to the accepted evidence, there is a real danger that the judge's statement of the law is misunderstood: so the jury's verdict may be upset on appeal because the judge's presentation of the law was unsatisfactory. Thus the really important function of the judge is to decide on the relevant law—and that is what the medieval Welsh judge did. He chose the rule of law which was to be applied, and called for the appropriate proof by the appropriate oaths: if these were duly given, the case was decided in one way, and if they were not duly given, it was decided in another way. The final result of the case could be the subject of what we may think of as appeal; but it is appeal only if we remember that the French word means "call". In the appeal of felony the man accused was called out, just like the man challenged to a duel. Moreover, it was the judge's ruling which was being doubted, and it was he who was challenged to defend it, by procedures involving oaths. A judge who was validly held to have given the wrong ruling would be disqualified for life and required to pay the legal value of his tongue, which was 176 kine, equal to £44 at the standard legal price for the cattle.

RULES ON PROOF

Our first samples of the limitations on oaths in litigation can be taken from the first chapters of the Iorwerth Test Book. These carry what all the redactions call the Three Columns of Law, the Nine Abetments of Homicide (*galanas*), Theft, and Arson.

The first Column of Law sets out the basis of liability under the nine heads, and the penalty for liability and the requirements for disproof of liability under three heads. Like the Powys version, the Gwynedd version has some words of linguistic interest; of these, only one will be noticed here, namely *tafawdrudd*, "red-tongued", which is clearly modelled on *llofrudd*, "red-handed". In contemporary Welsh, *llofrudd* means "murderer", and *llofruddiaeth*, "murder", is contrasted with *dynladdiad*, "manslaughter"; but for medieval Welsh "murder" is a wholly misleading translation.[42] For one thing, the contrast is not between murder and other forms of homicide, but between the principal offence and the abetments. For another thing, *llofrudd* is sometimes used for the principal offender in relation to other crimes: thus abettors of theft do not have "to pay anything to him who owns the goods, since they are not principal offenders" (*canyt ynt llourudyeyt*).[43]

[42] It has been used far too often by responsible scholars. The entry in GPC, *supra* n. 38, is confusing: it should have presented the medieval and later meanings under separate subheads.

[43] LTMW, *supra* n. 19, 157.11, translating Ior., *supra* n. 19, §111/13. A Wiliam's note is

The teaching lawyers may have been trying to devise a mnemonic system for the abetments, for as well as the red-handed and the red-tongued, we have in some manuscripts "the red-eyed", *llygadrudd*, who has watched or seen the killing and has not prevented it.[44] Any such mnemonic plan was not carried out, but the abetments of *galanas* were tidily arranged in three sets of three, of increasing seriousness. Of the nine as given in the Iorwerth Redaction:

> "[F]irst is pointing out the person who will be killed to him who will kill him, and he is called red-tongued; second is giving counsel to the person who kills the other, to kill him; third is agreeing with him and approving him. For each of those three points, the oath of a hundred men denies it; if he admits it, let him pay nine score pence. Fourth is being an onlooker; fifth is companionship with the person who kills the other; sixth is going to the townland where the person who will be killed is, with him who will kill him. For each of these three, the oath of two hundred men, or twice nine score pence if it is admitted. Seventh is, helping the person who kills the other, and that is called aid to violence; eighth is to hold the person who will be killed, until he who will kill him comes; ninth is to see the person killed in his presence, without protecting him. For each of these three, if it is denied, the oath of three hundred men, or thrice nine score pence if it is admitted".[45]

The Three Columns are concerned with prosecution by the ruler of abettors who are not being accused of the principal offence: it seems likely enough that the oaths to deny abetment needed more backing than the oath to deny the principal offence, or the principal offence and all abetments, as some passages put it. But the lawbooks do not speak with one voice, and a judge faced with advocates citing different lawbooks would find it difficult to decide exactly what proof should be offered. There is manuscript authority for requiring the oath of three hundred to deny "the principal offence of blood and wound and killing of a person";[46] that is as much as the backing required for the most serious of the abetments. The "revised edition" of this text, *Llyfr Colan*, has a different rule: "The oath of a hundred men denies homicide and the killing of a person, and that according to the law of Hywel",[47] and this edition seems to be claiming the strong authority of an

"'red-handed, guilty'. In this case, 'thieves'". The Welsh expression does not imply that the principal offender had been taken with the mainour: why do we speak in English of catching red-handed a person whose offence is not homicide?

[44] Nothing in the texts reveals whether the *llygadrudd* was the fourth or the ninth abettor; the latter seems more likely.

[45] LTMW, *supra* n. 19, 143.1–21, translating Ior., *supra* n. 19, §104/4–9.

[46] LTMW, *supra* n. 19, 149.1–3, translating *Llyvyr Du or Weun, Facsimile of the Chirk Codex of The Welsh Laws*, ed. by J Gwenogvryn Evans (Llanbedrog, issued to subscribers only, 1909 [rectius 1921]), 77.2–3 (= VC III.i.17A "Ll6*trychan6r a dau o genedyl y wadu llowrudyaeth gwaet a gwely a llad dyn.*"

[47] "*Llu canwr a guata llourudyaeth a llat dyn a henny herwyt* keureyth *Hewel*": Col., *supra* n. 19, §276.

older tradition for this rule. The Cyfnerth and Blegywryd Redactions go further: for them the denial of the principal offence of homicide needs the backing of only fifty men; but the wording in the two Redactions pulls in opposite directions. According to the Blegywryd Redaction:

> "Whoever denies homicide [*llofrudyaeth*] and its abetments wholly gives the oath of fifty men. And that is a compurgation of country [*reith gwlat*]; and it is called 'denying wood and field' [*diwat coet a maes*]. And like to that, whoever denies homicide apart from the abetments, or one abetment without anything else, gives the oath of fifty men".[48]

The expression *gwadu coed a maes* must imply denial of homicide, and the Cyfnerth Redaction uses only that expression in the rule "the one who denies wood and field, let him give the oath of fifty men without slave and without alien, and three of them under vow of abstinence from riding and linen and woman".[49] *Coed a maes* seems to look back; but we shall see that *rhaith gwlad* looks forward. For the moment we turn back to the abetments of homicide, and note that if the numbers of compurgators required seem incredibly large, there is evidence that in the aftermath of the Glyn Dŵr rising, people loyal to the English Crown were complaining that the kin of those killed by such loyalists were requiring:

> "that they would them excuse of the Death of such Rebels so slain by one Assache, after the custom of Wales, that is to say by the Oath of Three hundred men".[50]

The lawbooks' definition of the Three Columns confines them to the abetments, and the abetments of homicide may once have stood alone: but in the oldest surviving manuscripts there are substantial additions about various aspects of the law of homicide, beginning with rules for the distribution among the kin of the liability to contribute to the *galanas* payment and the right to share in it. There is confusion enough in these rules to confirm the belief that the whole system was breaking down in the thirteenth century. We may indeed doubt whether the ruler would allow the law to "release vengeance" if the compensation procedure was not carried through, as the Blegywryd Redaction provides;[51] but this passage makes it clear that we have to do with commutation of vengeance, as do other passages such as this from *Llyfr Colan*:

[48] Bleg., *supra* n. 5, 30.29–31.5; LatD, *supra* n. 25, 333.22–27 gives the same rule in Latin, with *llawrutyaeth, affeitheu,* and *diwad coed a mays* in Welsh; it does not mention *rhaith gwlad.*

[49] WML, *supra* n. 20, 37.17–20. The provision about abstinence is found elsewhere in special cases.

[50] 1 Henry V c.6 (1415).

[51] Bleg., *supra* n. 5, 110.3,6,9.

> "Neither a cleric nor a woman is entitled to share of *galanas*, since they are not avengers. They are bound to pay on behalf of their children unless they give their oath that they will never have children."[52]

The appended material also deals with special cases of liability, of which only one will be mentioned here:

> "If it happens that a person kills another with poison, he pays double *galanas*, for it is furious; or else let his life be forfeit for one *galanas*, and his manner of death will be at the will of the Lord, whether by hanging or burning; if he denies it, let him give the denial for killing a corpse, redoubled; that is the oath of six hundred men. The persons who make poison in order that others be killed with it are at the option of the Lord, whether they are banished or put to death; if they deny it, let them give the oath of six hundred men."[53]

As a further pendant to the abetments of homicide the Test Book has much to day about *sarhaed*, which in Welsh law corresponds closely enough to the *iniuria* of Roman law.[54] To kill anyone was prima facie *sarhaed*;[55] but the Iorwerth Redaction goes too far with "no one is killed without first suffering sarhaed",[56] for there were exceptions: if a blow aimed at an animal rebounded and killed someone, *galanas* was payable but not *sarhaed*. Perhaps we have pedagogic ingenuity in the case of the bowman whose arrow goes through his intended victim and kills another man behind him: *sarhaed* is payable only for the first.[57] The measure of *galanas* and *sarhaed* varied with the status of the victim, so that the lawbooks have to go into more detail than need concern us. According to the Test Book:

> "The legal measure of *galanas* is three times the *sarhaed* of the person killed, according to his status. Others say that for the person whose *sarhaed* is three kine and three score pence, the worth is three kine and three score kine; and similarly as every person's status rises".[58]

[52] Col., *supra* n. 19, §§ 299, 300: "*Ny dyly na gureyc nac escolheyc ran o alanas, canyt ynt dyalwyr. Wynteu a delaant talu tros eu plant ony rodant eu llu na bo plant udunt vyth.*" Cf. LTMW, *supra* n. 19, 150.22–9, translating Bleg., *supra* n. 5, 32.27–33.3.

[53] LTMW, *supra* n. 19, 151.15–26, translating AL, *supra* n. 14, IV.iii.12,13.

[54] In modern Welsh *sarhad* means "insult". Since the medieval form *sarhaed* has the double sense of the insulting act and the compensation payable for it, the medieval spelling is used for these senses. There is no sufficient authority for the spelling *saraad* used in the translation of *Ancient Laws*.

[55] Col., *supra* 19, § 297: "*Pan llader dyn, centaf y serheyr.*"

[56] LTMW, *supra* n. 19, 147.29, translating Ior., *supra* n. 19, § 108/1; cf. Col., *supra* n. 19, §297.

[57] LTMW, *supra* n. 19, 153.11–28, translating DwCol., *supra* n. 23, §§ 169–72.

[58] LTMW, *supra* n. 19, 144.15–20, translating Ior., *supra* n. 19, § 105/3,4. "Score pence" translates Welsh *ugain arian*, for which some scholars prefer "ounces of silver". The Latin texts have *unciae*, and of course twenty silver pennies did (or should) weigh one ounce Troy.

The others were certainly right: only the king and his "members" had a *sarhaed* of a third of the *galanas*. The Welsh theory of class and status is briefly expressed by the Blegywryd Redaction in triad form:

> "There are three kinds of man [*dyn*, that is, "human being"]: a king, a *breyr*, and a villein, and their members. The members of a king are those who are related to royal status though it does not belong to them".[59]

The Iorwerth Redaction is more definite: the king's members "are his sons and his nephews and his male first-cousins", and adds that these men

> "will be of that status until they take land, and after that their status will follow that of the land they take, except for this, that if it happens that they take villein-land the status of their land will rise to make it free land".[60]

The *breyr* was a free man who had come into his inheritance of land by the death of all his direct male ancestors: his status was higher than that of his descendants, but he was of the same gentry class. The class is defined by the Welsh word *bonheddig*, a derivative of *bôn*, "stock".[61] The three-unit status was that of the male *bonheddig* who had not yet inherited land: on his father's death he would rise to six-unit status, but he might in the interim have risen to four-unit status by becoming a member of the royal bodyguard (*teilu*), or to even higher status as a court officer. Most court officers were of six-unit status, and the chief officers were of a nine-unit status. An unmarried woman was of half the status of her brother: when she married, her *galanas* was unaffected, for it was her own blood relations who were concerned in any question of homicide: but her *sarhaed* would be one-third of the *sarhaed* of her husband, or of her last husband if she was a widow. The status of a villein depended on the class of his patron-lord: a king's villein was of three-unit status, a *breyr*'s villein of half the status of a king's villein.[62]

This relation between *galanas* and *sarhaed* applied to the gentry and villein classes, and to the class of settled aliens, though the triadic statement does not account for them. It did not apply to those above or below those

[59] Bleg., *supra* n. 5, 5.12–15.

[60] LTMW, *supra* n. 19, 7.1–2, 16–21. The final exception recalls the arguments in England about the relation of villein tenure to villein status.

[61] The word means "stock" both literally and metaphorically: it is today freely used for the trunk of a tree or the stub of a cheque. It is unfortunate that so many writers have regarded the *breyr* as a noble, perhaps under the influence of the *nobilis* of some Latin texts: the name *uchelwr*, an alternative for *breyr*, has had a similar effect, since in modern Welsh it is used of the squirearchy. *Breyr* can be translated by *paterfamilias* if we remember that his position was not exactly that of his Roman counterpart. The point of the name *bonheddig* is that the *bonheddig* is of identifiable stock; the gentry likewise belong to a known *gens*, and gentle behaviour is in origin that to be expected of people of a known stock.

[62] WML, *supra* n. 20, 44.18–22, among others.

two classes. It did not apply to those of royal class, nor to chattel slaves. The manuscripts' accounts of the rights of a king and his members vary significantly and suggestively: they may reflect the provenance of the manuscripts, and they are certainly evidence for change in political conditions. The reference to "the members of *a* king" shows that the Laws of Court were presented as laws for the court of any Welsh king, whose realm was, in modern language, a sovereign state.[63] But all the surviving manuscripts imply that if all rulers were royal, some were more royal than others. So the Blegywryd Redaction, after setting out in detail the way the *sarhaed* of a king was paid, adds that this is how *sarhaed* is paid to "a king who has a principal seat [*eisteddfa arbennig* ; Latin *sedes principalis*], as Dinefwr under the king of Deheubarth, or Aberffraw under the king of Gwynedd".[64] The Iorwerth Redaction Test Book gives the full royal *sarhaed* only to the king of Aberffraw; he is given less than some other texts give their more royal kings, but the measure is given in the same kind of terms:

> "a gold plate for him, as broad as his face and as thick as the nail of a ploughman who has been a ploughman nine years; and a gold rod as long as himself and as thick as his little finger, and a hundred cows for every cantred that he has, with a white bull with red ears for every hundred cows among them."[65]

For the king's "members" we turn to *Llyfr Colan*:

> "The *galanas* of the King's wife, and his son, and his captain of the household, and his *edling*[66] and his nephew, one third of the King's *galanas*, without gold and without silver; and the *sarhaed* of each of those is one third of his *sarhaed*."[67]

At the other end of society was the slave, to whom the principles of *galanas* did not apply because society did not regard him as having relatives: if he was killed, his value must be paid to his owner; but even he was entitled to *sarhaed*:

> "The *sarhaed* of a slave, twelve pence: six for a smock and three for breeches and one for a rope and one for a hedging-bill and one for brogues. His worth is a

[63] Here "king" means the ruler of any realm, however small; the designation *king* (*brenin*, Latin *rex*) was freely used for the rulers of every small realm until the Welsh found it tactful not to use it; in the lawbooks the ruler may be either *brenin* or *arglwydd*, "lord".

[64] Bleg., *supra* n. 5, 3.17–29.

[65] LTMW, *supra* n. 19, 154.12–18, translating Ior., *supra* n. 19, § 110/3.

[66] Here, the designated heir to the throne: *edling* is from OE *ætheling*, which applied to all those who would be "members" of a Welsh king; and the Welsh word had this wider meaning at first, but was later confined to the member who had been named by the king as his successor. The English word never came to have the narrower meaning: D N Dumville, "The Ætheling: A Study in Anglo-Saxon Constitutional History", (1979) 8 *Anglo-Saxon England* 1.

[67] LTMW, *supra* n. 19, 153.35–154.4, translating Col., *supra* n. 19, §§ 304,305.

> pound if he comes from this island; if he is from overseas, his worth will be six score pence and a pound."[68]

The female slave's *sarhaed* was the same but "if she is servient and does not go either to the spade or to quern, twenty-four pence".[69] The Blegywryd Redaction explains that the servient slave was a needlewoman.[70] Whereas there are wide-ranging parallels to the slave woman's working the quern, neither spade nor needle seems to appear: it is milking which is associated with milling in the Germanic texts.[71]

In the two other Columns, the abetments of theft and arson, there is no division into grades, and the provisions may well surprise the modern reader. For all abetments of theft the penalty was a *dirwy*, the larger penalty of twelve kine or £3, which is greater than the triple penalty for the gravest abetments of homicide: but we must remember that the essential secrecy of theft made it the most disturbing offence in early society, so that when the principal offender was liable to the death penalty, it was not unreasonable to penalise the abettor heavily. But if the abetments were denied, "their denial is as great as the denial of principal offenders".[72] And the measure of support for denial of theft is another surprise:

> "The oath of twelve men for a horse, and for three score pence, since that is the horse of least value in law .... To deny a horse's burden, and a steer (for a horse can carry a steer as its burden), six men are required of him, with himself as the seventh . . .To deny a pig, or a sheep, or a back-burden, his oath as one of five".[73]

The value of the stolen property was significant for the thief himself, since his fate varied with that value:

> "In the law of Hywel, he is a sale thief up to the value of fourpence, and from there on his life is forfeit. Others say that for every four-footed animal which is stolen, whether lamb or kid or piglet, his life is forfeit; nevertheless it is safer to say from fourpence".[74]

The "sale thief" (*lleidr gwerth*) was to be sold into slavery at the price of £7: he could and no doubt most often would redeem himself by paying that

[68] LTMW, *supra* n. 19, 155.34–8, translating Ior., *supra* n. 19, §110/16,17. F W Maitland, *Domesday Book and Beyond* (Cambridge, University Press, 1897), 31 and note 9, cites the *sarhaed* of the Welsh slave as a parallel to passages in *Leges Henrici Primi*; but the parallel is not very close, and gives no real clue to the source of the Welsh or English rules.

[69] LTMW, *supra* n. 19, 156.1–3, translating Col., *supra* n. 19, § 331.

[70] Bleg., *supra* n. 5, 59.25–27.

[71] J Grimm, *Deutsche Rechtsaltertümer*, ed. by A Heusler and R Hübner 4th edn (Leipzig, Mayer und Müller, 1899), vol. 1, 485. Cf. Exodus 11.5 and Luke 17.35.

[72] LTMW, *supra* n. 19, 157.17–18, translating Ior., *supra* n. 19, § 111/15.

[73] LTMW, *supra* n. 19, 157.19–33, translating Ior., *supra* n. 19, § 111/17–20.

[74] LTMW, *supra* n. 19, 164.16–21, translating Ior., *supra* n. 19, § 115/2,3.

price. For most items likely to be stolen, the lawbooks specified a legal value, and a passage in the Blegywryd Redaction is one of few references to legislation by a Welsh ruler:

> "For everything which has no legal value, sworn appraisal is allowed according to the law of Hywel. Rhys ap Gruffudd, the suzerain of Deheubarth, by agreement with his country, laid down sworn appraisal for every beast, to wit, that the owner should swear that the beast was worth the value he put on it, and that he would get that for it".[75]

That statement from a southern text meets the difficulty for which a Gwynedd manuscript has made special provision:

> "If it happens that a person swears to property in the hands of another person as being stolen, and that the thing has no legal value and because of that the defendant thief seeks, although the thing is worth much, to appraise it at little (since there is no right to put anyone to death save for the value of fourpence or more): then it is proper for the owner of the property to swear to it a second time. This is how he swears to it: that he would get so much for it, and that he would not give less than that".[76]

More will be said about the procedure in cases of theft when we look at *Llyfr Cynghawsedd*: here must be briefly mentioned the variants on unlawful taking. Surreption (*anghyfarch*) was "everything taken in absence which is not denied"; the name was also applied to other acts done without the appropriate permission. Robbery (*trais*) was "everything taken in presence against the will"; it was less serious than theft, and was not a capital offence. Fury (*ffyrnigrwydd*) was "spoiling the property both for himself and for him to whom it belongs", in modern terms "malicious damage to property"; the denial was "double the denial of other theft" and would or might carry the death penalty.[77]

The nine abetments of fire have a further surprise for us in their logical application of principle. The oath of fifty men is required to deny any of these; but there is a problem if the abetment was committed "by stealth" (*yn lladrad*). According to one view of that case, the *rhaith* was subject to a condition to which we shall return, but:

> "Others say that no compurgation in the world for stealth is more than twelve men, and that it is twelve men that deny stealth, . . . since the status of the stealth is greater than that of the burning".[78]

[75] LTMW, *supra* n. 19, 164.22–8, translating Bleg., *supra* n. 19, 93.23–4, 154.11–15.

[76] LTMW, *supra* n. 19, 164.29–165.1, translating DwCol., *supra* n. 23, § 304.

[77] LTMW, *supra* n. 19, 166.11–18, translating Ior., *supra* n. 19, § 115/12 and DwCol., *supra* n. 23, 286.

[78] LTMW, *supra* n. 19, 169.19–24, translating Ior., *supra* n. 19, § 116/12 (from manuscript C).

The same condition applied to the twelve as to the fifty. This invocation of the status of stealth gives expression to the fear in early society of the secret offender who undermines mutual confidence: the principle is applied in the rule "if a thief is found burning a house by stealth and is caught, let his life be forfeit",[79] a rule to be found, not in the Column, but appended to the values of kilns.

This reliance on the higher status of stealth has a doctrinaire look which gives some support to modern disdain for medieval methods: but the fact is that in our period the doctrinaire was struggling with the practical, and for the special rules which limited the swearers' freedom, we turn first to the Three Columns and to the general statements about the qualification and disqualification of testifiers. The Blegywryd Redaction uses two different words for two groups of disqualification: for one group, we can say that the testifier is "repelled", since Latin Redaction D has *repelli* for the Welsh *gwrthneu*: for the other group the Welsh word is *llysu*, which is in general use for all barring of testifiers. The distinction between the groups turned on the stage in the procedure at which objection was to be made: that could be important, as the triad of the three vain statements in law (*tair ofer ymadrodd*) shows:

> "Three vain statements which are said in court and do not thrive: denial before verdict, and objection before its time, and case put after judgment".[80]

"Denial before verdict" was in vain, because the verdict in question was the judge's ruling on the form of proof required by the case presented, and it was improper to offer denial before judgment made denial appropriate. "Objection before its time" was in vain, because the party would not know that the testifier's evidence was not favourable to him until he had heard what the testifier said, and a testifier who was prematurely challenged would stand as valid, even though there might be good ground for a bar.[81] The challenge must be made when the testifier gave his evidence in reply to the justice and swore by the relic: the Iorwerth Redaction makes the challenger counterswear and charge the testifier with perjury before he adds that the testifier's word is no word against him.[82] There seems to have been a traditional triad of the bars to a testifier, and these are named in the Iorwerth Redaction: *Llyfr Colan* on the other hand has drawn on

[79] LTMW, *supra* n. 19, 169.25–6, translating WML, *supra* n. 20, 104.1–2.

[80] "*Tri ofer ymadra6d a dywedir yn llys ac ny ffynnant; g6at kyn deturyt, a llys kyn amser, a chygha6s g6edy bra6t*": WML, *supra* n. 20, 125.24–126.1, re-punctuated. "Case put" seems to fit best the use of *cyngaws* in the Iorwerth land law tractate, and to make the best sense here. When final judgment has been given (following the success or failure of the proof required by the verdict), it is too late to state a case.

[81] LTMW, *supra* n. 19, 89.29–33, translating Ior., *supra* n. 19, § 77/13.

[82] LTMW, *supra* n. 19, 93.28–37, translating Ior., *supra* n. 19 § 79/10–12/1.

another source for something more analytical. The objections are said to be "in the law of Hywel according to the Book of the White House".[83] Since *Llyfr Colan* concludes its account of the objections by saying that if it is doubted whether all those objections are in the law of Hywel, "let the Latin books be looked up, and there they will be found"[84], it seems that this White House Book was in Latin.[85] That Latin source has not survived, and the earliest extant Latin manuscript which carries material similar to that in *Llyfr Colan* is the late medieval MS 454 of Corpus Christi College, Cambridge. The Latin text names three classes of *reprobacio*: natural, general and singular. It illustrates natural incapacity with the single example: a woman, who cannot testify against a man because of the instability of the sex. General incapacity is "as for a hand-having thief, even if he has made amends; a perjurer, and an excommunicate, who cannot testify anywhere." Singular incapacity arises "as of *galanas*, contention over inheritance, abuse of a wife, and *sarhaed* previously committed . . . and as yet unamended".[86] The distinction is between the natural incapacity, which is ingrained in the would-be testifier: the general incapacity, which applies in all cases, but has been acquired by the testifier: and the singular, which applies only *vis-à-vis* the particular party with whom the testifier has an unresolved dispute. The classification in *Llyfr Colan* is slightly different: this recognises "objection for offence, objection for nature, and objection for act." While its objections for offence are the same as the Latin cases of general incapacity, the objections for nature add to a woman "nearer kin, . . . and an alien against a Welshman". Again:

> "by reason of act there are in the law of Hywel these objections: those are land-feud and blood-feud and woman-feud, and those last count as one objection, for woman-feud is of the essence of enmity of kindred."[87]

These grounds of disqualification did not apply equally to all kinds of testifier:

> "There is no right to object to a maintainer if he is of status, for he charges no ill against anyone, but keeps for the owner what is his."

[83] LTMW, *supra* n. 19, 94.1–3, translating Col., *supra* n. 19, § 528.

[84] Col., *supra* n. 19, § 565.

[85] If the White House Book was indeed in Latin, it should probably be regarded as "the Whitland Book" and understood as a manuscript at (or from) the Cistercian abbey.

[86] LatE, *supra* n. 25, 457.13–20: "Causa autem reprobacionis est triplex: videlicet, naturalis, generalis, singularis. Naturalis: ut in femina, que non potest testificari super virum propter instabilitatem sexus. Generalis: ut in fure manifesto, licet sit emendatum, periurio, excommunicato, qui in nullo loco possunt testificare. Singularis: ut galanas, contencio hereditatis, abusio uxoris, et sarhaet ante factum, et in tribus de ea est conquestum, et adhuc inemendatum."

[87] LTMW, *supra* n. 19, 94, translating Col., *supra* n. 19, §§ 528–31.

Whereas "as an attestor charges ill against a person, that person can object to him".[88] That must depend on what the attestor has been called to witness to, and the exemption of maintainers from objection does not mean that they were exempt from all discredit. It was the *reprobacio singularis*, the "objection for act", which was inappropriate because it was personal to the party against whom the testimony was given, and as we shall see from the list of the cases in which maintainers are appropriate, the testimony of the maintainer for one party was given without reference to any other party. We are told, however, that maintainers must be "of status" (*breiniol*), which seems to mean that they must have a status recognised by their society, so that aliens and slaves were excluded: that hardly needed saying. A more important rule required all maintainers to be *addwyn*, for which the most useful English rendering will be "creditable".[89]

Maintainers can be discredited under several heads, some of which overlap other fields of disqualification. Discredited are an alien; the three persons whose word is no word (a religious who has broken his profession, a testifier who has given false testimony, a confessed coward);[90] a person not of age to answer, and a woman (since maintainers are not possible from those); and a blind man too, since he does not see what he maintains.[91] The "ways in which it is right that there should be maintainers" are:

> "First, to maintain land and earth for a man. Second is keeping before loss. Third is maintaining birth and rearing. Fourth is maintaining hospitality. Fifth is maintaining status. Sixth is maintaining an alien for a person".[92]

The maintainer had not only to be creditable: he must also be well-informed on the matter on which he testified: at least, he must have a named qualification which meant that he should know the truth. Keeping before loss and birth and rearing were special pleas in answer to a charge of theft: the defendant claimed in the one case that the animal had been born and reared in his care and had never left it, and in the other that the animal was in his keeping before the time at which the claimant asserted that he had lost it: neither

[88] LTMW, *supra* n. 19, 95.11–17, translating Ior., *supra* n. 19, § 80/5,6.

[89] There is confusion between two words which would be *addwyn* and *addfwyn* in modern Welsh, because almost any possible medieval spelling could represent either word. *Addfwyn* has survived: at Matthew 5.5 it corresponds to the "meek" of the authorised version, but has none of that word's suggestion of weakness. *Addwyn* has died out, and early dictionaries offer the English equivalents "honest, just" (1688) and "honest, virtuous, good, blameless" (1753): "creditable" is here preferred, as leading to "discredit" for the verb *anaddwyno*.

[90] The expression translates literally the Welsh *nid gair eu gair*, which reflects a concept found in various contexts in the lawbooks: thus the Prologue to the Cyfnerth Redaction records that Hywel Dda's word was a word over all within his dominions, where no-one's word was a word over him: his authority was paramount: WML, *supra* n. 20, 1.8–9.

[91] AL, *supra* n. 14, IX.i.19/7.

[92] WML, *supra* n. 20, 320.19–23 (re-translated). AL, *supra* n. 14, IX.xxxv.1 adds "to maintain disease in a beast".

plea implied that any other person had done anything wrong. For these pleas the maintainers must be men of the same status as the defendant, unless the defendant was not of status, for in that event the overriding requirement of status applied to them.[93] For hospitality, which meant liability for the goods of guests in the defendant's house, the maintainers must be the people of the house.[94] Cases of "land and earth" were brought by claimants to hereditary right in particular land: though the claim would usually be made when the claimant was not occupying the land, it did not necessarily imply wrong on anyone's part: the occupier might also have a hereditary right, or he might be occupying the land in virtue of some right less than hereditary proprietary right. In such a case the maintainers must be *uchelwyr o ambiniogau tir*, "landed proprietors holding adjoining land".[95]

This reference reminds us to look at the Iorwerth Redaction's account of procedure in cases relating to land. This gives a detailed account of the way the claim is to be brought to court and the date for the hearing is fixed, and then describes the layout of the court, illustrating it with a diagram:

> "And at that adjudged date it is proper for all to come to the land, both them and their aid. And then it is proper to make two parties and to sit legally. This is how they sit legally: The King, or the man who is in his place, sits with his back to the sun or the weather (lest the weather should disturb his face), with the court justice or the commote justice (whichever is the senior) sitting in front of him, with the other justice or justices who may be present on his left hand, and the priest (if any) or priests, on his right hand; and next to the King his two elders, with his goodmen from there on, on either side of him. From there a gangway for the justices, opposite them, for them to proceed to their judgment seat. The claimant's *cyngaws* with his left hand to the gangway, with the claimant next to him in the middle and his *canllaw* on the other side of him, and the serjeant standing behind the *cyngaws*. The other party on the other side of the gangway: the defendant's *cyngaws* with his right hand to the gangway, with the defendant next to him in the middle and his *canllaw* on the other side of him, and the serjeant behind the latter".[96]

Three points call for particular attention. First is the location of the hearing, on the land in question. We shall see that this may have some practical significance, but we shall also see (from *Llyfr Cynghawsedd*) that this location was not essential. For if the court in fact came together at some other place, though the defendant was entitled to call for a move, he must do so as soon as the claimant had presented his claim; if he put in an answer to the claim, he thereby waived the right to have the hearing moved. Second is the identity

93 AL, *supra* n. 14, IX.xxxvi.1.

94 AL, *supra* n. 14, IX xxxvi.2.

95 AL, *supra* n. 14, IX.xxxvi.3.

96 LTMW, *supra* n. 19, 84.26–85.9, translating Ior., *supra* n. 19, § 73/1–6. In the oldest manuscripts the diagram is a simple arrangement of the names; in later manuscripts it depicts the people of the court: the most imaginative (and perhaps more imaginary) picture is that of manuscript *S* (BL Add 22356), which is reproduced as the frontispiece of LTMW, *supra* n. 19.

of the elders and goodmen, and their function, to which we shall return. Third, and of the greatest interest to the legal historian, is the significance of the *cyngaws* and *canllaw*. It has never been shown what, if any, was the difference between the two; and what is more important, there seems to be a conflict between texts about their function. In the account of procedure in an action for land, both in the Iorwerth Redaction and in *Llyfr Colan*, the two representatives are named and the parties put "loss and gain in their mouth".[97] This seems to imply that, like the attorney in English law, the representative's act binds the party. Elsewhere in the classical law, the principal is allowed to repudiate the statements of his *canllaw* and *cyngaws*, which seems to imply that their function was that of the counter or narrator whose act did not bind the principal.[98]

With sureties given for law, the sureties being "pledges in the form of living persons, two or more from each party" who are held in the ruler's prison,[99] the hearing could go on and the parties would present their case. According to both the Iorwerth land law tractate and *Llyfr Cynghawsedd*, the claimant would tell the court that he was proprietor of the land claimed and was ejected from it by the defendant, and that he had maintainers to prove his proprietorship and knowers to prove the ejectment. On this two-handed plea the Iorwerth tractate comments:

> "If there are some who are surprised that maintainers and knowers are offered by the same party, the law says that it can be done until the defendant's answer is heard."

The old-fashioned Welsh lawyer no doubt felt that only one kind of testifier could be invoked at any one point in a case. *Llyfr Cynghawsedd* puts the point in more formal shape. The claimant pleads both elements, saying:

> "that he is proprietor by kindred and descent over this land, and that he was illegally driven from it, and that if there is anyone who doubts him he has enough who will maintain his proprietorship, and if there is anyone who doubts that he was illegally driven, that he has enough who know it."

If now "it is said against him that he has two pleas, maintainers and knowers, and it is said that it is not right to have them for the same claim", the passage turns to *oratio recta* for the claimant's reply:

[97] LTMW, *supra* n. 19, 85.29–86.6, translating Ior., *supra* n. 19, § 74/2–11; Col., *supra* n. 19, §§ 453–9.

[98] DwCol., *supra* n. 23, § 483: if different answers to a claim have been put forward by the defendant and his *canllaw* and *cyngaws*, and the claimant tries to choose the "worst answer", "the law says that it is right for the defendant to choose the plea he wishes from the three".

[99] LTMW, *supra* n. 19, 85.18–21, translating Ior., *supra* n. 19, § 73/7,8. According to Col., *supra* n. 19, §§ 460–2, the call for sureties is made by the claimant's *cyngaws* after the parties have been bound: but "others say that it is the claimant who should call for surety and on the law, and that before the two parties are legally bound", which is the Iorwerth rule. Of course the call could not be made by the *cyngaws* before he had been named.

> "God knows, wherever I am doubted about as much as I said, I want [*mynev a uenhaf*] maintainers where they are right and knowers where they are right to prove that what I said was true."

The text approves this argument as good law.[100] The mixture of direct and indirect speech shows that the Welsh courts did not apply "that hard rule, He who fails in a Syllable, fails in the whole cause", a rule which would not be applied when some institutions of English law were introduced by the Statute of Wales of 1284: here Welsh practice gave a better precedent.[101]

The whole field of theft law is illuminated by *Llyfr Cynghawsedd*; but its most important contribution is the principle of the three replications, already cited.[102] What is effectively a charge of theft arises when property is claimed by the claimant's laying one hand on it and the other on relics and asking who will "keep" it—who will resist the claim. If no-one responds, the claimant seeks the authority of a justice and takes the property: but anyone who responds has the three replications, to admit the claim and give up the property; to deny the claim and support denial by the appropriate oath; or to offer another plea (*arddelw*), which amounts to a denial of the offence without denying the taking ("asportation"), which is the defining element for theft. The commonest such plea is what an English lawyer would call "voucher to warranty": the defendant asserts that he acquired the goods from a named third person, who can be brought before the court in due course: if that vouchee admits that he transferred the goods to the defendant, the latter is freed from the charge and drops out of the case entirely. The claimant must then bring a fresh case against the vouchee, who has the same choice of pleas as the original defendant. If the vouchee denies the transfer, the defendant stands convicted, though he is given the opportunity to disprove the vouchee's refusal. The Welsh lawyers were perhaps not altogether happy with this kind of pleading, which took the proof away from the claimant who had made an assertion which he was prepared to prove: the name *cyfraith atgas*, "hateful law" was applied to some cases in which "the defendant takes the proof from the claimant for his own, and that is like upsetting law into its opposite".[103]

An example which the lawyer-historian may find more attractive is given in the treatment by *Llyfr Cynghawsedd* of a claim to land by mother-right (*mamwys*). Land could not be inherited by a woman: the basic thought was

[100] Wiliam, "*Llyfr Cynghawsedd*", *supra* n. 32, § 10; AL, *supra* n .14, VII.i.10.

[101] Statute of Wales 1284, c. 8: "it is necessary that the Demandant should count against the Deforciant, and express the Cause of his Demand, and this by Words that contain the Truth, without Exception to Words: Not following that hard rule, He who fails in a Syllable, fails in the whole cause."

[102] See *supra* at n. 31.

[103] *Cyfreithiau Hywel Dda yn ôl llawysgrif Coleg yr Iesu Rhydychen LVII*, ed. by M Richards (Cardiff, University of Wales Press, 1957, rev. edn 1990), 138, cf. ibid., 105. Did the difficulty arise because the defendant was proving something positive, rather than denying the

that daughters were to be given in marriage to husbands who held land or who would inherit land on the death of all direct male ancestors. In certain specified cases, however, a daughter could transmit a right to land to her son by an alien who held no land. In the case we are concerned with, a man is claiming a share of land with or from his maternal uncles because those uncles (and/or others of the kin) gave his mother to an alien. His claim can be met with a denial of the gift, for a woman who gave herself to an alien would not transmit any right to her son by that alien: but our pleading reveals a different possibility. The defendant is named in the singular, for the law provided for the appointment of a single representative for a group having the same rights. He admits that the kin gave the claimant's mother in marriage to an alien, but goes on to say that this alien (the claimant's father) had become a landholder—by making a successful claim to land by mother-right for himself. Since the no-longer-alien's land will pass from him to the claimant and to his other sons, the claimant has patrimony in another place, and has no right to inherit through his mother. The claimant may admit this assertion, and if he does so, there will be no need of proof: but if he does not, the proof promised by the defendant will be called for. Since the defendant is alleging that the claimant's father has landholding status, it might seem that maintainers should testify to that state of affairs: but the rule requires knowers, who will testify, not to the status but to the event which created it, the concession of mother-right to the claimant's father. [104] This is a good rule, for the claimant's father might have lost his right to the patrimony (by its being given up as *gwaetir*, "blood-land", if not in any other way) after the concession of mother-right: but that loss would not help the claimant, since it would not make the claimant's father an alien.

PROCEDURE IN COURT

We may now look a little more closely at the elders and goodmen of the Iorwerth land law tractate's court. If we assume that they were essential members of the court, who joined in expressing the final judgement, we still have to ask whether the elders were men specifically appointed to an office, or only elderly men who were picked up to strengthen the court because they would remember facts from an earlier period. We must also ask whether the

claimant's assertion, as the party impugned usually did? The explanation is probably the attempt of a later jurist to explain a traditional expression which he knew as defining a legal practice, though he did not know its origin. M Owen has suggested to me that *atgas* should be understood as "hate-causing", rather than in its modern sense of "hateful". Neither *Geirfa Barddoniaeth Gynnar Gymraeg*, ed. by J Lloyd-Jones (Cardiff, University of Wales Press, 1931–8) nor GPC, *supra* n. 38 offers light on the expression. A Owen has the neutral "untoward law" in both passages: AL, *supra* n. 14, V.ii.117, VII.i.45.

104 AL, *supra* n. 14, VII.i.25; Wiliam, "*Llyfr Cynghawsedd*", *supra* n. 32, § 15.

elders who were the appropriate maintainers for a claim of proprietorship were the same men as the court elders and what they were. To these questions we have no ready answer. There may be a clue in the Latin Redactions' translation of the Welsh words for "elder": this is sometimes *natu maior*, which must mean "older", and sometimes *senior*, which may mean either "older" or "senior" in the modern English sense of "of higher standing in some respect".[105] Leaving that question unanswered, we ask about the number of maintainers, and find that there is a minimum of two: in contrast with attestors, of whom two and only two are obligatory, the case will be the stronger for having more than two maintainers. Indeed, there is a general principle that where no number is specified, two are needed:

> "If he promises a particular number of testifiers, let him fulfil or fail. If he promises what will be a quota in law, two or three are enough, though more would be better. The testimony of one person is not testimony."[106]

To this last rule there were exceptions, set out in the ennead of the Nine Tongued-ones (*Y Naw Tafodiog*), which have become ten or more in some manuscripts.[107] Of these the most disturbing to us is "a thief at the gibbet as to his fellow-thieves".

Another significant refinement of the rules of evidence needs closer attention. We perhaps assume that when a maintainer supports a claim to proprietorship he does so by simply swearing that the claimant is a proprietor. The better view is that the maintainer would speak of his reasons for his belief: this is implied by the triad of the Three Dead Testimonies (*Tair Marw Dystiolaeth*):

> "One is, if a person claims land, and says that he is entitled to it and that his ancestors were on that land before him and left ditches or other works on the land, and if there were anyone who doubted it that he had maintainers who would be enough in law to maintain it; and that when it was desired to test the maintainers they returned that they had heard from their ancestors that it was the other's ancestors who made that stone work or the ditches or banks, that is taken as testimony."

If the hearing was being held on the land, as it should be, the "works" would be pointed out to the court.

> "Second is, if it happens that a person claims land by kindred and descent and puts that in the mouth of maintainers, and that the maintainers say that they heard from their ancestors that that was true, and did not see it, yet that is taken in place of testimony. Third is, if a person claims land and the defendant answers him and says that it was adjudged by law to his father and his grandfather, and

[105] Finding a satisfactory Welsh translation for "senior" is an unsolved problem in bilingual Wales today.

[106] LTMW, *supra* n. 19, 95.31–4, translating Ior., *supra* n. 19, § 81/1–3.

[107] LTMW, *supra* n. 19, 61.18–62.36, translating Ior., *supra* n. 19, § 56/1–9 with some variants from Bleg., *supra* n. 5 and WML, *supra* n. 20.

puts that in the mouth of knowers, and the knowers stand by him that they heard that from their ancestors before them and that they did not see it adjudged, that is a quota".[108]

There was a fairly general requirement that compurgators should be of the *galanas*-kin of the principal, and that two-thirds should come from the father's kin and one-third from the mother's. This requirement would reduce the likelihood of false compurgation for two reasons. On the one hand, if the compurgation failed for lack of the full number of compurgators, those who had sworn would stand convicted of perjury and would thereby suffer in prestige and lose the right to testify. On the other hand, a successful compurgation would define the swearers as liable to pay *galanas* in any later case.

The most important refinements take different forms in the southern and northern traditions, and both forms may be attributable to the thirteenth century. In the Iorwerth Redaction and *Llyfr Colan* many compurgations are required to include "designated compurgators" (*gwŷr nod*). The references are not as clear as might be desired, but they are definite enough to show that these compurgators were picked out by name in advance—as they were in many other countries. We cannot tell who did the naming: if the principal did it, he would be naming relatives without knowing whether they would indeed support him. The designated compurgators were at the heart of the process of proof:

"It is right for a designated compurgator to swear that the oath of the person with whom he swears is clean; and if one man from among the designated compurgators fails, the whole compurgation fails. It is right for another compurgator to swear that it is to his mind most likely that what he swears is true; and though a third of the ordinary compurgation fail, it is right to judge according to the two-thirds".[109]

The southern development is revealed in several passages in the Blegywryd Redaction. We have already seen that that redaction used the name "compurgation of country" (*rhaith gwlad*) for the oath of 50 which is required for denial of homicide and all abetments.[110] Elsewhere in the redaction there is a definition:

"Where a compurgation of country is appropriate, it is right for the King to compel compurgators to a relic, to swear with the denier or against him, at their option".[111]

This compurgation is further defined as "the oath of fifty landed men [*deg wyr a deu vgeint o wyr tiryawc*] under the king": while in contrast "where

[108] LTMW, *supra* n. 19, 98.8–31, translating DwCol., *supra* n. 23, §§ 339–42.

[109] LTMW, *supra* n. 19, 95.20–27, translating Ior., *supra* n. 19, § 80/7.

[110] See *supra* at n. 48.

[111] LTMW, *supra* n. 19, 377.27–30, translating Bleg., *supra* n. 5, 106.22–4.

compurgation of country is not appropriate, the denier is entitled to seek compurgators for himself as may be judged".[112] To judge by the number of casual references to *rhaith gwlad* in the Blegywryd Redaction, the older compurgation was being replaced by something very like the English jury, under a name which reminds us that the English defendant put himself "on his country". If we suppose that the 12 and 24 found in England are sacrosanct numbers for jury-like inquisitions, the sources studied by Brunner for *Die Entstehung der Schwurgerichte* will tell us that the numbers varied widely, though the Welsh 50 has no exact counterpart in any of them. In the relevant passages in Latin Redaction D *rhaith gwlad* is translated only once (as *iuramento in patria*).[113] The Cyfnerth Redaction's only reference is under the second head of the triad of the Three Fours (*Tri Phedwar*), which is also in the Blegywryd Redaction at two different points. This second head names the four shields which protect a man from *rhaith gwlad*.[114]

Since there are provisions for *rhaith gwlad* in the Blegywryd Redaction and Latin Redaction D, they must have been in the lost Latin text which lies behind the two, and since the references in Latin D almost all use the Welsh name, it seems fairly certain that the lost Latin text also used it. There is no real evidence of a source for the concept in any earlier text, and it thus seems to be the innovation of a lawyer thinking in Welsh terms and adapting a form which he will have known from some contact with English law. We of the "Celtic fringe" have been conditioned to think of all new developments as coming to us from the Continent through England, and we need to remind ourselves that before Macadam and Telford the Western Seaway was a much easier route to travel than the muddy roads of England. Whereas today we are told that, in terms of travel by public transport from London, Aberystwyth lies west of Chicago, in the Middle Ages Holyhead, Iona, and even Stornoway were nearer to Santiago da Compostella than to London. The use in the Latin Redactions of technical terms from the vocabulary of Roman law shows that our jurists knew enough Roman law to translate effectively: they seem also to have anticipated some well-known dicta of English judges. Every legal historian knows of the dictum of Brian CJ, who said in 1467 that "the thought of man shall not be tried, for the devil himself knoweth not the thought of man".[115] Some two centuries earlier, the nameless scribe of the Black Book of Chirk had noted the rule "testimony is possible for word and act and testimony is not possible for thought".[116] In about 1309, that medieval

[112] Bleg., *supra* n. 5, 106.25–9.

[113] LTWL, *supra* n. 19, 367.19, corresponding to Bleg., *supra* n. 5, 34.18.

[114] WML, *supra* n. 20, 124.9–10, Bleg., *supra* n. 5, 109.9. At Bleg. 44.8–13 the four shields are named without reference to the triad, and in a slightly different form.

[115] YB Pasch. 7 Edward IV, pl. 2, f. 2, cited T F T Plucknett, *A Concise History of the Common Law*, 5th edn (London, Butterworth, 1956), 447 at n. 5.

[116] Evans, *Chirk Codex*, *supra* n. 46, 121.2–4; DwCol., *supra* n. 23, § 10.

Lord Denning, Bereford CJ, said:

> "God forbid that he should get to his law about a matter of which the country may have knowledge; for then with a dozen or half-a-dozen ruffians he might swear an honest man out of his goods."[117]

Half a century earlier, the redactor of *Llyfr y Damweiniau* noted:

> "If it happens that a person does a public wrong and he seeks to deny it in the session, it is not right for the lord to allow that, either by denial or by attestors, for public testimony is greater than testimony of law".[118]

From one source or another the Welsh medieval lawyers were continually finding ideas which could be applied to their own legal problems, and so grafting them onto the native stock that they would bear fruit. It is because the Welsh lawyer who is hidden behind the Blegywryd Redaction and Latin Redaction D wrote about *rhaith gwlad* that our word for "juror" today is *rheithiwr*.

[117] *Yearbooks of Edward II. Vol.II. 2 & 3 Edward II. A.D. 1308–1309 and 1309–10*, ed. by F W Maitland, Seld. Soc., vol. 19 (London, 1904), 195; the original French is at *Yearbooks of Edward II. Vol.I. 1 & 2 Edward II. A.D. 1307–1309*, ed. by F W Maitland, Seld. Soc., vol. 17 (London, 1903), xvi at n. 2.

[118] DwCol., *supra* n. 23, §203.

3

Petit Larceny, Jury Lenity and Parliament

ROGER D GROOT (LEXINGTON)*

INTRODUCTION

The Statute of Westminster I in 1275 provided that one indicted for "Petty Larceny that amounteth not [above the Value] of twelve-pence" should be bailable. That statute is thought to have created the distinction between grand and petit larceny—the former a felony and the latter now a misdemeanour—based upon the value of the stolen goods.[1] In fact, for a half century prior to 1275 capital larceny was differentiated from minor larceny and the differential was based in value. This chapter argues that from the 1220s onward, there was a "rule" that minor larcenies were not capital felonies. For the "rule" to operate, the juries needed to report that, while the accused had stolen the goods, they were of little value. The justices had then to apply the "rule" by imposing some non-capital penalty. A number of cases demonstrate that the juries and the justices acted in precisely this way. As juries had the power to set value, they also had power to spare the accused the gallows; there is evidence that they did so. There are tantalising hints that they did so by declaring value, long before 1275, at less than twelvepence. Finally, then, this chapter argues that the Statute of Westminster I did not create a new rule about the substantive law of larceny and the attendant penalties. Rather, the statute simply recognised an existing rule and applied it to an earlier stage of the proceedings.

THE STATUTE OF WESMINSTER I

In its fifteenth chapter, the statute provided:

* I am grateful for comments, especially those of Paul Brand, received when this paper was presented at the Fourteenth British Legal History Conference. I am also indebted to Henry Summerson and Daniel Klerman who have provided both insights and additional cases. My colleague David Millon kindly provided me with helpful comments on a draft of this paper.

[1] In my state, Virginia, for example, stealing goods valued at $200 or more is grand larceny, a felony, while stealing goods valued at less than $200 is petit larceny, a misdemeanour. Virginia Code Annotated §§ 18.2–95, 18.2–96 (Charlottesville, Virginia, The Michie Co., 1996).

> "But such as be indicted of Larceny, by Enquests taken before Sheriffs or Bailiffs by their Office, or of light Suspicion, or for Petty Larceny that amounteth not [above the Value] of twelve-pence, if they were not [guilty] of some other Larceny aforetime, or [guilty] of Receipt of Felons, or of Commandment, or Force, or Aid of felony done; or [guilty of] some other Trespass, for which ought not to lose Life or Member, and a Man appealed by a prover after the death of the Prover, if he be no common thief, nor defamed, shall from henceforth be no let out by sufficient surety, whereof the Sheriff will be answerable, and that without giving aught of their Goods".[2]

This is not an easy text to read. It attempts to set out several classes of persons who should be bailed. The difficulty is in identifying the classes. As I read the statute there are five classes. First, those indicted for larceny by inquests of sheriffs or bailiffs and who are not recidivists or involved in a felony. Secondly, those indicted for larceny on "light Suspicion" who are not recidivists or involved in a felony. Thirdly, those indicted for petit larceny who are not recidivists or involved in a felony. Fourthly, those indicted for non-capital trespasses. Fifthly, those accused by approvers who have died and about whom there is no other suspicion.

Read in this way, the statute grants a right to bail to the different classes for different reasons that point to the same conclusion. Those against whom there is little evidence, the second and fifth classes, are likely to be acquitted and so are likely to appear if bailed. Those in the first class still have hope that they will escape presentment and so are unlikely to flee. Those in the third and fourth classes do not face the capital penalty and so are unlikely to flee.

My understanding that the "ought not to lose Life or Member" clause applies only to those accused of "other Trespass" depends, of course, on my belief that long before the statute petit larceny had been understood to be non-capital. I will make that case in the sections following. But, that still leaves open knowing how to divide larceny into its major and minor forms. There is no question that the statute defines a petit larceny as a larceny in which the value of the goods "amounteth not [above] . . . twelve-pence". The question is whether the statute is a restatement of an existing definitional understanding or whether it is creating a definition. I believe the former. Thus, I disagree with those authorities who understand the statute to have, first, created the distinction between major and minor larcenies and, secondly, to have set the value criterion at twelvepence.[3]

[2] 3 Edw. I, c. 15.

[3] E.g., R Perkins and R Boyce, *Criminal Law*, 3rd edn (Mineola, New York, Foundation Press, 1982), 335.

A NOTE ON VALUES

The larceny cases sometimes state a value. A salmon was valued at sixpence in Durham in 1242,[4] and in Liverpool in 1246, a thief stole meal worth threepence.[5] These cases inform both the petit larceny question and the value-criterion question. Other cases do not state a specific value, but use such phrases as "little value" (*parvi precii*)[6] or "the theft was a small one" (*latrocinum adeo parvum est*).[7] These cases inform the petit larceny question, but can inform the value-criterion question only if the stolen goods are specified in the case and a value can be assigned to them. Finally, there are cases that specify the goods, but give neither a value nor an indication of minimal value. In Berkshire in 1248, the thief stole hens[8] and in Durham in 1242, the stolen property was a pig.[9] These cases inform either question only if a value can be assigned to the stolen goods.

A general value for several kinds of livestock can be found directly in the rolls by reading the deodand cases. Horses and pigs were commonly deodand and were therefore valued at the eyre. Even setting aside changes in prices based on fluctuating economic conditions over time, it is also obvious that the value of a particular horse or pig depends upon a variety of factors such as age, sex, condition. Of course, there is also the risk that a false valuation was made for one reason or another. In Devon in 1238, the value of a deodand colt was placed at seven shillings and two men were amerced for falsely valuing it at four shillings.[10] Nonetheless, there is enough consistency over time that some useful conclusions can be made. Horses range in value from four to ten shillings, but the vast majority of deodand horses were valued at five or six shillings. I have noticed only one instance of a horse valued below twelvepence and that was a foal valued at sixpence.[11]

There is useful information in other places as well. Meekings has provided the prices paid for victuals and fodder by the judicial party in Wiltshire in 1249.[12] This information places the value of a chicken at one

[4] K E Bayley, *The Thirteenth Century Assize Rolls for the County of Durham*, part 2, Surtees Soc., vol. 127 (Durham and London, 1916), pl. 241.

[5] J Parker, in *A Calendar of the Lancashire Assize Rolls*, Lancashire and Cheshire Record Soc., vol. 47 (London, 1904), 82.

[6] *Curia Regis Rolls*, vol. 12, pl. 2098.

[7] *Curia Regis Rolls*, vol. 12, pl. 1582.

[8] M T Clanchy, *The Roll and Writ File of the Berkshire Eyre of 1248*, Seld. Soc., vol. 40 (London, 1973), pl. 891 (hereafter Clanchy).

[9] Bayley, *supra* n. 4, pl. 364.

[10] H Summerson, *Crown Pleas of the Devon Eyre of 1238*, Devon and Cornwall Record Soc., New Series, vol. 28 (Torquay, The Devonshire Press, 1985), pl. 602.

[11] Ibid., pl. 306.

[12] A F Meekings, *Crown Pleas of the Wiltshire Eyre, 1249*, Wiltshire Archaeological and Natural History Soc., Records Branch, vol. 16 (Devizes, 1961), 13.

penny and a quarter. Rogers' amazing work on prices begins in 1259.[13] It provides a value for virtually every commodity and therefore a cross-check on values derived from other sources. For example, Rogers values an adult sheep at approximately one shilling and a lamb at sixpence.[14]

WHY VALUE IS IN THE CASES

Larceny cases came before the justices in several ways. The victim of the theft might have appealed the thief. A captured and confessed brigand might have turned approver and appealed his erstwhile confederates. The presenting jury might have made a presentment against a suspected thief. A thief might have sought sanctuary, confessed and abjured the realm. None of these prosecutorial mechanisms, on their faces, depend upon value. One might expect, therefore, that larceny cases would not refer to value except to note the value of chattels forfeited by hanged or abjuring thieves. If there were no value-based distinction among larcenies one would expect, for example, that in the case of an abjuring thief the entry would state only that he confessed the theft and abjured before the coroners. To be sure, there are many entries of that kind. An abjuration entry which does state more might also simply be an example of an unnecessary fact being recorded. The same could be true of a presentment, an appeal in which the appellor was gilding the lily or a jury verdict.

But, in fact, there are cases in which coroners were amerced because the theft was too minor to support abjuration. Some accused thieves who had fled were permitted to return; they were not outlawed because their thefts were small ones. Some thieves appeared for trial and when convicted were remitted to alternative penalties because their thefts were minor. This seems to me to mean two things. First, larcenies were differentiated; secondly, they were differentiated by value.

APPEALS AND PRESENTMENTS

Because many local courts had jurisdiction over theft, it is difficult to know what fraction of prosecuted thefts never reached the royal courts. An appeal was a plea of the Crown made in the first instance before the coroners, royal officials. I have not noticed an instance in which coroners were amerced for enrolling an appeal of larceny that turned out to be a petit larceny. Thus, it

[13] J E T Rogers, *A History of Agricultural Prices in England, 1259–1793. Vol. 1, 1259–1400* (Oxford, Clarendon Press, 1866).

[14] Ibid., 351. Rogers also confirms the 1–1.5d value for a chicken given by Meekings: ibid., 356.

appears that all appeals of larceny were pleas of the Crown and should have been reported to the justices through the coroners' enrollment and the presenting juries' reporting of new pleas of the Crown. When there was no appeal, however, the interplay between local and royal courts is not clear. The roll of the 1242 Durham Eyre sheds a little light.[15] Geoffrey of Haswell was appealed of an unspecified crime by an approver. He was arrested and bailed, but was again arrested, this time with stolen corn worth twopence. He confessed that theft in the shire court. At eyre, the jury did not suspect him of the original charge, but did suspect him of stealing the corn. Geoffrey was acquitted, but ordered to leave the lands of the Bishop of Durham.[16] This case seems to place jurisdiction over the appeal in the palatine court and jurisdiction over the theft in the shire court. The theft of the corn was before the palatine justices only because of the appeal. It is worth noting that, whatever penalty was imposed upon Geoffrey by the shire court, he certainly was not hanged for twopence of corn.

However the jurisdictional rules worked, thieves were both appealed and presented in the royal courts. They occasionally appeared for trial. Hugh de la Mare was appealed at Durham in 1242 for a stolen salmon. The appeal was annulled because the appellor failed to plead why there should be trial by combat (*nichil dixit quaere formaretur duellem*).[17] Hugh was thereupon tried by the jury, which said he was guilty. He was placed in mercy and ordered to make restitution in the amount of sixpence, the value of the salmon.[18] Here is a clear case of guilt, but, because of low value, presumably set by the jury, Hugh escaped with minimal punishment.

Alice was accused of burglary and larceny along with her husband, William, and others at the Wiltshire Eyre of 1249. The jury said Alice was guilty of minor larcenies (*de minutis latrociniis*) and she was permitted to find pledges for good behavior. William was acquitted.[19] Thus, this is not a case of marital duress or of treating all defendants in the same case the same way. Whether Alice received leniency for her own crimes cannot be determined, but the jury clearly distinguished her from William.

Alice did, however, fare better than another Alice, a Cornish weaver. The latter Alice was indicted in Devon in 1238 for stealing two pairs of shoes. She was convicted and lost an ear; the shoes were returned to their owner.[20] The value of the shoes is not stated. Together, both pairs were probably

[15] Durham was a palatine jurisdiction. An eyre there was not a royal eyre, but is essentially indistinguishable. A general description of the Bishop of Durham's jurisdiction can be found in G Holmes, *The Later Middle Ages 1272–1285* (Edinburgh, T Nelson, 1962), 60.

[16] Bayley, *supra* n. 4, pl. 130.

[17] Ibid., pl. 241.

[18] Presumably the salmon could not be returned. See n. 20, *infra*.

[19] Meekings, *supra* n. 12, pl. 116.

[20] Summerson, *supra* n. 10, pl. 555. The shoes were returned to the owner. There is a similar case, *Curia Regis Rolls*, vol. 12, pl. 2098, in which a linen cloth was returned to the owner. This contrasts with the more general rule that stolen goods were forfeited to the Crown.

worth between fivepence and eightpence.[21] Alice's mutilation was shared by others. Agnes, Richard's daughter, was arrested with a stolen cloak in London in 1220. Because the cloak was stolen, but had little value (*parvi precii est*), Agnes also lost an ear.[22] Likewise, Henry of Newcastle, arrested in London in 1230 with canvas and other small things (*pannum canevacium et alie minute rebus*), lost an ear.[23] Robert Crock probably came closer to the gallows. He was also arrested in London in 1230 while in flight with stolen linen towels (*lintheaminibus mantugeriis*), and he used a knife to resist arrest. Robert lost an ear.[24] But another Robert, Alexander Malherbe's son, was a true tempter of fate. He had been found to be of ill fame (*de malo recto*) and exiled from London unless he found pledges for his good behaviour in the city. He apparently left, but returned and in 1230 was arrested in flight with two stolen caps or capes (*duabus capellis*). This Robert also escaped the noose, but he did lose an ear.[25]

Robert Malherbe's case brings together two of the dispositional threads in these cases. He was first exiled from the city of London and when he returned he had an ear excised. The case of Alice, the Cornish weaver, notwithstanding, ear cropping seems to occur most commonly in London.[26] Internal exile, too, is most commonly found in the rolls of the central courts. Ralf of Canterbury was arrested in London in 1226 with a linen cloth (*uno lintheamine*) proven to be stolen. Because the cloth was of little value (*parvi precii est*), Ralf was released but required to remove himself (*exeat de patria*).[27] The same phrase was used at Middlesex in 1230. Edred was accused of various offenses. The jury said it knew nothing of him but good, except for theft of some meal and other small things (*cybariis et minutis rebus*). Eldred was ordered to find pledges or leave the area (*vel exeat patriam*).[28] I understand *patria* in this context to mean "locality" or "countryside" as it does in the phrase *ponit se super patriam*. This is not abjuration of the realm; rather it is exile from the locality.[29] The order in

[21] Rogers, *supra* n. 13, 585 (one pair of shoes valued at 2.5d to 4d.).

[22] *Curia Regis Rolls*, vol. 9, 7–8.

[23] *Curia Regis Rolls*, vol. 13, pl. 2786.

[24] *Curia Regis Rolls*, vol. 13, pl. 2782.

[25] *Curia Regis Rolls*, vol. 13, pl. 2784.

[26] The only other instance I have noticed of ear-cropping ordered by a court is from the 1242 Durham Eyre: see Bayley, *supra* n. 4, pl. 355. In Cambridge, 1260, a woman who had previously lost an ear abjured the realm. W M Palmer, *The Assizes Held at Cambridge, A.D. 1260* (Linton, Eagle Printing Works, 1930), 40.

[27] *Curia Regis Rolls*, vol. 12, pl. 2098.

[28] *Curia Regis Rolls*, vol. 14, pl. 446.

[29] This internal exile seems to be a way to rid the community of social irritants rather than, strictly speaking, a penalty. See, for example, the case of Gregory Sale; he was arrested on suspicion of theft because he carried himself foolishly; he was not seized of stolen goods, no one sued against him and no one knew evil of him; he was acquitted but exiled (*ne de cetero veniat in comitatu illo*). *Curia Regis Rolls*, vol. 13, pl. 2780. See also *Curia Regis Rolls*, vol. 12, pl. 2096, in which an accused thief was acquitted for lack of evidence and was exiled (*exeat a*

Edred's case is evocative of that in Geoffrey of Haswell's case, already described. Geoffrey was ordered not to be found in the lands of the Bishop of Durham except with the Bishop's permission (*non inveniatur magis in terra Episcopi, nisi per licenciam domini Episcopi*).[30]

There are, however, cases of minor larceny in which the verdict and judgment can best be described as guilty, but unpunished. Robert of Hillendon was tried at Berchamsted in 1225 after having been arrested for two stolen geese. Robert was simply released because the theft was a small one (*latrocinium adeo parvum est*).[31] The two geese were worth approximately fivepence.[32] Edith of Shropshire, tried at the same place and time, having been taken with a piece of *chanevaz* (canvas?) was freed because of its small value (*eo quod parum valet*).[33] A very interesting Surrey case from the same year comes to the same result. The jury said of a man indicted that he may have taken wool from sheep in sheepfolds and that he took sheaves at harvest and other small things. The judgment, which released the defendant, includes this statement: "since this is not a larceny upon which he should suffer judgment, nor do they know any grand larceny of him . . . let him be delivered".[34] This is the first use, of which I am aware, of the term "grand larceny". Although this defendant did entirely escape judgment, the petty thieves already described did not. The conclusion that he should suffer no judgment is intriguing. It might mean that he should not suffer the usual judgment upon thieves—hanging. It might also be related to the jury's statement about taking sheaves in harvest.

The taking of sheaves at harvest seems to have been universally excused. These cases generally do not specify value or the type, weight or volume of the grain. It is therefore impossible to know if these cases were based on value or if there was a special social dynamic at work. Perhaps the gleaning-in-the-fields story from the Book of Ruth was the model. In any event, these are cases falling into the category of minor theft. Walter Goddrich, tried at the Wiltshire Eyre of 1249, presents a case like the Surrey case of 1225 just described. Walter was appealed of burglary and homicide. The jury said Walter was not guilty of any misdeed except taking sheaves at harvest (*de garbis in autumpno*); Walter was released to pledges.[35] Another Surrey case, this one from 1235, seems even stronger. Maud, Kenting's daughter, was

villa), and *Curia Regis Rolls*, vol. 12, pl. 1581, in which a man arrested for false preaching and other foolishness was freed and exiled (*exeat de patria*).

[30] Bayley, *supra* n. 4, pl. 130.

[31] *Curia Regis Rolls*, vol. 12, pl. 1582.

[32] Rogers, *supra* n.13, 356.

[33] *Curia Regis Rolls*, vol. 12, pl. 2079. Bracton's report states that Edith was later arrested at London with a purse she had cut containing 3s.6d., and she lost her right thumb. F W Maitland, *Bracton's Note Book*, (London, C J Clay and Sons, 1887), vol. 3, pl. 1725.

[34] JUST 1/863 m. 4. I have taken the case as it is reported in C A F Meekings and D Crook, *The 1235 Surrey Eyre*, Surrey Record Soc., vol. 32 (Guildford, 1983), 559.

[35] Meekings, *supra* n. 12, pl. 32.

accused of larceny by the vill of Micham. When the case came on to be heard, the vill of Micham admitted it knew no ill of Maud except that she stole sheaves at harvest (*furata est garbas in autumpno*). Maud was acquitted and the vill of Micham was placed in mercy.[36] This seems almost to say that taking sheaves at harvest was not larceny at all. At the very least it says that the offence is known to be so minor that prosecution should not be brought.

One case of sheave-stealing does specify what was taken. Richard, John Raven's son, was accused at the 1256 Eyre in Northumberland of stealing a thrave of sheaves. The jury said that Richard was not guilty of any misdeed except that he took about twelve sheaves from a rick. Richard was acquitted, but was required to find pledges.[37] A thrave, the amount Richard was accused of stealing, consisted of twenty-four sheaves.[38] Thus, the jury's verdict reduced the charged amount by one-half. This is clearly not a case of gleaning in the fields. Yet the jury's verdict seems either to have put the case into the sheaves-at-harvest category or sufficiently reduced the value that it fell into the minor theft category. It is also worth noting that Richard's father had made himself scarce because he feared being convicted of receiving a felon. As the father was not suspected of anything other than receiving his son, he was permitted to return. The father's flight may indicate the original accusation was closer to the truth of the matter than was the jury's verdict. This may well be a case of jury lenity.

FLIGHT AND OUTLAWRY

Flight, or at least failure to appear, was a popular solution to criminal accusation in medieval England. The usual judicial response was to order the fugitive exacted and outlawed and order forfeiture of his chattels. There are a fair number of cases in which persons who might have expected acquittal or some other form of lenient treatment at the eyre nonetheless fled.[39] When the jury later reported facts that would have dictated leniency or acquittal, the fugitive might be permitted to return, sometimes under pledges, but his chattels generally remained forfeited because of his flight. The case of John Raven, the father of Richard the sheaf thief, is an example of this general pattern. Larceny cases involving small thefts follow the first part of this pattern; they sometimes follow the second part as well.

[36] Meekings and Crook, *supra* n. 34, pl. 533.

[37] W Page, *Three Early Assize Rolls for the County of Northumberland*, Surtees Soc., vol. 88 (Durham, London, Edinburgh, 1891), 100–1.

[38] *Webster's Third New International Dictionary* (Springfield, Webster, 1986), 2381.

[39] For example, Meekings notes 44 acquittals of absent defendants at the 1249 Wiltshire eyre: Meekings, *supra* n. 12, 99.

Six men who had been arrested for larceny in Berkshire were released to sureties. They failed to appear at the 1248 Eyre in that county. The jury said it did not suspect any of them of anything except petty things (*de parvis rebus*). The sheriff is told that, if he can find these men, he is to put them on pledges for good behavior. There is no mention of their chattels.[40]

In Cambridge in 1260 Henry, William's son, had been arrested with stolen corn. The jury reported that it did not suspect him of any theft, not even the theft of the sheaves of corn with which he had been arrested. Unless, as is noted above, taking of sheaves was not larceny, this verdict is difficult to swallow. But the justices swallowed it. They adjudged that Henry could return, but his chattels were forfeited.[41] At the same eyre, Godwin of Ixninge who had been arrested with butter and cheese stolen from a named house, was presented. He also had escaped and failed to appear. This jury also said it did not suspect Godwin. He was permitted to return and he had no chattels to forfeit.[42] There seems little doubt that the theft in each case was real. But they were probably minor thefts. In addition, these are thefts of food and there had been a famine in Cambridge in the years immediately preceding this eyre, a fact which is noted in and seems to control other larceny cases.[43]

But famine cannot be the only explanation because there are too many similar cases in which the fact of theft is verified by the jury. Roger de la Heath was accused of larceny at the 1248 Berkshire Eyre. He did not appear. The jury said he was suspected only of stealing geese and of other small misdeeds (*parvis maleficiis*). It was adjudged that Roger could return and he had no chattels to forfeit.[44] Thomas Zonarius, appealed of some unspecified offence at the 1247 Bedford Eyre, also failed to appear. His jury suspected him only of stealing fowl and of other small matters. He was also permitted to return and had no chattels to forfeit.[45] Recall that a goose was worth a little more than twopence and that a chicken was worth a little more than one penny. These are petit larceny cases, as is the case of Adam de Scheyl, arrested in Liverpool in 1246 for stealing threepence worth of meal. Adam escaped, but his jury did not suspect him of any *other* misdeed. He was permitted to return, but his chattels were forfeited.[46]

Four cases from the 1242 Palatine Eyre in Durham produced slightly different judgments. Matthew, Alan's son, broke into a house and stole bread; the value (or amount) was not known (*nescitur summa*). Alwin of Branspath had stolen one sheep. Neither appeared, but both were permitted

[40] Clanchy, *supra* n. 8, pl. 725.
[41] Palmer, *supra* n. 26, 3.
[42] Ibid., 10.
[43] See text at notes 61–64, *infra*.
[44] Clanchy, *supra* n. 8, pl. 747.
[45] G H Fowler, *Calendar of the Roll of the Justices on Eyre, 1247*, Bedford Historical Record Soc., vol. 21 (Aspley Guise, 1939), pl. 628.
[46] Parker, *supra* n. 5, 82.

to return upon finding pledges.[47] These cases seem to go beyond the norm. Matthew's case appears to involve housebreaking, but it is treated as one involving the theft of bread. Alwin was accused of stealing sheep. Sheep thieves were regularly hanged and outlawed.[48] Of course, Alwin's case is specific that he had stolen only one sheep. But sheep were generally valued at twelvepence. If the twelvepence marker was in place by 1242, Alwin came perilously close to crossing the line. In the third case, Ralf Cokeman had stolen a pig, but its owner did not sue against him. Ralf did not appear, apparently because he feared presentment. Clearly his case was presented, and although his chattels were forfeited, he was permitted to return.[49] The most common deodand value for pigs is eightpence, but it can go higher. Ralf, like Alwin, may have been the beneficiary of a close decision. So might Nicholas Hathering who fled after stealing a half-bushel of wheat from a barn. The jury did not suspect him of *any other* theft so he was permitted to return upon finding pledges.[50]

As proof that this whole line of cases is about value, I offer the case of Jordan, Walter's son. Jordan was accused at the Devon Eyre of 1238 of the theft of two firkins of honey. He did not appear. The honey was said to be worth four shillings and Jordan was outlawed.[51] I believe the value is correct. A firkin of honey was worth approximately twenty-eight pence;[52] this would value two firkins at a little over four shillings. Even though honey is food, if there is enough value (and that may be the same thing as a commercial quantity), the line must be drawn.

ABJURATION

Abjuration cases, of course, are very common and typically very terse. The common formula is:

> "X fled to the church, confessed himself to be a thief and abjured the realm before the coroners. His chattels . . . ."

Abjuration required confession and confession was conviction. Thus, every person who abjured for theft was in a significant way a convicted thief.

[47] Bayley, *supra* n. 4, pls 86, 231.

[48] See for example, Peter Ode, who was hanged at this eyre for stealing sheep, geese, chickens and wheat: ibid., pl. 234. William, Robert's son, was placed in exigent for stealing one sheep: ibid., pl. 367.

[49] Ibid., pl. 364.

[50] Ibid., pl. 350. Rogers values wheat at 560d per quarter in 1259. This value would place Nicholas' theft at well above 12d. The 1259 price may, however, be inflated by the famine reported many times in the roll of the 1260 Cambridge Eyre.

[51] Summerson, *supra* n. 10, pl. 194.

[52] Rogers, *supra* n. 13, 418. Honey is valued at 3d per gallon. A firkin is a type of container, but its volume seems to be 8–9 gallons: *Webster's Dictionary*, *supra* n. 38, 856.

Yet there are four mid-century cases in which coroners were amerced for improperly forcing abjuration upon petty thieves. At the 1249 Wiltshire Eyre one Helen put herself in the church and confessed to stealing a "rochet" (smock?). The coroners and bailiffs were placed in mercy for requiring abjuration for so small a crime (*pro tam modico delicto*).[53] Two cases come from Berkshire, the first from 1241 and the second from 1248. In the first, judgment was taken against a coroner who had compelled abjuration for the theft of sixpence worth of corn.[54] In the second, William le Sopere was forced to abjure for stealing only hens. Recall that a chicken was valued a little over one penny. The coroner was placed in mercy.[55] Somerset in 1242 provides the fourth case. Henry of Stanford had confessed the theft of two fish called hake and abjured. The coroners were placed in mercy.[56] The case does not spell out the coroners' defalcation, but noticing that one hake was worth approximately one penny sets the value of Henry's theft at twopence.[57] Comparing the case to the three preceding it makes reasonably clear where the coroners went wrong.

All of these cases taken together convince me that larceny had become divided as early as the 1220s and that the division was based on value. Unfortunately, when values are specifically stated in the cases they are values falling substantially below twelvepence. While I have tried to assign values where none is specifically given, I confess the speculative nature of those values. Even then, the value assigned is generally substantially below twelvepence. The one case that is extremely close is that of Alwin of Branspath, the Durham thief who stole a single sheep.

Cases like that one are crucial for two reasons. First, deciding when the twelvepence marker came into existence can only be determined if a value is known; if it is, the value and outcome can be compared and conclusions drawn. Secondly, without knowing what value was determined and comparing that with the value that separates the two forms of larceny, no real estimate can be made about whether juries reported low(er) values to save the necks of their neighbours who were not bad enough to hang.

THE TWELVEPENCE MARKER

The case following was heard at Westminster in 1220:

> "Peter of Lindsey appeals Robert Copeland of association in larceny in that they were thieves together at the Isle of Ely in the house of Thomas

[53] Meekings, *supra* n. 12, pl. 557.

[54] JUST 1/776, m. 27. I have taken the case from Meekings, *supra* n. 12, 55.

[55] Clanchy, *supra* n. 8, pl. 891.

[56] C E H Chadwyck-Healy in *Somerset Pleas: Part I*, Somerset Record Soc., vol. 11 (London, 1897), pl. 797.

[57] Rogers, *supra* n. 13, 617.

> of Eydon of tunics and supertunics and capes, of which Robert had as his part twelvepence and more, and at Luton they were thieves of clothing, of which Robert had as his part one tunic of a value of twelvepence and more."

The entry goes on to accuse Robert of two homicides and aiding the theft of a horse. Peter offered to prove by his body. Robert denied and offered to prove by his body. The duel was adjudged, both were sent to jail and ordered to appear armed on a later date.[58] The outcome is not recorded.

I think this case is important. An approver was a confessed and therefore convicted person. He could save his own neck only by putting the neck of another in the noose. He had a powerful incentive to state his appeal in a way that would ensure it would not be nullified. He was also, by definition, negotiating with officialdom about his own status and fate. This must have provided opportunities to find out exactly what he needed to say to state a nullification-proof appeal. The way the values are stated in this appeal seems to me to be generated by all of those circumstances. In brief, Peter had been instructed to allege that Robert's share of each theft was more than twelvepence. That, in its turn, means that there was some sense that something important turned on stating the value in that way. I am not suggesting that this case means that the twelvepence marker had been finally and unalterably fixed by 1220. Rather, I am suggesting an understanding that a value in excess of twelvepence was always enough to make out a capital larceny.

JURY LENITY

As already noted, a determination that a theft was a minor one could generate a variety of judicial responses—dismissal, finding pledges for good behavior, internal exile or ear cropping. To the extent juries manipulated facts to report thefts as minor ones, the juries cannot have been quite sure what penalty, if any, would be imposed. I am quite sure, however, that those juries knew that the capital penalty would not be imposed.

I would therefore suggest that while juries were constrained to report verdicts limited to substantive issues—the accused did or did not steal the goods, the goods had a certain value—the juries were actually making a much larger decision. In effect, the juries were deciding who should live and who should die. I would also suggest it was living rather than dying that was foremost in the minds of the jurors. Outside of London, almost all defendants convicted of minor thefts were returned to the community. Thus, the juries must have been aware that the probable outcome of a minor-theft verdict was that the defendant would continue to be in their community. Finally, then, I would suggest that the juries were deciding whether they were

[58] *Curia Regis Rolls*, vol. 9, 99.

willing to have the defendant amongst them. There is hardly any other explanation for the difference in treatment of two men, each of whom had stolen one sheep and failed to appear, at Durham in 1242. Alwin of Branspath was permitted to return; Peter Ode was placed in exigent.[59]

The Cambridge Eyre of 1260 is particularly interesting. Recall that Cambridge juries in the cases of two different men who had been arrested in possession of stolen goods said that they did not suspect them even of stealing the goods with which they were arrested. The judgment in each case permits the defendant, who had escaped, to return.[60] Recall also that the stolen property was food, corn in one case and butter and cheese in the other. In two other cases, Cambridge juries accomplished the same result in a different way. Richard Balding and his wife had been arrested on suspicion of stealing corn, but had escaped. The jury said they were suspected only of stealing corn during a great famine (*magna carista*). They were permitted to return.[61] Mildo, Richard Bernard's son, was arrested in a bakehouse stealing bread. He also escaped. His jury said that he was suspected only of small thefts at the time of the famine.[62] Finally, two children of Margaret Childerle stole a half bushel of peas worth twopence and a half during the famine. Because of this theft, Margaret's supertunic was seized. The jurors presented the matter as an accusation upon the man who had seized the supertunic; he was required to make restitution to Margaret and placed in mercy for *his* transgression.[63] One way to understand these verdicts is as statements by the juries that they were willing to have these petty thieves in their community.

A similar case in 1241 in Berkshire is even stronger because it points directly at the existence of and jury manipulation of the twelvepence marker. Two persons had stolen four and one half sheep carcasses. Their jury said they had stolen through want and poverty and the carcasses were worth eleven pence and a half. The defendants were then released upon finding pledges.[64] This case almost certainly means that the jury knew that twelvepence was the dividing line between capital and non-capital larceny, that it thought the defendants should be excused, that it was willing to have these defendants in the community, and that it reported a manipulated value.[65] These jurors, by setting value at elevenpence and a half, stayed safely below twelvepence.

59 Bayley, *supra* n. 4, pls 251, 367.

60 See text at notes 42 and 43, *supra*.

61 Palmer, *supra* n. 26, at 3.

62 Ibid., 19.

63 Ibid., 4. In a somewhat similar case from the 1235 Surrey Eyre, a woman appealed a man of wounding her and stealing her clothing. The jury said she was very poor and was stealing brushwood from the wood of the appellee's lord. The appellee was ordered to return the clothes and to be in custody: see Meekings and Crook, *supra* n. 34, pl. 556.

64 JUST 1/776 m. 27d. I have taken the case from Meekings, *supra* n. 12, 55–6.

65 A live sheep was worth approximately twelvepence. As the case speaks of four *and a half* carcasses, these sheep apparently were butchered rather than simply dead.

The jurors in a Rutland case from 1256 were not as careful. Two Richards were accused of larceny and other misdeeds. The jury reported that it did not suspect one of them, but the other, Richard Miller, had stolen geese and chickens worth twelvepence. Richard was ordered to be in custody until he found pledges.[66]

The first of these cases is quite clearly a jury lenity case; the second probably is. In any event, these cases make clear the twelvepence marker was operating by mid-century. It probably was not certain whether petit larceny was less than twelvepence or twelvepence or less, but the importance of the amount is obvious.

Jury lenity was probably also operating in a number of the cases described in earlier sections. Two of them are good examples. The Surrey defendant whose jury reported that he *might* have taken wool from sheep and that he took sheaves at harvest may have been the beneficiary of jury lenity.[67] The special status of sheaves at harvest has already been noted; the jury's equivocation about the important part of the case looks like an effort to avoid convicting. There is also the case of a Northumberland man accused of stealing a whole thrave of sheaves and whose father had fled from fear of having received a felon. The jury in that case reduced the amount of the theft by half. The defendant was released to pledges and the father was permitted to return.[68]

In this section I have not distinguished those cases in which the defendant appeared for trial from those cases in which he did not. I suspect that in these larceny cases defendants who did not appear had not fled very far. When a jury returned a verdict of minor larceny, the defendant who was present was generally released or released to pledges while the defendant who was absent was permitted to return. In practical effect, the outcome is the same—the defendant would rejoin the community. The effect of the abjuration cases in which coroners were amerced for compelling abjuration upon confession of minor thefts is not so clear. It is clear that the abjuration should not have occurred, but none of the cases say what effect that has on the abjurer. In addition, the role of the jury in reporting the facts causing the abjurations to be declared improper is far less clear than it is in other kinds of cases.

THE STATUTE OF WESTMINSTER I REVISITED

This was apparently not the only statute of its kind and time. The roll of the Hampshire Eyre of 1280 reports a case in which the suitors to a local court are placed in mercy because they hanged a man for stealing chattels worth

66 JUST 1/1185 m. 5d. I am indebted to Daniel Klerman for this case.

67 Meekings and Crook, *supra* n. 34, 559.

68 Page, *supra* n. 37, at 100–1.

less than twelvepence, "and this after the king's statute of the seventh year".[69] The roll of the Sussex Eyre for the preceding year reports a similar case. The suitors of a private court hanged a man for stealing a linen sheet worth sixpence, "and as [they] hanged him for a value of less than 12d and contrary to the statute . . .", they were required to make a fine.[70] The statute in question cannot be Westminster I because the reference to the king's seventh year dates this statute to 1278–9. Even if the date were the same as that of Westminster I, that statute is about bail and this one seems to be about penalty.

I suggest this sequence. By the middle half of the thirteenth century a rule had developed that minor larcenies were not capital larcenies. During the same period the marker that divided the two forms of larceny became understood to lie at twelvepence. The Statute of Westminster I did not create the division or the marker. Rather, it dealt with precisely what it purports to deal with—pre-trial disposition of those accused of the minor form of larceny. Stated another way, Westminster I did not create petit larceny, but it was made necessary by the fact that petit larceny had been created. The sole contribution of Westminster I to the substantive law of larceny was to clarify that the dividing line was less than twelvepence on the one hand and twelvepence or more on the other. The later statute forbidding local courts to impose the capital penalty for thefts involving less than twelvepence was not an extension of Westminster I. It was an extension of the pre-existing substantive rules applied in the royal courts.

CONCLUSION

I believe a general division of larcenies into a major, capital form and a minor, non-capital form was in place by 1220. I also believe that by 1220 there was an understanding that what divided the two forms of larceny was value and that the value was about twelvepence. The whole series of London cases from 1220 clearly show that the justices were acting on the distinction. The case of Peter of Lindsey, the approver, is some evidence of the understanding about value. By mid-century juries had understood both the distinction and the value criterion. They manipulated the latter to spare the gallows to those of their neighbours with whom they were willing to continue to live. The Statute of Westminster I, c. 15, took the logical step of making bailable those accused thieves who did not face the capital penalty and, incidentally, clarified the value marker.

[69] JUST 1/786 m. 31d.

[70] JUST 1/921 m. 10d. I am indebted to Henry Summerson for this and the preceding case. The quoted material in each is Summerson's translation.

4

The Jury in English Manorial Courts

MAUREEN MULHOLLAND (MANCHESTER)

INTRODUCTION

The manorial courts of medieval and early modern England have long been the study of economic and social historians. Because such thorough records were kept of all manorial affairs and because so many of these records have survived, we have inherited an invaluable historical resource, since they reveal much precious information about the society in which they operated. Legal historians, however, have devoted comparatively far less time to the study of these records: it is one hundred and thirteen years since Frederick Maitland produced his masterly volume on the manorial courts.[1] But his wish that the Selden Society should continue the work that he began remained for long unfulfilled. Perhaps because of the rapid and overpowering predominance of the King's justice and the centralisation of the common law courts, and the consequent decline of manorial justice, English lawyers have not been eager to study the anatomy of manorial justice, and where they have done so their consideration has often been limited to its significance in relation to the common law, rather than as a subject of legal historical analysis of the courts in themselves. The work of Professor John Beckerman and more recently of Professors L R Poos and Lloyd Bonfield has to some extent remedied this situation, providing new and fascinating insights into these courts, which, for centuries, were the most important and meaningful legal tribunals in the lives of the ordinary people of England.[2] Further, the manorial courts often mirror developments in the common law. After the thirteenth century, the office of steward of the manorial court had become a stage in the legal career of many a young aspiring common lawyer, and it is surely legitimate to presume that there may have been some cross-fertilisation between common law and manorial justice and that such

[1] *Select Pleas in Manorial and other Seignorial Courts. Volume I: The Reigns of Henry III and Edward I*, ed. by F W Maitland, Seld. Soc., vol. 2 (London, 1889).

[2] J Beckerman, "Customary Law in English Manorial Courts in the Thirteenth and Fourteenth Centuries" (unpublished Ph.D. thesis, University of London, 1972); idem, "Procedural Innovation and Institutional Change in Medieval English Manorial Courts", (1992) 10 *LHR* 197; *Select Cases in Manorial Courts 1250–1550*, ed. by L R Poos and Lloyd Bonfield, Seld. Soc., vol. 114 (London, 1998).

a lawyer may perhaps have carried some aspects of his manorial practice to his practice in the courts in London, having brought his legal training from the Inns of Court to his role as steward of the manor.

The manor was a socio-economic unit and the records produced by manorial officials were primarily designed for accounting and management purposes. In addition to manorial extents and accounts, the court rolls and court books had a clear economic function, noting the fulfilment of feudal services and the many fines ("amercements") imposed on tenants for manorial offences and leet offences and for non-attendance at court. Although of minor importance at the time, at least until they became essential for the purpose of establishing copyhold tenure in the fifteenth century, the court rolls are an invaluable resource for the study of the substantive and procedural rules applied in the manorial courts. In addition to the court rolls, a further valuable source of information on the procedures of manorial courts are the courtkeepers' manuals and books of instructions, printed for the benefit of stewards and bailiffs in the sixteenth and seventeenth centuries, some of which date back to the thirteenth century.[3]

The jury in the manorial courts has, in particular, been the focus of study by historians in search of the nature of medieval manorial society. The personnel of the courts, especially the suitors and juries in these courts, their social status and occupations and the changes in these over the centuries, as well as the economy of the manor and the events and ordering of agricultural society are revealed in the manorial records, through extents, accounts, court rolls and court books. This paper looks from the point of view of the lawyer at the jury in the manorial courts—its composition, its function and its importance during the medieval and early modern period. Of necessity, within the scope of this paper it is possible to cite only a few examples of manorial juries, but the records are numerous, many of them untranslated and some still unresearched.[4]

MANORIAL COURTS

It is customary to speak and write of "manorial courts", but the term is a general one, covering several different courts. In analysing and classifying

[3] A valuable source of these is *The Court Baron: Being Precedents for Use in Seignorial and Other Local Courts, Together with Select Pleas from the Bishop of Ely's Court at Littleport*, ed. by F W Maitland and W P Baildon, Seld. Soc., vol. 4 (London, 1891). See also *Walter of Henley's Husbandry*, ed. by D Oschinsky (Oxford, Clarendon Press, 1971); N J Hone, *The Manor and Manorial Records* (London, Methuen, 1906); S Ratcliff, A Collins, and B Schofield (eds) *Legal and Manorial Formularies* (Oxford, University Press, 1933).

[4] In addition to the examples cited, there are numerous collections in libraries and public record offices throughout England and Wales, as well as collections still in private hands. The author is researching such a collection—the papers of the manorial court of Dunham Massey, held by the John Rylands Research Institute, University of Manchester.

them, the classic distinction is between the different kinds of jurisdiction exercised by these courts. The seignorial or domanial jurisdiction is that which was intrinsic to feudal landholding;[5] it was the duty and the right of the lord to hold a court for his vassals—his tenants. Such a duty was part of the reciprocal bond between lord and vassal, the latter similarly having the reciprocal right to the lord's justice and the duty to attend the lord's court. The duty to attend ("suit of court") applied after the Conquest to all tenants, free and unfree, although in the case of free tenants the duty may have depended on the terms of the original grant of tenure.[6] The courts which exercised seignorial or domanial jurisdiction were the court of the honour, the court baron, and the court customary or "halmote."

The court of the honour was the principal court of the lord and originally the most prestigious, since it was the court for the principal manors and the most important of the lord's immediate tenants. It might, perhaps, have become a superior court of appeal from lesser manorial courts, but, after 1259 and 1267, such a development was no longer possible. The court of the honour was the first of the seignorial courts to wither away and it therefore was insignificant in the development of the manorial jury. The court baron was the lord's court for all free tenants, who were the suitors to the court and also constituted the homage. This body declared custom and on occasion therefore created manorial law in the process. Hence, like the *Curia Regis*, it could be said to have judicial and legislative functions. It dealt primarily with matters relating to feudal landholding and with questions of feudal rights and duties. The court customary (usually described as the "halmote") was the court held by the lord for his unfree tenants. The constitution of this court differed from that of the court baron: indisputably the villeins were bound to attend as a feudal obligation. They were not suitors and judges of the court, though they increasingly had a role in its work, even before the development of the jury, in that they made presentments to the court, but the presiding official, who represented the lord, was the steward or bailiff of the manor. This court was essentially a court for "domanial" matters and was especially concerned with the duties of unfree tenants with regard to their lord, including failures to perform manorial services and also to disputes between them—minor "civil litigation" including debt, trespass and defamation, and the punishment of certain "moral offences" such as adultery and fornication. Gradually in its records we can trace the development of the jury which became a regular part of its proceedings. As the court

[5] An alternative classification is to divide the feudal or seignorial jurisdiction into two: the baronial pertaining to matters concerning the relationship of the lord and his vassal, and the domanial, concerned with questions of the manor: e.g. W O Ault, *Private Jurisdiction in England* (New Haven, Yale University Press, 1923).

[6] Bracton stated that, with the exception of certain specified cases (e.g. the writ of right), a free tenant was not bound to attend the lord's court in the absence of a special stipulation in the grant from his lord.

baron, with its composition only of free tenants, declined, it was the halmote which became the most common form of domanial court and this lowly tribunal was to survive as the most common form of manor court, attended by all tenants without difference of tenurial status. These courts therefore provide a wealth of examples of the jury as it developed, performing its duties of presentment, acting as an inquest, and even serving as a "trial jury".

The franchise jurisdiction of the lord was conceptually of an entirely different kind. Here the lord's right to administer justice was not his as a feudal right but by royal grant. The franchise court of the manor was in effect the hundred court in private hands and it was therefore only by the king's permission that that jurisdiction could be wielded by the lord. This was in a sense "public jurisdiction" as against the "private jurisdiction" of the seignorial courts proper. By 1272, when Edward I established the *quo warranto* commission, 358 out of 628 hundred courts (about 57 per cent) had been transferred to private ownership and were therefore franchise courts and the numbers were ultimately little affected by the *quo warranto* enquiry.[7] The lord's jurisdiction in one of these courts—the "courts leet"—was exercised on the lord's behalf by his bailiff or steward. Although conceptually the court leet was originally quite distinct from the halmote or court customary, the distinction was by no means always clear. Here, as in the true "seignorial" courts, the jury was used to present tenants for a widely ranging number of offences (the "articles of the leet") and particularly to "police" the Assizes of Bread and Beer. One of the most important functions of the hundred court since the Conquest was to take a "view of frankpledge" to ensure that every man over the age of 12 years was in frankpledge and the term "*visus francpledgii*" was often used to describe the court itself. The pledges, whose task it was to present persons to the court, were eventually superseded by the jury. At first, the pledges were the jury, but gradually it becomes evident from the rolls that the jury consisted of different persons from the pledges. The leet jury was accepted with enthusiasm by the lords and can be seen in the court performing the historic duty of presentment and also acting as an inquest to pronounce on questions of fact and even on occasions as a "trial jury" to decide questions of guilt or innocence.

To some extent, the distinctions between the different manorial courts were rationalisations constructed in later centuries and the classifications of the manorial courts, particularly the "seigniorial", "feudal" or "domanial" courts were not clear, even as early as the thirteenth century. It is indisputable, however, that first the court of the honour and then, to a lesser extent, the court baron faded as living institutions. The reasons for their decline are well established: the developments of the reign of Henry II, par-

[7] It is now acknowledged that Edward's policy was rather to assert his authority rather then to attempt a serious reduction in the number of franchises. In the late 1830s there were still 56 manorial courts leet in operation: see J P Dawson, *A History of Lay Judges* (Cambridge, Mass. Harvard University Press, 1960).

ticularly the writ of right, the grand assize, the petty assizes, the increasing use of tolt and *pone* and the increasing awareness of the king's justice, all directed freehold tenants to the *Curia Regis* or to the king's justices. Indeed, many of the lords themselves were taking advantage of the new developments and the trend towards the king's justice grew with the increased issue of *praecipe* writs. *Quia Emptores* played its role in limiting the growth of feudal estates and the manorial courts accompanying them, and the Statute of Marlborough of 1267 released free tenants from suit of court as an obligation. Once suit of court was no longer compulsory for them, free tenants often ceased to attend the manor court and since freehold land increasingly became the business of the king's court, much of the free tenants' business was no longer dealt with in the lord's court. Social and economic change brought about a loosening of feudal bonds; the growth of towns and of trade, the Peasants' Revolt in 1381, the rebellion of Jack Cade, the Thirty Years' War with France and the Black Death in 1348 all helped to bring about a change in the nature of English society. Later, this social mobility was enhanced and, by the fifteenth century, the decline of villeinage and the recognition by the common law courts of copyhold tenure resulted in a society in which the old certainties of status were no longer applicable. All these developments had a profound effect on the manorial courts. The distinction between the court baron and the court customary, in so far as it was clearly defined, became blurred, and, as early as the thirteenth century, we find the "halmote" composed of free and unfree tenants.[8] By the fifteenth century at the latest, the (apparent) rule that there had to be two free tenants to constitute the court baron had vanished;[9] as the court baron became less important, its remaining jurisdiction was dealt with in conjunction with the business of the halmote. The name "court baron" was often used where the business of that court and the halmote were dealt with at the same session but the terms are used loosely in the court rolls: there was an overlapping of function and increasingly it is not evident from the court rolls which tenants were free tenants and which unfree. It is against this background that the position of the manorial jury must be examined.

THE MANORIAL JURY

The terminology used in the manorial records to describe the personnel of the court is varied. The suitors were those free tenants who attended the

[8] The Statute of Gloucester 1278 is credited with bringing about the decline of the manorial courts, but the 40 shilling limit did not drastically affect the work of the halmote dealing with manorial offences. Even in relation to litigation, the sum was far from negligible, especially for lower tenants.

[9] Though Coke states that there can be no court baron without freeholders and that without a court of freehold tenants there is no "manor": Co. Lit.58a, quoted in Maitland, *supra* n. 1, lxi.

lord's court, typically the court baron. Where all free tenants were stating custom or making presentments, this was described as "the whole court" (*tota curia dicit per sacramentum suum*), though this is rare after the thirteenth century. Another term used of this body of suitors is "the homage", while the suitors are also described in some rolls by their ancient name of "doomsmen". By 1300, the jury (*juratores, jurata*) are being consistently mentioned in the rolls and gradually the term replaces the older descriptions. Although in its literal meaning this means "they who swear an oath", they were evidently always quite distinct from the compurgators or oath-helpers who took part in wager of law and their function was distinct from the affeerors who fixed the amount of amercements. Nor were the jurors exactly the same as the doomsmen and pledges who gradually yielded to the jury. It seems that the manorial courts "borrowed" the jury from the king's courts: it certainly became the prevailing body for performing the functions formerly performed by the old doomsmen, suitors and pledges. The term "jury" sometimes seems to be a mere synonym for "suitors", or "the homage", but increasingly the jury becomes a recognised entry in the court rolls. In the court baron it is distinct from the suitors, as only some of the suitors present have the duties of jurors. In the halmote, the jurors are elected along with the other officials of the manor. Maitland's view was that the role of suitors was different from that of jurors; whereas suitors laid down the law and decided on mode of trial (for example, how many oath-helpers for wager of law), they did not find facts, whereas the jurors, as in the common law courts, were finders of fact. In his view, the advent of the jury meant the demise of suitors as an institution; this is doubted, however, by—among others—Ault, whose view is borne out by many of the thirteenth-century manorial cases.[10] The two institutions seem to have co-existed for centuries, though ultimately the references in the court rolls to the jury increase and those to the suitors (often in the form "the whole court") decline.

The court rolls of the manorial courts describe the jury as being "elected". The precise manner in which this took place is not described, but in the halmote they are among many officials elected as a matter of course at the beginning of every court. In the leet, they are, at first, the chief pledges, but later they appear to be elected by the court and are sworn in by the steward or bailiff. The usual number of jurors in the manorial courts is 12, and the names are frequently set out in the roll. It seems that the verdict of the jury had to be unanimous. The case might be postponed to another day if the jury could not agree.[11] Although it may have been usually implicit rather than expressed, there seems to have been an acceptance by the community

[10] Ault, *supra* n. 5, 167.

[11] M K McIntosh, *Autonomy and Community: The Royal Manor of Havering, 1200–1500* (Cambridge, University Press, 1986), 199 cites a plea of trespass in the manor court of Havering in 1386, in which the jury was unable to agree on whether the plaintiff had established her claim and the case was therefore postponed to the next session of the court.

that jurors should be impartial, at least to the extent that immediate relatives were excluded, and either party had the right to exclude potential jurors.[12]

Membership of the jury in the manorial courts, like the courts themselves, changed with the decline in distinctions of status. Although there are suggestions that there must always be at least some free men on the jury,[13] it is evident from some manorial court rolls, even as early as the thirteenth century, that the jury in the leet and in the halmote consisted of unfree tenants. In 1278, in the court of the Abbot of Ramsey two tenants objected to serving on the jury on the ground that they were free men. Their objection was overruled because the court held that they were not in fact free. But their proposition that free men should *not* be compelled to serve on a jury was not challenged. Their reluctance was understandable, since, as at common law, to be a member of the jury was by no means easy and could be onerous. A parallel concept to that of attaint existed. A jury could be fined ("amerced") for making mistakes in its report, for refusing to give a verdict or for contempt.[14] Maitland gives the example of the manor of Little Stukeley in 1290 when the jury was fined fourpence for "saying that all the brewsters had broken the assize of beer whereas one had kept it and for other concealments".[15] The jurors, however, were not merely docile "yes men" and in the reign of Henry III, when the Earl of Warenne's steward imprisoned a woman for a whole year for oppressive reasons, the jury condemned the act as a demonstration of the steward's "innumerable and devilish oppressions".[16]

The manorial rolls of the fourteenth and fifteenth centuries reveal increasing resort to special juries, convened by the lord's steward, to secure information on matters relating to the lord. In addition to the jury appointed by the court, in the court baron and the halmote as early as the thirteenth century, the lord frequently took payment for granting a jury to one of the parties before the court. An example occurs in the rolls of the manorial court of Ogbourne, one of the manors of the Abbey of Bec in 1249:

> "Adam Moses gives half a sextary of wine to have an inquest as to whether Henry Ayulf accused him of the crime of larceny and used opprobrious and contumelious words of him".[17]

Examples of such payments included disputes as to possession or "private right" to unfree land as in the manor court of Weedon Beck in 1275:

[12] In "the court baron" a typical challenge to the jurors is made by the accused man to the effect that "these men have their hearts big against me and hate me much". He is then told by the bailiff: "thou canst oust from among them all those whom thou suspectest of desiring thy condemnation." See Maitland, *supra* n. 1, 63.

[13] *Inter alia* by Coke: see *supra* n. 9.

[14] Ault, *supra* n. 5, 174.

[15] Maitland, *supra* n. 1, 90, 97, 217.

[16] Ault, *supra* n. 6, 175.

[17] Maitland, *supra* n. 1, 19.

> "John Mabeley gives the lord 3s to have the judgment of twelve men as to certain land whereof Noah deforces him . . . The said jurors say that Noah the Fat has right".[18]

THE FUNCTIONS OF THE MANORIAL JURY

The functions of the jury in the medieval and early modern manorial courts can be analysed into three: first, declaration of custom, secondly, presentment and thirdly, deciding issues. As in many medieval institutions, not only were these functions not always clearly differentiated, but also, as in many medieval institutions, there may be an overlap of function within one court hearing. Moreover, a reader of the rolls soon becomes aware that the language used may be describing one function under the name of another, while it is not always immediately clear from the court roll which function is being performed.

In deciding custom, the jury succeeded the old doomsmen as custodians of and invaluable authorities on local custom, in an age when literacy in the population at large would be minimal and documentary evidence scarce. The members of the jury were the ultimate arbiters of custom and sometimes legislators, since, by stating a custom, or preferring one custom to another, they were in reality creating the customary law of the manor.[19] The court rolls are rich in examples of jurors stating the custom of the manor, such as, for example, in the manor court of Barnet, Hertfordshire in 1349:

> "The jurors, being asked whose testaments, or the testaments of those of what condition, ought to be proved before the cellarer, all answered unanimously, the testaments of all neifs and neif tenants. Being further asked from what time this custom began, they answered, from time out of mind, and that all cellarers without interruption have thus used and enjoyed it".[20]

Sometimes the statement of custom is in the form of presentment:

> "[The jurors present] that strangers coming from without, who hire houses from divers persons and hold nothing of the lord, called 'Undersettles'.... [E]very undersettle shall mow half an acre of corn in the autumn and bind and dry it without food from the lord".[21]

The second duty of the jury—that of presentment—was one of the ancient functions of the manorial courts. In the earlier court rolls, presentment in the court baron was by the whole court *(tota curia)* and, in the halmote, often by a manorial official. In the leet, it was at first the duty of the chief pledges in the frankpledge system. The rolls show that these pledges are, at first, synonymous with the jury, but later, the individuals named as the

18 Ibid., 24.
19 Poos and Bonfield, *supra* n. 2, lxiii, 20 (no.18).
20 Ibid., 157 (no 211).
21 Maitland and Baildon, *supra* n. 3, 146.

jurors are different from those named as pledges. As the distinctions between the different manorial courts broke down, presentment became one of the major roles of the jury in all of them. A tenant might be presented at the halmote because he or she had failed to perform a feudal obligation, or had acted in a way contrary to manorial custom, or had damaged or inconvenienced his fellow tenants. Thus, a typical roll of such a court begins with a list of persons presented for failing to attend court, who were duly fined, and proceeds to report presentments for a variety of manorial offences. Tenants were often presented for such manorial misdemeanours as: failing to pay toll or to use the lord's mill; allowing their livestock to escape and damage the fields and crops of their neighbours and therefore of their lord; failing to obtain the necessary licence from the lord to marry; receiving strangers; and failing to acknowledge status as the lord's villein tenant. The court of the Bishop of Ely at Littleport provides a number of examples.[22] Already by the thirteenth century, the sessions of the court leet and the halmote were often combined at the same sessions.[23] For example, on various occasions from 1316 until 1320, the jurors in the court of the Bishop of Ely presented:

> "[T]hat the Brethren of the Hospital [of St John] have pastured their sheep in autumn before the gleaners against the by-law and that the said Brethren keep two dogs which run in the lord's warren which give rise to suspicion."

At another session, the jurors presented:

> "[T]that Thomas Brokenhorn and Ralph Shepherd have taken hay from the lord's rick and set it before their impounded beasts without leave. And that John Swineherd has a dog which ate a rabbit of the lord."

In addition, there were frequently customs particular to the manor and its location, such as that "the jurors present that William Fisher sold 500 of sedge outside the commune". Or again that:

> "The jurors present that Alan Rushpiller (2d) John Kiggel, William Godloke [etc] habitually collect bitterns' eggs and export them out of the fen to the great destruction [etc]".[24]

Presentment was all important in the court leet: in Maitland's words, "the lords grasped at the presenting jury and made it the active force of their leets". Presentment in the court leet was for any of the numerous offences which fell within the list of "articles of the leet". In particular, there are constant and numerous presentments in the rolls for the breaking of the Assizes of Bread and Beer, for minor trespasses and offences, and sometimes also for moral offences, where there was an overlap of jurisdiction both with the church courts and with the domanial courts of the manor. By the fifteenth

[22] Ibid., 59, 88, 94, 99, 102, 127, 131, 143; see also the courts of the Abbots of Bec and Ramsey in Maitland, *supra* n. 1, 45–6, 94.

[23] Ault, *supra* n. 5, 166.

[24] Maitland and Baildon, *supra* n. 3, 125–31.

century, presentment was still being made by the jury, as, for example, in the court rolls of the Manor of Dunham in 1485:

> "It was presented to the bailiff by Hamo that Richard de Thorle made an affray on Alice on the day after Easter. The same Hamo is presented that he made an affray on John Lyam on the Monday before the feast of St George. [It was also presented to the bailiff] that the wife of John Malleson made an affray on Alice the wife of Richard W on Monday before the feast of St George".[25]

In its third function of deciding issues the jury resembled the trial jury of the common law courts. The jurors were first of all acting from their own knowledge as finders of fact (as an inquest) and this method was frequently used in deciding questions relating to possession of land. For example in the manor court of Weedon Beck in 1248:

> "[The] twelve jurors come and say that Guner Lutting has no right in a half virgate of land which Richard Oppmel holds".[26]

Similarly in the manor court of Methley in 1352:

> "It was found by twelve jurors that William the son of Henry Dogson is the nearer heir of the same Henry, and that each heir may be accepted to have his inheritance at all times, whenever it should please him to show his right. Therefore it was decided that the said William should recover seisin of one messuage and one oxgang of land with the appurtenances in Houghton".[27]

There are numerous examples in the collection of manorial cases collected by Poos and Bonfield of juries making decisions and deciding disputes on matters of possession of and inheritance to land, some of them extremely complex. Such work often demanded of the jurors a knowledge not only of factual happenings but also of law. In one case, we feel sympathy for the jury which states, on being questioned as to the custom of the manor, that they do not know, "because this situation never occurred among them".[28] Many of the cases involving property disputes were settled with the approval of the jury, just as, in cases of litigation involving debts, trespasses, defamation and other disputes, the court would grant "love-days" for the parties to compromise or settle their differences. However, on occasions the jurors inevitably had to choose between conflicting statements and to decide between them; here they were truly acting as a "trial jury". [29]

Similarly in litigation involving wrongs such as trespass the issue was sometimes simply decided: "The jurors say that Simon Chacede has made

[25] University of Manchester, John Rylands Research Institute, Court Rolls of the Manor of Dunham Massey. These unpublished court rolls tend to support the prevailing notion that the 15th century was particularly violent!

[26] Maitland, *supra* n. 1, 16

[27] Poos and Bonfield, *supra* n. 2, 28 (no. 27b).

[28] Ibid., 133 (no. 173).

[29] As in ibid., 17–18 (no. 16) in a dispute over land. See also ibid., lxiii.

default, 12d., likewise Isabella of Weston, 12d." But an example of a conflict of evidence is revealed by a case in the same court:

> "[The jurors] say that the ploughman of Sir Ralph Rastel beat and ill treated John Scot the man of Brother W Margaret whereupon the hue was raised."

Subsequently the jurors did not believe John Scot's evidence, stating that William, the ploughman, had acted lawfully since he had acted as he had in the course of rescuing sheep which belonged to his lord.[30]

CONCLUSION

The heyday of the jury in the manorial courts was the reign of Edward II, though its use in manorial courts can be traced back at least to the thirteenth century. As in the common law courts, wager of law continued to exist, in practice and in theory, until the nineteenth century, but there is a marked increase in the use of the jury from the thirteenth century; the fact that parties chose to put themselves on the country and that they would often buy the right to a jury indicates that, as in the common law courts, the jury was regarded with favour by the "clients" of manorial justice. Its use was undermined to some extent by the development, in the courts of the manor, of documentary evidence and references to the court roll and by the growth of copyhold tenure. The functions of presentment and of acting as a "trial jury", deciding on the outcome of the case were often blurred and increasingly the role of deciding the issue became subordinate to the presentment, which was non traversable. By the fifteenth century, the jury was primarily being used in the manorial court for that purpose and its function in litigation was much reduced. Also, the court leet, like the hundred courts, became less important, especially with the rising importance of the justices of the peace. Nevertheless, the jury was still active in the manorial courts of the fifteenth century and even in the sixteenth, albeit primarily as a body to present and as an inquest on occasions.[31] The rich crop of manorial records will yet yield important discoveries about manorial courts, juries and procedure from which (in Maitland's metaphor) more sickles will reap a fascinating harvest.[32]

[30] Maitland, *supra* n. 1, 96.

[31] For an account of several active manor courts, see C Harrison, "The Manor Courts in Tudor England", in M Lobban and C Brooks (eds), *Communities and Courts in Britain* (London and Rio Grande, The Hambledon Press, 1997), 43.

[32] In addition to the many works on manorial justice there are also many published and edited collections, e.g. *Court Roll of Chalgrave Manor 1278–1313*, ed. by M K Dale, Bedfordshire Historical Record Soc., vol. 28 (Aspley Guise, 1950); *Court Rolls of the Wiltshire Manors of Adam de Stratton*, ed. by R B Pugh, Wiltshire Record Soc., vol. 24 (Devizes, 1970); *Court Rolls of the Abbey of Ramsey and of the Honour of Clare*, ed. by W O Ault, (New Haven, Yale University Press, 1928); *Court Rolls of the Manor of Ingoldmells*, ed. by W O Massingberd (London, Spottiswoode,1902); *Manorial Records of Cuxham, Oxfordshire, circa 1200–1359*, ed. by P D A Harvey, Oxfordshire Record Soc., vol. 1 (London, HMSO, 1976).

5

Jurors, Evidences and the Tempest of 1499

DAVID J SEIPP (BOSTON)

Jurors are the unsung heroes of the common law. Jurors gave the verdicts that made the whole system possible. Without the enforced co-operation of jurors, the tiny number of royal justices—usually 12 or 13 at any one time—could not possibly have resolved the thousands of disputes that came to judgment every year in the expanding jurisdiction of the common law.[1]

Jurors rarely got a speaking role in the Year Books, our principal sources for the early history of the common law. Jurors were always just off-stage in the pages of the Year Books, a silent, unseen presence. Litigants sued, defended, and compromised always with an eye to what a jury of 12 would someday say. Lawyers expended their considerable skill in framing new, narrower issues to be presented to jurors, questions that lawyers thought had a better chance of being answered favourably for their clients. Judges in the Year Books time and again pushed lawyers back to the general issue—to guilty or not guilty, and to total reliance on jurors.[2]

When jurors did make an appearance in the Year Books, it was usually because something had gone wrong with the jury process. Jurors had not behaved as judges and lawyers expected, or others had behaved toward jurors in improper ways. Our best sources for understanding the trial jury in fourteenth- and fifteenth-century England are roughly one hundred cases in the Year Books and Abridgments about jurors who misbehaved. In those cases, judges and lawyers revealed their assumptions and expectations about how jurors were supposed to behave when everything went right.

In a nutshell, these cases show that trial jurors in fourteenth- and fifteenth-century England, in civil and criminal suits, were virtual prisoners of the court once they were sworn. Before the trial, they were fair game for all sorts of communication of evidence and arguments by the parties and their counsel. Then, as soon as they were sworn, they were isolated and subjected to physical discomfort until they delivered their verdict.

[1] J P Dawson, *The Oracles of the Law* (Ann Arbor, Michigan University Press, 1968), 1–4; J P Dawson, *A History of Lay Judges* (Cambridge, Harvard University Press, 1960), 130–1.

[2] J H Baker, *An Introduction to English Legal History*, 3rd edn (London, Butterworths, 1989), ch. 5, "The Jury and Pleading".

In 1499, in a case that ended before all the justices of England in Exchequer Chamber, just about everything that could go wrong among jurors did go wrong. The case provides a good framework for discussing the varieties of jury misbehaviour and what they meant.

As reported in the Year Book, the suit was between a bishop and the Earl of Kent.[3] What bit of land or other matter was in dispute was not recorded in the Year Book, and did not matter to the reporter or to readers of the Year Book. The Plea Roll record of the case reveals that the actual plaintiffs were Mary and Joan Lucas, daughters of Thomas Lucas of Wavendon, Buckinghamshire.[4] The actual defendants were Joan Cesse, widow of John Cesse, and Henry Leesechylde, also of Wavendon. The Lucas sisters brought an action under the Statute of Forcible Entry to recover 40 acres of meadow, 20 acres of wood, and treble damages.[5] Defendants Cesse and Leesechylde pleaded a gift from George Grey, Earl of Kent. The Lucases' connection with William Smith, the Bishop of Lincoln, is not clear, but as will be seen shortly, the jurors understood that the bishop stood behind the Lucases.

According to the Year Book, the suit was pleaded to issue, and a panel of prospective jurors were summoned to give their verdict at *nisi prius*. The Plea Roll shows that the action, originally brought in Common Pleas, came before Chief Justice Fyneux and Justice Rede, both of King's Bench, at *nisi prius* in Aylesbury, Berkshire, probably on 16 July 1499. A jury of 12 were chosen from the sheriff's panel, were examined for kinship with the parties or for other grounds of challenge and were sworn to render their true verdict, all as usual.

Then, after the jurors were sworn, but before they gave their verdict, while the parties were showing their evidence to the jury in the presence of the justices at the King's Head Inn in Aylesbury, the heavens suddenly opened and there came a tempest of thunder, lightning and rain. Some or all of the jurors took fright and ran out of the hall, without first getting permission from the justices. That was the first problem. Amidst the thunder, rain, and lightning, one of the jurors took shelter in a house, not surprisingly an alehouse, where a stranger there remarked to the juror that he should take care what he did on that jury, because the Earl of Kent's matter was better than

[3] YB Trin. 14 Hen. VII, pl. 4, f. 29-31 (1499); YB Hil. 15 Hen. VII, pl. 2, f. 1–2 and *Select Cases in the Exchequer Chamber before all the Justices in England* ed. by M Hemmant, Seld. Soc., vol. 64 (London, 1948) 183–4 (1500). Further details of the case were reported in *The Reports of Sir John Spelman. Volume I*, ed. by J H Baker, Seld. Soc., vol. 93 (London, 1976), 222, Verdit pl. 5.

[4] CP 40/948 mm 395–6. I thank Prof. J H Baker for supplying this reference. W Page (ed.), *The Victoria History of the County of Buckingham* (London, St Catherine Press, 1927), vol. 4, 492 and n. 10, cites Early Chancery Proceedings bundle 212, no. 38, relating to Mary and Joan Lucas, daughters of Thomas Lucas of Woburn, Bedfordshire, who held a manor of Wavendon, perhaps the Passelewe manor, between 1485 and 1500.

[5] 8 Hen. VI, c. 9 (1429).

the Bishop's. That was the second problem. Then this stranger who sided with the Earl offered the juror a drink. He drank it, and that was the third problem.

The storm ended, everyone returned to court, and the parties finished showing their evidence. The jurors were charged, they were sent to a house to deliberate, and they returned to court to give their verdict. At that point, either the plaintiff or the defendant could still have objected. The jurors' behaviour during the storm was cause for challenge, and either could have insisted on summoning a new jury and starting over. Neither party did, so the jurors gave their verdict. Plaintiffs the Lucas daughters and the Bishop of Lincoln's matter won; defendants Cesse and Leesechylde and the Earl of Kent's matter lost.

Only at that point did the defendants move in arrest of judgment, objecting that the verdict should not be received. The jurors were questioned, and they admitted each of these small matters—the departure, the remark and the drink. Each of these matters gave rise to arguments that the verdict should not be received or that the jurors should be punished, that is, imprisoned, until they paid fines assessed by the justices. The departure, the remark, and the drink represent three different images of juror misbehaviour. Each had a long history in prior Year Book cases and each illuminates a different feature of the late medieval jury. The justices were in doubt whether the verdict was valid or void, so the matter came to Exchequer Chamber.

This paper has three main parts. The first deals with the problem of runaway jurors, with who could be jurors and with the coercion necessary to get jurors into court and keep them there. The second part is about the problem of communications with jurors after they are sworn, about how jurors were informed of the matters in dispute, and about what to do with a wrong verdict. The third part treats the problem of jurors drinking or eating after they were sworn, jury bribery, and how the courts secured a unanimous verdict from jurors.

RUNAWAY JURORS AND COERCION

The departure of jurors from court without permission was a serious matter, so serious that, in the discussion in Exchequer Chamber in 1499, Justice Vavasour and Chief Justice Bryan of Common Pleas and Chief Baron Hody of Exchequer would have thrown out the verdict. Jurors, Vavasour said, are like prisoners after they are charged, until they deliver their verdict. When jurors were sent off to deliberate, they were in the custody of guards appointed to keep them all together. When in 1350 jurors had gone "at large" and then returned, the justice at *nisi prius* would not take their verdict.[6] The jurors in

[6] YB Hil. 24 Edw. III, pl. 41, f. 51 (1350).

1499 had not yet been charged when the thunderstorm struck, but by departing from court without permission, Chief Baron Hody said, they had disabled themselves from giving a verdict.

Justices Wood and Danvers of Common Pleas took a different position in 1499. They would have imposed a fine on the jurors but would have left the verdict in place, at least on this account. When one juror went missing during deliberations in a trespass case in 1360, leaving 11 to deliver their verdict, the verdict was received.[7] In that case, Justice Knyvet warned the 11 that after they were sworn, they each ought to be guardian of the others, and none ought to depart. The 11 escaped paying a fine because the wandering juror returned to court, and was himself fined 40 pence.

Serjeant Thomas Kebell suggested in Exchequer Chamber in 1499 that the unusual circumstance of the thunderstorm justified the jurors in making their escape from court. All the Justices of King's Bench—Rede, Tremayle, and Chief Justice Fyneux—agreed with Kebell. If the courtroom were on fire, if the roof were beginning to fall, if a fight had broken out, it would not be reasonable to expect the jurors to await a grant of permission before running out. Even prisoners, Kebell pointed out, would not be prosecuted for escaping gaol under such circumstances. Chief Justice Bryan of Common Pleas considered that rain was a feeble excuse for such misbehaviour by jurors. But Chief Justice Fyneux countered that the parties to the action and their counsel had also fled the courtroom, and the case could not go on without them.[8]

The departure of jurors from court without permission was a serious matter because it was so hard to get jurors *to* court in the first place. Jurors were precious commodities, and getting the right sort of jurors into court at the right time was a tremendous problem. Many disputes never came to judgment because term after term a jury did not appear, until the parties finally gave up or died.[9]

Ordinarily, the justices sent the sheriff a writ of *venire facias*, and the sheriff was supposed to return a "panel", a small piece of parchment, containing the names of 24 prospective jurors who would appear on the appointed day.[10] These 24 were called collectively the "array" or "panel". The *venire facias* was rarely enough, so plaintiffs secured further writs of distraint or of *habeas corpora jurtaorum* to get the panel into court.

Prospective jurors had to be from the county where the suit arose, the "venue". In the fourteenth and fifteenth centuries, at least four of the

[7] YB Mich. 34 Edw. III, Fitzherbert Office del Court, pl. 12 (1360).

[8] This 1499 storm does not seem to have been the sort of crop-destroying, house-flattening, steeple-toppling storm that got into the chronicles and local history lore. I have found no trace of it in county histories, in J M Stratton, *Agricultural Records* (London, John Baker, 1969), or in T H Baker, *Records of the Seasons* (London, Simpkin Marshall, 1883).

[9] E.g., YB Mich. 13 Hen. IV, pl. 31, f. 10 (1411).

[10] YB Trin. 15 Edw. II, pl. 1, f. 467 (1323).

panel of 24 had to come from the hundred where the land in dispute was located or the transaction or wrongdoing was supposed to have occurred.[11] Some writs made careful provision that these prospective jurors would get a "view" of disputed land before coming to court. Lawyers took venue very seriously, often arguing that jurors could not know of matters in a different county. Jurors still brought their personal, local knowledge into court and the absence of one juror could deprive the rest of information they needed.

The *venire facias* also required that the prospective jurors should not be related to the parties. Once in court, individual members of the panel could be challenged by either party. The grounds for challenge included consanguinity, affinity and interest in the outcome. These were the same sorts of objections that canon lawyers made against witnesses in the church courts, as the Glanvill treatise noted in the late 1180s.[12]

Jurors also had to meet a property qualification set out in statutes of 1285, 1414 and 1429.[13] A juror in most suits had to hold lands worth at least 40 shillings a year. Jurors who failed to appear when summoned by the sheriff were liable to be fined the same amount, their yearly income from land, as valued by their fellow jurors. Richer landholders bought exemptions from jury duty, so that potential jurors were largely drawn from the middling stratum of society.[14]

Sheriffs no doubt sometimes filled out juries with men who did not meet the qualifications, and parties no doubt sometimes withheld their challenges in order to get on with the case. When still there were not enough jurors, the justices issued writs of *tales* to summon an extra eight or ten prospective jurors, or a writ of *tales de circumstantibus* for the sheriff to haul in any hapless bystanders in or near the courtroom, "talesmen", to join the jury immediately. Nobody thought of swearing alternate jurors in case one or two of the twelve would run away during the trial.

The entire system depended on coercion. Jurors were not volunteers. They were compelled to appear, compelled to swear and compelled to remain until their duty was done. Jurors, as Vavasour said in 1499, were virtually prisoners of the justices, responsible for each other's behaviour and subject to prison and fines for any breach of their duty. This treatment sharply differentiated the subordinate status of jurors from the lofty status of the justices, although jurors, to a much greater extent than justices, exercised the real

11 YB Pasch. 11 Hen. IV, pl. 14, f. 62 (1410); YB Mich. 26 Hen. VI, Statham Enquest, pl. 5 (1447); J Fortescue, *De Laudibus Legum Angliae* (c. 1465), ed. by S B Chrimes (Cambridge, University Press, 1942), 60 (ch. 25).

12 *Glanvill* (c. 1189), ed. by G D G Hall (London, Oxford University Press, 1965), 32 (bk 2, ch. 12).

13 Westminster 2nd, 13 Edw. I (1285), c. 38; 2 Hen. V, stat. 2, c. 3 (1414); 8 Hen. VI, c. 9 (1429).

14 See S L Waugh, "Reluctant Knights and Jurors: Respites, Exemptions, and Public Obligations in the Reign of Henry III", (1983) 58 *Speculum* 937.

sovereign prerogative of choosing who would win and who would lose their suits.

BELABOURED JURORS AND EVIDENCES

In the tempest of 1499, a stranger in an alehouse said to a juror:

> "I advise you take heed what you do, for my lord of Kent's matter is good and my lord of Lincoln's matter is not so good."

These were the words recorded in English in the Latin Plea Roll. Wavendon, where these events took place, was near the home base of the Grey family, the earls of Kent, and they must have had their local supporters. A remark about who should win the case, made to a juror who had left the court during presentation of the evidence, was seen as less of a problem in 1499 than the jurors' departure without permission or the drink that this juror then received.

None of the justices in Exchequer Chamber thought that the stranger's remark to the juror was enough on its own to invalidate the verdict, which in any case went against the Earl of Kent and his alehouse supporters. Justice Wood of Common Pleas said that the remark did not literally express a desire for the juror to be favourable to the Earl. Justices Rede and Tremayle of King's Bench agreed with Wood that the remark did not "entreat" the juror to be partial, but merely said that the Earl had the better cause. It did not prove the juror to have been partial or favourable or corrupted in any way, so the verdict stood. If the verdict had been for the Earl, some of the justices would probably have found that the communication itself was reason to reject the verdict.

The remark would have been a more serious matter if it had been made at a slightly later stage in the trial, after the jurors had been charged on the issue between the bishop and the earl and had retired, under guard, to deliberate together. The *Fleta* treatise from the 1290s, a petition to Parliament in 1354, and Year Book reports of 1465 and 1498 all repeated what must have been a standard prohibition that no one was allowed to approach or have speech with a jury during its deliberations, except their guards, on pain of imprisonment.[15] The guards not only kept the jurors from escaping, they insulated them from last-minute promises and threats.

In 1310, Baron Foxley of the Exchequer, a justice of assize, was accused of going in and speaking to jurors during their deliberations.[16] This was con-

[15] *Fleta Volume III: Book III and Book IV*, ed. with trans. by H G Richardson and G O Sayles, Seld. Soc., vol. 89 (London, 1972), 66 (bk 4, ch. 9, f. 89); Rot. Parl., vol. 2, 259, ch. 30 (1354); YB Mich. 5 Edw. IV, Long Quinto pl. 3, f. 61 (1465); YB Mich. 14 Hen. VII, pl. 5, f. 1 (1498).

[16] *Reports from the Lost Notebooks of Sir James Dyer. Vol. II*, ed. by J H Baker, Seld. Soc., vol. 110 (London, 1994), 342 (pl. 424.15).

sidered so serious a slander that the accuser was imprisoned in the Tower until he paid a large fine to the king and 200 pounds to Foxley. In 1411, a defendant's counsel told jurors during their deliberations to be well-advised about their verdict, because the plaintiff's complaint was not true.[17] In 1411, as in 1499, the verdict went against the side that communicated improperly to the jury. The jurors and their guards were fined in 1411, and the defendant's damages were increased by the court. If parties wished to show more documents to the jury, or if jurors wished to hear more argument, then the jury should return to court.

Several more Year Book cases deal with written evidence smuggled in to jury deliberations. Charters, a list of costs and damages, a court roll, a letter, a "church book" and other unspecified writings were discovered among the jurors, and led to rejection of verdicts and to fines imposed on jurors and their guards.[18] One scoundrel was caught in 1347 who had arranged with parties to get himself named as a juror on more than one case and had brought along a book that he called variously "Domesday Book" and the "Book of Fees" to overawe his fellow jurors.[19]

Most mentions of evidence in the Year Books referred to charters, deeds and other writings, to "evidences" rather than evidence.[20] These were what was supposed to be presented by the parties in open court. Jurors would take these writings with them during their deliberations.[21] Jurors in a case in 1390 were discovered to have a thirteenth fellow among them. When questioned, they said that none of them could read the deeds delivered to them, so one of them found a stranger who could read them aloud and explain them "in the mother tongue".[22] The justice at *nisi prius* refused to accept the verdict, but the full court disagreed and took it.

It seems to have been much more common for parties or their counsel to show written evidences formally in open court than to offer witnesses who would testify under oath in court. Evidence, in the sense of live oral testimony in court, was not the essence of the trial. When a deed or charter was disputed, and the document named witnesses attesting to its creation, these witnesses were summoned to court and were sworn. But then these witnesses, like the

[17] *Select Cases in the Court of King's Bench under Richard II, Henry IV and Henry V*, ed. by G O Sayles, Seld. Soc., vol. 88 (London, 1971), 199 (Hil. 12 Hen. IV; 1411).

[18] *Select Cases of Trespass from the King's Courts, 1307–1399*, ed. by M S Arnold, Seld. Soc., vol. 100 (London, 1985), xxviii, n. 132 (1371) (charter); YB Pasch. 12 Ric. II, pl. 21, Ames 186 (1388) (list of costs); *Select Cases*, supra n. 17, 125 (Trin. 3 Hen. IV; (1402) (roll); YB Hil. 9 Hen. VI, pl. 21, f. 65 (1431) (list of places wasted); YB Hil. 35 Hen. VI, Fitzherbert Examination, pl. 17 (1457) (letter).

[19] *Select Cases in the Court of King's Bench under Edward III. Volume VI*, ed. by G O Sayles, Seld. Soc., vol. 82 (London, 1965), 58 (Trin. 21 Edw. III; 1347).

[20] E.g., YB Hil. 12 Hen. IV, pl. 1, f. 11 (1411); YB Pasch. 11 Hen. VI, pl. 36, f. 41 (1433); YB 14 Hen. VI, pl. 32, f. 7 (1436); YB Mich. 6 Edw. IV, pl. 14, f. 5 (1466).

[21] YB Hil. 34 Hen. VI, pl. 2, f. 25 (1456); YB Mich. 21 Edw. IV, pl. 1, f. 37 (1481).

[22] *Select Cases, supra* n. 17, 66 (Hil. 13 Ric. II; 1390).

deed, went with the jurors during their deliberations.[23] As late as the 1570s, jurors during their deliberations could send for anyone who had been sworn to testify in the case, and question them in private.[24] The information supplied by sworn witnesses to the jurors was not something that the justices and parties needed to see in open court.

The Year Books reveal that a large part of the process of informing juries about matters in dispute in the fourteenth and fifteenth centuries took place informally, outside of court, and before the day of trial. In 1412, for example, we hear that on the Saturday before an assize in Middlesex, one J Beke who was of counsel to the plaintiff and one R Sheffield who was of counsel to the defendant brought all the prospective jurors of the panel together at a certain place "to show their evidences" to them.[25] Whether counsel for one of the parties also gave the panel six shillings eightpence for their dinner was the issue in that Year Book report. In the same year, in an action for covenant in Colchester, an attorney for a defendant "made a great speech" to prospective jurors on the day of trial.[26] This was presumably not in court, because the attorney was also alleged at the same time to have given each of the jurors two or three fish. In 1450, Chief Justice Fortescue said that, if jurors came to a man who lived in the countryside, so that the man could inform the jurors of the truth of the matter in dispute, neither the jurors nor their informant had committed any wrong.[27]

The process of summoning a jury panel made such pre-trial contacts possible. The writ of *venire facias* told prospective jurors the names of the parties and, in very brief form, the matter in dispute. A statute of 1368 required the sheriff to deliver to court (and thereby to the parties) the names of the 24 prospective jurors at least four days before the day of trial.[28] Chief Justice Gascoigne repeated this requirement in 1407.[29] In 1427, the Commons petitioned that the sheriff should provide the names of prospective jurors to the parties at least six days in advance of trial.[30]

Parties and their counsel customarily used those days to inform and attempt to persuade some or all of the prospective jurors about the truth of their suits. Two dozen Year Book cases litigated the proprieties of communications with and among jurors, in and out of court, in the context of prose-

[23] *The Eyre of Northamptonshire. 3–4 Edward III, A.D. 1329-1330*, ed. by D W Sutherland, Seld. Soc., vol. 98 (London, 1983), 592 (1329); YB Mich. 11 Edw. III, RS 339 (1337); YB Mich. 14 Edw. III, pl. 72, RS 189 (1340); YB 23 Edw. III, Lib. Ass, pl. 11, f. 110 (1349); YB Mich. 12 Hen. IV, pl. 16, f. 9a (1410); YB 5 Hen. V, Statham Enquest pl. 19 (1417); YB Mich. 5 Hen. VII, pl. 19, f. 8 (1489).

[24] T Smith, *De Republica Anglorum* (c. 1577), ed. by L Alston, (Cambridge, University Press, 1906), 101 (bk 2, ch. 12).

[25] YB Hil. 13 Hen. IV, pl. 4, f. 12 (1412).

[26] YB Hil. 13 Hen. IV, pl. 12, f. 16 (1412).

[27] YB Pasch. 27 Hen. VI, pl. 1, f. 6 (1450).

[28] 42 Edw. III, c. 11 (1368).

[29] YB Hil. 8 Hen. IV, pl. 7, f. 20 (1407).

[30] Rot. Parl., vol. 4, 328, ch. 30 (1427).

cutions for maintenance. Letters in the Paston and Plumpton correspondence show that the proprieties were not always observed.[31]

Statements of serjeants and justices form a consistent picture of what was allowed and what was not. It was forbidden for the parties, their counsel, or anyone else to bribe jurors, promise them future favours, threaten them, "embrace" them, or "procure" them.[32] It was permissible for parties, their counsel, their relatives, in-laws, lords, grantors, and servants to inform prospective jurors of the truth of the matter, to show the party's title deeds and other evidences, and thus to "labour" them by trying to persuade them that the party had the right or the better matter.[33]

On the other hand, it was forbidden for *strangers* to "labour" prospective jurors in any of these ways, whether at the request of a party or otherwise.[34] For someone not in the party's camp to "show the truth of the matter" to prospective jurors before trial, or to sworn jurors in court, was equally maintenance and equally wrongful.[35] This effectively barred witnesses not related to the parties who volunteered their testimony.[36] Jurors too could be guilty of maintenance if they bribed their fellow jurors, but not if they merely "exhorted" or "preached" to their companions that one party had the right.[37] Juries were most often called "enquests" or "quests", and those who made a regular business of manipulating them were condemned as "questmongers" by William Langland, Geoffrey Chaucer, and later writers,[38] as

[31] N Davis (ed.), *Paston Letters* (Oxford, Clarendon Press, 1976), pt. 1, 526–7 (2 June 1464), pt. 2, 388–9 (28 Oct. 1468), 493–4 (16 Dec. 1488 or 1494); T Stapleton (ed.), *Plumpton Correspondence* (London, Camden Society, 1839), 130–3 (28 Jan. to 12 Feb. 1499), 141 (21 Nov. 1499), 159-61 (Sept. 1501).

[32] YB Hil. 13 Hen. IV, pl. 12, f. 16 (1412); YB Mich. 21 Hen. VI, pl. 30, f. 15 (1442); YB Mich. 19 Edw. IV, pl. 9, f. 3 (1479).

[33] YB Hil. 13 Hen. IV, pl. 12, f. 16 (1412); YB Mich. 19 Hen. VI, pl. 60, f. 31 (1440); YB Mich. 21 Hen. VI, pl. 30, f. 15 (1442); YB Mich. 35 Hen. VI, pl. 25, f. 15 (1456); YB Mich. 6 Edw. IV, pl. 5, f. 2 (1466); YB Mich. 6 Edw. IV, pl. 14, f. 5 (1466).

[34] YB Hil. 32 Hen. VI, pl. 11, f. 24 (1454); YB Mich. 20 Hen. VII, pl. 21, f. 11 (1504).

[35] YB Pasch. 11 Hen. VI, pl. 36, f. 41 (1433); cf. YB Pasch. 11 Hen. VI, pl. 33, f. 39 (1433).

[36] YB Pasch. 27 Hen. VI, pl. 1, f. 6 (1450); cf. YB Pasch. 18 Edw. IV, pl. 11, f. 2 (1478).

[37] YB Mich. 8 Edw. III, pl. 35, f. 68 (1334); YB Mich. 17 Edw. IV, pl. 2, f. 5 (1477).

[38] W Langland, *Piers Plowman* (1377), ed. by W W Skeat (London, EETS, 1869), vol. 2, 360 (B text, pass. 19, ln. 367: "lyeres and questmongeres that were forsworen ofte"); G Chaucer, *The Parson's Tale* (c. 1390), in J M Manly and E Rickert (eds), *The Text of the Canterbury Tales* (Chicago, University of Chicago Press, 1940), vol. 4, 443 (ln. 797: "ware yow questemongeres and notaries certes for fals witnessing"); *The Anonimalle Chronicle* (1381), ed. by V H Galbraith (Manchester, University Press, 1927), 140 ln. 21 (f. 344v); R Pecock, *The Repressor* (c. 1449), ed. by C Babington (London, RS, 1860), 516 (pt 5, ch. 6: vnpiteful questmongers and forsworen iurers); *The Towneley Plays* (c. 1460), ed. by G England (London, EETS, 1897), 205 (play 20, ln. 25: "all fals indytars, Quest mangers and Iurers"); ibid., 244 (play 22, ln. 24: "Quest gangars and Iurors"); *ibid.*, 373 (play 30, ln. 185: "bakbytars and fals quest-dytars"); R Fabyan, *The New Chronicles of England and France* (1494), ed. by H Ellis (London, F C and J Rivington, 1811), 530 (1381: "they … slewe as many men of lawe and questmongers as they myght fynde"). See also ch. 7 *infra*.

"leaders of enquests" in a 1412 Year Book and as "embracers" in other Year Books and statutes.[39]

Historians of the jury have debated whether medieval English juries were ever truly "self-informing" and when they ceased to be so.[40] Year Books of the fifteenth century suggest that parties could and certainly often did "labour" prospective jurors in advance of trial, and that jurors could and perhaps did seek out such information for themselves. Fifteenth-century jurors were not the "naïve" jurors of the present day who need to hear everything about the dispute in court. The privately-informed or pre-informed or informally-informed jury might be a better term for these belaboured panels of jurors.

Jurors had the formal character of witnesses down through the sixteenth century. Like witnesses they were sworn to tell the truth, though witnesses were sworn to tell the truth as they had seen and heard it, and jurors were sworn to tell the truth according to their consciences.[41] The Bracton treatise in the mid-thirteenth century instructed judges to interrogate jurors individually to discover the basis of their verdict, sifting eyewitness knowledge from hearsay.[42] Judges did not do so. They questioned juries rarely, and only when their verdict was incomplete or confused. Thomas More, in a tract of 1533, made a sharp distinction between jurors and witnesses,[43] but Christopher St German, with whom More was debating, made none.[44] One of Dyer's reports for 1557 assumed that jurors would give more credence to the personal knowledge of one of their number than to the testimony of four or five witnesses given in court.[45] A report of 1598 says that during deliberations a juror might declare to his fellows "as a witness" what he knew to be true, and might show them any writings he brought in, so long as they did not come from a party.[46]

[39] YB Hil. 13 Hen. IV, pl. 12, f. 16 (1412). Also 38 Edw. III, stat. 1, c. 12 (1364); YB Trin. 40 Edw. III, pl. 16, f. 33 (1366); YB Pasch. 41 Edw. III, pl. 3, f. 9 (1367); YB Trin. 41 Edw. III, pl. 5, f. 15 (1367); YB Mich. 7 Hen. IV, pl. 16, f. 2 (1405); YB Trin. 37 Hen. VI, pl. 12, f. 31 (1459); YB Mich. 6 Edw. IV, pl. 14, f. 5 (1466); 11 Hen. VII, c. 24, preamble (1495).

[40] See principally T A Green, *Verdict According to Conscience: Perspectives on the English Criminal Trial Jury, 1200–1800* (Chicago, University of Chicago Press, 1985); J S Cockburn and T A Green (eds), *Twelve Good Men and True: The Criminal Trial Jury in England, 1200–1800* (Princeton, University Press, 1988).

[41] *Fleta, supra* n. 15, 66 (bk 4, ch. 9, f. 89); YB Mich. 5 Edw. IV, Long Quinto pl. 3, f. 61 (1465); YB Mich. 21 Edw. IV, pl. 1, f. 37 (1481); YB Mich. 32 Hen. VIII, pl. 19, 1 Dyer 48a, 73 ER 106 (1540).

[42] *Bracton* (c. 1250), ed. by G E Woodbine and S E Thorne (trans.) (Cambridge, Mass. Harvard University Press, 1968), vol. 2, 404 (f. 143–3b).

[43] T More, *The Debellation of Salem and Bizance* (1533), in idem, *Complete Works* (New Haven, Yale University Press, 1987), vol. 10, 149.

[44] C St German, *Salem and Bizance* (1533), in More, *Complete Works, supra* n. 43, vol. 10, 360.

[45] *Dyer's Reports, supra* n. 16, 410, pl. 37 (1557).

[46] *Graves* v. *Short*, Cro. Eliz. 616, 89 ER 857 (1598).

Judges did not control the process of informing jurors about matters in dispute, since much of this happened outside court before the day of trial. In the tempest case of 1499, Justice Vavasour said in passing that parties need not present any evidence at all between the time the jurors were sworn and the time they were charged to bring in their verdict. This made sense only in a process in which parties had ample opportunity to labour prospective jurors in advance of trial. It follows from this that judges could not overturn jury verdicts that were inconsistent with the evidence presented at trial. Jurors could be deciding on the basis of information about which the justices were completely unaware. This was the position still being taken by Chief Justice Vaughan in 1670 in the case of that most famous of English jurymen, Edward Bushel.[47]

All that could be done to overturn a jury verdict in 1499 was to bring a writ of attaint against the jury. This meant summoning a second jury of 24 to try the first 12. Justices, when they charged trial juries, warned them not only about the solemn and sacred character of their oath but also about the grave consequences of perjury in this world.[48] Chief Justice Fortescue, in his *De Laudibus*, recounted the punishment for attaint: the 12 shall be committed to the public gaol, their goods shall be confiscated, their possessions seized into the king's hand, their habitations and houses shall be pulled down, their woodlands shall be felled, their meadows shall be plowed up, and they shall forever thenceforward be deemed infamous in the eyes of the law.[49] It sounded like a formula that justices intoned many times from the bench when charging juries. This harsh punishment left attaint juries so extremely reluctant to convict that it was reduced in 1496 to a monetary fine. Even so, attaint was hardly ever successful in the sixteenth century, and the punishment of false jurors passed to Star Chamber.[50]

The practice of informing jury panels before trial was beginning to change in the course of the sixteenth century. Parties began to use subpoenas to compel witnesses to testify in the common law courts. Statutes confirmed this practice in 1552 and 1563.[51] Witnesses who were compelled to testify in court were safe from prosecution for maintenance. Demurrers on the evidence and motions for new trial began to be heard, based solely on the evidence that was introduced at trial. To find the origins of judicial control over live oral testimony, of the law of evidence in our modern sense, we need look no further back than the sixteenth century. Fifteenth-century jurors came to court belaboured by information and argument provided informally by the parties in the days leading up to the actual trial.

[47] *Bushel's Case*, 1 Freeman 1, 89 ER 2; Vaughan 135, 124 ER 1006 (1670).

[48] E.g., *The Eyre of Northamptonshire. 3–4 Edward III, A.D. 1329-1330. Volume I*, ed. by D W Sutherland, Seld. Soc., vol. 97 (London, 1983), 289 (1330).

[49] Fortescue, *supra* n. 11, 60–2.

[50] Smith, *supra* n. 24, 111.

[51] 5 & 6 Edw. VI, c. 11, s. 9 (1552); 5 Eliz 1, c. 9, s. 6 (1563).

THIRSTY JURORS AND UNANIMITY

Coerced to remain until discharged, belaboured beforehand and again in court, jurors were further beset by rules designed deliberately to cause them discomfort. In the thunderstorm at Aylesbury in 1499, the drink given by a stranger to one juror, named Robert Legynggam in the Plea Roll, was the gravest offence of all in the eyes of the justices in Exchequer Chamber. Three of the justices, two of them from Common Pleas, said that the drink taken by that one juror invalidated the verdict of 12. Four of the justices, three of them from King's Bench, would have levied fines on account of it. Two justices and Serjeant Kebell would have fined all 12 jurors because one had taken a drink, and two justices would have fined only Legynggam. Two justices agreed to let the verdict stand and mentioned no fine, but they would have rejected the verdict on account of that drink if it had gone the other way.

A rule withholding food and drink from jurors after they were charged appeared in the *Fleta* treatise in the 1290s.[52] The rule was enforced consistently in Year Book cases.[53] Four Year Book cases before 1499 rejected verdicts because the jurors had eaten or drunk while they were deliberating.[54] Justice Vavasour of Common Pleas rejected such a verdict in 1498, just one year before the tempest in Aylesbury.[55] Another four cases fined the jurors and their guards but let the verdicts stand.[56] The rule was broadened by 1346 to prevent jurors from eating or drinking not just during deliberations but at any time after they were sworn.[57] Justices relaxed the rule if a juror was ill,[58] or if the jurors had reached their verdict after court had adjourned for the evening.[59] If a juror or two died after they were charged and before they delivered their verdict, a chief justice proposed in 1410 that they could be replaced by two new jurors summoned by a *tales*.[60]

In the sixteenth century, we see the rule again and we hear for the first time what sort of foods jurors smuggled into courtrooms. Between 1500 and 1588 jurors were caught with comfits, dredge, sugar-candy, raisins, plum

[52] *Fleta*, *supra* n. 15, 66 (bk 4, ch. 9, f. 89).

[53] Early applications of the rule are YB 21 Edw. I, RS 273 (1293) (Rothbury J) and Mich. 4 Edw. II, pl. 74 (1310) (Stanton J) in *Year Books of Edward II. Vol. IV. 3 & 4 Edward II. A.D. 1309-1311*, ed. by F W Maitland and G J Turner, Seld. Soc., vol. 22 (London, 1907), 188.

[54] YB Hil. 24 Edw. III, pl. 10, f. 24 (1350); *Select Cases of Trespass*, *supra* n. 18, xxviii-xix (1359); YB Hil. 35 Hen. VI, Fitzherbert Examination pl. 17 (1457); case cited *infra* n. 55.

[55] YB Mich. 14 Hen. VII, pl. 3, f. 1 (1498).

[56] YB Mich. 34 Edw. III, Fitzherbert Office del Court pl. 12 (1360); YB Trin. 11 Ric. II, pl. 10, Ames 34 (1387); *Select Cases*, *supra* n. 17, 199 (Hil. 12 Hen. IV; 1411); Trin. 9 Hen. V, in *Dyer's Reports*, *supra* n. 16, 428 (1421).

[57] YB Trin. 20 Edw. III, pl. 8, 1 RS 487 (1346).

[58] YB Mich. 14 Hen. VII, pl. 5, f. 1 (1498).

[59] YB Trin. 2 Hen. IV, pl. 2, f. 21 (1401).

[60] YB Mich. 12 Hen. IV, pl. 18, f. 9 (1410).

jam, dates, figs, pippins, preserved barberries, more sugar-candy and liquorice.[61] For these Tudor snack foods, jurors sometimes paid fines of up to five pounds, but their verdicts were accepted. The rule persisted in one form or other until 1870.[62]

Even panels of prospective jurors had limits on what they could eat and drink. If they had received food or drink from one of the parties to the case after they were impanelled, they could be challenged for cause.[63] This was a problem, because jurors had to travel to the assize town or to Westminster, and sometimes had to stay for some nights, all at their own expense. In 1334, Serjeant Robert Parvyng protested this: "The plaintiff will never have an assize if he does not bring [the jurors] at his cost".[64] Chief Justice Herle of Common Pleas replied:

> "It was Law before we were born, that those who come at the costs of the party, will not be put on the inquest for the presumption that there is against them. And we would not change that law."

Serjeant Parvyng said "Sir, then a man will never have his recovery." The Chief Justice said "Sue then in Parliament to make new Law". Parliament began allowing jurors reimbursement for their expenses 615 years later, in 1949.[65] Around 1380, John Wycliffe preached against jurors who forswore themselves "for their dinner and a noble" (six shillings eightpence) or "for twelve pence and their dinner".[66] By 1499, when jurors were discovered to have had any food or drink during deliberations, the justices wanted to know first of all whether one of the parties had paid for it. If so, the justices would throw out the verdict. If not, they would merely fine the jurors. And after the verdict, it was customary and lawful for the winning party to provide a good dinner for all the jurors, as Thomas Smith recounted in 1577.[67] Food and justice seemed locked in an eternal struggle.

One might think that the reason for this rule was to prevent a common and rather petty form of bribery. Bribery of prospective jurors was enough

[61] *Earl of Arundel's Case*, in *The Reports of Sir John Spelman. Volume II*, ed. by J H Baker, Seld. Soc., vol. 94 (London, 1978), *113* (1500); YB Mich. 16 Hen. VII, Rastell, *Entrees*, f. 268 (1500); *Littleton* v. *Hunkleton*, 1 Dyer 78a, pl. 41, 73 ER 167 (1552); *Mounson* v. *West*, 1 Leon 132 at 133, 74 ER 123 (1558); *Welcden* v. *Elkington*, 2 Plowd. 518 at 520, 75 ER 766 at 768 (1576).

[62] W R Cornish, *The Jury* (London, Allen Lane, 1968), 70.

[63] YB Mich. 22 Ric. II, Fitzherbert Challenge pl. 177 (1398); YB Hil. 13 Hen. IV, pl. 4, f. 12 (1412); YB Pasch. 13 Hen. IV, Statham Challenge pl. 45 (1412).

[64] YB Mich. 8 Edw. III, pl. 35, f. 68 (1334).

[65] Cornish, *supra* n. 62, 53.

[66] J Wycliffe, *The Grete Sentence of Curs Expounded* (c. 1380), in *Select English Works* ed. by T Arnold (Oxford, Clarendon Press, 1871), vol. 3, 301 (ch. 22: "Men of lawe and jurours han non conscience to forswere hem for twel pens and her dyner"); J Wycliffe, *Three Things Destroy This World* (c. 1380), in *English Works* ed. by F D Matthew (London, EETS, 1880), 183 ("yit iurrouris in questis wolen forsweren hem wittyngly for here dyner & a noble").

[67] Smith, *supra* n. 24, 80.

of a problem that statutes of 1346, 1360 and 1364 finally made the corrupt juror and the briber each liable for ten times the amount of the bribe, half to the king and half to the person who discovered and prosecuted the offence.[68] In more than 30 Year Book cases, jurors were charged with receiving amounts that varied widely between two pence and 20 pounds "to say their verdict".[69] Twenty shillings seems to have been the most common bribe for a juror, far more than the price of a dinner.

The original motivation for the rule forbidding food and drink to jurors was not merely to prevent petty bribery, not merely to keep them sober and awake, but rather to force them to agree on a verdict. Even before the common law required unanimous verdicts, justices were locking up jurors without food or drink in order to compel the jurors to agree. Verdicts of 11 were received until 1367, and in six Year Book cases through 1367 the stubborn lone dissenter was sent to prison.[70] When this option was outlawed, the justices added a threat that starving jurors who still failed to agree when the session ended would be carried in a cart to the next county.[71]

In Exchequer Chamber in 1499, Serjeant Kebell explained that, if all 12 jurors were allowed to eat and drink, they would never agree. Keble added that if one juror had some food or drink after they were sworn, as Legynggam did in the tempest case, that one could hold out against hunger and thirst longer than the others, and so compel the rest to agree with his view of the case. Whether or not one of the parties provided the food or drink, letting some jurors have sustenance while depriving the rest would skew the result. Christopher St German's Doctor of Divinity in 1530 vividly described how a juror who knew the truth to be with one party might be forced by hunger and thirst to join in a verdict against his conscience.[72] Although St German's Student of the Common Law denied the possibility, this is precisely the result that the rule against food and drink was designed to achieve. Hunger and thirst would overcome a dissenting juror's scruples. As Alexander Pope wrote in 1714, "wretches hang, that jurymen may dine".[73]

With this rule against food and drink in mind, other features of the late medieval trial, such as the remarkable speed of the proceedings, make more

[68] 20 Edw. III, c. 4 (1346); 34 Edw. III, c. 8 (1361); 37 Edw. III, stat. 1, c. 12 (1364) (*decies tantum*).

[69] E.g., YB Trin. 40 Edw. III, pl. 16, f. 33 (1366) (20s); YB Pasch. 41 Edw. III, pl. 3, f. 9 (1367) (£20); YB 14 Hen. VI, pl. 30, f. 6 (1436) (2d); YB Pasch. 9 Edw. IV, pl. 16, f. 4 (1466) (20s).

[70] Nottingham Eyre, 3 Edw. III, Fitzherbert Verdict pl. 40 (1329); YB 8 Edw. III, Lib. Ass. pl. 35, f. 19 (1334); YB Mich. 20 Edw. III, pl. 110, 2 RS 557 (1346); YB 29 Edw. III, Lib. Ass. pl. 4, f. 156 (1355); 41 Edw. III, Lib. Ass. pl. 11, f. 253 (1367); YB Mich. 41 Edw. III, pl. 36, f. 31 (1367).

[71] YB 41 Edw. III, Lib. Ass. pl. 11, f. 253 (1367); YB Hil. 20 Hen. VIII; Iour pl. 1, in *Spelman's Reports vol. I, supra* n. 3, 155 (1529); *The Times*, 21 July 1848, p. 7.

[72] [C St German] *St. German's Doctor and Student*, ed. by T F T Plucknett and J L Barton, Seld. Soc., vol. 91 (London, 1974), 292–3 (pt 2, ch. 52) (1530). An Italian visitor made a similar observation about 1500: *A Relation or Rather a True Account, of the Island of England* (c. 1500), ed. by C Sneyd (London, Camden Society, 1847), 32–3.

[73] A Pope, *The Rape of the Lock*, canto 3, ln. 22 (London, 1714).

sense. In 1504, for example, after the jurors were sworn, the parties gave them their evidence "for the space of five hours and more", according to the Year Book report, and then begged the justices to allow the jurors some food and drink.[74] The justices relented in 1504, allowing the jurors refreshment under judicial supervision. But five hours of evidence in court must have been an unusual departure from the normal practice.

A party who excessively prolonged the time that jurors must spend in court without food and drink would not have been popular among the jury. Much better to present evidence and arguments to the panel of prospective jurors at leisure, before the day of trial. In court, jurors forbidden food and drink from the moment they were sworn until after they came back with their verdict, had reason to want the parties' counsel to get through their challenges and arguments, the clerk to read out the issue, and justices to charge them—all as quickly as possible. The rule against food and drink kept common law litigation humming along with almost indecent haste. By this means, a pair of justices could get through several trials in a single day.[75]

CONCLUSION: THE JURORS' PREDICAMENT

The judges of the common law, not yet willing or able to control the information upon which jurors would decide cases, nevertheless felt impelled to discipline and to subordinate jurors in the ways outlined here. Jurors were coerced to appear and to remain. They could be informed in a variety of ways before trial, but they deliberated in strict isolation. And they were compelled to agree by hunger and thirst. All three of these features of the trial jury in late medieval England fall into place when seen in light of the jurors' larger predicament.

Never forget that jurors had to make the hard choices in the courts of common law. When the jurors gave their verdict, judgments followed. Tracts of land changed hands. Possessions were seized and sold so that damages could be paid. Felons were hanged. Winning parties bought the jurors a good dinner. But the parties who lost by a jury's verdict would find it easy to blame the jurors personally for that verdict and that loss. To the extent that winners and losers viewed verdicts as the free choice of the jurors, verdicts made enemies. Losing parties, their relatives, their patrons and their friends might retaliate against the jurors who caused their loss. Year Books show that some jurors were threatened before trial,[76] and some were assaulted

[74] YB Mich. 20 Hen. VII, pl. 10, f. 3 (1504).

[75] R B Pugh, "The Duration of Criminal Trials in Medieval England", in E W Ives and A H Manchester (eds), *Law, Litigants and the Legal Profession* (London, Royal Historical Society, 1983), 104–8.

[76] *Select Cases, supra* n. 17, 233 (Pasch. 3 Hen. V; 1415); ibid., 235 (Trin. 3 Hen. V; 1415); YB Mich. 19 Hen. VI, pl. 60, f. 31 (1440); YB Mich. 21 Hen. VI, pl. 30, f. 15 (1442); Swaffham petition (1451), in *Paston Letters, supra* n. 31, pt. 2, 528–30.

after trial.[77] Popular literature in those centuries displayed a remarkable hostility toward jurors, perhaps more so than toward judges or lawyers; some preachers and writers treated "juror" and "perjurer" as synonymous.[78] Jurors had good reason to want to shift the responsibility for deciding guilt, liability and entitlement away from themselves.

Some jurors tried to shift the responsibility to the person of the judge, a powerful outsider, but judges resisted this. In Year Book cases from 1314, 1406, and 1468, and a petition to Parliament in 1348, juries tried to return "verdicts at large", giving lengthy statements of facts and asking the judges to draw the legal conclusions, but each time the judges forced the jurors to answer the question of liability as the lawyers framed it.[79] This is the same pattern we see in Year Book pleading. Judges rarely decided questions of law arising on demurrer, and commonly forced the parties back to the general issue, a question for the jury alone to decide.[80]

English judges, in their more candid moments, realised that courtroom decisions were difficult and could be dangerous. It was safer for judges if jurors took the blame, especially in criminal cases. In 1883, Justice James Fitzjames Stephen wrote that trial by jury:

> "saves judges from the responsibility—which to many men would appear intolerably heavy and painful—of deciding simply on their own opinion upon the guilt or innocence of the prisoner".[81]

Maitland quoted these words of Stephen, and added that trial by jury:

> "saved judges of the middle ages not only from this moral responsibility, but also from enmities and feuds. Likewise it saved them from that as yet unattempted task, a critical dissection of testimony".[82]

Chief Justice Matthew Hale wrote in the 1670s:

> "It were the most unhappy case that could be to the judge, if he at his peril must take upon him the guilt or innocence of the prisoner".[83]

[77] YB Mich. 19 Edw. III, pl. 73, RS 453 (1345); *Select Cases*, *supra* n. 19, 64 (Hil. 22 Edw. III; 1348); YB 39 Edw. III, Lib. Ass. pl. 1, f. 231 (1365); 41 Edw. III, Lib. Ass. pl. 25, f. 256 (1367).

[78] E.g., J Wycliffe, *Against the Orders of the Begging Friars* (c.1370) (Oxford, J Barnes 1608) 53; J Berners, *The Book of St. Albans*, ed. by W Blades ([London, 1486] sig. Fvj b; London, Elliot Stock, 1881), 82 (collective noun, "a damning of jurors").

[79] *Year Books of Edward II. Vol. XVI. 7 Edward II. A.D. 1313–1314*, ed. by W C Bolland, Seld. Soc. vol. 39, 160 (Trin. 7 Edw. II, pl. 1; 1314); YB Pasch. 7 Hen. IV, pl. 2, f. 11 (1406); YB Hil. 7 Edw. IV, pl. 14, f. 29 (1468); Rot. Parl., vol. 2, 203, ptn 18, ch. 22 (1348).

[80] *Select Cases of Trespass*, *supra* n. 18, xxvi.

[81] J F Stephen, *History of Criminal Law* (London, Macmillan, 1883), vol. 1, 573.

[82] Pollock and Maitland, vol. 2, 627.

[83] M Hale, *Historia Placitorum Coronae* (c. 1675), (London, printed by Eliz. R Nutt and R Gosling (assigns of Edward Sayer, Esq.,) for F Gyles, T Woodward and C Davis 1736), vol. 2, 313 (ch. 42).

And Thomas More, Lord Chancellor of England, in the 1530s said that common law judges "see that they may, by the verdict of the jury, cast off all quarrels from themselves upon them, which they account their chief defence".[84] Elsewhere More wrote that judges wisely "for the avoiding of obloquy" refrained from deciding cases, though More himself would rather trust one judge than two juries.[85] By placing the responsibility for deciding cases squarely on the shoulders of jurors, royal justices shifted the blame from themselves.

Many features of the jury system combined to help insulate the jurors from this blame. There was, of course, safety in numbers: each juror was just one voice, one conscience, among a dozen. The fact that jurors were coerced to appear, coerced to remain and to perform their duty provided further protection against reprisals. Thomas More wrote that "commonly no man was so angry" with opposing witnesses "when it is against their wills" that they are forced to swear and testify.[86] The same could be said of jurors.

The loose, informal methods of informing the jury before trial and the strict isolation of jurors during their deliberations also gave the jurors some protective coloration. In the fourteenth and fifteenth centuries, the facts upon which the jurors based their verdict could not be fully known by anyone else. Jurors were not limited to the evidence presented in open court in the presence of both parties. Every juror could and should have private communications and bring personal knowledge to bear on their verdict. Justices would not inquire where or from whom jurors got their information.

Justices would not know how the jurors reached their verdict. No one would know but the jurors themselves. And so the peculiar rule forcing jurors toward a unanimous verdict through hunger and thirst provided an additional measure of plausible deniability for each juror. When cornered by an angry, disappointed, vengeful litigant, each could say: "I was on your side, but the others forced me to go along with them." The common law was built on the backs of jurors, but it provided some devices to protect jurors from retribution and reprisal.

Juries pose one of the most interesting puzzles in English legal history. Judges and lawyers talked in the Year Books as if there were substantive rules of law that would have real effect in the real world. But the only mechanism applying those rules to real disputes in the Year Book period was the verdict of jurors.[87] Jurors had enormous discretion to apply local customary norms, or *ad hoc* notions of appropriateness, or group prejudices, or whatever they liked.

[84] Quoted in W Roper, *The Lyfe of Sir Thomas Moore* (c. 1557), ed. by E V Hitchcock (London, EETS, 1935), 45.

[85] More, *supra* n. 43, vol. 10, 95.

[86] Ibid.

[87] This point is well made in D Millon, "Positivism in the Historiography of the Common Law", (1989) *Wisconsin Law Review* 669.

But with this power came the responsibility of accounting for their decisions to losing parties and to the wider community. Jurors in the Year Books were coerced, belaboured, hungry, thirsty men who did not relish the powers of local self-government that they momentarily held. Jurors in the Year Books sought to apply the judges' and lawyers' rules as best they understood them. They were hungry and thirsty for effective rules of law that would shift the blame away from themselves. Jurors were at once the prisoners of the common law and its final and indispensable arbiters.

6

No Link: the Jury and the Origins of the Confrontation Right and the Hearsay Rule

RICHARD D FRIEDMAN (ANN ARBOR)*

The rule against hearsay has long been one of the most distinctive elements of the common law of evidence, and indeed—except for recent changes on the civil side in many jurisdictions—of the common law system of trial. Observers have long believed that the rule, like most of the other exclusionary rules of the common law of evidence, is "the child of the jury system".[1] Though Edmund Morgan argued vigorously to the contrary,[2] the received understanding is that the jury's inability to account satisfactorily for the defects of hearsay explains the rule.[3] A famous, and perhaps seminal, expression of this view was that of Chief Justice Mansfield in *Re Berkeley*:

> "[I]n England, where the jury are the sole judges of the fact, hearsay is properly excluded, because no man can tell what effect it might have upon their minds".[4]

In recent years, the abolition of the hearsay rule as a doctrine of exclusion in civil litigation in Britain has been predicated on the near-total absence of the

* This paper is largely based on research I have been doing with Mike Macnair. I am, however, responsible for the contents of this paper and any mistakes in it.

[1] This is the celebrated term applied to the law of evidence in general in J B Thayer, *A Preliminary Treatise on Evidence at the Common Law* (Boston, Little, Brown, 1898), 266, based in part on the danger that the evidence is "likely to be misused or overestimated by that body".

[2] "The essays of the great Thayer, the rationalisations of the judges beginning in the third or fourth decade of the 19th century and the acceptance of these by Wigmore have combined to make orthodox the fallacy that the exclusionary rules of evidence, and particularly, the hearsay rule, are results of the jury system." Foreword to American Law Institute, *Model Code of Evidence* (Philadelphia, American Law Institute, 1942), at 36.

[3] See C Tapper, "Hearsay in Criminal Cases: An Overview of Law Commission Report No. 245", [1997] *Crim LR* 771 at 777 and n. 43.

[4] 4 Camp. 401 at 415, 171 ER 128 at 135 (1811). Mansfield distinguished the situation in Scotland, where judges were the finders of fact, and could "trust themselves entirely" to give hearsay such weight as they thought it deserved.

jury from such litigation.[5] Colin Tapper, a highly sophisticated scholar of evidence, has expressed the perplexity that:

> "[W]hile the absence of a jury from most modern civil proceedings has been a major contributory factor to the separate development of the hearsay rule in civil and criminal proceedings, the comparable difference between summary proceedings and trials on indictment within the area of criminal proceedings has failed to lead to a comparable separation of development".[6]

Even on its face, this emphasis on the role of the jury in explaining the hearsay rule is a rather curious one: there is no reason to believe that, as a general matter, the jurors will so over-value hearsay that the truth-determination process is improved by shutting their ears to it. Indeed, the empirical evidence suggests that jurors tend to *under*-value hearsay.[7] More fundamentally, this view ignores history, which demonstrates rather clearly that at the core of the hearsay rule is the fundamental right of a litigant, especially a criminal defendant, to confront the witnesses against him. This right has a scope much narrower than the modern rule against hearsay, and it does not explain or justify all of hearsay law. But it has roots that are deep and broad. It is one of the cornerstones of the common law system of adjudication, and it is not substantially affected by whether or not the trier of fact is a jury.

Any adjudicative system based on evidence must determine how witnesses are to give evidence. A particularly common requirement, one shared by the common law as well as many systems that do not rely on a jury, is that a witness testify under oath. And throughout history many systems, whether they use the jury or not, have required that a witness give testimony in the presence of the accused. Thus, in Acts, 25.16, the Roman governor Festus declares:

> "It is not the manner of the Romans to deliver any man to die, before that he which is accused have the accusers face to face, and have licence to answer for himself concerning the crime laid against him."

Here we see an early, but quite clear, expression of the confrontation right: when a witness testifies, she must do it "face to face" with the accused, pre-

[5] Civil Evidence Act 1995, s. 1, which provides that "[i]n civil proceedings evidence shall not be excluded on the ground that it is hearsay", resulted from a recommendation by the Law Commission for England and Wales, which emphasised "the greatly reduced use of juries in civil trials other than for defamation proceedings". The Law Commission for England and Wales, *The Hearsay Rule in Civil Proceedings*, Consultation Paper No. 117 (London, HMSO, 1991), 52. The 1995 Act was foreshadowed by a similar development in Scotland. See Civil Evidence Act, 1988, c. 32, s. 2 (abolishing the rule against hearsay in civil cases); Scottish Law Commission, *Evidence: Report on Corroboration, Hearsay and Related Matters in Civil Proceedings*, Report No 100 (Edinburgh, HMSO, 1986), 16–17 (emphasising the limited use of the civil jury), 23 (recommending the abolition of the rule against hearsay).

[6] Tapper, *supra* n. 3, 777.

[7] P Miene, R C Park and E Borgida, "Juror Decision Making and the Evaluation of Hearsay Evidence", (1992) 76 *Minnesota LR* 683.

sumably in front of the trier of fact. It is not acceptable for her to testify through intermediaries.

This confrontational method of giving testimony has not been universal. To minimise the dangers of intimidation, traditional Continental systems took testimony out of the presence of the parties, though they protected the right of cross-examination through written interrogatories. But this was not the English norm. In the middle of the sixteenth century, Sir Thomas Smith described the heart of a criminal trial as an open "altercation" between accuser and accused.[8] And repeatedly, over hundreds of years, English judges and commentators declared the superiority of English law in this respect. For example, in the *Case of the Union of the Realms*, Lord Chief Justice Popham, arguing for the superiority of English over Scots law, contended that "the Testimonies, being viva voce before the Judges in open face of the world", were "much to be preferred" over "written depositions in a corner".[9]

To be sure, even in England, the norm of confrontation was not always followed. But the situations in which it was not followed reveal the strength and ultimate triumph of the principle that testimony must be given in the presence of the adverse party—and the irrelevance of the jury to that norm.

First, the common law courts shared an uneasy coexistence with the courts of equity and other courts that followed Continental procedures. One advantage of those procedures was that a deposition could preserve the testimony of a witness if the witness was unable later to testify at trial. Common law courts came to accept these depositions as a second-best alternative to trial testimony in the case of an unavailable witness. Indeed, by the middle of the seventeenth century the courts developed a sophisticated body of law determining when depositions were acceptable and ensuring that a deposition could not be used as evidence unless the adverse party had an adequate opportunity of cross-examination through written interrogatories.[10] Thus, Sir Geoffrey Gilbert, commenting in the first years of the eighteenth century on a case from several decades earlier, wrote:

> "A Deposition can't be given in Evidence against any Person that was not Party to the Suit, and the Reason is, because he had not Liberty to cross-examine the

[8] T Smith, *De Republica Anglorum*, ed. by M Dewar (Cambridge, University Press, 1982), Bk 2, ch. 15.

[9] Moore (KB) 790 at 798, 72 ER 908 at 913 (1604). See also, e.g., S Emlyn, Preface to *State Trials* (London, J Walthoe, Sen., 1730); M Hale, *History of the Common Law*, ed. by C M Gray (Chicago, University of Chicago Press, 1971), 163–4; W Blackstone, *Commentaries on the Laws of England* (Oxford, Clarendon Press, 1765–69), vol. 3, *373.

[10] *Fortescue* v. *Coake*, Godb. 193, 78 ER 117 (Com. Pleas, 1612); *Anon.*, Godb. 326, 78 ER 192 (KB 1623); *Rushworth* v. *Countess de Pembroke & Currier*, Hardres 472, 145 ER 553 (1668). This law developed more rapidly and systematically in civil cases. This disparity presumably occurred in part because of the presence of counsel in civil cases and in part because of the use, discussed in the text below, in criminal cases of examinations taken before magistrates.

Witnesses, and 'tis against natural Justice that a Man should be concluded in a Cause to which he never was a Party".[11]

Similarly, magistrates acting pursuant to statutes passed in the reign of Queen Mary took statements from accusing witnesses in felony cases. It seems rather clear that the expectation, and at least the usual practice, was for the accused to be present when this accusatory statement was taken.[12] Quickly, the practice arose of taking these statements under oath, the understanding being that doing so would preserve the testimony for use at trial if the witness died beforehand. As William Lambarde, writing a manual for justices of the peace in 1581, explained:

> "[I]f these informers bee examined upon *Oath*, then although it should happen them to die before the Prisoner have his *Triall*, yet their information may bee given in evidence, as a matter of credite, whereas otherwise it wold be of little or no weight at all, & therby offenders shold the easlier escape unpunished".[13]

It was clear that, if the accuser was not dead, or unable to travel, or put out of the way by the accused, this pre-trial statement could not be used; the witness must testify live at the trial.[14] And in 1696, the justices of the Courts of King's Bench and of Common Pleas determined after a consultation that this practice should not be extended to misdemeanour cases, where it was not supported by tradition and statutory authority—and they did so specifically on the basis that:

> "the defendant not being present when [the statements] were taken before the [examining authority, in this case the mayor], and so had lost the benefit of a cross-examination".[15]

Finally, of great significance was the practice in treason cases and other politically charged trials. The Crown, eager to use the criminal law as a

[11] G Gilbert, *The Law of Evidence* (London, 1754), 47. Mike Macnair has dated the writing of the treatise, which was published long after Gilbert's death, to the first decade of the century.

[12] The statutes required the magistrate to take a statement from the accused as well as from the person who brought him in, so the statements were presumably taken in close time proximity. Professor J M Beattie, who has studied the reports of these statements extensively—though without addressing this question—says that the accused's familiarity with the accusatory statement appears to be a presupposition of the accused's statement.

[13] W Lambarde, *Eirenarcha: or Of the Office of the Justices of Peace* 210 (London, Imprinted by Ra. Newbry and H Bynneman, by the ass. of Ri. Tot[ell] & Ch. Bar[ker], 1581), quoted in J H Langbein, *Prosecuting Crime in the Renaissance: England, Germany, France* (Cambridge, Mass. Harvard University Press, 1974), at 27. The principal statute, 1 & 2 Ph. & M., c. 13, required examination of those that "bring" the accused; it did not refer explicitly to accusing witnesses, and most often it was the constable who brought the accused to the justice of the peace. But it appears that the constable was usually accompanied by the accusing witnesses, and this was the practice recommended by Lambarde—presumably because of the opportunity it offered for preserving testimony. See Langbein, *supra*, at 11–12.

[14] See the notes following *R* v. *Paine*, 1 Salk. 281, 91 ER 246 (1696).

[15] *R* v. *Paine*, 5 Mod. 163 at 165, 87 ER 584 at 585.

means of controlling its adversaries, sometimes used testimony taken out of the presence of the accused. Thus, it is in the treason cases of the Tudor and Stuart period that the battle for the confrontation right was most clearly fought. As early as 1521, treason defendants, often using the term "face to face", demanded that the witnesses be brought before them.[16] Sometimes these demands were heeded,[17] sometimes not—but what is most notable is that they found recurrent support in acts of Parliament, which repeatedly required that accusing witnesses be brought "face to face" with the defendant.[18] By the middle of the seventeenth century, the battle was won, and courts clearly understood that treason witnesses must testify before the accused, subject to questioning by the accused.[19]

Well into that century, prosecutorial authorities often tried to use confessions of alleged accomplices of the accused that were not made according to the usual norms of testimony, under oath and before the accused. The case of Sir Walter Raleigh is the most notorious, but far from the only one. The theory was that self-accusation was "as strong as if upon oath".[20] But the judges soon realised the iniquity of allowing an exception to the usual norms of testimony simply because the accomplice accused himself as well as another.[21] In 1662, shortly after the Restoration, the judges of the King's Bench ruled unanimously and definitively that,

[16] E.g., *Seymour's Case*, 1 How. St. Tr. 483 at 492 (1549); *Duke of Somerset's Trial*, 1 How. St. Tr. 515 at 520 (1551).

[17] According to E Hall, *The Union of the Two Noble and Illustre Famelies of Lancastre & Yorke* (London, 1548), published under the title *Hall's Chronicle* (London, J Johnson, 1809), 623, the witnesses against the Duke of Buckingham in 1521 were produced at his request. Hall's account of Buckingham's trial appears to be the ultimate source for the one offered by Shakespeare and Fletcher in *King Henry VIII*, II,i. John Spelman, a justice of the King's Bench, was careful to note in his report of a treason trial of 1531 that the accuser confronted the defendant "face to face." *R* v. *Rice ap Griffith*, in *The Reports of Sir John Spelman*, ed. by J H Baker, Seld. Soc., vol. 93 (London, 1976), vol. 1, 47.

[18] 5 & 6 Edw. VI, c. 11, s. 9 (1552), and 1 & 2 P. & M., c. 10, s 11 (1554), required witnesses to be "brought forth in person" before the accused. 1 Eliz. I, c. 1, s. 21 (1558), 1 Eliz. I, c.5, s. 10 (1558), 13 Eliz. I, c. 1, s. 9 (1571), and 13 Car. II, c.1, s. 5 (1661), all used the "face to face" formulation.

[19] For example, in the celebrated case of John Lilburne in 1649, there was no doubt that the witnesses would testify live in front of Lilburne; "hear what the witnesses say first," said the presiding judge in postponing one of Lilburne's arguments: 4 How. St. Tr. 1270 at 1329. When the witnesses did testify, Lilburne was allowed to pose questions to them, through the court: ibid. at 1333, 1334, 1335, 1340. In *John Mordant's Case*, just nine years later, there does not seem to have been any doubt that he could question the witnesses directly, which he did, 5 How. St. Tr. 907 at 919–21. Indeed, at one point the presiding judge solicitously inquired whether Mordant wished to ask a witness any questions, ibid. at 922, a practice that soon became routine: e.g., *Colledge's Case*, 8 How. St. Tr. 549, at 599, 603, 606 (1681).

[20] *Earl of Somerset's Case*, 2 How. St. Tr. 966 at 986 (1616) (Coke, CJ).

[21] In 1631, the judges concluded that, at the trial of a peer before the House of Lords, "[c]ertain Examinations [clearly confessions from the context] having been taken by the lords without an oath ... could not be used until they were repeated upon oath." *Lord Audley's Case*, 3 How. St. Tr. 401 at 402 (1631).

though a pre-trial confession was "evidence against the Party himself who made the Confession" and, if adequately proved could indeed support conviction of that person without witnesses to the treason itself, the confession "cannot be used as evidence against any others whom on his Examination he confessed to be in the Treason".[22] This fundamental principle quickly became canonical.[23]

Thus, there was a clear—though not entirely uncluttered—norm that guided English civil and criminal trials, that witnesses should give their testimony in open court, face to face with the adverse party. Nowhere in the development of this norm of confrontation does any deficiency on the part of the jury appear to have been mentioned. The concern was not the jury's inability to deal with secondary evidence but rather the fact that such evidence did not conform to proper procedural conceptions. And only rarely was such evidence referred to as hearsay. As is apparent from Gilbert's perfunctory treatment, hearsay had a limited meaning, one conforming closely to what even now is probably the common lay understanding of the term—a witness's account of what another person had said. Even quite late in the eighteenth century, the term hearsay would not have been used to refer to written transcriptions of previously taken testimony, or indeed to other writings offered as evidence.[24]

Furthermore, the norm of confrontation did not extend the full breadth of the modern legal conception of hearsay. Under that conception, hearsay is any statement made out of court and offered to prove the truth of a matter that the statement asserts. The confrontation norm, however, was a principle that governed the procedures for the giving of *testimony*. Around the beginning of the nineteenth century, probably because of the growing role of lawyers in criminal trials, courts and treatise writers became far more sensitive to the absence of cross-examination with respect to out-of-court statements that were not made for the purpose of giving testimony. Hearsay became the rubric under which this concern was expressed, and the category of hearsay expanded to include writings.[25] Almost inevitably, then, the

[22] *Case of Thomas Tong and Others*, Kelyng 17 at 18, 84 ER 1061 at 1062 (1662).

[23] *See* Gilbert, *supra* n. 11, 99; W Hawkins, *A Treatise of the Pleas of the Crown* (London, printed by Eliz. Nutt and R Gosling, assigns of Edward Sayer for J Walthoe jun., 1721), vol. 2, 429.

[24] Cf. F Buller, *An Introduction to the Law Relative to Trials at Nisi Prius* (London, printed by W Strahan and M Woodfall for C Bathurst 1772), 235–6 (saying that depositions can be admitted "in general in all Cases where Hearsay and Reputation are Evidence; for undoubtedly what a Witness, who is dead, has sworn in a Court of Justice, is of more Credit, than what another Person swears he has heard him say").

[25] T Peake, *A Compendium of the Law of Evidence* (London, E and R Brooke and J Rider, 1801), 10. Peake says, in the course of his discussion of hearsay, that certain written memoranda made in the ordinary course of business are admissible as "not within the exception as to hearsay evidence". The backhand suggestion appears to be that other writings would be "within the exception" - that is, objectionable as hearsay. By 1815, S M Phillipps made the principle clear: The exclusionary rule "is applicable to statements in writing, no less than to

hearsay rule also expanded to include the long-established rules governing when depositions of a witness, taken under oath before trial, could be introduced in lieu of trial testimony.[26] And eventually the expansion included conduct that did not assert the proposition at issue but appeared to reflect the actor's belief in it.[27] Now the modern shape of the hearsay rule was complete.[28]

The expansions that yielded this form of the rule could not all be justified on the basis of the need to protect the conditions under which testimony is given, because conduct that was *ante litem* was not testimonial in nature. Perhaps for this reason, it is in this same era that we first see the justifications for the hearsay rule being laid at the feet of the jury. The analysis here suggests, however, that the jury had very little to do with the development of the hearsay rule. Nor should it have much to do with the question of whether, or in what form, the rule ought to be retained.

On the one hand, at the core of the hearsay rule is a noble principle that it is critical to preserve. This principle is the confrontation norm—the requirement that a witness must testify openly, in the presence of the accused and subject to cross-examination. The modern hearsay rule is too poorly articulated, too broad, and too riddled with exceptions to protect that principle ideally well. Not only does the principle remain valid, however; it may be considered a fundamental aspect of fair criminal procedure, whether a jury is present or not. Indeed, in a highly ironic development, the European Court of Human Rights—operating outside the context of a system that has either the jury or hearsay law—has recognised the significance of the confrontation right and issued a series of decisions protecting it.[29]

On the other hand, to the extent that the hearsay rule excludes evidence where the confrontation norm is not at stake—for example, statements made *ante litem*—the justification for the rule seems dubious. Certainly the rule has significant costs, most notably in the loss of valuable information to the truth-determining process. Perhaps other justifications, such as the creation of incentives to present live testimony, justify limited application of an exclusionary rule. But whether this is true or not, the presence or absence of the jury as trier of fact should have very little bearing. Perhaps in time there will be persuasive reason to believe that juries tend to over-value hearsay

words spoken", the only difference in this respect being that there is greater facility of proof in the case of writings than of oral statements: S M Phillipps, *A Treatise on the Law of Evidence* (New York, Gould, Banks and Gould, 1816), vol. 1, 173. Phillipps' analysis does not appear to have gained immediate universal acceptance.

[26] Phillipps, *supra* n. 23, 177–8 (discussing the celebrated *Berkeley* case, 4 Camp. 401, 171 ER 127 (1811)).

[27] *Wright* v. *Tatham*, 5 Cl. & F. 670, 7 ER 559, 47 Rev. Rep. 136 (HL 1838).

[28] See, for example, the quite modern-sounding explanation in T Starkie, *A Practical Treatise on the Law of Evidence* (Boston, Wells and Lillie, 1826), vol. 1, 47 (Pt. I, § 28).

[29] E.g., *Van Mechelen* v. *Netherlands*, 25 EHRR 647 (1998).

evidence by so much that truth-determination is advanced by shutting their eyes and ears to such evidence. I doubt it, though, and until such time the jury-defect theory should be considered as nothing more than an unsupported rationale accepted unquestioningly in a bygone era.[30]

[30] See *supra* n. 7.

7

"A Quest of Thoughts": Representation and Moral Agency in the Early Anglo-American Jury

J R POLE (OXFORD)*

In the forty-sixth sonnet, which begins:

> "Mine eye and heart are at a mortal war,
> How to divide the conquest of thy sight"[1]

Shakespeare sets up a lawsuit between heart and eye to settle a dispute as to which of them has the better title to the loved object. To decide this title he impanels:

> "A quest of thoughts, all tenants to the heart."

A "quest" is an inquest; and, by extension, it is the jury.[2] But this jury consists of thoughts, and it will not escape notice that the jurors are all tenants to one of the parties to the suit—perhaps a comment on the art of jury selection. But why a quest of thoughts? The function of thought is to reason, and reason is the divine power distinguishing humanity from the brutes; so this jury is required to apply its reasoning powers to a philosophical dispute involving the faculties of perception and emotion, subjects which interested Shakespeare for reasons that had no bearing on the law. Since neither heart nor eye can benefit without the other, the outcome is an eminently reasonable compromise. Shakespeare is not making fun of the jury as he does of country justices and constables. He knew law and court proceedings well, and knew the strengths and weaknesses of the gentry who were called to serve as jurors; their views would reflect those of a cross-section of the community from which they were drawn. There is, of course, a characteristic touch of irony in his lines, yet no suggestion that it might be incongruous to impose on the inquest the responsibility for settling disputes with a moral dimension. It is

* The author wishes to acknowledge the support of Slaughter and May (London) and Getty, Meyer and Mayo (Lexington, Kentucky).

1 H Vendler, *The Art of Shakespeare's Sonnets* (Cambridge, Mass. Harvard University Press, 1997), 233.

2 "But is this law?" "Ay, marry, is't, crowner's quest law." i.e., coroner's inquest law. *Hamlet,* V, ii.

significantly the jury, who represent the local community, not the judge, that serves as the crucial instrument in the local dispensation of justice; the jury is required to draw on its moral as well as intellectual powers, which are here presumed to qualify it to resolve linguistic and metaphysical problems.

MORALITY AND THE JURY

The English jury was getting on for 500 years old when Shakespeare wrote the Sonnets. It is worth noting from the beginning that once the jury had come into normal existence it served the interests of central government far more effectively than any other system of local order would have done, since it proved to be both a practical and an economical instrument for the conduct of county administration. No troops or additional taxes were needed to run the county judiciary, whose functions extended to a wide variety of local problems requiring adjudication; it nourished loyalty to the realm as a political whole by drawing members of the community into a share of control of their local affairs. At critical moments, moreover, its criminal jurisdiction involved delicate and politically sensitive moral judgments. The jury's judgment would represent the community's moral sense. It would, however, be a cruel injustice to innocent victims to suggest that juries were invariably honest or disinterested; long after Shakespeare, Alexander Pope, who was far from being a committed social reformer, dropped the cynical couplet:

> "The hungry judges soon the sentence sign,
> And wretches hang that jurymen may dine".[3]

But juries also notoriously mitigated the severities of the law by finding guilt of lesser crimes than those charged, where these could lead to the death penalty, and often showed a propensity to side with those accused of social crimes. The passage of the game laws in 1672 brought these inclinations out in the clearer light of conflicts which extended through the eighteenth century over the rights of the community against the interests of increasing aggregations of landed property. Douglas Hay records that the farmers and tradesmen who made up the panels of common jurors at quarter sessions and assizes were often among the poachers, and a steward preparing a prosecution complained in 1791 that "there is no answering for a Common Jury . . . as they have in general a Strong Byass upon their minds in favor of Poachers, being professed enemies to all Penal Laws that relate to Game." It was for this reason that Parliament removed most game offences from the jury's authority and made them tryable by justices of the peace or judges sitting alone.[4]

[3] *The Rape of the Lock*, canto III, 21–2.

[4] D Hay, "Property, Authority and the Criminal Law", in D Hay, P Linebaugh, J G Rule, E P Thompson and C Winslow (eds), *Albion's Fatal Tree: Crime and Society in Eighteenth Century England* (New York, Pantheon Books, 1975), 3; and idem, "Poaching and the Game Laws on Cannock Chase", in ibid., 211.

While it is true and was well understood that jurors were drawn from and in that sense *represented* elements of society with a stake in the security of property, it is a crude simplification to regard all owners of any type or amount of property as having similar interests. Juries might sometimes see themselves reflected among the accused. Adversarial relations, feelings of being threatened, seem to have become more intense on both sides as landowners enclosed the commons in the mid-eighteenth century. As a result, juries found themselves increasingly charged with the problem of defining what constituted guilt, which involved some attempt to unravel and determine motive, and to bear such considerations in mind when apportioning responsibility. Gradually, in one of the more significant if largely unnoticed transformations associated with the diffusion of enlightenment, the concept of guilt metamorphosed into a socially modulated and psychologically more subtle concept of responsibility. The process was partly concealed by the fact that the courts retained, unmodified, the concept of personal culpability implied by the question addressed to the accused, "How say you: Guilty or Not Guilty?" Questions of what state of mind constituted "guilt" were often charged with a moral dimension from which juries, even if they wished, found it hard to disentangle themselves.

By the 1590s, when Shakespeare's Sonnets were written, English adventurers and religious dissidents were on the verge of setting out to plant colonies in America, where they would revive or reinvent many English institutions. It did not all happen like the opening of a book; the English jury had a fitful reawakening in the colonies; through the seventeenth century, most cases both civil and criminal were heard by magistrates.[5] In England, the jury, by now a long trusted and revered instrument in the defence of the liberty of the subject, was about to enter into a gradual process of transformation; yet, once restored to active life in the colonies in the first two or three decades of the eighteenth century, it would remain recognisably the same institution on both sides of the Atlantic, on both sides deriving some of its appeal from its antiquity, often claiming origins in Magna Carta. This claim was actuated by ideology: Henry II had made the jury an agency of royal governance in 1178. But Magna Carta does say that every free man (*liber homo*) is entitled to trial by his peers. Since the early English kingdom, certainly in Norman times, a free man had been known as one who had a right to be heard in the king's court as well as the lord's, a point which would later have some bearing on individual rights at common law. Under the aegis of Magna Carta, trial by one's peers in a society differentiated by rank must

[5] For this subject in general, but with special reference to New England, J M Murrin, "Magistrates, Sinners, and a Precarious Liberty: Trial By Jury in Seventeenth Century New England", in D Hall, J M Murrin and T W Tate (eds), *Saints and Revolutionaries: Essays on Early American History* (New York, Norton, 1984), 152; and A G Roeber, *Faithful Magistrates and Republican Lawyers: Creators of Virginia Legal Culture,1680–1810* (Chapel Hill, University of North Carolina Press, 1981).

mean trial by a body of men, however selected and constituted, who are of the same rank as the accused; but it appears to exclude villeins and other unfree men, who were numerous in the labouring ranks of the feudal order. Sir James Holt has noted that medieval interpretations of Magna Carta were strikingly varied; in 1215 *liber homo* embraced a wider spectrum than in the more stratified society that had developed by the fourteenth century.[6] The outlines of something resembling a jury can be discerned in this provision in the original, but the concept of trial by one's peers would later have become more specific. For extraneous reasons, however, the year 1215 was portentous: it also saw the Lateran Council's rejection of criminal trial by ordeal: it was now held impious to subject God to human interrogation. The practical consequence of abolishing trial by compurgation and ordeal was a need for a procedure for finding the facts of guilt or innocence. In England, where the concept of trial by one's peers had been formulated, this gave a new impetus to the function of the jury, jurors being men of the neighbourhood sworn to the truth; and in doubtful cases, the jury was also charged with the obligation not only of determining the facts, but of finding what the facts meant in law, a question which often gave rise to differences of opinion. This difficulty was clarified by an early Statute of Westminster in 1230, which defined the responsibilities of the jury by giving it the right to render a general verdict, covering both the facts and the law relating to those facts; in which they were to seek the counsel of the justices. As Professor J H Baker has observed, it was the emergence of the jury that really forced recognition of a distinction between fact and law, leading in turn to refinement in the principles of law; not surprisingly, trial judges were soon giving directions to the jury on points of law.[7] When British subjects in the American colonies invoked the right to trial by jury as derived from Magna Carta they may have spoken from an excess of historical enthusiasm; but allowing for a distance upwards of 500 years, they were not far from the mark; and they stood in a line with English radicals including—perhaps starting with—John Lilburne, who, in the mid-seventeenth century, was twice tried before a judge and jury and twice acquitted by London juries.

[6] J C Holt, "The Ancient Constitution in Medieval England", in E Sandoz (ed.), *The Roots of Liberty: Magna Carta, Ancient Constitution, and the Anglo-American Tradition of Rule of Law* (Columbia, University of Missouri Press, 1993); P Wormald, *Legal Culture in the Early Medieval West: Law as Text, Image and Experience* (London, Hambledon Press, 1999), 332.

[7] J H Baker, *An Introduction to English Legal History*, 3rd edn (London, Butterworths, 1990), 6–7, 96, 110, 579; T A Green, *Verdict According to Conscience: Perspectives on the English Criminal Trial Jury 1200–1800* (Chicago, University of Chicago Press, 1985), 8; P Brown, "Society and the Supernatural: a Medieval Charge", (Spring 1975) *Dædalus*, 133: it is important to bear in mind that the ordeal was not intended to leave things to chance, but to maximise certainty: ibid., 139.

FROM THE MEDIEVAL TO THE EARLY MODERN JURY

Since its inception in the thirteenth century, profound changes have taken shape in the form, composition and to some extent the functions of the trial jury. The modern jury is sequestrated from the rest of the court, with which it is normally permitted no dialogue in the course of the trial. Any exceptions are matters for the judge. The modern jury, moreover, is deliberately selected of persons who have no connection with the case or the persons involved. A prospective juror may be challenged by counsel and disqualified by any such connection. In the United States this method of selection is often permitted even when the perceived connection is remote. Members of the medieval and early modern jury often sat about at random in the room or public space assigned to the court, not even withdrawing to confer; and throughout the eighteenth century, jurors could summon and question witnesses on their own initiative. This paper will argue that the changes to the modern from the medieval and early modern character of the jury have not conflicted with but rather, have enabled the jury to maintain crucial attributes of this essential role of representative moral agency. This agency, moreover, has had and to some extent still retains an element of political responsibility. It became a commonplace in the eighteenth century that the role of the jury was *representative* in a clearly political sense. Modernisation has not transformed the medieval principle that an accused person is entitled to be tried in the place or county where the offence was alleged to have been committed, except when, in highly contentious cases, the defence might be prejudiced by local hostility. This is a further example of the continuity of purpose just referred to. The principle of trial in the locality became particularly important to colonial New Englanders when they feared removal for trial in England on allegations of treason.

The transformation from the medieval to the modern idea of the jury has not been the result of any aim, programme or thought-out intention; no one envisaged a transformation in English jurisprudence, at least until Bentham took the whole question in hand; nor has it been firmly dated or fully explained. Its beginnings, however, have been credibly linked to seventeenth century advances in the concept of evidence, which came increasingly to depend on reliable verification rather than on circumstance, local suspicions or diabolical influence.[8] Scientific ideas were slow to transmit themselves to social processes, but if the process cannot be dated with precision, this is in part because the great transformation has never been quite as decisive or, indeed, as complete as is usually supposed. It certainly did not mature in the seventeenth century. When, in 1670, Chief Justice Vaughan delivered his

[8] B J Shapiro, *Beyond "Reasonable Doubt" and "Probable Cause": Historical Perspectives on the Anglo-American Law of Evidence* (Berkeley, University of California Press, 1991); and see in general JM Mitkin, "From Neighbour—Witness to Judge of Proofs: The Transformation of the English Civil Juror", (1988) 32 *AJLH* 201, to which I am much indebted.

famous judgment in Bushel's Case, exonerating jurors from being punished for rendering a verdict contrary to the court's instructions, he gave as one justification of the jury's independence that its members might possess personal knowledge enabling them to evaluate the evidence before the court.[9] From the whig-historical point of view, this profoundly important decision represented "progress"; but in fact it was not a "modernising" judgment: on the contrary, Vaughan looked back to the medieval fact-finding role of jurors, who were expected to be self-informing and to make their own enquiries.[10] Clearly, the "modern" jury was not conceptually exclusive; it seems unlikely that any change in the jury's relationship to society was perceived at the time. Nevertheless, by affirming the jury's right to independent judgment, Vaughan had assisted its passage towards a fuller independence in the modern sense. Of course a jury might err, but the Chief Justice added for good measure that a judge might err; and, if a judge was to find the facts, why should not the jury do so? The argument really turned on the question of why the jury was there at all. The process of transformation was so gradual that as late as 1880, a jury seems to have acted on their own knowledge as witnesses in the case of a woman charged with keeping a disorderly house.[11]

In this way, the principle of the jury's independence from the bench seems to have merged by a process of logical but quiet extension into that of the jury's independence from all local circumstances of the case. While it was no doubt facilitated by the sequestration of the jury, the main instrument was the ancient right of the defendant to challenge prospective jurors. This right, probably devised to prevent jury packing, extended in principle to the whole panel. Selection by balloting has proved the only way to immunise a jury against prejudicial selection.[12] Though the presumption of innocence until proved guilty had not yet entered into English jurisprudence, early modern trial procedures were designed to ensure fair play. But the right of challenge was seldom exercised until trial proceedings assumed a resemblance to their modern form towards the end of the eighteenth century. Challenges were and have remained rare in English courts; it is in the United States that the right has been developed to make jury selection "a fine art", as it has been called. From the attorney's point of view, it is also a useful art: in the process of extended questioning, the attorney can learn much useful information about the jury he has to convince, enabling him to adapt his style to the jury as much as to the evidence.[13]

[9] C Grant Robertson, *Select Statutes, Cases and Documents* (London, 1947), 362–6.

[10] Green, *supra* n. 7, 19; M Constable, *The Law of the Other: the Mixed Jury and Changing Conceptions of Citizenship, Law and Knowledge* (Chicago, University of Chicago Press, 1994), 2–14.

[11] J F Stephen, *A History of the Criminal Law of England* (London, Macmillan, 1883; repr. New York, Burt Franklin [1964]), vol. 1, 271. (From Stephen's account, this may have been a grand jury.)

[12] P Devlin, *Trial by Jury* (London, Stevens, 1966) 26–30.

[13] Ibid., 33.

The essential key to this transformation was the increasing role of lawyers in the conduct of trials. It was only in 1730 in England that defendants were allowed legal representation by attorney in court; before that date, the judge was expected to ensure that the defendant was fairly treated, and to ask the kinds of question that would later come from a defence attorney; but the assumption, as Pope's couplet shows, was clearly failing. Once attorneys were actual participants in the trial, it becomes easy to see how they extended their influence by taking up the right of challenge. The process was so seamlessly consistent with the exercise of common law rights that it left no trace in court records. But, by 1843, when Francis Lieber edited his *Encyclopædia Americana*, a long article on the jury explained the permissible grounds of challenge in terms so extensive that they would satisfy a modern American court. They covered almost all possible kinds or suspicions of prejudice or bias.[14] Essentially the same ground was covered in a compendious textbook of Virginia law by Henry St George Tucker, son of the famous Chancellor St George Tucker. Quoting a widely held opinion, Tucker stated that the jurors' oath to find on the evidence "according to their knowledge" was construed to include their own knowledge. But Tucker reports that this doctrine "has been gradually exploded in England" and in Virginia explicitly repudiated by legislation, by which any juror possessing local knowledge was required to tell the court.[15] We also learn from Tucker that it was not the custom for the judge to sum up in Virginia, as it was in England and in some sister states; Virginia juries would have regarded this as an intrusion on their privileges.[16] There is at least a hint here of a democratic influence on the courts, akin to Andrew Hamilton's argument a century earlier in the Zenger trial in New York that the popular element in colonial government enhanced the rights of juries at common law.[17]

For explanation of the extensive exercise of the right of challenge in more recent times, a right which has been both explored and exploited, sometimes occupying days of court time, we would need to look to the increasing specialisation of trial lawyers and their open market competitiveness. The longer the trial, moreover, the higher the fees accruing to the attorneys. This would also explain why the practice has become so much more extensive in the United States than among England's more secluded legal profession. Even in the United States, the state has been allowed by the Supreme Court to limit the number of challenges to ten.[18] But the Supreme Court has also

[14] *Encyclopædia Americana*, ed. by F Lieber (Philadelphia, Thomas, Cowperthwait and Co., 1843), vol. 7, 87–8.

[15] H St G Tucker, *Commentaries on the Laws of Virginia*, 3rd edn (Richmond, Colin and Shepherd,1846; repr. with introd. by D Cobin and P Finkelman, Union, New Jersey, Lawbook Exchange, 1997), vol. 1, 291.

[16] Ibid.

[17] Discussed *infra*, text at notes 62–63.

[18] *Ashe* v. *United States ex. Rel. Valotta* 270 US 424 at 425 (1926).

ruled that it is not unreasonable to select on the basis of intelligence and comprehension, a procedure that does not contradict the aim of selecting a cross-section of the community.[19]

Another convention, associated with the principle of the separation of the "powers" or branches of government to protect the judiciary from political intervention, ascribes to the judicial system a role secluded from the political aspects of government. This fiction has the potency of dogma in the United States, where it has seldom been sustainable. In both civil and criminal causes, juries have so often been called on to judge political questions, and it is in any case so often impossible to separate the political from other elements, that this principle will not survive scrutiny. On scrutiny, the doctrine is no more plausible in England; certain crimes, from high treason downward, are inherently political; but in ordinary, non-political criminal cases, the jury's independent powers of judgement might be called on not only to decide whether the offence alleged had been committed, but, if it had been committed, whether it was criminal. A moral judgement would here enter into the formulating of law. The jury's power to determine the defendant's fate, says Professor Green, "was virtually absolute".[20]

The composition of the jury, which was likely to be a factor of considerable relevance to the outcome, was historically designed to express a subtle mixture of elements; it must have seemed obvious to the medieval and early modern mind that if the verdict was to be reached impartially as demanded by the law's sense of justice, that impartiality was to be achieved not by studious distance from the characters and circumstances, but by a substantial admixture in the composition of the jury itself, of relevant elements of the community. This principle corresponded to a *representation* of the community and its values, and representation was an essential element in the political scheme. The demands of impartiality have not been of the kind to obscure, as I hope to make clear, that from its medieval origins, the jury has been known and expected to be a highly political animal.

POLITICS, COMMUNITY MORALITY AND THE JURY

None of these changes detracted from the jury's essential role of moral agency. As society changed, credulousness sustained by faith was gradually supplanted by confidence in proof by verification, which in turn came to depend on more impersonal procedures; but this in no way diminished society's need of the kind of service that the jury could provide. In order that English society might cling to the belief that justice was the birthright of all conditions of men, involving at least procedural equality in the legal process,

[19] W R Cornish, *The Jury* (London, Allen Lane, 1968), 34.

[20] Green, *supra* n. 7, 19.

the jury had to adapt; the real key to understanding the transformation is not to see it as an inexplicable anomaly, but to recognise that it contained profound elements of continuity, enabling the jury to survive vast social changes while remaining a secular moral agency. Whatever the limitations of the modern jury, it has been able to preserve its agency for both ascertaining and evaluating the information that enables the court to make a judgment. If it had lost this purpose it must in time have withered away.

The community which sent a member to represent its interests in a parliament had much in common with the community as reflected in an assize jury. They were likely to be drawn from the same sort of people. The quarter sessions were in many respects the county's principal public event.[21] When the court assembled, there was a general coming together, with morris dancing, drinking, gossip, organised and informal games, buying and selling, deals and local politics, as well as the formalities of the law. In eighteenth century England, with the spread and popularity of cricket and horse racing, these events frequently followed immediately on the assizes. [22]

The concept of the *representativeness* of the judicial process, already implied in the work of T A Green and Cynthia Herrup, has more recently been deepened with more specific reference to the jury in Marianne Constable's illuminating account of the legal recognition of "other" communities.[23] England's prosperity depended on imports, exports and financial operations that required the presence of permanent resident alien communities; inevitably, disputes arose both within such groups and between individual members and English people. As far as internal disputes were concerned, the English authorities were generally content to leave matters to be resolved within the alien community; alien ideas of justice or procedure did not affect their hosts. But litigation could also involve an alien against an English person, and to ensure fairness in such cases, the Statute of the Staples was enacted in 1353 to give the affected alien community a right to be represented on the jury.[24] The statute did not alter common law or other English procedures, but it implicitly recognised that different communities had their own customs, moral perspectives and codes, which were entitled to consideration by English law. Aliens would also know the facts of a situation within their own communities. As Constable has pointed out, members of such "other" groups were not being treated as individuals but were identified as members of their own community.[25] It was fitting to judge

[21] C B Herrup, *The Common Peace: Participation and the Criminal Law in Early Modern England* (Cambridge, University Press, 1987), 7.

[22] D Underdown, *Start of Play: Cricket and Culture in Eighteenth-Century England* (London, Allen Lane, 2000).

[23] Constable, *supra* n. 10, 2–14; cf. F W Maitland, *The Constitutional History of England* (Cambridge, University Press, 1919), 71.

[24] 28 Edw. III, c. 13.

[25] Constable, *supra* n. 10, 13–14.

a person according to the laws and customs of his (or her) own country. There was policy as well as humanity in this procedure; the goodwill of alien merchants had its value to English economic well-being.

In more political language, aliens deserved some kind of representation. But here we are speaking a political rather than a legal language; a litigant was normally to be represented by his attorney, not by the jury or by officers of the court. The foreign communities, however, had no access to the political recourse of parliamentary representation. But even for the natives, the county court offered opportunities for the cut and thrust of *personal* representation, which came much closer to home than that of the distant, relatively infrequent and inaccessible meetings of a parliament, usually summoned because the king needed a vote of supplies. The political business of the county was effectively transacted at the assizes, whose character as instruments of political representation was well understood; not for nothing were they known as in medieval and early modern England as "the parliaments of the shires".[26]

The representative character of the jury, translated to American conditions, appeared in a Massachusetts colonial case (later alluded to by Justice William Cushing) in which an Indian who had been indicted in a county court was allowed a jury of six Indians and six English.[27] But this reference appeared in the course of an opinion rejecting a similar claim by indicted British soldiers for a British presence on the jury. This little stratagem was clearly a dodge by the defence; in colonial America, British subjects could not be considered "aliens."

In feudal society, the problem of defining an accused person's "peers" was one of rank; but the principle of social status wore a new guise when racial distinctions were at issue after the end of Reconstruction in the United States. Under the aegis of the Fourteenth Amendment's imperative, "the equal protection of the laws", courts were obliged to ask whether an African American could expect a fair trial from a jury composed by official action exclusively of whites? In *Strauder* v. *Virginia* (1880) the question went to a Supreme Court not notably sensitive to the civil rights of black persons. But in this case the answer was clear:

> "The very idea of a jury is a body of men composed of the peers or equals of the person whose rights it is selected or summoned to determine, that is, of his neighbours, fellows, associates having the same legal status in society as he holds,"

[26] Herrup, *supra* n. 21, 7; Green, *supra* n. 7, 103–5.

[27] Indictment of W Brooks, Buchanan and Ross for murder, Worcester, April Session, 1778, Harvard Law School, Cushing Papers. Recently published research shows that this was standard practice in New England and also in Pennsylvania, where William Penn negotiated such arrangements with the Lenni Lenape Indians. K Hermes, "'Justice Will be Done to Us': Algonquin Demands for Reciprocity in the Courts of European Settlers", in B H Mann and C L Tomlins (eds), *The Many Legalities of Early America* (Chapel Hill, University of North Carolina Press, 2001), 133 n. 28.

wrote Mr Justice Strong for the Court. He cited Magna Carta and Blackstone and for good measure, Bentham, as well as the Constitution. Under the Fourteenth Amendment, it would have been inappropriate to designate African American citizens as inferiors in legal status; indeed, Strong's opinion followed the dubious reasoning of Justice Miller in *The Slaughterhouse Cases* (1872), which had held that the Fourteenth Amendment did *not* apply in that case because the Amendment was specifically intended to protect the Negro race. But it was only too clear that the social position of blacks rendered them collectively vulnerable to white hostility; to have subordinated that reality to the legal fiction of equality before a racially prejudiced jury would have been a travesty of the explicit meaning of the Amendment; and it would have violated the logic of the Constitution even before the Amendment. The judge resolved this problem by drawing an analogy with the well known practice of removing trials from the vicinity of local prejudices. In this sense a fair trial could not be expected, and the conviction was overturned.[28] The real issue, of course, was not rank or class but race. The Constitution was a constitution for politically and legally equal individuals; American jurisprudence could not officially admit the idea that a forbidden distinction of rank or class was inherent in the distinction of so-called races. In principle, the requirement of an equal black presence on the trial jury was identical to the principle of alien representation under the Statute of the Staple in medieval England.

CHARGES TO THE GRAND JURY

The early modern court performed many functions of local government, such as issuing or refusing licences, ordering the repair and maintenance of roads and bridges, while generally addressing itself to transgressions against the moral tone and religious observances of the county. The assizes also served as a meeting ground between judges from Westminster and the people of the shire in their various ranks and with their communal or personal concerns, grievances, demands. The judges, on circuit from the centre of government, were able to take soundings of local opinion as well as promulgating government policies. For such occasions, when the court had assembled, a grand jury of 23 men summoned by the lord lieutenant of the county was empanelled from a group of substantial landowners and merchants. Presiding over the session sat the judge, the one officer of the court who represented no section of the local community. Notwithstanding a measure of judicial independence, the judge was an officer of the crown and, until 1701, liable to dismissal by the crown.

The presiding judge opened proceedings with a solemn charge to the grand jury. The formal purpose was to instruct the grand jury in the duty of

[28] *Strauder* v. *West Virginia*, 100 US 303.

presenting indictments for crimes of varying degrees of gravity, to inform them of the differences in law between felonies and misdemeanours, and other points of law that might call for their consideration—a charge frequently laced with warnings of the sins of godlessness, drunkenness, disorder and sexual licentiousness by which the county was in imminent danger of attracting the wrath of a vengeful deity. Sin, which put the whole community at risk, was high on the catalogue of crimes, the more so in the earlier generations of settlement in North America; but gradually, in a society of deepening complexities and a widening variety of activities, though sin did not lose its hold, it began to yield primacy to concern for material interests. Coke had ruled that a contract made on the Lord's Day was invalid. But even in Massachusetts, Chief Justice Cushing declared in 1783 that "by the practice of modern times this rule had been exploded" and a contract could not be held invalid merely because it had been entered into on a Sunday.[29] On the other hand, forestalling, regrating, charging unfair prices and committing unfair dealings in the market, were sins described in market language, but still *sins*, and therefore likely to provoke God's anger. The religious meanings underpinning both English and American society's moral order gave way only gradually from the seventeenth to the mid-eighteenth centuries to issues of more frankly secular concern. Judges varied their language and emphasis from time to time, but the charges are more striking for their consistency and continuity than for any dramatic departures. We shall notice in a moment that these themes run on parallel courses in England and her American colonies. The grand jury considered the evidence brought up on complaints from members of the community; whenever they were satisfied that there was a case to answer, they were to draw up an indictment for trial by the petty or traverse jury in the next phase of the session. But that was not all. It fell to the grand jurors to act as a sort of schoolmaster to their neighbours. The moral surveillance then exercised had important political dimensions; any signs of discontent, subversion or rebelliousness were to be made the subject of indictments.

The charge to the grand jury was an instrument whose importance, familiar though it may be to specialists, is under-valued when historians concentrate their attention exclusively on the power of the crown and the development of parliament.[30] Lines of communication between the central government and the populace were essentially limited to two major organs. The most important was the church. When church attendance was compulsory and when its elders received instructions from Lambeth Palace, which was in close communication with Whitehall, the sermon and the notice board on the parish church door were the principal means of transmitting

[29] *Norton* v. *Bartlett*, Plymouth, May 1783, Harvard Law School, Cushing Papers.

[30] But see R D Younger, *The People's Panel: the Grand Jury in the United States, 1634–1941* (Providence, R.I., Brown University Press, 1963), 2, for an anticipation of these arguments.

government policies and of inculcating general principles, obligations and loyalties into the people. The other, and hardly less important channel, however, was the grand jury. The judge's charge began as a homily on fundamentals. At the Staffordshire quarter sessions in 1587, the judge instructed the grand jury in the importance of the connection between the rule of law and the necessity for obedience, a doctrine, as Christopher Brooks points out, which firmly endorsed the convention of divine right monarchy.[31] At the opening of the Norwich quarter sessions in 1606, the grand jury received from Sir Edward Coke a veritable education in constitutional law, religious doctrine and economic policy. The Chief Justice expounded the king's title to the throne, explained and justified the recusancy laws and warned the jurors against the error that religious toleration would bring peace; he then went on to expound his own passion for free trade by telling them to root out monopolists. The grand jury also concerned itself with social conditions, on occasion in hard times ordering local magistrates to provide poor relief.[32] Grand jurors were the men of influence and respect among their rural neighbours; the channels of authority ran down from them throughout the county. The interaction between judge and grand jury was usually respectful and harmonious, and, both in England and America, the grand jury, after respectfully seeking permission, often authorised publication of the judge's charge.

In the wake of the Revolution Settlement and particularly after the Hanoverian succession, the presiding judges often introduced political philosophy, amplified by lessons in English history. In 1690, the Leicester grand jury heard from the Earl of Stamford that the monarchy was not of "meer divine right, but by Human Consent".[33] Men were by nature equal, and government could be established only by consent—express or implied, this was a recurrent theme.[34] The common law was founded on consent:[35] the origin of government was in contract, as Westminster heard in 1728,[36] at the beginning of a long disquisition on history ancient and medieval; invoking Bracton and Fortescue, the judge reminded the grand jurors that the laws of England were the subject's birthright. The essential need to inculcate loyalty to the Hanoverians, undoubtedly prompted by Jacobite rumblings and the recent memory of the rising of 1715, reflected the importance of the connections between the Protestant religion, constitutional and political stability and

[31] C W Brooks, "The Place of Magna Carta and the English Constitution in Sixteenth Century Legal Thought", in Sandoz (ed.), *supra* n. 6, 69.

[32] *Charges to the Grand Jury, 1689–1803*, ed. by G Lamoine, Camden Society 4th ser., vol. 43 (London, Royal Historical Society, 1992), 34; *Western Circuit Assize Orders, 1629–1848*, ed. by J S Cockburn, Camden Society 4th ser., vol. 17 (London, Royal Historical Society, 1976; hereafter cited as *WCAS*), 21 (no. 89 (1631)); Herrup, *supra* n. 21, 52–3.

[33] *Charges to Grand Jury*, *supra* n. 32, 34.

[34] Ibid., 67 (Norfolk, 1709).

[35] Ibid., 142 (Wiltshire, 1720).

[36] Ibid., 254.

good government; but these oft-repeated and strenuously whiggish views, which emphasised the Bill of Rights and the principle of consent found in representative institutions commonly believed to have existed before Parliament, could from a social standpoint be expressions of a deep conservativism. They overlooked, or intentionally averted attention from the divisive implications of changes in the laws of England such as the recent Black Act or, even from a constitutional view, the passage of the Septennial Act in 1716.

At the end of the century, the rise of radicalism and the news from France brought forth some of the most explicit political indoctrination of the century. "Unlawful meetings and assemblies for altering the laws and changing the Constitution" were denounced by William Mainwaring Esq. before the Middlesex Grand Jury in 1792; adding that its *Purpose* made such an assembly unlawful.[37] Sir William Ashurst in Middlesex, also in 1792, denounced pamphlets currently circulating which disclaimed any idea of subordination, while in Dublin, Robert Day Esq. extolled the system which afforded equality of justice to rich and poor alike.[38] Sir James Eyre, Lord Chief Justice of the Common Pleas, went as far as to say that even to seek the reform of Parliament was high treason.[39] Differing personal opinions found expression in these charges. In a philosophical address to the Gloucester grand jury in 1797, the Rev. John Foley analysed the distinction between the social and moral causes of poverty, urging the need to provide care.[40] Five years later he was recommending manufacturers to provide employment for discharged soldiers and sailors.[41] Many of the social and economic changes of the era can be traced in the record of concerns that came before the grand juries of England, Wales and Ireland. Throughout these records, the representative role of the jury system is always visible and often explicit. There is no sense that the functions of the judiciary ought to be physically separated or morally distinguished from those of political institutions; they are all interdependent and often interlocked. Thus, in 1751, the Norfolk borough court grand jury was told that the judicial part of the constitution should be preserved by the jury "who are a fair and unexceptionable representative of the people and Country";[42] next year the same note was struck with, "the Jury are the representatives of the People of England".[43] In Virginia, as Gwenda Morgan has shown, "great care was taken to achieve a balance between different sections of the county so that all precincts were represented".[44] By the 1760s,

[37] Ibid., 454, 448–9, 468–9.

[38] Ibid., 534–5.

[39] Ibid., 526.

[40] Ibid., 553–60.

[41] Ibid., 587–91.

[42] Ibid., 367.

[43] Ibid., 376.

[44] G Morgan, "Law and Social Change in Colonial Virginia: the Role of the Grand Jury in Richmond County, 1692–1776", (1997) 95 *Virginia Magazine of History and Biography* 61. For a survey on the representational thesis, Younger, *supra* n. 30.

Richmond County grand juries were willing to castigate members of the upper gentry who were given to loose living and were neglecting their official duties.

The grand jury, unlike the petty jury, was able to address itself to matters of policy. This function remained remarkably stable with the passage of centuries. John Morrill thus tells us of the Cheshire grand jury in the mid-seventeenth century that:

> "They could be called upon to join the Justices in petitioning Parliament and the Crown as the authoritative voice of the County."

In the next century, at the York assizes of 1764, the grand jury voted thanks to the Yorkshire MPs for their stand for Wilkes on the issue of General Warrants.[45] The principles were similar, although the role of the crown's authority in the person of the presiding judge, and that of the grand jurors as representatives of the people, were now facing each other on opposing sides in Middlesex County, New Jersey, when, at the opening of quarter sessions in April, 1776, Chief Justice Smyth issued a strong warning not to exceed lawful bounds in protest against Parliament. The chief justice had said in his opening charge that all their liberties depended on the law—by which he meant British law—but the grand jurors demurred, preferring to affirm their belief that although liberty "was defined and protected by law, we nevertheless think that it is built on the rights of human nature".[46] This microcosmic replication of the great transatlantic debate reveals the grand jury as standing in as representatives of the popular cause in a situation in which the ordinary channels of political action were no longer available, or, if available, no longer adequate.

The debates on ratification of the Constitution have generally been traced by historians through the newspapers and pamphlets of the period. As a source of political direction, however, the judge's charge to the grand jury is a clue too long overlooked; the deference owed to a judge and the hierarchical scale down through the petty jury to the people may help to explain the Federalist advantage in many districts. The grand jury in Edenton, North Carolina, which met in November 1787 for the Michaelmas session, issued a long statement advocating ratification. One does not immediately think of this as Federalist territory; yet, after affirming the need for a firm and lasting union, they observed:

> "We admire in the new Constitution a proper jealousy of liberty mixed with a due regard for the necessity of a strong and authoritative government."

[45] J S Morrill, *Cheshire 1630–1660: County Government and Society During the English Revolution* (London, Oxford University Press, 1974), 12; J Beattie, *Crime and the Courts in England 1660–1800* (Oxford, Clarendon Press, 1986), 322, n. 24.

[46] A Speech delivered by Frederick Smyth, Esq., Philadelphia, American Philosophical Society, Philadelphia, Frederick Smyth Papers.

The statement was drawn up with the assistance of the judge, James Iredell, soon to be a justice of the new Supreme Court.[47] (In that capacity, when charging the federal grand jury in Savannah in 1792, Iredell expressed the legalistic view that juries should confine themselves to finding the facts, leaving questions of law to the court).[48] In supporting the Constitution, and ten years later in explaining and defending the controversial Alien and Sedition laws,[49] Iredell was taking a more interventionist part in constitutional realignment than even that of the English judiciary in connection with the Glorious Revolution.

PARTICIPATION, COMMUNITY AND THE JURY

The grand jury was a potent player in the judicial team. In the eighteenth century, its representative role was so well understood that only men of considerable property were permitted to exercise so much political influence; but, ever since the Middle Ages, the keynote of the assizes, as Mariannne Constable has emphatically said, was participation.[50] Both the high public duties in which men of some property were called to play their parts, and the social aspects of the occasion must have intensified the integrative function of these sessions. They bound men into a sense of community and gave both men and women an opening in which they were free to speak with their own voices.[51] It was a remarkably economical and effective way of running local government while maintaining the bonds with the centre which mixed discipline with allegiance. This system of local participation, not so much exported as reconstructed, did much of the practical governing in the American colonies; it was not based on theory, but it amounted to an active engagement for which I have proposed the name "the sociology of consent".[52]

There is, however, a caveat. Both in early modern England and in its early colonies, community had its limits as well as its internal distinctions; the population of manual and agricultural labourers, the very extensive though poorly defined classes known as servants, and, so far as jury service was concerned, all women, were excluded. So, in the colonies, were slaves, and, in all

[47] *Life and Correspondence of James Iredell*, ed. by G J Macree (New York, Peter Smith, 1949), 180–2.

[48] Ibid., 551–2.

[49] S Hadden, "Grand Jury Charges and Presentments of the Eighteenth Century: Regional and Temporal Comparisons", (Unpublished paper read at Cambridge, September 2000). I am much indebted to Dr Hadden for letting me see this paper.

[50] Constable, *supra* n. 10, 7.

[51] Herrup, *supra* n. 21, 43.

[52] J R Pole, "Reflections on Law in the American Revolution", (1993) 1 *William and Mary Quarterly* 144. That this was not a late colonial development, but an institutional and social habit is confirmed by W Offutt, Jr, "The Limits of Authority: Courts, Ethnicity, and Gender in the Middle Colonies, 1690–1710", in Mann and Tomlins (eds), *supra* n. 27, 359.

probability, Indians and African-descended persons even when free. In England the system had a basic unity which was lacking in the colonies. The judges were "the eyes of the kingdom",[53] who would return to Westminster, leaving the county communities aware of the existence of an overarching authority. Appeals from colonial courts to the privy council in London, though not unknown, were comparatively rare; although the colonies received and frequently cited the English reports, and were in a sense united by the common law, they lacked the centralising link between law and the actual policies of British governments; this failure of linkage with a central authority facilitated the appearance of differing practices in the different colonies. Each colony was in a strong sense its own jurisprudential authority.

Throughout the centuries, the government in every era needed all the information it could get; England had emerged under the Tudors in many respects as a divided nation, whose social order was frequently threatened by rural and regional unrest and by deep religious divisions; the introduction of the Reformation was a very incomplete process—as William Shakespeare himself, with his Catholic connections, had reason to know. Policing the Reformation was one of the functions of the judicial system.[54]

This judicial system, and with it the jury, became involved in almost every phase of the series of political crises that afflicted England during the first century of American colonisation. The irrepressible John Lilburne was twice, in 1649 and 1653, subjected to political trials for alleged offences against the state and twice acquitted by irrepressible London juries. His supporters struck a commemorative medal bearing the legend:

> "John Lilburne, saved by the power of the Lord and the integrity of the jury, who are judges of law as well as fact".[55]

The distinction between law and fact was not new; Coke had earlier laid down the lawyerly doctrine that the jury was to determine the facts, leaving it to the bench to declare the legal meaning of the facts.[56] Law, according to Coke's extremely specialist jurisprudence, could be known only through many years of erudite study, a view which necessarily placed legal interpretation beyond the powers of the laymen who made up the jury, whose primary obligation was simply to find the facts. The idea of a distinction between law and fact seems to have developed gradually with increasing sophistication in the concept of proof, involving, as we have noticed, more tangible ideas of verification; but as a distinction between judge and jury, it

[53] Green, *supra* n. 7, 176.

[54] G R Elton, *Policy and Police: The Enforcement of the Reformation in the Age of Thomas Cromwell* (Cambridge, University Press, 1972); A Holden, *William Shakespeare: His Life and Work* (London, Little Brown and Co., 1999), ch. 3.

[55] Green, *supra* n. 7, 176.

[56] *Coke on Littleton* (1628), s. 366, in E Coke, *The Institutes of the Laws of England* (London, printed for the Society of Stationers, 1628–1644), vol. 2; Green, *supra* n. 7, 170.

does not seem to have troubled the thinking of medieval generations. As Lilburne's medal shows, the issue carried political overtones; but it does not follow that lawyers were necessarily taking sides politically when they sought to protect the prerogatives of their profession. When, as in Lilburne's case, the charge was treason, sedition or libel, the politics of the charge necessarily entered into the legal distinction. Radicals or opponents of the regime claimed that the juries spoke with the voice of the common people, from whom they were drawn and to whose ranks they would return when the court adjourned. It is hardly going too far to say that, at least to the end of the eighteenth century, in both the English kingdom and the American republic, the trial jury's claim to judge law as well as fact, particularly in trials for treason or libel, was the critical issue in the debates which involved legal principles in political controversy.

The problem was incisively analysed by Sir John Hawles, whose treatise, *The Englishman's Right*, published in 1680, became a textbook, republished at intervals through the eighteenth century, for what may be called the popular or whig position; and since Hawles became solicitor general under William and Mary, his views evidently carried considerable weight, and proved, incidentally, that lawyers did not all think alike when their profession engaged with politics. *The Englishman's Right* was a purported dialogue, modelled no doubt on Christopher St German's famous text of the 1520s, *Doctor and Student*, between a lawyer urging the duty of public service and a prospective, but reluctant, juryman. In a sustained attack on the idea that the work of the jury was confined to finding the facts of the case, Hawles maintained that the distinction between "fact" and "law" was logically indefensible. Experience, he observed, showed that the jury often judged both, as for example in a homicide, "whether it is *murther, manslaughter per infortunia or se defendendo*". These were distinctions in which "facts" could not be separated from "law" because the legal category would itself define the facts. Examples are easy to construct: A kills B in a fight (Fact). Though A may have started the fight, he may not have intended the outcome; or, again, he may have seized a weapon and killed B in self-defence when B fought back. (This qualifies the nature of the act, therefore requiring interpretation of the original fact.) The first fact is that B is dead; and it is not disputed that A's blow was the immediate cause of B's death. But how far back does the "cause" go? Is there evidence that, when A started the fight, he intended to kill B? Where a life was at risk, the law was curious about these questions. May the fact that A was pursuing B from his (A's) wife's bed be entered into the causative catalogue of relevant facts, raising the question of motive; and may the parties' motives be regarded as organic elements of the original fact? May they, then, transmute fact itself into justification? The jury must ponder all these questions, and can hardly reach a verdict without making a finding in law—called a general verdict. The judge will have given technical instruction; but the verdict belongs to the jury. This particular reconstruction does not come from Hawles, but as he shrewdly pointed out, if a jury were really confined to declaring fact, it would return a verdict of "done" or "not done". The word "guilty" in itself implied a moral judgement; a verdict of "guilty" or "not guilty" was in itself a judgment of *law*. As Richard Beattie's researches have shown, it often fell to the trial jury to decide whether the case was one of murder or manslaughter.[57]

Hawles's prolonged influence is indicated by the editor of the fourth edition, published in the late eighteenth century, who noted that Blackstone had here drawn on Hawles.[58] In ordinary criminal law, the judges had little difficulty in leaving both fact and law to the jury; and in civil actions, which came to involve complex commercial transactions, insurance claims and disputes over the feudal refinements affecting land titles, post-colonial American as well as English juries might need the same sort of guidance from the bench. The charges that politicised the issue, with profound constitutional implications, were those involving treason or seditious libel. Suppose, Hawles proceeded, a man is accused of treason for failing to remove his hat when passing the king's statue. The evidence—the fact—is simply that he did not remove his hat. But would you find him guilty of treason? Hawles's juryman thinks not, because he would not think the omission constituted treason.[59] The jury, Hawles might have said, must apply both heart and eye. At the local level, the moral agency of juries is exemplified by the fact that they would often forgive sheep steeling in bad times; and, in capital cases, judges would collude with juries in the cause of leniency.[60] The duty of service which the lawyer urges on his interlocutor is essentially a political duty. If, as has been suggested, the notion of a distinction between fact and law had originated with the emergence of the jury, it had not appeared to raise serious or divisive issues of legal principle;[61] but now, in the turbulent politics of Stuart England, the technical argument involving law and fact in the same bundle had the ulterior purpose of strengthening the independence of juries against the crown in a period of growing threat to freedom of expression. Hawles, invoking England's heroic record in the history of liberty, cited Fortescue on the role of juries in maintaining the peoples' liberties, and Coke on the duty of fearless attachment to doing right according to the law. "The end of juries is to preserve men from oppression", says the barrister; and Vaughan's judgment on Bushel's case is played into the argument. But the situation now had a topical urgency. Certainly English government had been unstable in Henry VI's reign, but

[57] J Hawles, *The English-man's Right: A Dialogue between a Barrister at Law and a Juryman* (London, printed for Richard Janeway 1680; reprinted seven times to 1844); Beattie, *supra* n. 44, 104.

[58] Hawles, *supra* n. 56, 26–32.

[59] Ibid., 14–15, 77, 31, 32.

[60] Beattie, *supra* n. 44, 211.

[61] Baker, *supra* n. 7, 6–7, 110.

even rivalry for the throne between baronial houses, serious enough to precipitate civil wars, was nevertheless different and less formidable in character than the threat feared by Protestants from the impending succession of James II. It seems remarkable that the language had changed so little over some 200 years of changing political realities; yet, the central role of the jury maintained a significant consistency. Sir John Hawles was now insisting on a specifically political responsibility for the jury. Vaughan's judgment established the principle of jury independence and the fundamental principle that the jury's verdict must be accepted by the court (and Hawles repeated Vaughan's point about local knowledge);[62] but the struggle might begin again at any moment. The trials of Lilburne some 30 years earlier had brought the issues into sharp focus; the bullying and imprisonment of juries by tyrannical judges since the 1660s were recent memory. Hawles was in effect codifying for the future the general principle, already proclaimed by Fortescue, that the jury was the people's instrument in protecting their liberties whenever and by whomever threatened; and in these modern circumstances this claim made the jury an instrument in the process of political representation.

Only seven years later, James II proved Hawles's point by committing the Archbishop of Canterbury and six bishops to the tower for petitioning the king against an order in council requiring them to promulgate the king's Declaration of Indulgence. This cause led to the Trial of the Seven Bishops. That James's desire to extend religious toleration should have precipitated a struggle for individual freedom in the cause of suppressing religious minorities was a historical irony probably not appreciated by any of the participants. The charge against the Seven Bishops was seditious libel: their petition had brought the government into contempt. This doctrine proved to have great stamina: in the United States, over a hundred years later, the administration of John Adams would bring the same charge against its press critics in 1798–1799; and this notwithstanding a First Amendment expressly prohibiting any curtailment of the freedom of the press. A change of regime had done little to mitigate the character of the law or the sensitivities of governments whether of kingdom or republic. It was in seditious libel that the courts contested the jury's claim to determine both fact and law. In the Bishops' case, the King's Bench was divided, which must have encouraged the London jury to bring in their celebrated verdict of "Not Guilty".[63]

Between the trial of the Seven Bishops and the flurry of prosecutions under George III, the most important jury trial in the Anglophone world in which the law of seditious libel was used as an instrument for restraining the press occurred in 1735 in New York, when John Peter Zenger, the editor of a partisan newspaper, was indicted by the council for political attacks on

[62] Hawles, *supra* n. 56, 55–6.
[63] Grant Robertson, *supra* n. 9, 388–406; 12 How. St. Tr. 183.

Governor William Cosby. This indictment followed the refusal of the grand jury to present Zenger for prosecution, a striking case of political action by that body. Unfortunately for the governor, Chief Justice DeLancey, recently appointed by Cosby as an ally, made the tactical blunder of banning Zenger's attorneys from the court. The defence brief was at once offered to the famous Philadelphia lawyer Andrew Hamilton, who rode post-haste to New York to seize the opportunity. Hamilton was ready for the familiar arguments for judicial authority: according to the Chief Justice, the role of the jury was restricted to the finding of the fact of publication; it was for the bench to decide whether the content of the publication constituted a libel. But what if the allegations proved to be true? It made no difference: libel consisted in damage; DeLancey held that publication of a truth could be a libel. Hamilton replied that, in libel, truth was a defence, and the jury's province included a right to determine the truth. This argument seized for forensic purposes and turned against its official defenders the conventional legal principle that the jury determined fact; as Hawles had argued 50 years earlier, the definition of "fact" *included* the question of the truth of the alleged libel. Departing from strict common law, Hamilton also advanced the novel point that the jury could claim a higher prerogative in the colonies on account of their more popular form of government; this was in all probability the first appearance of an argument that colonial law might differ in principle from English law on account of colonial circumstances. Such a course might have serious implications for legal theory, apparently deriving legal authority from a popular source rather than from the books of law; but it was a view which both colonial and early national judges declined to follow. Hamilton also deftly introduced an allusion to the trial of the Seven Bishops, citing the London jury's view that truth was a defence, with an implied hint that the prosecution of Zenger was a similar act of tyranny. These arguments satisfied the New York jury, who achieved historical fame by acquitting Zenger.[64]

The passage of a century, more or less, since the trial of the Seven Bishops produced remarkably little change in the issues of principle. A cluster of trials began with John Wilkes's action against the Secretary of State, Lord Halifax, following the notorious search and seizure of his premises under cover of a general warrant, spurring a new and aggressive radical movement to reclaim the jury for the people as an explicit instrument of political action. As editor of the aggressively satirical journal, *The North Briton*, Wilkes had certainly succeeded in pouring contempt on George III's government, in the government's view justifying a case against him for seditious libel. London juries famously responded in *Wilkes* v.

[64] P U Bonomi, *A Factious People: Politics and Society in Colonial New York* (New York, Columbia University Press, 1971), 116–18; J Alexander, *A Brief Narrative of the Case and Trial of John Peter Zenger*, ed. by S N Katz (Cambridge, Bellknap Press, 1963); *Journal of the Legislative Council of New York* (Albany, N.Y., 1861), 642–2.

Wood by awarding both Wilkes and his printers heavy damages against the crown, and by vindicating the liberty of the press in the kindred case of *Entick* v. *Carrington*.[65] In the history of British liberties, the case was notable for Lord Chief Justice Camden's thundering pronouncement of the common law principle that officers of government are subject to the law and cannot take refuge under the doctrine of "state necessity". The jury itself justified the radical criterion: it was a *participatory* jury, which drew strength from its rejection of any idea that it might be a merely passive recipient of information, and insisted on the right to question and cross-examine the accused.[66] This claim was consistent with the jury's medieval origins; but when energised by a new emphasis on its positive role as a supplementary instrument of representation, this amounted to a new challenge to government, and a claim for a dramatic turn in constitutional law. This right was still practised in South Carolina at the end of the century, where juries were known to return verdicts contrary to the judge's direction.[67] When the crown prosecuted Wilkes, the radicals supplied jurors with pamphlets on press freedom and an account of the Zenger case in New York.[68] Rather than seeking a process of separation between English and American law, the radical perspective insists on an empire of *common* law in a literal sense. The radicals had no doubts or hesitations about treating jurors as moral agents of public opinion, publishing in the newspapers their names, addresses, employments and connections. When the government prosecuted the printers Almon and Woodfall for sedition, the latter (the famous parliamentary reporter who preceded Hansard) for publishing one of Junius's *Letters* critical of government policy in the American colonies, Almon's jury convicted, but Woodfall was found guilty of publishing *only*. Lord Mansfield having laid down the line of distinction between law and fact, the core of radical argument was that libel was a matter of public opinion and therefore appropriate for a jury, a claim that picked up Hamilton's defence of Zenger.[69] Interrogation from the bench failed to elicit a verdict that the publication complained of was seditious as charged.[70] After the verdict, the jurors' names were blazed forth from on the Guildhall in gold letters.

[65] 19 How. St. Tr. 987; 1167; 1044. Grant Robertson, *supra* n. 9, 440–72.

[66] J Brewer, "The Wilkites and the Law, 1763–1774", in John Brewer and John Styles (eds), *An Ungovernable People: The English and their Law in the Seventeenth and Eighteenth Centuries* (London, Hutchinson, 1980), 154.

[67] *State* v. *Josiah Querret* (murder) in South Carolina Historical Society, Cases Determined in Constitutional Courts at Charleston and Columbia, 1798–1803, 43. The jury had taken evidence on their own initiative but were overruled because the witness had not been sworn, citing 4 Blackstone 348. In *Stephen Shackleford* v. *Warner Bierowth* (?) April 1795, in ibid., 9, the jury "thought proper to find against the judge's direction". The court was upheld on appeal.

[68] Brewer, *supra* n. 65, 156.

[69] Ibid., 157.

[70] 20 How. St. Tr. 803.

The central importance of the issue of fact and law was the theme in 1769 of a significant letter to *The New-York Chronicle*. By signing himself "Britannicus", the author identified American liberties with British law, and the letter claimed to be copied from *The* [London] *Political Register* and addressed to a juryman. The letter assumes an immediate relationship between the issues in the colonies and those on which the Wilkite radicals were fighting in England. The author may not have been a lawyer, for he thought the restriction of jury power to finding the facts had only recently been asserted. He asked:

> "O what can tend more to overthrow our laws and liberties? For if this pernicious doctrine should be allowed, juries would be so far from being a security to the subject, that they would be then a snare."

With the jury compelled to find only the facts, the judge, a royal officer, could impose what punishment he chose. He added a warning that juries should be careful to act only on a grand jury indictment, not on an "information", which might emanate from the crown.[71]

The prosecution in 1783 of Dr William Davies Shipley, Dean of St Asaph, who had published an allegedly seditious pamphlet written by his brother-in-law, gave rise to a trial remarkable principally for one of Erskine's most brilliant and passionate defences of freedom of the press and of conscience. The prosecution was again frustrated by a jury which would only find that the defendant had in fact published the offending material, but refused to condemn the material published. On being asked the jury's finding, the foreman answered: "Guilty of publishing only." Buller J responded:

> "I believe that is a verdict not quite correct. You gentlemen of the jury must explain one way or the other, whether you find the meaning of the innuendoes."

Later, Mr Erskine asked: "Would you have the word *only* recorded?" To which one of the jury replied: "Yes." Buller J said:

> "But I must tell you the law is this: if you find the defendant guilty of publishing, without saying any more, the question of libel or not is open to the consideration of the Court; But if you say he is guilty of publishing only, it is an incomplete verdict."

One of the jury then stated: "We certainly mean to leave the question of libel or not to the consideration of the Court." Erskine accordingly asked: "Do you find the sedition?" Again, one of the jury: "We give no verdict upon it." Buller J:

> "When you understand your verdict yourselves, I will take it in the manner you state it. If you say guilty of publishing only, there must be another trial, because the verdict will be imperfect".[72]

[71] *The New-York Chronicle*, 26 Oct. 1769.
[72] 20 How. St. Tr. 946–55.

The significance of the word "only" seems clear enough; but on the verdict, there appear to have been uncertainties among the jurors; the government did not risk a second trial.

Whigs and radicals were committed to the view that juries had always represented the people and, in questions of sedition or libel, had a right to enter into questions of law; no judge could take this power from them. For this reason, when, in 1792, Fox's Libel Act settled full power on the jury to determine law and fact, it claimed to be an act declaratory of existing law.[73]

John Brewer's account of these events emphasises the political nature of law and its use as a principal instrument of government policy. Law was "the main vehicle of state power", but it was not the absolute property of the governing class.[74] The radical programme, in effect, was to accept this thesis, seize control of the law through the instrumentality of the jury, and turn it against the government. The culmination of this programme in Fox's Libel Act was a famous victory, but it was not the end of the struggle; it would be an over-indulgent error to suppose that this act brought an end to political prosecutions or convictions. The record of repression under Pitt, followed by numerous sentences of transportation for various radical activities and working class combinations in the early nineteenth century, testify that juries could convict as well as acquit.

In a trial of a group of cordwainers (shoemakers) in New York in the first few years of the nineteenth century, the State found itself in the peculiar position of having no local statute on which to base the prosecution. The State therefore fell back on the English common law of conspiracy; according to this assumption, the common law, far from having been Americanised, remained a seamless Anglo-American fabric; this doctrine was now as useful to the State as it had recently been to English radicals. The defence now rejected the radical view and ridiculed the prosecution's reliance on English common law, which they denounced as a feudal relic with no part to play under America's republican government; but the jury of propertied citizens was no longer called on to stand up for the peoples' rights against the crown or its agents. Juries in this and a similar trial in Philadelphia seem to have been unmoved by the defence's strictures on the employment against the rights claimed by American workers of the old common law of conspiracy, which had never been recognised as state law. In both trials, local juries found for the prosecution. The jury was asked to adjudicate between the cordwainers' right to act collectively to protect (or improve) their standard of living, and the state's invocation of the traditional common law of conspiracy.[75]

[73] 32 Geo. III, c. 6 (1792).

[74] Brewer, *supra* n. 65, 13, 20.

[75] There is a complete record of the New York trial in New York Public Library, Box 91–3562 R-2 Pos. See also C L Tomlins, *Law, Labour and Ideology in the Early American Republic* (Cambridge, University Press, 1993), 136–7.

A few years earlier, newspaper records suggest that all the Republican and opposition editors prosecuted for political dissent under the Sedition Act of 1798 were convicted.[76] As citizens of the new American Republic, the jury had been domesticated rather than liberated.[77]

THE JURY, MORALITY AND COMMON LAW IN AMERICA

When the American Constitution was in its infancy, James Wilson, the Philadelphia lawyer and leading nationalist and now a justice of the newly constituted Supreme Court, gave a course of lectures in the College of Philadelphia, one of which was devoted to the jury, which (though admitting to uncertainty as to its origins) he eulogised as being "in the nature of things". The jury's moral agency was Wilson's central theme. It was clear to Wilson as to other lawyers that the jury's role was to find the truth, but, he explained, the truth might include intention; while acceding to the popular principle, Wilson entered the important reservation that, in forming their opinion on the law, juries were not free to exercise discretionary powers, but must adhere to common law rules; this involved observation of precedent (on which they would obviously need to be guided by the judge).[78] However, Wilson, borrowing from Rousseau the theme of the nation as a moral person, maintained that the power exercised by the people through their participation in the legal system was an exercise of delegated sovereign power (a rare use on his part of the concept of sovereignty).[79] Juries, he admitted, were liable to error, but they were not liable to building their errors into a system, as could happen when judicial error became sanctified as precedent. Randomly chosen and constantly changing juries could not develop an *esprit de corps*.

Whether or not the lawyer and the politician contended with each other in Wilson's mind, he conceded to the jury the right of determining legal questions. But the concession was guarded:

> "The discretionary powers of jurors find no place for exertion here; these powers they possess as triers of facts because, as we have already observed, trial of facts depends on evidence; and because the force of evidence cannot be determined by any general system of rules. But law, particularly the common law, is governed by precedents, and customs, and authorities, and maxims . . . alike obligatory upon jurors as upon judges, in deciding questions of law."

[76] D H Stewart, *The Opposition Press of the Federalist Period* (Albany, State University of New York Press, 1969), 471–86.

[77] A thorough analysis reflecting the radical perspective is Norman L Rosenberg, *Protecting the Best Men: an Interpretive History of the Law of Libel* (Chapel Hill, University of North Carolina Press, 1986).

[78] *The Works of James Wilson*, ed. by R G McCloskey, (Cambridge, Mass. Harvard University Press, 1967), 541–2.

[79] Ibid., 547. Professor J H Burns has suggested Burlamaqui as a more likely source.

After admitting Lord Hardwicke's emphasis on the distinction between findings of fact and law, Wilson concluded in favour of "harmonious co-operation".[80]

In the years before colonial protest turned into revolt and revolt into revolution, skirmishes between local crowds and customs officers were followed by trials in which it is hardly an exaggeration to call the New England coastal juries an arm of the resistance.[81] Even normal domestic litigation was infected by the imperial crisis. This point was particularly well illustrated in 1765 in the prominent New York case of *Forsey* v. *Cunningham*.[82] Forsey had taken a writ for assault and battery against Cunningham; the jury awarded Forsey the enormous damages of £1,500. When Lieutenant Governor Cadwallader Colden agreed to hear Cunningham's appeal to the provincial council, the public outcry had no relation to the merits of the dispute, and was almost certainly fuelled by sensitivities inflamed by the Stamp Act. The spectacle of a crown officer taking the decision out of the hands of the New York jury struck many New York citizens as an unprecedented threat to their liberties. Colden's decision drew criticism from the Supreme Court, and the council, and the legal profession in New Jersey and Pennsylvania as well as New York, where the grand jury congratulated the judges for defying the lieutenant governor. When John Adams met John Morin Scott in 1774, he was impressed by the information that Scott, "an eminent Lawyer", had drawn up the answer of the council to Governor Colden's reasons for sending an appeal to England.[83]

The importance of the general issue of the English right to trial by a jury of the vicinity had gained in urgency from recent British legislation which appeared to threaten Americans with transportation for trials in London; historians have always been aware of and have given varying degrees of prominence to the perceived threat to these constitutional rights in the building up of colonial anxieties and resentments. In *The New-York Chronicle*, "Britannicus" had pointed to the danger hidden in the doctrine which confined the jury to the facts, but seems to have overlooked or chosen to ignore that this restriction normally applied to charges of sedition or libel; however, the boundaries had never been tightly drawn, and might be moved to include other charges.[84] In the context of conflict between the British and the colonies, the policy of taking law-finding out of the jury's hands was a policy of locating it in the hands of their oppressors. This

[80] Ibid., 542.

[81] J P Reid, *Constitutional History of the American Revolution: The Authority of Rights* (Madison, University of Wisconsin Press, 1986), 53–4.

[82] M M Klein, "Prelude to Revolution in New York: Jury Trials and Judicial Tenure", (1960) 4 *William and Mary Quarterly* 439 at 456–7.

[83] *Diary and Autobiography of John Adams*, ed. by L H Butterfield, The Adams Papers, Series I Diaries (Cambridge, Bellknap Press, 1961), vol. 2, 105.

[84] *The New-York Chronicle*, 26 Oct. 1769.

theme had, as we have seen, a long history, dating at least from the trials of Lilburne; it was not perhaps the most prominent of causes but must have added its weight to the general suspicion of British intentions. Historians with their sights focused on the broader constitutional controversy, involving taxation, representation, quartering of troops and other familiar grievances, have neglected the implications of this by no means trivial issue.

One reason why colonial spokesmen themselves failed to deploy this argument more emphatically may well have been that it divided the legal profession. It would be a mistake to award the whole argument to the radicals. Lawyers were trained in the law, and as a memorandum in the 1750s by William Kempe, attorney general of New York, on a case involving the writ of trover and conversion showed, in ordinary jurisprudence the courts themselves held conventional views. The court, according to Kempe, was to direct the jury in the matters of law "arising from the Evidence"; the jury was to have regard for the court's direction. But even this left too much to the jury:

> "for what is a conversion and what is not a conversion is a matter of law, and not proper for a jury who are ignorant of such matters . . . ."

Kempe went so far as to say that the court should set aside a perverse general verdict given against the direction of the court.[85] This doctrine was not advanced as a rejection of whig or republican principles; the records from South Carolina in the 1790s show several examples of appeals in which the higher court upheld the bench over the trial jury, and precisely the same point was made by Henry St George Tucker in Virginia as late as the 1840s.[86] These cases did not range the crown or the state government against the people; rather, they reflected a consciousness of public obligation to maintain professional standards. The issue simply would not die down, and was the subject of renewed controversy in the 1820s in both Britain and South Carolina.[87] This kind of legal thinking, however, could never persuade the increasing numbers of dissidents, and may have contributed to the legal profession's unpopularity.

The stubbornly persistent issue of the jury's power in libel bore a heavy charge; it involved the right of citizens to criticise their government and thus trenched on the wider issue of press freedom. Since criticism of government had become an American habit during the long controversy with British authorities, and showed no tendency to disappear when the authorities were American, and American governments proved no less sensitive than their predecessors, the controversies on this theme survived not only the transition

[85] New York Historical Society, John Tabor Kempe papers, Lawsuits C-F.

[86] See South Carolina Historical Society, *supra* n. 66; Tucker, *supra* n. 15, vol. 2, 292–3. A re-trial would be granted if the jury ignored the judge's direction to bring in a special verdict, i.e. on the facts alone.

[87] (1825) *Westminster Review*, 43–92, reviewing G Worthington, *An Inquiry into the Power of Juries to decide incidentally into Question of Law*; A Blanding and D J McCleod, (1831) 1 *The Carolina Law Journal*.

from British rule to self-government but also the transition from Federalist to Jeffersonian administration. But the law was far from self-explanatory. In February, 1789, Chief Justice Cushing of Massachusetts sought the opinion of John Adams in a long letter replete with references to Coke, Blackstone and the Seven Bishops. By the law of England, he observed, a civil action for damages required that the libel be false as well as scandalous; it ought to follow that the truth of an accusation might be pleaded in defence. Cushing had studied the record closely and noted that the indictments against the Bishops, which initiated a criminal action, accused them of a libel that was *false* as well as scandalous. By analogy with the civil principle, the case, then, turned on the truth or falsehood of the assertion that the king had acted illegally. Mr Justice Powell had held that to make the petition a libel, it must be false. He held the position of the bishops true and right; so truth could be pleaded in mitigation. Mr Justice Allybone took the view that a private man writing about the government was an intruder and a libeller. Happily, however, the jury had set them all right. But a single jury verdict did not overturn the law; and this left the law of England holding (where Lord Mansfield had placed it, though Cushing did not say so) that the truth could not be pleaded in bar of indictment. Where, then, did it leave Massachusetts and the constitutional protection of the liberty of the press? Cushing found the English position incompatible with the liberty of a republic; citizens must be free to criticise their rulers. "Why", he asked, acknowledging Gordon (co-author of *Cato's Letters* in the 1720s) but distantly echoing Milton's *Areopagitica*, "need any honest man fear the truth? The guilty only fear it . . . ." Adams agreed that it would be safest to let the jury hear evidence as to the truth of the allegations, "and if the jury found them true and they were published for the Public good, they would readily acquit." The motive of publication was to be a consideration—which was consistent with Erskine's emphasis on *intent*; but the jury would be the judges of motive, vindicating their brief as society's moral agents.[88]

The same issue was reopened under the republican ægis of Jefferson's presidency. *The People* v. *Croswell* arose from a journalistic criticism of the president, held by the administration to be exactly the same kind of libel that had brought scandal and contempt onto earlier and more regal governments; and the trial judge restricted the jury to finding the fact of publication, as British governments had tried to do with Woodfall and the Dean of St Asaph. The jury followed the judge and convicted. On appeal, Alexander Hamilton, who was so soon to lose his life in a duel, argued that it was *intent* that constituted the crime, and intent was itself one of the *facts* of the case:

> "Texts taken from the holy scriptures, and scattered among the people, may, in certain times . . . become libellous, nay, treasonable . . . surely the time, manner, and intent are matters of fact for a jury."

[88] "Cushing-Adams Correspondence", (1942) 27 *Massachusetts LQ* 12.

He agreed that the jury ought to pay respectful regard to the opinion of the court; but the jury might conclude from their own reading and on their own judgment that "the law arising from the case is different from that which the court advances."[89] Chancellor James Kent, giving judgment for the appellant, stated that the Sedition Act itself had specifically decreed that the jury who tried the cause should have the right to determine the law and the fact, under the direction of the court; the Supreme Court had set similar precedents.[90] Alexander Hamilton had made his last contribution to American liberty and one that may be said to have matched his better known achievements.

The issue was fought through on several further occasions, in each of which the same precedents were cited.[91] State legislation or constitutional revisions eventually tidied up the question in the jury's favour, an almost unnoticed step in the passage to more democratic government in the United States usually—though very loosely—associated under the umbrella of Jacksonian Democracy.[92] When Alexis de Tocqueville visited the United States in the early 1830s, he had not yet been in England and had no previous experience of the Anglo-American jury, but observed proceedings in the courts, and was impressed by the political value of the jury system. The feature he particularly noted was not so much the trial as a method of finding the truth, but the binding force of the jury in the structure of government. Like John Adams in the previous century, Tocqueville regarded the jury as the authentic location for the expression of popular sovereignty, a fundamental binding force to which the democratic experiment owed its hopes of success.[93]

The word "jury", however, is not synonymous with the word "justice", and the habits of a community are not invariably derived from instincts of fairness, an ability to weigh evidence or a capacity to absorb scientific advances; a jury called together from the locality of the alleged crime could be fallible, prejudiced and ignorant. English country juries persisted in believing in witchcraft and resented the dictates of enlightened justices from London who told them there was no such thing. White American juries went on fighting the Civil War through Reconstruction deep into the twentieth century. And deep into the twentieth century, in ex-confederate states, any black man accused of an offence against a white woman and tried by a white

[89] *The People* v. *Croswell* (1803) 3 *Johnson's Cases*, 354–5.

[90] Ibid., 375; 3 Dallas 4.

[91] *Commonwealth of Massachusetts* v. *Buckingham* (Boston, 1822).

[92] Law reform took an uneven course, with the focus mainly on the disputed status of the common law. See C M Cook, *The American Codification Movement: A Study in Antebellum Legal Reform* (Westport, Conn., Greenwood Press, 1981); L S Pangle and T L Pangle, *The Learning of Liberty: The Educational Ideas of the American Founders* (Lawrence, University of Kansas Press, 1993), 218–22.

[93] A de Tocqueville, *De la Démocratie en Amérique*, ed. by J-P Mayer (Paris, Gallimard, 1961), vol. 1, 286–7.

jury was a victim, not a beneficiary, of the trial process, putting a new gloss on the concept of trial by one's peers, which, as the Supreme Court had observed in the Strauder case, needed amendment to mean trial by a jury of one's own colour or race; failing which, the medieval mixed jury might be revived to accommodate representatives of each race. To some extent the Supreme Court took the place once occupied in England by the courts of Westminster; but federal jurisdiction did not supplant the state systems. The democratic credentials of the jury drew deeply on its claims as a representative of dominant local opinion, renewing the principle that law itself emanated from custom. Whether the jury, responding to local customs and mores, gave fairer justice or better government would depend, not only on the combination of the heart and the eye, but on whether the heart was in the right place.

8

Jury Research in the English Reports in CD-ROM

JAMES OLDHAM (GEORGETOWN)

Recently the entire set of The English Reports became available in electronic format, compressed onto two compact disks. This paper is designed to illustrate, in the context of the history of the jury, the new vistas that stretch before legal historians as a result of this new resource. Nothing presented in this paper is profound, yet the potential of the CD format for generating new understandings of past practices and institutions that appear in the printed reports may be extraordinary. The simple reason is, of course, the ability to search case reports by key word. The indexes published as part of the nominate reports were, as was true of those reports themselves, variable in quality. Even at best, the indexes were blunt instruments as finding aids. Until now, the most dependable solution was to turn the pages, one-by-one. Yet even that wearisome work did not ordinarily extend to the actual *reading* of the text of each page—the pages would be scanned (by eye) in search of cases that looked relevant to the subject being researched.

Researchers can now be free of such inelegant drudgery. In literally a matter of seconds, the computer will reveal, from the CD-ROM, the number of times any word or phrase or word combination appears in the printed reports. Simultaneously, a "hit list" will be produced showing the cases, and, for each case, the lines of text containing the search words, with the search words highlighted. Immediately available on screen as well is the full text of any case on the hit list.

The advantage of the new technology in finding and counting cases containing words or terms of interest is apparent, but it bears demonstrating, and that is the objective of this exercise. The approach that seemed to me to be best was to go over prior work that I have done on the history of the jury and to look for two things—what I missed, and what I never searched for because there was no practicable way to do so. Despite the multitude of textual errors in the CD-ROM as it now stands (more on that later), the findings are significant.

One starting point would be to search for terms that *were* indexed in the nominate reports, in the expectation that cases would be retrieved beyond those displayed in the indexes, both because the alphabetical indexes often did not capture every case in the volumes relevant to the index terms and because the index terms used by different reporters were by no means uniform. More interesting, however, is to search for expressions that would *not* normally have been used by contemporary case reporters and indexers. I will illustrate this in three ways: first, by tracing the trajectory of a specific writ; secondly, by searching for an unofficial type of special jury—the jury of merchants; and thirdly, by searching for jury material in decisions by the Court of Chancery, a court where there were no juries.

THE SPECIFIC WRIT

Some years ago I did a study of the jury of matrons—a jury of women that for centuries served the purpose of physically inspecting female parties to litigation to see if they were pregnant.[1] Most applications were on the criminal side, where female defendants who had been convicted of felonies "pleaded their bellies", claiming to be pregnant in order to gain a reprieve from the hangman until after the supposed baby was born, and to give them time to seek a pardon or clemency (usually transportation to the colonies, after transportation emerged). The women on the juries in criminal cases were usually empanelled on the spot at the Old Bailey or on assize, and no writ to the sheriff was needed. On the civil side, a woman occasionally claimed after the death of her husband to have been left pregnant by him, raising questions of inheritance. When this happened, a jury of matrons was summoned by the sheriff with a specific writ—*de ventre inspiciendo*, "to inspect the belly". I thought I had discovered every appearance of this writ in the printed reports. Not so, it turns out, for two reasons—first, the familiar problem of variant spellings of the parties' names by different reporters when there was more than one report of the same case, and secondly, because of not looking thoroughly enough in Chancery cases.

One Chancery case that I did find was *Ex Parte Aiscough*.[2] Decided in 1730, Lord Chancellor King saw no way to avoid issuance of the writ—it was, after all, "in the *register*".[3] A note by Pere Williams in his report explains that two writs were needed—one to see whether the widow be with child, and then a second whereby she would be removed "to a castle where the sheriff is to keep her safely" (this in order to avoid, as Blackstone put it, a "suppositious birth")[4]—but in the principal case

[1] J Oldham, "On Pleading the Belly: A History of the Jury of Matrons", (1985) 6 *Criminal Justice History* 1.

[2] 2 P. Wms. 591, 24 ER 873 (1730).

[3] 2 P. Wms. 593, 24 ER 874, referring to the *Registrum Brevium* (London, apud R. Totellim 1553), f. 227.

[4] W Blackstone, *Commentaries on the Laws of England* (Oxford, Clarendon Press 1768), vol. 3, 362.

"the *Lord Chancellor* said, there was no occasion to execute the writ in that strict manner, provided people of skill had from time to time free access to her, and might be present at the birth".[5]

There are, I discover, two additional reports of this decision, one by Cooke and one by Mosely. I failed to locate them because the Pere Williams version is what is referenced in later cases and in secondary sources, and because Cooke recorded the case as *Ascough* v. *Chaplin (Lady)*,[6] and Mosely called it *Ex Parte Ayscoughe*.[7] The variant spellings of the name of the case resulted in Pere Williams' report being entered on page 15 of the first volume of the index to the English Reports, Cooke's report on page 46, and Mosely's report on page 81.

Mosely quotes Lord Chancellor King as saying:

"The chief thing is to prevent a suppositious child, but the first writ issues, to see whether she is pregnant or not, because you cannot otherwise come at the second; and if the sheriff returns that she is with child, then the second, which is the material writ, issues out of the Court of King's Bench or Common Pleas".[8]

Also, remarking that it would be hard on Lady Chaplin to confine her to the country when she desired to live in town, King said:

"[Y]ou cannot hinder her, for the first [writ] does not confine her, but she may go where she pleases, till the second writ issues, which cannot be had till *Michaelmas* term; and there is no fear of her being brought to bed immediately . . .."[9]

Cooke's report pertains to the second writ. The co-heirs of the deceased, who challenged Dame Elizabeth Chaplin, the widow, are all identified, and after indicating that the first writ "was returned that the lady was with child", the co-heirs moved

"for the safe custody of her until her delivery", pointing out that "the lady's mother was likewise with child, and therefore neither she nor any other woman with child were proper persons to be with her . . .."[10]

And instead of the relaxed formula suggested by Lord Chancellor King (occasional visits by people of skill), the Court of Common Pleas ordered that a clause be inserted in the writ to prevent other women with child from being with Lady Chaplin,

"and ladies were named on the part of the prosecutors or heiresses, to attend the lady during her pregnancy and till her delivery, but they must not name any spinster; and the mother was allowed to visit only".[11]

[5] 2 P. Wms. 593, 24 ER 874.
[6] Cooke, C.P. 62, 125 ER 958.
[7] Mosely 391, 25 ER 458.
[8] Mosely 393, 25 ER 459.
[9] Ibid.
[10] Cooke, C.P. 62, 125 ER 958–9.
[11] Cooke, C.P. 62, 125 ER 959.

In the nineteenth century, after the medical profession had acquired a little sophistication, the writ *de ventre inspiciendo* was thought a scandal. When the writ was requested in an 1835 case, the editor of the *Medical Gazette* was outraged, noting that by the terms of the writ, the inspection of the woman was to be by a jury of twelve women *and two knights*, a procedure called "disgustingly indecent".[12] The knights actually did not participate in the inspection,[13] but in any event I had thought this gasp of editorial indignation was the end of the trail of *de ventre inspiciendo*. I now discover that in 1845, ten years after the *Medical Gazette* outcry, the Vice-Chancellor ordered the writ in the case of *Blakemore* v. *Blakemore*.[14] There, a gentleman described as "of dissolute and intemperate habits", but worth some money, had married a barmaid of an inn in Wales, but after a time, he left her in the country and returned to the city, where he died. The widow claimed to have been left pregnant by her late husband, even though she had been living with her husband's groom since before he died. At the Chancery hearing, Vice-Chancellor Knight-Bruce blandly inquired, "The subsisting connection is one of sin?" He was told: "There has been no second marriage." The Vice-Chancellor's ruling was: "Let the ordinary course be followed. The jury is a jury of women."

THE JURY OF MERCHANTS

In past work I have wrestled extensively with the history of the special jury.[15] In England this type of jury took shape in common law practice in the seventeenth century; was endorsed by statute in 1730; was used effectively by Lord Mansfield in the second half of the eighteenth century in mercantile cases; flourished during the first half of the nineteenth century, especially under Lords Ellenborough and Campbell; then fell subject to abuse and disintegrated. The best-known chapter in the life of the special jury is the instrumental part it played in the formative era of English commercial law, and in these cases the special jurors were customarily merchants. Mansfield's reliance on, or perhaps it is better to say teamwork with, merchant juries became famous.[16] Yet acknowledging this is one thing; under-

[12] *Medical Gazette*, 15 Aug. 1835, pp. 698–9.

[13] See Oldham, *supra* n. 1, notes 96–8 and accompanying text.

[14] 1 Holt Eq. 328, 71 ER 769 (1845).

[15] See J Oldham, "The Origins of the Special Jury", (1983) 50 *University of Chicago LR* 137; idem, "Special Juries in England: Nineteenth Century Usage and Reform," (1987) 8 *JLH* 148; idem, "The History of the Special (Struck) Jury in the United States and Its Relation To Voir Dire Practices, the Reasonable Cross-Section Requirement, and Peremptory Challenges", (1998) 6 *William and Mary Bill of Rights Journal* 623.

[16] I discuss this in J Oldham, *The Mansfield Manuscripts and the Growth of English Law in the Eighteenth Century* (Chapel Hill and London, University of North Carolina Press, 1992), vol. 1, 93–9.

standing the workings of the process is another. How often were "juries of merchants" formed, and how did this happen? And what part did the merchant jurors' expertise actually play in the decisions and in the formulation of common law doctrine in commercial cases? Both of these questions can be addressed through the CD-ROM resource by searching for appearances in the cases of the expression "jury of merchants", a term not used in the indexes to the nominate reports.[17]

There was no entitlement to a jury of merchants. The 1730 statute on special juries endorsed them without definition other than by reference to the practice of empanelling special juries already established in the courts and by describing the procedure—producing a panel of 48 names which was then reduced to 24 by the parties' taking turns striking out names. In my study of the Mansfield manuscripts, I describe a 1773 case involving the Goldsmiths Company in which the Recorder of London had summoned a jury of merchants.[18] Barrister John Dunning challenged this, remarking:

> "With the same propriety that the order specifies a Jury of Merchants, it might have specified a Jury of Goldsmiths to be summoned . . . ."[19]

Opposing counsel, Serjeant Burland, observed that orders for juries of merchants had frequently been made; Dunning said perhaps this was so, but only with consent. In the case being argued, "it was agreed to have a Special Jury not confined to Merchants only".

Reported cases confirm Serjeant Burland's remark that juries of merchants were frequently empanelled. Sometimes special juries or juries of merchants were ordered by the Court of Chancery in referring a question to law for jury trial resolution. In an anonymous case in 1722 in which Chancery referred a question to law, the Court remarked:

> "[I]t is proper to move the Court of Chancery for a special jury, if the circumstances of the case require it; and the court will grant the same, as they did in the case of *Attorney General* and *Snow*."[20]

At common law, special juries were empanelled only at the request of one of the parties, but since questions referred by Chancery to the law courts were

[17] Some reporters did index "special jury" cases, especially in the nineteenth century, but even when this was done, the cases that were identified were ordinarily those in which some question about special jury entitlement or procedure had arisen—many other cases in which special juries were used were not identified. Also, some case reports refer to juries of merchants without ever mentioning the fact that the juries were special.

[18] Oldham, *supra* n. 16, vol. 1, 95.

[19] Ibid.

[20] *Anon.*, 2 P. Wms. 68, 24 ER 643 (1722). The only printed report of *Attorney General* v. *Snow* is of a case in Exchequer, noted briefly at Bunbury 96, 145 ER 608 (1721), but there is no mention of proceedings in Chancery or of a special jury order. Other cases where the Court of Chancery specified in its order referring a question to law for a jury trial that the jury should be special include *Lord Falmouth* v. *Innys*, Mos. 87, 25 ER 287 (1729); *Earl of Thanet* v. *Pattison*, Cas. t. Hard. 454, 25 ER 1029 (1738).

designed, according to the common expression, "to inform the conscience of the Court of Chancery", orders from Chancery calling for special juries or juries of merchants were ordinarily complied with.[21]

But what, exactly, did juries of merchants do? We can imagine models at two extremes, one passive and one active. The first would be a jury of impassive experts upon whom the court would rely to do the right thing. The second would be a jury of experts who were permitted, perhaps encouraged, to participate in the trial and to articulate, where relevant, mercantile practices. Both models find support in the cases, but as I will show, the active model came to dominate as the eighteenth century ended, continuing well into the nineteenth century.

The question of how active the jurors were is of interest in considering how common law principles and doctrine came to be articulated and agreed upon in a system with jury trial as its mainspring. The problem of the inarticulateness of the general verdict has often been recognised as an impediment to the formulation of the common law. As Lord Mansfield remarked in *Vallejo* v. *Wheeler*, "it is not easy to collect with certainty from a general verdict, or from notes taken at Nisi Prius, what was the true ground of decision";[22] and for this reason Mansfield, in *Vallejo* "as in all doubtful cases, . . . wished a case to be made for the opinion of the Court".[23] As to merchant jurors, perhaps Mansfield's best-known observation is that in *Lewis* v. *Rucker*, where he stated:

> "The special jury, (amongst whom there were many knowing and considerable merchants) found the defendant's rule of estimation to be right, and gave their verdict for him. They understood the question very well, and knew more of the subject than any body else present; and formed their judgment from their own notions and experience, without much assistance from any thing that passed".[24]

This, of course, suggests more of the passive model of the jury of merchants than the active.

[21] In the nineteenth century, there was much statutory attention to special juries, and, in an 1841 case, it was argued that one section of an 1825 statute removed the power of the Court of Chancery to order a special jury. The Master of the Rolls observed that "though the direction for a special jury was thought imperative on the parties, it was only an intimation to the Judge at common law, of the course considered expedient, and that this Court would not feel satisfied with the finding of any other jury than that specified in the order." See *Fowler* v. *Wood*, reported in n. (1) to *Ellis* v. *Bowman*, 13 Beav. 316, 51 ER 112 (1851).

[22] 1 Cowp. 143, 98 ER 1012 (1774), Lofft 631, 98 ER 836.

[23] 1 Cowp. 153, 98 ER 1017 .

[24] 2 Burr. 1167, 87 ER 769 (1761). See also Lofft's report of *Vallejo* (styled "Vallezjo") v. *Wheeler*, Lofft 631, 640, 98 ER 836, 841, where Mansfield remarked: "I should pay great respect to the gentlemen of the special jury who were considerable merchants, the proper judges of a cause of this nature." Mansfield was not, however, content to rely on the special jurors; in the final judgment, delivered after the case had stood over for a term, Mansfield stated: "As it was a matter of a commercial nature, and turned greatly upon the usage and custom of merchants, I consulted an eminent merchant of whose skill and experience I have a great opinion." Lofft 644, 98 ER 843.

Another example on the passive side is a 1744 decision, *Banbury* v. *Lisset*, presenting the question of whether a document drafted by the parties constituted a bill of exchange.[25] Chief Justice Lee observed:

> "[I]t was not within the power of the parties to make what form they please pass for such a bill, but it ought to be agreeable to the lex mercatoria: the privilege arises from the convenience to trade, which is not consulted in this case . . . : however, being a mercantile transaction, he left it to the special jury of merchants: who found it to be no bill of exchange . . . ."[26]

In the post-Mansfield era, a more active pattern for juries of merchants can be discerned, especially after the chief justiceship of King's Bench had passed from Lord Kenyon to Lord Ellenborough. Looking back on this time in a case in the Court of Session, involving the sharing of profits between partners, Lord Chancellor Brougham remarked in 1831 that the question

> "comes with peculiar advantage under the cognizance of a learned judge like Lord Ellenborough, and a special jury of merchants in the city of London, who declare what is the result of the facts: no judge ever had greater experience in mercantile law, and no men are better able than those juries to decide by their good sense and mercantile habits".[27]

Clearly Ellenborough believed in the active model of the jury of merchants. In *DeTastet* v. *Baring*, a dishonoured bill of exchange had been drawn from London to Lisbon while Lisbon was blockaded by a British squadron, and the question was whether any exchange or re-exchange of the bill could be allowed, given the state of war between the two nations.[28] Ellenborough was the trial judge, and in presenting the case to the Court of King's Bench for argument:

> "[He] stated the manner in which he had left the case to the jury: which he observed was a special jury consisting of many eminent merchants conversant with the subject, and therefore he had encouraged them to take an active part in the examination of the witnesses; which they had done: and they had drawn their conclusion from the whole evidence, in favour of the defendants against the claim of re-exchange."[29]

I do not know how often merchant jurors were encouraged to participate in the examination of witnesses, though I am certain that the *DeTastet* case was not a singular instance. Repeatedly, in cases covering well over half of the nineteenth century, deference by the judges to the merchant jurors is shown in the case reports. For example, in *Prescott* v. *Flinn*,[30] the Court of

[25] 2 Str. 1211, 93 ER 1134 (1744).
[26] Ibid. at 1212, 1135.
[27] *Thompson* v. *Williamson*, 7 Bligh NS 432, 443–4, 5 ER 833, 837 (1831).
[28] 11 East 265, 102 ER 1006 (1809).
[29] Ibid. at 267, 1007.
[30] 9 Bing. 19, 131 ER 521 (1832).

Common Pleas declined to order a new trial on a question of a clerk's authority to endorse checks because at the first trial,

> "the evidence on this subject was left to a special jury of merchants, who have the right to bring their own knowledge of the general course of business in aid of their judgment on the particular occasion, and they have declared themselves satisfied that the Defendants have, by their conduct, shewn that this clerk had authority to indorse . . .."

And in *Foster* v. *The Mentor Life Assurance Company*,[31] requiring an interpretation of a life insurance policy, Lord Campbell stated:

> "Upon the whole, I am of opinion that a special Jury of the city of London, gentlemen more familiarly acquainted with such transactions than we are, have arrived at a right Conclusion, and that their verdict ought not to be dist-urbed."[32]

There are many other instances in the reports of deference by the judges to juries of merchants. Some illustrations follow:

Justice Grose (King's Bench):

> "Now it must be remembered, that this cause was tried by a special jury of merchants of London, persons peculiarly conversant in commercial transactions, and who perfectly well knew the ordinary risk of such a voyage, and what would vary that risk; and they were of the opinion that the underwriter was not liable."[33]

Chief Justice Eyre (Common Pleas):

> "If I had continued to doubt I should be unwilling to interfere with a verdict of a special jury of merchants on a subject of this kind, unless I clearly saw that some principle of law had been mistaken; or unless I was bound by authorities to pronounce that verdict wrong."[4]

Justice Chambre (Common Pleas):

> "Whether that explanation would have been satisfactory to any of us, sitting as jurymen, I do not know; it has been submitted to a special jury of merchants, who are very competent judges, and they have found on it, and . . . I think they have judged rightly".[35]

Chief Baron Abinger (Exchequer):

> "There was no misdirection upon the letter, the meaning of which, as part of a mercantile correspondence, was left to the judgment of a jury of merchants."[36]

[31] 3 El. & Bl. 48, 118 ER 1058 (1852).
[32] Ibid. At 82–3, 1072.
[33] *Middlewood* v. *Blakes*, 7 T.R. 162 at 168, 101 ER 911 at 914 (1797).
[34] *Driscol* v. *Passmore*, 1 B. & P. 200 at 203, 126 ER 858 at 860 (1798).
[35] *Langhorn* v. *Allnutt*, 4 Taunt. 511 at 518–9, 128 ER 429 at 432 (1812).
[36] *Stewart* v. *Aberdein*, 4 Man. & G. 211 at 227, 150 ER 1406 at 1413 (1838).

Chief Justice Tindal (Common Pleas):

> "The whole case as to the debt due to the factors was summed up, and left to the consideration of the jury, as mercantile men, to draw their own conclusion whether there was a debt or not . . .. [P]laintiffs objected altogether to the principle on which the account was made up by the factors. But, without entering into a discussion on the point, we think this matter was a question peculiarly for the consideration of a jury of merchants; and we cannot see that they have come to a wrong conclusion."[37]

Lord Chancellor Cottenham:

> "It does appear to me to be, of all others, a case which ought to be decided by a Court of law with the assistance of a jury of merchants, who are familiar with the subject-matter, and much better competent than any Judge can be to put a construction upon mercantile terms, and to take a right view of the transactions as between merchants who are in the habit of dealing with questions of this sort."[38]

Justice Crowder (Common Pleas), in chambers, ordered a change of venue from Middlesex to London in a contract dispute over the sale in London of indigo, remarking:

> "I certainly thought that the action would, from its nature, be more satisfactorily tried by a jury of merchants."[39]

Justice Crowder (Common Pleas):

> "The question as to the amount and mode of estimating the damages was very fully gone into. The evidence upon the subject was that of mercantile men, peculiarly conversant with the matter: and the jury was a special jury of Liverpool merchants, than whom none could be more fit to decide such a question. And I must say that I do not consider the amount excessive."[40]

Justice Keating (Common Pleas):

> "Whether or not there had been a breach of contract was for the consideration of the jury . . .. Now, here was a special jury of London merchants, who must be taken to be perfectly well aware of the rule of law that a man must at all events perform his contract: and they came to the conclusion that this defendant did not absolutely refuse to proceed to Copenhagen."[41]

Further manifestations of the active model of the jury of merchants are found in case reports containing volunteered observations by jurors about mercantile practices, often strongly influencing the outcome, and in a case in which insurance companies changed their practices in response to the verdict. The latter case was before Chief Justice Ryder in King's Bench in 1754,

[37] *Bonzi* v. *Stewart*, 4 Man. & G. 295 at 325–6, 134 ER 121 at 133 (1842).
[38] *Malcolm* v. *Scott*, 2 H. & Tw. 440 at 443, 47 ER 1755 at 1757 (1849).
[39] *Begg* v. *Forbes*, 13 C.B. 614 at 615–6, 138 ER 1340 at 1341 (1854).
[40] *Fletcher* v. *Tayleur*, 17 C.B. 21 at 28–9, 139 ER 973 at 976 (1855).
[41] *Pole* v. *Cetcovich*, 9 C.B. N.S. 430 at 440, 142 ER 169 at 173 (1860).

Cantilton v. *The London Assurance Company*, where a jury of merchants was of the opinion that a term of a policy ("unless the ship be stranded") constituted a condition.[42]

In *Hoare* v. *Dickson*, a case coming before Baron Parke at the Surrey assizes in 1849:[43]

> "the jury (a special jury) expressed so strong an opinion—in which the learned judge coincided—that there was no ground for the action, that the plaintiff's counsel consented to be nonsuited."[44]

And in *Rucker* v. *Lunt*, at the London sittings of the Court of Exchequer at Guildhall in 1863, insurance brokers sued to recover a commission of ten per cent:[45]

> "One of the jurymen said that he himself and one or two of his colleagues had experience in like matters, and were convinced that such was the understanding in London."

Baron Martin recollected that such a custom had been "found by a special jury at Guildhall about thirty years ago". Defendant's counsel threatened to call witnesses to express the contrary view, but after plaintiffs called two witnesses who endorsed the custom, defendant's counsel said that he could not hope for a verdict, and the jury found for the plaintiffs.[46]

A good example of the volunteered comment by a merchant juror is found in *Brough* v. *Whitmore*, an action on an insurance policy for coverage of the loss of a ship's stores and provisions which had accidentally burned up while in a warehouse during ship repairs.[47] At the trial before Lord Kenyon, the defendant claimed that the provisions were not protected by the policy:

> "but one of the [special] jury said that it had been determined in Lord Mansfield's time that they were included under the word 'furniture', under which decisions the merchants in the city had since acquiesced; on which the plaintiffs obtained a verdict."

Other instances are supplied in cases tried before Lord Ellenborough in the King's Bench. In *Wright* v. *Shiffner*, Ellenborough stated his understand-

42 Unreported, but discussed by Lord Kenyon in *Burnett* v. *Kensington*, 7 T.R. 210 at 222, 101 ER 937 at 943 (1797).

43 7 C.B. 164, 137 ER 67 (1849).

44 Ibid. at 167, 68.

45 3 F.& F. 960, 176 ER 437 (1863).

46 An interesting variation is shown in *Poingdestre* v. *Royal Exchange*, Ry. & Moody 378 at 379, 171 ER 1055 at 1056 (1826), when Serjeant Bosanquet proposed to call merchants and insurers to prove an insurance usage applicable to the facts, but: "Best, C.J. interposed and said that it would scarcely be insisted upon by the plaintiff, that witnesses should be called to establish that usage before a special jury of London, every one of whom must be perfectly cognizant of the fact of the usage. The jury assented to this . . . ." The verdict, therefore, went for the defendants.

47 4 T.R. 207, 100 ER 976 (1791).

ing of the application of the terms of an insurance policy written on a voyage from Surinam in the West Indies to London,[48] after which:

> "Mr. Taylor, a special juryman, said, that this was the construction universally put upon these policies in the city of London."

This gave the plaintiff the verdict. In *Gantt* v. *Mackenzie*, the question concerned damages payable by the drawer of a dishonored foreign bill of exchange:[49]

> "Lord Ellenborough left this upon the custom of merchants, to the gentlemen of the special jury: who said, the holder of the bill was entitled to £10 per cent damages, and that interest was to be allowed only from the time when the bill was presented for payment . . . ."

In another case, the jurors explained a practice in legal terms. Plaintiff in *Spear* v. *Travers* sued successfully for undelivered goods that had been paid for, and in giving its verdict:

> "The gentlemen of the special jury observed, that in practice the indorsed dock warrants and certificates are handed from seller to buyer as a complete transfer of the goods."[50]

Numerous comparable examples of influential merchant juror opinions appear in the reports.[51]

One case in the Court of Common Pleas in 1832 shows how blurred the line was between merchant juror and witness. In *Elton* v. *Larkins*, the question was whether a person buying a policy of insurance was obliged to state to the underwriter facts that were contained in Lloyd's List, which the underwriter could inspect.[52] The court ruled that disclosure was required, and in reaching the decision, heard the testimony of a witness named Willis. At the time, Willis was serving as foreman of the special jury in a cause being heard by the Court of King's Bench, but Chief Justice

[48] 2 Camp. 247, 249, 170 ER 1145, 1146 (1809).

[49] 3 Camp. 51, 170 ER 1303 (1811).

[50] 4 Camp. 251 at 252–3, 171 ER 80 at 81 (1815).

[51] See, for example, *Baring* v. *Vaux*, 2 Camp. 541 at 543, 170 ER 1245 (1810) ["The gentlemen of the special jury said, they were clearly of opinion the ship was not to be considered as in port when she was captured, and immediately found a verdict for the plaintiff"]; *Pearce* v. *Cowie*, 4 Camp. 363 at 365, 171 ER 116 (1814) ["The gentlemen of the special jury corroborated this statement, and observed that many cargoes of cotton from Amelia Island had been allowed to be imported both into London and Liverpool, in neutral vessels of European build"]; *Levi* v. *Barnes*, Holt 412 at 415, 171 ER 288 at 289 (1816)["The jury (which was a special jury of merchants) found a verdict for the plaintiffs, and stated that it was their unanimous opinion that the allowance was a gratuity merely"]; *Friere* v. *Woodhouse*, Holt 572 at 574, 171 ER 345 at 345–56 (1817)["The jury, which was a special jury of merchants, said, that inasmuch as the arrival of the 'Victorioso', and of the other vessels was noticed in Lloyd's List at the time the insurance was effected, and as these Lists were in the hands of the underwriters, they were of opinion that there was no concealment"].

[52] 5 Car. & P. 385, 172 ER 1020 (1832).

Tenterden permitted Willis to leave the jury box to come into the Common Pleas to be examined, where Willis stated, among other things:

> "It is my practice, in an extensive connection as a broker, to communicate all information as to the time of sailing."[53]

A final question about the jury of merchants cases, perhaps the critical question, is how the legal community viewed the merchant juror pronouncements. Were they law? If so, how so? I earlier mentioned the case of *Brough* v. *Whitmore*, where a special juryman explained that a ship's stores and provisions came within the term "furniture" in an insurance policy.[54] Lord Kenyon's opening remarks in his opinion in the case were a bit forlorn; he stated:

> "On the trial of this cause I had nothing to guide my judgment on the construction of this instrument but the words of the policy; and when it was stated that 'provisions' were included in the word 'furniture', I confess I was somewhat at a loss to know to what extent the underwriters were liable on words so indefinite as these which are used."

He then wondered aloud about whose job it was to say what the words meant, observing:

> "But then I thought, and still continue to think, that the rule of law is to be given (not by merchants) but by the Court; though, when a question arises on the construction of the words of an instrument which are in themselves ambiguous, it is a matter fairly within the province of those who alone act upon such instruments to declare the meaning of them."[55]

He added that only help from Lombard street on the uniform practice of merchants and underwriters rendered insurance policies intelligible.

Years later, in the case of *Lucas* v. *Dorrien*, the question before the Court of King's Bench was whether an indorsement of the delivery checks or warrants of the West India Docks would pass the property in the goods covered by the warrants.[56] Both sides naturally referred to the case of *Spear* v. *Travers*,[57] where the special jurors had said that indorsed dock warrants effected a complete transfer of goods. In *Lucas*, Serjeant Best tried to shake off the earlier case by observing:

> "The special jury [in *Spear*] certainly mentioned the practice. The usage of merchants is undoubtedly part of the law of the land; but these ephemeral practices are not."[58]

[53] Ibid. at 390, 1023.
[54] 4 T.R. 206, 100 ER 976 (1791), *supra* n. 47.
[55] Ibid. at 208, 977.
[56] 7 Taunt. 278, 129 ER 112 (1816).
[57] *Supra*, n. 50.
[58] 7 Taunt. 287, 129 ER 115.

The court, however, was not persuaded, and in his opinion, Justice Dallas observed:

> "I have been several times stopped by a special jury, they being satisfied that the goods pass from hand to hand by indorsement of these instruments. All special juries cry out with one voice, that the practice is, that the produce lodged in the docks is transferred by indorsing over the certificates and dock warrants . . . ."[59]

Clearly, therefore, merchant jurors played an important role in articulating mercantile practices that had legal implications. It is too much, however, to say that undisputed merchant practices that were brought out in litigation automatically became part of the common law. Practices might do so, as in *Spear* and *Lucas*, where they made sense to the court and offended no established legal principle, but not otherwise. In a case before Lord Kenyon, for example, a special juror stated that the practice with underwriters was to subscribe a slip or short memorandum of proposed insurance which was considered binding in the ordinary course of business, but Kenyon said:

> "[W]hatever obligation of this kind there might be in point of honour and good faith, the underwriter certainly would not be bound in law, for the assured in order to support his claim in a Court of justice must produce a stamped policy."[60]

And in *Rickford* v. *Ridge*, Lord Ellenborough simply rejected as nonsense a banking practice that everyone agreed was uniformly followed.[61] Bankers from Fleet Street testified that they often waited overnight to present for payment cheques that came in the post after the banks' daily shipment of cheques for payment had gone out, but a special juror

> "observed (and it was on both sides allowed to be so), that the practice is different with all London bankers east of St. Paul's, who present for payment all checques [sic] and bills the very same day they receive them by the post."

Ellenborough said:

> "I cannot hear of any arbitrary distinction between one part of the city and another. It is not competent to bankers to lay down one rule for the eastward of St. Paul's, and another for the westward."[62]

In the *Rickford* case, the result reached by the special jury—that it was reasonable to wait until the next day to present the late-arriving cheques for payment—was agreeable to the court. Some years earlier, however, precisely

[59] Ibid. at 290, 117.

[60] As noted in J Arnould, *Treatise on the Law of Marine Insurance and Average, with References to the American cases and the Later Continental Authorities*, 2nd edn (London, Stevens and Norton, Sweet & Maxwell, 1857), vol. 1, 50–1, quoted in *Parry* v. *Great Ship Company*, 4 B. & S. 556, 122 ER 568 (1864).

[61] 2 Camp. 537, 170 ER 1243 (1810).

[62] Ibid. at 539, 1244.

the same issue came before King's Bench in a series of cases in which special juries stubbornly insisted on what we can call, for short, "same day deposit". I discuss these in the Mansfield volumes, because they exhibit a struggle within the Court of King's Bench with whether the court had the power to declare as a matter of law what a reasonable time should be for making the deposits, thereby sweeping away jury verdicts consistently going wrong.[63] Justice Buller argued strongly that the court should declare the matter one of law, characterising the cases as "a disgrace to Westminster Hall". Lord Mansfield ultimately agreed with Buller, but, perhaps in deference to special jurors with whom he had worked for so long, was very hesitant to take the step. Yet it was a step that had to be taken; otherwise juries, special or not, would be empowered to insist upon verdicts that in the eyes of the judges were senseless. A good example of the difficulty, and a last case in this discussion of the jury of merchants, is *Scrimshire* v. *Alderton*, decided by the Court of King's Bench in 1743.[64] There, the question was whether a farmer who had consigned goods to a factor had an action against a buyer who had arranged purchase of the goods from the factor, after which the factor had failed before being paid by the buyer. Chief Justice Lee thought the action was valid and directed the jury to find for the plaintiff farmer, but the jury

> "went out and found for the defendant; were sent out a second, and a third time to re-consider it, and still adhered to their verdict; and being asked man by man, they separately declared they found for the defendant."

Lee granted a new trial, and the case came on again, this time before a special jury. Lee "declared, that a factor's sale does by the general rule of law create a contract between the owner and buyer".[65] Nevertheless, the jury found for the defendant, telling the court that under the circumstances proved, they thought the buyer answerable to the factor only. There the case ended, however unsatisfactorily to the court.

CHANCERY CASES

Many Chancery cases have been mentioned already in discussing juries of merchants, but there are three further matters on which the CD-ROM search of "jury" appearances in Chancery cases proved illuminating. The first relates to the earliest appearances in English law of the special jury.

[63] See the discussion of *Metcalf* v. *Hall*, *Appleton* v. *Sweetapple*, and *Tindal* v. *Brown* in Oldham, *supra* n. 16, vol. 1, 158–60; also case transcriptions *ibid.*, vol. 1, 371–7. Interestingly, in the *Metcalf* case, Mansfield noted that there was evidence of different customs east and west of Mansion House.

[64] 2 Str. 1182, 93 ER 1114 (1743).

[65] Ibid. at 1183, 1115.

The second relates to an issue of current importance in the United States on the scope of jury trial preserved in civil cases by the Seventh Amendment to the US Constitution. The third pertains to the rule in English practice that disqualified parties to litigation from testifying under oath in their own cases.

The early appearance of the special jury

The common law practice that became the special jury was described in the 1665 edition of *Trials per Pais* as applicable to cases involving "matters of great consequence":

> "[I]n such Cases (everyone knowes) the Court most commonly orders the Prothonotary to chuse 48 out of the Sheriff's Book of Freeholders, of the most substantial men in the County, and the parties strike out 12 a piece, then the Sheriff returns the rest."[66]

In my study of the origins of the special jury, I speculated about what evidence there was that, as of 1665, this procedure was indeed something that "everyone knowes". I wrote:

> "An examination of the reports from King's Bench, Common Pleas, and Exchequer throughout the 1600s yields only a handful of such cases . . . ."

Moreover, those cases were far from clear.[67] Conspicuously absent from my search of the case reports was the Court of Chancery, and I now discover two Chancery cases, one decided in 1670 and the other 1677, conforming exactly to the formulation in the 1665 edition of *Trials per Pais*. In the first, *Yeavely* v. *Yeavely*, there was a question of whether one Anthony was dead on a specific date.[68] Lord Keeper Bridgman referred the question to a trial at law at the Derby assizes,

> "and the Sheriff of the County was to attend the Prothonotary with the Book of Freeholders, who is to return forty-eight Persons, out of which each is to strike twelve, and the remaining twenty-four to be impanel'd as an indifferent Jury to try the said Issue . . . ."

A virtually identical order was issued in 1677 in *Devenreux* v. *Devenreux*, specifying as well that depositions of dead witnesses should be read, plus those of witnesses unable to attend the trial.[69]

[66] S E, *Trials per Pais* (London, 1665) 73. As I have previously noted, the "S.E." stands for Samson Euer, but the work quickly became identified with Giles Duncombe, who is the author of subsequent editions. Whether Euer or Duncombe wrote the first edition is unclear. See Oldham *supra* n. 15, at n. 30.

[67] Oldham, "Origins", *supra* n. 15, 183–4.

[68] 3 Ch. Ca. 44, 21 ER 741 (1670).

[69] Rep. t. Finch 324, 23 ER 178 (1677).

The Seventh Amendment and the jury

The Seventh Amendment issue relates to an ongoing debate in American constitutional law on whether it would be constitutional to dispense with the jury in complex civil litigation.[70] The Supreme Court once hinted that this might be possible, but despite a little activity in the lower federal courts, the proposition has not been established. The Seventh Amendment provides that, in suits at common law involving more than twenty dollars, the right to jury trial shall be preserved. What right to jury trial? Justice Story, in an opinion in 1812, thought the answer obvious—the right to jury trial that would have been available according to "the common law of England, the grand reservoir of all our jurisprudence".[71] Later, the Court said that the benchmark year for the right to jury trial in England was 1791, the year the Seventh Amendment became effective.[72] This has come to be known as "the historical test", and the Supreme Court strongly adheres to it to the present day.[73]

In one skirmish in the federal circuit courts, an attempt was made to persuade the court to rule that a jury was not required, and legal historians Morris Arnold and Patrick Devlin were commissioned on opposing sides to carry out studies of the question.[74] These were published in the *Pennsylvania Law Review* and the *Columbia Law Review*, and Lord Devlin followed up with another article in the *Michigan Law Review* several years later.[75] One of the central points of contention was whether it could be shown that there was in the English law of the applicable period, a recognised principle that, if a case was complicated, the Court of Chancery did not have to send it to the common law courts, even though there were contested questions of fact. Devlin claimed that this could be demonstrated; Arnold disagreed. In their original opposing articles, the debate revolved around two cases, *Clench* v. *Townley* and *Blad* v. *Bamfield*.[76] With the help of John Baker, Arnold effectively showed that *Clench* could not stand for

[70] I have written about this in a recently-published *Festschrift* for Brian Simpson. See J Oldham, "The Seventh Amendment Right to Jury Trial: Late-Eighteenth-Century Practice Reconsidered", in K O'Donovan and G R Rubin (eds), *Human Rights and Legal History* (Oxford, University Press, 2000), 225. I revisit the issue here to feature the CD-ROM discoveries.

[71] *United States* v. *Wonson*, 28 F.Cas. 745, 750 (C.C.D. Mass. 1812).

[72] *Thompson* v. *Utah*, 170 U.S. 343 (1898).

[73] See, e.g., *Markman* v. *Westview Instruments, Inc.*, 517 US 370 (1996).

[74] The case was *In re. Japanese Products Antitrust Litigation*, 631 F.2d 1069 (3d. Cir. 1980).

[75] The original articles were P Devlin, "Jury Trial of Complex Cases: English Practice at the Time of the Seventh Amendment", (1980) 80 *Columbia LR* 43; M Arnold, "A Historical Inquiry into the Right to Trial by Jury in Complex Civil Litigation", (1980) 128 *Pennsylvania LR* 829. Lord Devlin's follow-up article was P Devlin, "Equity, Due Process and the Seventh Amendment: A Commentary on the *Zenith* Case", (1983) 81 *Michigan LR* 1571.

[76] Respectively, Carey 23, 21 ER 13 (1603); 3 Swans. 604 at 607, 36 ER 992 at 993 (1674).

much, certainly not what Devlin claimed. And Arnold brushed aside *Blad* as standing "for the simple proposition that suits involving foreign relations ought to be tried in prerogative courts".[77]

Devlin, in his later article, placed heavy emphasis on an 1804 Irish Chancery case, *O'Connor* v. *Spaight*,[78] decided by Lord Redesdale, who, in his pre-titled life as John Mitford, had written *A Treatise on the Pleadings in Suits in the Court of Chancery*, first published in London in 1780, and substantially revised for a 1789 edition.[79] In the treatise, Mitford explained that courts of equity had assumed jurisdiction "in a variety of complicated cases of account [and other matters]" and

> "seem by degrees to have been considered as having on these subjects a concurrent jurisdiction with the courts of common law . . .."[80]

And in *O'Connor*, Lord Redesdale (Mitford) stated:

> "The ground on which I think this is a proper case for equity, is, that the account has become so complicated that a court of law would be incompetent to examine it upon a trial at *Nisi Prius*, with all necessary accuracy . . .. This is a principle upon which courts of equity constantly act . . .."[81]

In his *Columbia Law Review* article, Devlin deals briefly with the case of *Gyles* v. *Wilcox*, decided by Lord Hardwicke in 1740;[82] yet the case seems to me to have more persuasive force than is suggested by the half-page devoted to it.[83] Devlin mentions only one of the two published reports, and omits any reference to the arbitration feature of the case.[84] *Gyles* was a copyright infringement case brought under the Statute of Queen Anne. Fletcher Gyles was a bookseller who published an edition of Matthew Hale's *Pleas of the Crown*. Wilcox then published a volume called *Modern Crown Law*, which Gyles claimed was nothing but his book with a few obsolete statutes omitted and with all the Latin and French quotations translated into English. Lord Hardwicke, in Atkyns' report, observed that the question was whether Wilcox's work was a fair abridgment, which it would not be if merely "colourably shortened". He then stated:

[77] Arnold, *supra*, n. 75, 846.

[78] 1 *Sch. & Lef.* 305 (1804).

[79] See Devlin, "Equity, Due Process and the Seventh Amendment", *supra* n. 75, 1571, n. 3.

[80] J Mitford, *A Treatise on the Pleadings in Suits in the Court of Chancery*, 2nd edn (Dublin 1789) 111, quoted by Devlin, "Equity, Due Process and the Seventh Amendment", *supra* n. 75, at 1629.

[81] 1 *Sch. & Lef.* at 309, quoted by Devlin"Equity, Due Process and the Seventh Amendment", *supra* n. 75, at 1628.

[82] 2 Atk. 141, 26 ER 489 (1740), Barn. C. 368, 27 ER 682, with further proceedings reported at 3 Atk. 270, 26 ER 957 (*sub. nom. Gyles* v. *Wilcocks*).

[83] See Devlin, "Jury Trial of Complex Cases", *supra* n. 75, at 73.

[84] In ibid., 77–80, Devlin discusses the arbitration features of the Common Law Procedure Act of 1854 and subsequent reform legislation, mainly as they related to actions of account.

"Mr. Attorney General has said I may send it to law to be determined by a jury: but how can this possibly be done? It would be absurd for the chief justice to sit and hear both books read over, which is absolutely necessary, to judge between them, whether the one is only a copy from the other.

The court is not under an indispensable obligation to send all facts to a jury, but may refer them to a master, to state them, where it is a question of nicety and difficulty, and more fit for men of learning to inquire into, than a common jury.

This I think is one of those cases where it would be much better for the parties to fix upon two persons of learning and abilities in the profession of the law, who would accurately and carefully compare them, and report their opinion to the court.

The House of Lords very often, in matters of account which are extremely perplexed and intricate, refer it to two merchants named by the parties, to consider the case, and report their opinions upon it, rather than leave it to a jury; and I should think a reference of the same kind in some measure would be the properest method in the present case".[85]

Accordingly, a reference to arbitration was agreed to.[86]

The *Gyles* opinion, of course, is not dispositive of whether there was, in equity, a generalised "complexity exception" to the practice of sending factual questions to law for jury determinations. In an 1803 case involving tithes owing on land, Lord Eldon observed:

"Beyond all question, it belongs to the constitution of a Court of Equity to decide upon matters of fact, if they think proper . . .."

He added, however, that:

"Courts of Equity have for a great number of years, where questions of fact have been disputable, thought it a more proper exercise of their jurisdiction, to have them determined by a jury."[87]

Nevertheless, Lord Hardwicke's language in *Gyles*, the preeminence of Hardwicke as both a common law judge and as Lord Chancellor, and the fact that the case was *not* the typical problem of accounts combine to make the case a strong precedent. Also forceful is the version of Hardwicke's opinion in Barnes' report of *Gyles*. According to Barnes, Hardwicke acknowledged that:

[85] 2 Atk. at 144, 27 ER at 490–1. Only the first two paragraphs of this passage were quoted by Lord Devlin, "Jury Trial of Complex Cases", *supra* n. 75, at 73.

[86] In a brief note at 3 Atk. 269, 27 ER 957, the agreement to arbitrate is indicated. With consent of the parties, Lord Hardwicke issued an order referring all matters in dispute to the award and determination of Mr Cay and Mr Thomas Stephens, with the customary terms of such an order set out. On this procedure, see H Horwitz and J Oldham, "John Locke, Lord Mansfield, and Arbitration During the Eighteenth Century", (1993) 36 *Historical Journal* 137.

[87] *O'Connor* v. *Cook*, 8 Ves. Jr. 535 at 536, 32 ER 463 (1803). See also Lord Eldon's earlier opinion in the same case, *O'Connor* v. *Cook*, 6 Ves. Jr. 665 at 671 31 ER 1247 at 1250 (1802). Where there was no reasonable doubt, however, Chancery would keep the case, as shown in *Short* v. *Lee*, 2 Jac. & W. 464, 37 ER 705 (1821), esp. at 502, 719.

"Whether the second Book is the same Book with the former is a Matter of Fact, and a Fact of Difficulty to be determined."

Then:

"It has been hinted, that as this is a Matter of Fact the Court may send it to be tried before a Jury, but the Court is not confined to send all Matters of Fact to be tried in that Way. Where the Matter indeed consists of a single Fact, or of two or three Facts, the Court does take that Method to determine them, but where the Facts are of an extensive Nature, as Matters of Account, or the like, the Court does not take that Method to determine them, but directs them to be inquired into before the Master. ... And in order that the Master may better determine the Matter, his Lordship said that he did not see but he ought to direct, that the Master should be attended by two Persons skilled in the Profession of the Law, to assist him. And Directions of this Sort have been made in Mathematical and Algebraical Inquiries. But his Lordship said he should choose, that two Persons should be agreed upon by Consent of both Parties to attend the Master in this Matter, rather than the Court should appoint them; for which Reason his Lordship said, he would direct that the Matter should stand over for a Week . . .."[88]

Disqualification of parties

In past work I have argued that the "party witness rule"—the rule in the common law courts that, until late in the nineteenth century, prevented parties to litigation from testifying under oath because they were considered too interested in the outcome to be trustworthy—had a perverse effect, impeding the discovery of the true facts in dispute.[89] I have also pointed out how it came to be standard in Lord Mansfield's orders referring cases to arbitration to provide that the parties should testify under oath before the arbitrator.[90] These orders were issued with consent, to be sure, but the fact that it became standard to provide for the parties' sworn testimony signifies, I think, that Mansfield understood long before its demise that the party witness rule made little sense. This perception, it turns out, may have grown out of Chancery practice.

In the Seventh Amendment discussion above, the practice of the Court of Chancery in not sending to law matters of account was noted, as was the standard reason given—that accounts can be quite complex. Yet another reason was given by Fleming James in a 1963 article on the right to jury trial in civil actions. James first noted that:

"At law the parties to an action were neither competent nor compellable to testify, whereas in equity each party could offer his own sworn statements and also

[88] Barn.C. 368, 27 ER 682.

[89] See J. Oldham, "Truth-Telling in the Eighteenth-Century Courtroom", (1994) 12 *Law and History Review* 95 at 107–17.

[90] See Oldham, *supra* n. 16, vol. 1, 154.

> 'probe the conscience' of his adversary by propounding written interrogatories, which had to be answered under oath."

He then observed:

> "Where an accounting between business associates was sought, if the inquiry was to have the benefit of the testimony of the parties (the two witnesses who could shed the most—sometimes the only—light on the matter), it would have to be conducted in equity, where the chancellor would decide questions of fact without a jury."[91]

Even more interesting than James' pragmatic observations is the realisation that even while the party witness rule persisted in the law courts, the Court of Chancery sometimes ordered that the parties give sworn testimony in cases sent to law. This required some explaining. In a 1706 case, *Ibbotson* v. *Rhodes*, the referral order said that the plaintiff should admit the defendant's answer to be read at trial, not as evidence, which it could not be, and not as an admission that it was true, but just so that the oath the defendant took could "weigh with the Jury"—so that the defendant could have the benefit of his oath at law as he does in Chancery.[92] William Fortescue, Master of the Rolls, later declined to follow *Ibbotson*;[93] by Lord Eldon's time, however, the procedure had revived.

In *De Tastet* v. *Bordenave*,[94] the Master of the Rolls referred the case to King's Bench for a jury trial and included an order for the examination of the parties under oath. The trial was conducted at the Guildhall; both parties were examined, and the verdict was for the defendant. Plaintiff petitioned for a rehearing on the Master of the Rolls' order that the parties be examined, and moved as well for a new trial. Counsel for plaintiff contended:

> "that the order for examining both parties at trial was unprecedented, and that such orders could not be made, except by consent, or in bankruptcy, where the course of proceeding is altogether different, the affidavits of the parties interested being admitted."[95]

Absent consent or a bankruptcy matter, plaintiff's counsel contended that a party could be examined at law only where he was a nominal party without interest,

> "or if he be interested, where the opposite party is desirous of interrogating him before a jury, for the purpose of eliciting from him admissions against himself,

[91] F James, Jr, "Right to a Jury Trial in Civil Actions", (1963) 72 *Yale LJ* 655, at 662 (footnotes omitted).

[92] 1 Eq. Cas. Abr. 230, 21 ER 1010 (1706).

[93] *Only* v. *Walker*, 3 Atk. 407, 26 ER 1095 (1746). Fortescue refused to order that defendants' answers be read at the common law jury trial.

[94] Jacob 515, 37 ER 945 (1822).

[95] Ibid. at 518, 946.

hoping to prove his story fabricated, by subjecting him to the scrutiny of a rigid cross-examination"

—which would be "quite analogous to the usual course in equity: it is only substituting a *viva voce* for a written examination." But in the case being argued, counsel pointed out that there was not much other evidence than the statements of the parties, and:

> "A court of equity cannot . . . act upon evidence of this description: the statements of the parties themselves could be of no effect at the hearing, except as against themselves; then upon what principle can such proofs be let in through the medium of a jury?"[96]

The Master of the Rolls (Sir Thomas Plummer) denied both the petition and the motion, observing that,

> "An issue [sent to law], being intended to inform the conscience of the Court, may be tried in any manner and with any qualifications which the Court thinks fit."[97]

The case was then appealed to Lord Eldon.

Lord Eldon first observed that an order for the examination of the parties in cases referred to the law courts was very common in bankruptcy and in other causes as well, and when the order (as in the case before him) was imperative, there was no option—both parties had to be examined. He remarked:

> "This matter is often mistaken at common law. Where the parties are to be examined, it is not meant that they should be witnesses for themselves or for the other side, but they are witnesses for this Court."[98]

Later in his opinion, he explained that, when a bill for an injunction rests upon an affidavit that is directly contradicted by another affidavit, "the Court [of Chancery] does not know how to deal between the two", and thus would have to be neutral, so that plaintiff could not prevail. One possibility, however, would be to refer the case to law, as the Master of the Rolls had done in the case at bar, apparently thinking:

> "that if there should be a verdict for the Plaintiff, the affidavit of the Defendant would be displaced by it, and that he would then be able to act upon the affidavit of the Plaintiff, which he could not do while it was contrasted with the other."

Then Lord Eldon concluded that the Master of the Rolls,

> "was quite right, that upon this application, with these affidavits, it was very fit that the jury should try the credit of these parties; and it should be understood

96 Ibid.
97 Ibid. at 521, 947.
98 Ibid. at 520, 947.

that when they are ordered to be examined, they are not to be considered as the witnesses of either side but of this Court which orders them to be examined".[99]

CONCLUSION

I have explored cases pertaining to the jury by searching for appearances of a specific writ (*de ventre inspiciendo*), of an unindexed but recurrent type of jury (the jury of merchants), and of the jury in Chancery cases. I trust that these examples amply demonstrate the exceptional value of the CD-ROM version of the English Reports as a finding aid. Many other paths might have been taken. On a number of additional topics I ran searches and produced "hit lists", but must leave them for future research opportunities. These topics included the writ *de medietate linguae*,[100] the writ of inquiry,[101] hundredors,[102] "juries of gentlemen", and "excessive damages". Your imagination will supply other topics that would be of interest to explore.

Finally, I promised a word about the mistakes in the CD-ROM text. There are hundreds, no, thousands, of mistakes. Presumably these will be culled out in time, but, at present, the ocean of mistakes produced by whatever scanning technology was used means that it is not safe to purchase the CD in lieu of the printed volumes. A few examples may prove the point, and these are recorded more or less at random: Appearing at times instead of "cases" is "cages"; instead of "bad" appears "had"; instead of "existence" appears "exist once"; "do one" shows up instead of "no one"; "ill grounded"

[99] Ibid. at 522, 947. For an earlier case showing Lord Eldon's struggles with the problem of differences in evidentiary rules between the equity and law courts, including the complications of the party witness rule, see *The East India Company* v. *Donald*, 9 Ves. Jun. 274, 32 ER 608 (1804). It is interesting that the Court of Chancery in some circumstances trusts common law juries to "try the credit" of the parties notwithstanding the parties' interests (since, as Lord Eldon pointed out, the testimony is being given not on behalf of either side but for the Court of Chancery), while in other contexts, Chancery points out that parol evidence would be too prejudicial to be permitted to go before a jury. Thus in a note appended to *Countess of Gainsborough* v. *Earl of Gainsborough*, 1 Eq. Cas. Abr. 230, 21 ER 1010 (1691), parol evidence of a Testator's intent was said to be allowable before a court (where "it can do no hurt, being to inform the Conscience of the Court, who cannot be biased or prejudiced by it") but not before a jury ("lest the Jury might be inveigled by it"); ibid. at 230, 1011. Likewise, in *Newton* v. *Preston*, Prec. Ch. 103, 24 ER 50 (1699), parol evidence was permitted, "for tho' at law it is not to be allowed, where a jury may be inveigled by that which is not proper evidence, yet here is no such danger." These examples are admittedly long before Lord Eldon's time, but they were only a few years ahead of the *Ibbotson* case, *supra* n. 92.

[100] Literally, "of the half-tongue", a writ used to call a mixed jury of Englishmen and foreigners when the defendant was a foreigner. See Oldham, "Origins", *supra* n. 15, at 167–71.

[101] This is the writ that customarily issued when plaintiffs recovered default judgments, and a jury was to be called to assess damages. The "hit list" here is quite long, and it is a subject that seems to hold potential for fruitful study.

[102] In early times, there were requirements that a specified number of "hundredors" (residents of the "hundred") be on juries. See Oldham, "Origins", *supra* n. 15, at 164–7.

becomes "ingrounded"; and two favourites—instead of "left out" we have "left gut," and instead of "stated the manner", we have "stated the mariner".

This problem, nonetheless, interferes little with the power of the CD-ROM as a search engine. In preparing this paper, I have learned a great deal about the jury topics searched, and I expect the word-search procedure to become an indispensible part of any research project that utilises printed case reports to any significant extent. We will, I am sure, appreciate the benefits of CD-ROM research, just as legal historians did when the convenience of 176 volumes of The English Reports materialised. We will also, just as surely now as then, succumb to a melancholy nostalgia for days gone by—for the smell, the dust, the historical *presence* that seems to live on in the nominate reports.

9

The Limits of Discretion: Forgery and the Jury at the Old Bailey, 1818–21

PHILIP HANDLER (LEICESTER)

The crime of forging Bank of England notes was rife in the first twenty years of the nineteenth century. The Bank's suspension of cash payments and first ever issue of small notes in 1797 had unleashed an epidemic of forgeries and an avalanche of prosecutions. In the period 1818–21 the situation reached a crisis point. Two juries at the Old Bailey refused to convict any of the prisoners charged with the capital offence of uttering forged notes in December 1818. The evidence was complete, the judge had given clear instructions to convict and yet the jurors acquitted. Trial juries in eighteenth- and early-nineteenth-century criminal trials frequently used their discretion to mitigate the severity of the law, but seldom rejected it in such a direct and open manner. The acquittals precipitated a crisis within the criminal justice system that was not fully resolved until the Bank withdrew all its small notes from circulation in 1821. Central to the whole of the crisis was the trial jury and its ability to frustrate the operation of the law in defiance of the judiciary and the Bank of England. This right to nullify the law was particularly controversial at the time, as the debate over criminal law reform gathered pace in Parliament. In 1819, a House of Commons Select Committee produced a report that was to pave the way for many of the reforms that were to transform the role of the jury over the ensuing decades.[1] By mid-century penal law reforms and procedural changes had drastically restricted the extent of the jury's discretion in criminal trials, rendering impossible the sort of outright rejection of the law exhibited in the forgery trials of 1818. This paper investigates the picture, which the forgery crisis reveals, of the early-nineteenth-century criminal trial jury on the eve of its reform.

The discussion is divided into four sections. The first is concerned with the circumstances that made forgery such a dangerous offence at the beginning of the nineteenth century. The second examines the composition of the Old Bailey juries and the context in which their decisions were taken, to try

[1] *Select Committee on the Criminal Laws as Relates to Capital Punishment* PP 1819 (585) VIII, 5 (hereafter cited as SC 1819).

to reconstruct the motives behind the verdicts. The jurors had particular, economic interests in the problem of forged notes and the acquittals of December 1818 offered a clear illustration of the power that juries possessed to express those interests. This aspect forms the third section where the jurors' discretion to reach a verdict according to their own, rather than the judicial, conception of the law is examined. Finally the discussion turns to the effect that the forgery crisis had both inside and outside the courtroom. The acquittals brought the Bank's whole system of prosecutions to the verge of collapse and had a crucial influence on the criminal law reform movement and the decision to resume cash payments in 1819.

THE PROBLEM OF FORGED BANK NOTES

The 1797 Bank Restriction Act, prompted by a shortage of gold during the Napoleonic wars, suspended cash payments and forced the Bank of England to issue £1 and £2 notes for the first time.[2] Prior to 1797, notes of under £5 had been illegal and £5 notes had only been introduced in 1793. The result of the restriction was that bank notes now had to be used in numerous petty transactions by people unused to dealing with paper money. Further, the Bank of England had not made any plans to issue notes and consequently the first batch it issued was of poor quality, printed using old and worn plates.[3] The ease with which these notes could be forged and their widespread use provided much greater scope for the commission of the crime. In the eighteenth century forgery had been a rare crime, the preserve of literate middle class offenders who needed skill to execute the forgery and audacity to carry it off. Following the restriction, complex criminal operations developed involving forgers, sellers, and utterers of counterfeit notes. In the 21 years prior to the restriction there were six prosecutions for offences relating to the forgery of Bank of England notes, in the 21 years after there were 860.[4]

The Bank of England adopted a new system of prosecution to deal with this increase in which two charges were brought against each prisoner, one capital and one minor. The capital offence was for forging, or uttering a bank note, knowing it to be forged; the minor was for possessing a note, knowing it to be forged.[5] Most prisoners were allowed to plead guilty to the offence of possession, punishable with 14 years transportation, in which

[2] 37 Geo. III, c. 45.

[3] A Mackenzie, *The Bank of England Note: A History of its Printing* (Cambridge, University Press, 1953), 47.

[4] 1 Parliamentary Debates XXXVIII (1818), 697.

[5] The capital indictments were founded upon 45 Geo. III, c. 89. This statute superseded 15 Geo. II, c. 13 and changed the wording from "uttering and publishing" to "disposing and putting away" as the latter was more inclusive. The indictments for the minor offence of possession were founded upon 41 Geo. III, c. 39.

case the Bank declined to proceed on the capital charge. If the prisoner refused to plead guilty, or if the Bank viewed the crime as being particularly serious, a capital trial would follow. In this way the Bank was able to maintain a balance between terror and mercy in the pre-trial process in the same way as pardons were used after conviction.

The Bank paid the expenses of the prosecution and took an active role in the detection of offenders. The majority of the prosecutions were still initiated by private traders who had taken a forged note, but the Bank also employed agents to entrap suspected utterers into selling or passing forged notes. The traders and agents were the key witnesses in the trials, along with the Bank inspector who gave evidence that the note in question was a forgery. The Bank prosecutions attracted little criticism in the press or in Parliament until the number of counterfeit notes in circulation rose from 25,000 in 1816 to 31,000 in 1817.[6] The rise prompted the Bank to appoint a committee to examine plans to improve the notes and, in April 1818, a Royal Commission was set up to enquire into the mode of preventing the forgery of bank notes.[7] The crucial development however, came in the case of *Brooks* v. *Warwick*, in June 1818.[8] In this case Lord Ellenborough ruled that a trader had a right to retain a forged note that came into his possession. Previously, the Bank had retained all forged notes to help to trace the utterers and to ensure that the note did not re-enter circulation. Following *Brooks*, traders were allowed to keep notes, provided that they were marked forged by the Bank, and use them to compare with other notes. According to the Bank's solicitor, Kaye, it was this factor that led to the huge increase in forgery prosecutions in 1818, when there were more than three times the number than for any of the previous six years.[9] Utterers apparently thought that the Bank would no longer be able to trace them and, as long as they passed single notes, they would avoid prosecution. In fact, increased diligence from traders armed with forged notes and a willingness on the part of the Bank to prosecute for single note passing, saw 14 sentenced to death at the September sessions at the Old Bailey for forgery related offences, where previously the average was between two and three.[10]

The forgery cases dominated the September sessions and awakened press interest in the trials. The Bank was attacked for the arbitrary manner in which it conducted its prosecutions and jurors started to express doubts about the evidence that the Bank adduced to prove its case. A crisis point

[6] Mackenzie, *supra* n. 3, 56–8

[7] For details of the Report that the Commission presented, see *infra* text at n. 64.

[8] 2 Stark. 389, 171 ER 682.

[9] Statement delivered by Mr Kaye to the Commissioners for enquiring into the means of preventing forgery of bank notes 6 November 1818 (Bank of England: Freshfields Files, F2 85). There were 152 prosecutions in London and Middlesex for forgery related offences in 1818, compared to 49 in 1817 (SC 1819, *supra* n. 1, Appendix Number 3).

[10] *Old Bailey Sessions Papers* (hereafter *OBSP*), Sept. 1818.

was reached in December 1818 when two juries refused to convict the only four prisoners arraigned on the capital charge. In the cases of John Dye and John Williams the jury could not accept the testimony of a Bank agent employed to buy forged notes from the prisoners. In William Howard's case the jury did not think the prisoner had the requisite guilty knowledge and in the trial of William Connor it refused to accept the Bank's evidence that the note in question was a forgery. In all bar Howard's case, the juries ignored the judge's direction to convict.[11] These acquittals produced a sensation in the press and speculation that the system of Bank prosecutions was about to collapse. The reform press seized on the acquittals as an expression of popular disgust at the death penalty.[12] The evidence suggests a less clear cut explanation for the verdicts.

THE MOTIVES AND COMPOSITION OF THE JURY

The 1819 *Select Committee on the Criminal Laws* reported a growing reluctance on the part of jurors to convict for property offences that carried the punishment of death. Forgery was not seen as an exception, indeed it was singled out by the Committee as the offence in which jurors were least willing to convict:

> "There is no offence in which the infliction of death seems more repugnant to the strong and general and declared sense of the Public, than forgery; there is no other in which there appears to prevail a greater compassion for the offender, and more horror at capital executions."[13]

Historians have generally accepted this appraisal despite the fact that it was based on pre-packaged evidence tailored to suit the cause of reform.[14] There are other reasons to doubt the proposition that, for forgery of all kinds, jurors had become increasingly unwilling to convict. In the period 1812–18, out of a total of 131 capital trials for forgery at the Old Bailey for which true bills were found, there were 84 convictions and 47 acquittals.[15] Thus approximately two out of every three prisoners were convicted. The figures available for the eighteenth century show that, between 1770 and 1779, approximately one out of every two forgers was convicted.[16] When it is

[11] *OBSP*, *supra* n. 10, 6, 7 Dec. 1818; *The Morning Chronicle*, 7, 8 Dec. 1818; *The Times*, 7, 8 Dec. 1818. The London jury tried three of the cases, the case of Connor was tried by one of the two Middlesex juries.

[12] See for example *The Morning Chronicle*, 9 Dec. 1818.

[13] SC 1819, *supra* n. 1, 13.

[14] See J Beattie, *Crime and the Courts in England 1660–1800* (Oxford, Clarendon Press, 1986), 410; L Radzinowicz, *A History of English Criminal Law 1750–1950* (London, Stevens, 1948), vol. 1, 538.

[15] SC 1819, *supra* n. 1, Appendix No. 3.

[16] P Baines, *The House of Forgery in Eighteenth Century Britain* (Aldershot, Ashgate, 1999), 187.

considered that there were many more offenders in the nineteenth century, the Committee's conclusions look even more problematic. It is possible, of course, that in the specific case of the bank note forgeries of 1818, the jurors' apparent concern with the evidence masked their genuine concern for the fate of the offender, but this seems unlikely. In his evidence before the 1819 Select Committee, Thomas Shelton, who had been clerk to the arraigns at the Old Bailey since 1784, was asked specifically about the forgery cases of December 1818. He maintained that the acquittals were on account of the jury not being satisfied as to the bank notes being forged. On being asked, by a typically leading question, about whether the prisoners would have been acquitted of the minor charge of possession, Shelton stuck to his story:

> "I rather think not; for one or two of the gentlemen on the jury seemed very attentive, and asked a great number of questions with regard to whether the bank notes were actually forged or not; and one of them threw out doubts which he communicated to his brethren."[17]

There was plenty of opportunity for objectors to the death penalty for forgery to express their discontent in the six years prior to December 1818, when 47 out of a total of 134 executions in London were for forgery offences.[18] The idea that a suddenly acquired distaste for the death penalty was behind the Old Bailey jurors' actions at the end of 1818 is inadequate. Their motives were of a more selfish nature.

Old Bailey jurors were drawn from the middling ranks of retailers and small traders who were most vulnerable to the crime of uttering forged bank notes.[19] Shelton stated that the trial jurors were generally tradesmen and shopkeepers, frequently taken from Tottenham Court Road or Oxford Street.[20] Forged notes posed a serious threat to these people's livelihoods. In a typical case, the offender would go into a shop and get change for a counterfeit note by making a small purchase. Crucially, if the shopkeeper failed to detect the forgery straight away, he had to bear the financial loss because the Bank refused to pay on forged notes. In 1821, one London MP reported to Parliament that his constituents had sustained a loss of £31,000 in the last year because of forgeries.[21] The problem of forged notes was particularly

[17] SC 1819, *supra* n. 1, 25. As well as indicating where the main concern of the jury lay in the forgery trials, this testimony provides a useful insight into how the jury at the Old Bailey deliberated. It supports Beattie's theory that one or two of the more experienced jurymen dominated the London juries' deliberations. See Beattie, *supra* n. 14, 425.

[18] SC 1819, *supra* n. 1, Appendix No. 3.

[19] Beattie in his study of Old Bailey jurors at the end of the seventeenth century found that 70% of the jurors were in wholesale or retail trades: J Beattie, "London Jurors in the 1690s", in J Cockburn and T Green (eds), *Twelve Good Men and True: The Criminal Trial Jury in England, 1200–1800* (Princeton, University Press, 1988), 214 at 239–52.

[20] SC 1819, *supra* n. 1, 25.

[21] *The Times*, 27 Mar. 1821.

acute in London, where the absence of country bank notes meant that the circulation was heavily dependent on the Bank of England notes.[22] It was much easier for utterers to pass forged notes undetected in the great metropolis of London, where transactions between strangers were commonplace, than in many of the more close knit communities in the localities. Furthermore, the middling ranks of traders were the only class of people who suffered seriously from the problem. The upper classes, the wealthier merchants and substantial men of commerce were not affected, because they conducted their business using bankers' drafts.[23]

The jurors at the Old Bailey then, had a particular, economic interest in the problem of forged notes. After the case of *Brooks* in June 1818, many jurors referred during the trial to how, as retailers, they could not tell the difference between a forged and a genuine note. Thomas Wooler's radical publication, the *Black Dwarf*, exploited this concern in a campaign designed to turn the jury against the Bank and subvert its prosecutions. By 1817 the *Black Dwarf* was the leading radical periodical with a circulation of around 12,000 and an actual readership of considerably more, given that there was more than one reader per copy.[24] Two days prior to the start of the September sessions at the Old Bailey, it printed the first in a series of essays and letters vehemently criticising the "Old Hag of Threadneedle Street". The focus of its attack was the quality of the evidence that the Bank adduced to show that the notes in question were forged:

> "Juries, in future, will do well to pause on such trials before they convict. They can demand the necessary evidence, and if that evidence is not forthcoming, their duty is evident."[25]

In the September and October sessions at the Old Bailey the juries openly expressed doubts about the evidence for the first time, asking the Bank inspector to give details as to how he knew the note to be forged.[26] On each occasion the judge denied the request by saying that it might be prejudicial to the public interest to disclose the information. The jurors also asked for the signing clerk to be called, as well as the Bank inspector, to give evidence that it was not his signature on the note. In one case this provoked a severe rebuke from the judge, Mr Baron Garrow, who said that the law was clear and that the oath of the inspector was sufficient. He added that a:

[22] In most areas of the country, with the notable exception of Lancaster, country bank notes were a viable alternative to Bank of England notes and they proved much more difficult to forge. Forged Bank of England notes did circulate all around the country but the scale of the problem in London made it the focal point for the crisis.

[23] For a letter from a merchant making this point and suggesting the withdrawal of £1 and £2 notes from circulation see *The Times*, 29 Jan. 1819.

[24] R Hendrix, "Popular Humour and the Black Dwarf", (1976) 16 *The Journal of British Studies* 112.

[25] *Black Dwarf*, 9 Sept. 1818.

[26] See for example the case of *John Jones* (*The Morning Chronicle*, 17 Sept. 1818).

> "most foolish notion had some how or other got possession of the public mind that the Bank had a private mark of their own which no person but those in the privity of the Bank knew,"

this was "folly in the extreme".[27] The strong language that Garrow felt obliged to use in this incident signifies the growing force of opinion against the Bank and the effect it was having on the trial. This was also reflected in the tone of the jurors' questions, which was hostile and occasionally sarcastic. In January 1819 one juror actually brought a note into court that was genuine but had not been signed by the Bank clerk. He asked the inspector if that was a frequent occurrence and prefaced his question by saying:

> "I believe you do things with the greatest accuracy at the Bank—it is almost impossible to make a mistake."[28]

The *Black Dwarf* clearly influenced the increasingly irreverent attitude that jurors were exhibiting and no doubt prompted the jurors to ask some particular questions, but the jurors themselves showed a good deal of initiative. They displayed detailed knowledge of methods of printing bank notes and were able to question the Bank witnesses at some length about each stage of the process. A favourite question was how common it was for a forged note to deceive the bank inspectors themselves. In one exchange the juror was not satisfied when the inspector said such an occurrence was rare and asked whether the inspector had ever been a paper maker or engraver, or whether he had ever seen the watermark made.[29] Underlying the jurors' suspicion of the Bank inspectors and preoccupation with the detail of the notes was a deeper fear concerning the reliability of the currency. The doubts and insecurities that forgery engendered are manifest here; if the Bank could not be relied upon to distinguish between forged and genuine notes, how could any note be trusted?

The Bank's system of detection and prosecution gave rise to other reasons to doubt the testimony of witnesses. The Bank paid many of the witnesses to come to court or brought its agents, who had entrapped the prisoners, to testify. In the trials of John Williams and John Dye in December the jury could not believe the evidence of one such agent, Underwood, and acquitted the prisoners as a result. On average the Bank would pay witnesses between £10 and £20; Underwood, however, received £20 for his work, notwithstanding the acquittals.[30] This "blood money" bred corruption amongst those assigned to detect offenders. The *Black Dwarf* speculated that the reason that the forgers of the notes were never caught was that Bank agents declined to follow up such leads in case the trade in forged notes ceased and

[27] *The Morning Chronicle*, 3 Nov. 1818.

[28] Case of *Thomas Watson* (*OBSP*, *supra* n. 10, 15 Jan. 1819).

[29] Case of *John Kingston* (*OBSP*, *supra* n. 10, 16 Dec. 1818).

[30] Bank Law Committee Meeting, 24 Dec. 1818, Bank of England: Committee for Law Suits M5/321.

they were deprived of their blood money. It attacked the Bank with its "host of spies, and traps, of fallible clerks and infallible inspectors" to undermine its public credibility.[31] It seems to have had an effect: the dominant feeling of jurors in the forgery trials towards the end of 1818 was distrust of the Bank and the paper system it was concerned to protect.

THE CONSTITUTIONAL ROLE OF THE JURY

The juries' actions in the trials brought them into direct conflict with the judiciary. By refusing to accept the evidence of the Bank, the juries in December 1818 acted against clear directions from the bench that the cases had been made out against the prisoners. They also rejected the legal standard of proof that had been sufficient to convict forgers and utterers in previous years. This sort of conflict with the judge and outright rejection of the established law was rare. Legal historians have stressed the essentially harmonious relationship that existed between judge and jury in eighteenth- and early-nineteenth-century criminal trials.[32] The expeditious rate at which Parliament enacted new capital statutes during the century gave juries plenty of opportunity to exercise their age old discretion to mitigate the severity of the law in the offender's favour. This might involve undervaluing stolen property or interpreting facts in such a way as to avoid a capital conviction. These "pious perjuries" had enjoyed at least tacit official acquiescence, not least because the reduced charge still meant that the offender was transported, a serious punishment in itself.

Hay has argued that the reason for the general agreement between judge and jury was that the jurors' interests as middling men were more closely aligned to those of the ruling classes than they were to those of the victims of the criminal law. The elite and middling ranks shared an interest in using the criminal law to control the poor and protect property, thus the "social history of the English jury from 1730 to 1825 is a history of carefully structured inequality".[33] Whilst not all historians share Hay's views about the decisive influence of class, research into jury composition indicates that jurors, especially those in London, were men of substantial property.[34] They

[31] *Black Dwarf*, 4 Nov. 1818.

[32] Beattie, *supra* n. 14, 410. For the relationship between the judge and the jury in the eighteenth century criminal trial see T Green, *Verdict According to Conscience: Perspectives on the English Criminal Trial Jury, 1200–1800* (Chicago, University of Chicago Press, 1985), 267–311; J. Langbein, "The Criminal Trial before the Lawyers", (1978) 45 *University of Chicago LR* 263 at 284.

[33] D Hay, "The Class Composition of the Palladium of Liberty: Trial Jurors in the Eighteenth Century", in Cockburn and Green (eds), *supra* n. 19, 305 at 355.

[34] See Beattie, *supra* n. 19; P King, "'Illiterate Plebeians easily misled': Jury Composition, Experience and Behaviour in Essex 1735–1815", in Cockburn and Green (eds), *supra* n. 19, 254; Hay, *supra* n. 33.

were more likely therefore to share a community of interest with the judge than the prisoner, although the attitude of the jury may have displayed distinctive middle class values or have been shaped by influences other than class. It is perhaps most useful to think in terms of what Langbein has described as a "moral consensus" between judge and jury about the purpose of the substantive criminal law, which had emerged over centuries.[35] The jury-based mitigation that did take place then, "occurred within a highly managed and routine processing of cases that left room for few surprises".[36]

Green has described the jury's right to adjust its verdict to take account of the harsh law of sanctions as a "modest" version of law finding, modest because the jury applied the law more or less as it was stated by the bench.[37] The role of the jury in the forgery crisis does not fit into this tradition. In the first place, there was no opportunity in forgery trials for the jury to reduce the charge for the benefit of the offender. More importantly, there was a clear conflict of interests between judge and jury that did not relate primarily to the question of punishment. As the *Quarterly Review* commented in 1821, the crisis had "scarcely any perceivable connexion [*sic*] with the general question about the propriety of capital punishment for forgery".[38] This was not a breakdown of Langbein's "moral consensus" and certainly does not reveal a class split, in which a new distinctive middle class view on punishment challenged the traditional elite position. The crisis cannot therefore be integrated into accounts of penal law reform that argue that there was an increase in jury reluctance to convict on the basis of a widespread loss of faith in hanging amongst the middle classes.[39] If the juries' role is to be understood, the terms of humanitarianism or squeamishness that are usually employed to explain acquittals in routine eighteenth- and early-nineteenth-century property trials must be discarded.

The forgery crisis reflects the confusion that had come to surround the role of the trial jury in early-nineteenth-century England. This confusion centred on the extent to which the jury was entitled to apply the law according to its own, rather than the bench's, conception of justice. In the vast majority of ordinary criminal trials, because judge and jury agreed, the question did not arise and the exact extent of the jurors' discretion did not need to be formally delineated. The one exception to this rule was in seditious libel cases where the jury was restricted, until Fox's Libel Act in 1792,[40]

[35] J Langbein, "The English Criminal Trial Jury on the Eve of the French Revolution", in A P Schioppa (ed.), *The Trial Jury in England, France, Germany 1700–1900* (Berlin, Duncker and Humblot, 1987), 13 at 39.

[36] T Green, "The English Criminal Trial Jury and Law-Finding Traditions on the Eve of the French Revolution", in Schioppa (ed.), *supra* n. 35, 41 at 50.

[37] Ibid., 46–8.

[38] (1820–21) 24 *Quarterly Review* 210.

[39] Beattie, *supra* n. 14, 619. See also R McGowen "The Image of Justice and Reform in Early Nineteenth Century England", (1983) 32 *Buffalo LR* 89 at 114, 123.

[40] 32 Geo. III, c. 60.

to reaching a verdict strictly on the facts. It was left to the judge to determine as a matter of law whether the act was done with criminal intent and whether the writing was seditious. A number of high profile seditious libel trials in the late seventeenth and early eighteenth century gave rise to a debate in which pro-jury writers urged a jury right to find law, and not just to apply it in terms dictated to them by the bench. Green calls this the "radical law-finding or nullifying role of the jury—its asserted duty to nullify the law in cases involving executive or judicial tyranny".[41] He argues that, by the end of the eighteenth century, the modest law finding tradition had become entangled with this second more radical tradition. Pro-jury writers in the seditious libel debate used the analogy of common run property cases, where the jury had the right to find a general verdict on all the facts, to make their case. In doing so, they mixed the modest discretionary and radical nullifying roles of the jury without clearly separating the two.[42] In the forgery crisis the analogy was effectively reversed. The jurors' actions amounted to a radical nullification of the law and yet they occurred in an ordinary criminal trial. The justification for the right of the jurors to reject the law was a duty to provide a safeguard against the tyranny of the Bank.

It was the *Black Dwarf*'s influence that, more than any other factor, gave rise to the perception of the Bank as a tyrannical force that needed to be stopped. According to Wooler, the "Old Hag", sitting on her paper throne, had profited endlessly from the restriction whilst ruthlessly hanging forgers and utterly failing to improve the printing of its notes. He blamed the paper system and the desire of those in power to maintain it, for all problems associated with the forgery laws. Justice was a casualty of the all-consuming evil of the paper currency. Wooler did not object to the normal operation of the criminal laws but to its pernicious abuses by the Bank and the government. The problem of forged notes was merged with the political question of cash payments in the *Black Dwarf's* unrelenting vitriol:

> "The Bank therefore is the criminal cause of the necessity of a paper currency. And this necessity is the basis of the crime of uttering forged notes. In addition to this the Bank has been for years endeavouring to simplify the means of forgery and to make its notes as easy of imitation as possible."[43]

The political climate that Wooler was operating in was ideal for his purposes. The post-war social and economic unrest in the country made the radicals' attack on "old corruption" in government particularly effective. A few high profile acquittals in libel trials, particularly those of William Hone, the radical bookseller, at the end of 1817, had also given the radical press a degree of immunity from prosecution. Thompson comments that "1816–20 were

[41] Green, *supra* n. 36, 46. For a full discussion of the seditious libel debate see Green, *supra* n. 32, 318–55.

[42] Green, *supra* n. 36, 67–72.

[43] *Black Dwarf*, 31 Mar. 1819.

above all years in which the popular Radicalism took its style from the hand-press and the weekly periodical".[44] The Bank was certainly worried about the *Black Dwarf's* influence. The government refused its request to pursue a libel prosecution against Wooler for his articles on the forgery prosecutions. The Bank considered pursuing its own prosecution, but decided against it in view of public feeling, despite being certain of its case in law.[45] Wooler knew of these attempts, but, gleefully aware of his own virtual immunity, he continued to portray the Bank as a tyrant with devastating effects. The impact of his campaign against the paper currency was critical. *The Courier* acknowledged as much when it complained that the December acquittals were encouraged by "inflammatory discussions which have taken place recently upon the subject".[46] *The Morning Chronicle* reported the Old Bailey courtroom as being crowded to excess during the forgery trials in September and December 1818 and described how the assembled crowd applauded loudly when the not guilty verdicts were announced in December.[47] In the heated and constrained atmosphere of the courtroom, such participation from the crowd must have generated pressure on the jury to acquit.

The government's desire to control the jury in the seditious libel trials of the eighteenth century arose out of a fear of exactly this sort of popular passion. The jurors were eulogised in the press for having saved the people from the Bank. Immediately after the acquittals there was speculation that the Bank capital prosecutions had been discontinued completely and that the laws relating to the crime of forgery had been invalidated. The *Morning Chronicle* hailed the acquittals as proof of the "inseminable value of trial by jury" and stated that:

> "There is no one of the institutions of this country so deservedly dear to the people . . . . When all other protection has failed them here they have found their safety."[48]

Conservative newspapers, in contrast, lamented the acquittals that had arisen from "a mistaken, though perhaps amiable, conception of the province of the jury".[49] In particular, they complained that the juries had allowed their own opinion of the justice of the law to prevail over their duty as jurors to enforce it.[50]

The forgery trials then, brought the question of the jurors' duty and relationship to the law and the judges into sharp focus. The two traditions, of modest law finding in everyday criminal trials and radical

[44] E P Thompson, *The Making of the English Working Class* (London, Gollancz, 1963; Harmondsworth, Penguin Books, 1991), 739.

[45] See Black Dwarf Libel Correspondence, Bank of England: Freshfield Files F2/204.

[46] *The Courier*, 9 Dec. 1818.

[47] *The Morning Chronicle*, 15 Sept., 7 Dec. 1818.

[48] *The Morning Chronicle*, 9, 10 Dec. 1818.

[49] *The Courier*, 8 Dec. 1818.

[50] See *The New Times*, 14 Dec. 1818; *The Courier*, 15 Dec. 1818.

law finding in political trials, came together clearly in the crisis. Green argues that the merging of these two traditions made the question of whether the jury-based discretion in ordinary criminal trials was judge or jury controlled of crucial importance.[51] The forgery trials suggest that the jury possessed a substantial power to shape the course of a trial. In one case the jury requested the prosecution witnesses to be excluded from court prior to giving testimony on the grounds that it had frequently observed that "witnesses seemed to act as if they thought it indispensably necessary to deviate in no respect from the evidence that went before on the same side". The recorder expressed surprise, and said that such an application was an insinuation that the witnesses were guilty of perjury, but submitted to the request when four or five of the jurymen rose to their feet.[52] The jurors were persistent and ultimately successful in many of their demands for more evidence. In December they insisted on the Bank inspector giving evidence that pointed to some "specific mark" in the note that proved it to be forged. In response the inspector discussed the watermark, the type of paper used and the way in which the figures were engraved on the note, but even this was not sufficient.[53] The acquittals were a registration of the dissatisfaction that the jurors felt with the evidence and an implied threat of what would happen if things were not improved. The standard of evidence produced was not maintained consistently in the trials after 1818, but it was not ignored. At the end of 1819 there was no formal separation of witnesses in the forgery trials, but witnesses were criticised for repeating what had already been said.[54] The Bank inspector had reverted to giving sketchy evidence as to the forgery but the signing clerk was usually called and jurors occasionally still requested and invariably received further details as to how the inspector could be sure that the note was a forgery.[55]

The jury's confidence to challenge the authority of the judges, the law and the Bank was rooted in the tradition of the jurors' role to provide protection for the people against tyranny. The Old Bailey jurors were prompted to assume this role certainly, but to view their decisions as an unthinking response to radical propaganda and popular feeling would be to undervalue the jury's role in shaping events. Many of the jurors came to court with questions prepared and occasionally, as in the case where the juror brought an unsigned note to court, evidence.[56] In another case, a juror had gone out of his way to carry out some detective work:

[51] Green, *supra* n. 36, 68.
[52] *The Times*, 9 Dec. 1818.
[53] *The Morning Chronicle*, 7, 8 Dec. 1818.
[54] Case of *Voss and Keaton* (*OBSP*, *supra* n. 10, 4 Dec. 1819).
[55] See for example the case of *William Saul* (*OBSP*, *supra* n. 10, 15 Jan. 1820).
[56] See *supra* text at n. 28.

> "I have a paper in my hand, which states that at an examination before the Lord Mayor, the clerk to the Solicitor of the Bank said there was no signing clerks of the name of Middleton - I have three notes in my hand signed Middleton."

Conveniently for the Bank, the clerk concerned was in the court and recalled that in the examination he had said that there was no clerk named Meddleton.[57]

It is striking that both this case and the one involving the unsigned note occurred in the January sessions of 1819. Further, the foreman of the London jury in that session had presented a petition to Parliament on the subject of preventing the forgery of bank notes.[58] During one of the trials he said that whilst the jurors were satisfied as to the evidence adduced by the prosecutors "they cannot but deeply lament the facility with which bank notes can be imitated, and express their ardent desire for an alteration of the notes". He went on to say that he had seen some notes from America that were excellently engraved and virtually impossible to imitate and that he had felt it his duty to put those notes into the hands of some distinguished members of Parliament.[59] It seems reasonable to infer from this evidence that there was some manipulation of jury selection in this session at least. The jurors chosen clearly had a particular interest in the question of forged notes, but the fact that they were willing to convict in spite of their concerns, may be a sign of other types of dealing behind the scenes. Following the sensation that had attended the acquittals in December, it was essential for the Bank to obtain capital convictions to restore faith in the integrity of the system.

The jurors did not see their roles as being limited to trying their peers according to the evidence. They viewed the trial as an opportunity to perform a public service in subjecting the Bank to some scrutiny. One juror asked the Bank witnesses to state the difference between genuine and forged notes as a matter of justice "not only to him but to the public".[60] Jurors frequently referred to their duty to the public and refused to be deterred by judges telling them that the courtroom was not the proper place to discuss matters other than the case at hand. In the absence of any alternative, the Old Bailey became the forum in which this issue of public concern was debated. The press and reform campaigners could write as many pamphlets as they liked, but, short of lobbying a reactionary Parliament, there was little that they could do. The forgery trials provided a rare opportunity to offer a more direct challenge to the authorities and it was the jurors who held the power to do so. It is not surprising then, to find reformers and radicals seizing on the acquittals as a great triumph and using them to further their own campaign towards reform.

[57] Case of *Dorothy Neaves* (*OBSP*, *supra* n. 10, 15 Jan. 1819).

[58] *The Times*, 18 Jan. 1819.

[59] *The Morning Chronicle*, 18 Jan. 1819.

[60] Case of *John Jones*: *The Morning Chronicle*, 17 Sept. 1818.

THE EFFECTS OF THE CRISIS

Faith in the forgery trials and the integrity of the criminal justice system was at a dangerously low level following the December acquittals. Immediately after the trials, the execution of Driscoll, Weller and Cashman, three utterers of forged notes convicted in September on the evidence rejected by the juries in December, brought the public mood to a fever pitch. The Bank employed a body of guards at the execution and between 50 and 60 constables were stationed within the walls of Newgate to guard against the possibility of an attack by the public.[61] A few days later, amidst speculation in the press that the system of Bank prosecutions had collapsed completely,[62] 12 prisoners who had already pleaded guilty to, and been convicted on, the minor charge, petitioned the court successfully to have their cases reopened. The Bank declined to prosecute on the capital charge; thus, remarkably, the prisoners were tried for an offence for which they had already been convicted. The cases were brought before the second Middlesex jury, the only one that had not been involved in any of the earlier acquittals. It found the prisoners guilty, but again seemed dissatisfied with the evidence brought by the Bank and questioned its inspector at some length.[63] In fact the convictions may have restored some faith in the law, as, at the very least, they illustrated that the Bank could still obtain a conviction for a forgery-related offence.

The authorities had to act quickly to restore faith in the trials and try to retain public confidence in bank notes. In January 1819, the Royal Commission presented its report, which recommended a plan to print notes that were much more difficult to forge.[64] A month after the report of the Royal Commission, an Act was passed which authorised the Bank to print the new notes whenever it was ready.[65] The Twelve judges gave a ruling on the December cases in which they held that the system of bringing two charges was legal and that there was no need for the signing clerk to give evidence that the note was a forgery, as long as the inspector was acquainted with the clerk's handwriting.[66] In the January Old Bailey Sessions, the Bank felt able to resume its capital prosecutions and secured the conviction of four prisoners for passing bad notes, including Thomas Watson who was aged 15.[67] The jurors were still concerned with the state of the Bank's evidence, as

[61] *The Times*, 16 Dec. 1818.

[62] See (1818) 31 *The Edinburgh Review* 214; *The Times*, 10 Dec. 1818.

[63] *The Times*, 17 Dec. 1818; *OBSP*, *supra* n. 10, 16 Dec. 1818.

[64] *Report of Commission appointed to inquire into the Means of Preventing the Forgery of Bank of England Notes* PP 1819 (2) XI, 303.

[65] 1 Geo. IV, c. 92.

[66] *Bank Prosecutions*, Russ. & Ry. 376, 168 ER 854.

[67] *OBSP*, *supra* n. 10, 15 Jan. 1819.

discussed above, but they did convict. The Bank, however, did think it prudent to reduce the number of capital prosecutions it undertook in 1819, when there were only 33 capital convictions, just over half the number that there had been in 1818. The apparent ease with which the Bank was able to resume its prosecutions is partly explained by these measures, but the reaction to the chaos of December played at least as significant a part.

Many of the middling ranks of traders, who had found themselves riding the wave of popular resentment of the Bank, may have paused to consider the monster that they had created. *The Courier* announced:

> "We may expect to hear soon of multiplied forgeries upon the Bank of England for, by the wise conduct of Juries that Corporate body is now placed beyond the protection of the law."[68]

The idea of forgers carrying on their trade with impunity was not one that the middling ranks were willing to entertain for too long, no matter what their feelings were about the ease with which notes could be forged. No doubt this largely explains why, in January 1819, the juries were willing to convict the offenders in questions of forgery, despite expressing exactly the same sort of concerns that had been articulated in December 1818. It is also tempting to believe Wooler's allegations about the Bank of England having friends at court who could influence proceedings.[69]

The impact of the forgery crisis continued to be felt outside the courtroom long after order had been restored within it.[70] It bridged two of the crucial political issues of the day, namely, the question of the return to cash payments and the issue of penal law reform. The Parliamentary discussions of these two questions in the early part of 1819 took place against a backdrop of widespread public anger directed primarily against the Bank and its notes. In the cash payments debate this contributed to the feeling that the Bank was an incompetent "company of merchants" that needed to be stripped of its unwarranted power to control the financial affairs of the nation. Less obviously, but no less importantly, the feelings of insecurity and doubt about the paper currency engendered by the forgery crisis contributed to the overwhelming desire to return to the solidity of gold. The final decision to resume was as much an emotional one as it was a rational one. The Prime Minister, Lord Liverpool, said that "policy, good faith and common honesty" called on the state to return to "the ancient standard of value". In contrast the paper system had given "encouragement to speculation, to unsound dealings, to the accumulation of fictitious capital".[71]

[68] *The Courier*, 9 Dec. 1818.

[69] *Black Dwarf*, 25 Nov. 1818.

[70] In the discussion that follows there is only space to sketch out briefly some of the consequences of the forged notes crisis. There is much more on these themes in my unpublished PhD thesis: "Forgery and Criminal Law Reform in England, 1818–1830" (The University of Cambridge, 2002).

[71] 1 Parliamentary Debates XL (1819), 613, 622.

In 1819 Parliament adopted a plan, recommended by two secret committees, to resume cash payments gradually over a period of four years, with full resumption due by 1823.[72] The committees dealt with the forgery problem by placing faith in the plan for a new note that had been recommended by the Royal Commission.[73] By 1821, however, it had become apparent that the plan to produce an improved note had failed. The Bank by this time had enough gold in its coffers to resume cash payments immediately and was grateful to be able to do so, being fearful of a possible repetition of the 1818 crisis. There were more cases in the year 1820 than there had been in 1818 or at any time previously;[74] jurors were still expressing doubts about the quality of the Bank's evidence, and the *Black Dwarf* had renewed its interest in the issue.[75] Constant promises of a new note from the Bank were beginning to sound empty and finally, in March 1821, the Chancellor of the Exchequer brought a bill into Parliament for the immediate resumption of cash payments, on the basis of the failure to find a new, improved note.[76] An act was passed and within a year the forged notes problem was almost completely solved.[77]

The criminal law reform movement received a vital boost from the publicity that the forgery crisis generated. Immediately after the December trials, the City's Court of Common Council resolved to present a petition to Parliament on the subject of the criminal laws. One of the aldermen, Samuel Favell, in proposing the motion, said that the experience of the last four days made it impossible to deny "that public opinion called for a revision of the criminal law".[78] *The New Times* suspected that the real motive of the petition was "to raise a cry for factious purposes, against the Bank of England, and to cast an odium on that most important and respectable corporation, on account of the recent trials for forgery".[79] The petition was a

[72] 59 Geo. III, c. 49.

[73] There was one secret committee from each House of Parliament and both heard evidence from experts and expressed themselves satisfied with the plan for a new note. CSC, *Second report of the Secret Committee on the Expediency of the Bank resuming Cash Payments* PP 1819 III, 17; LSC *Second report of the Secret Committee on the Expediency of the Bank resuming Cash Payments* PP 1819 III, 388.

[74] There were 352 convictions for forgery offences in England and Wales in 1820, as compared to 227 in 1818: *Statement of the Number of Persons convicted of the Forgery of the Notes of the Bank of England 1790–1820*, PP 1821 264 XVI, 187).

[75] *Black Dwarf*, 5, 12 Apr. 1820, 7 Mar. 1821.

[76] 2 Parliamentary Debates IV (1821), 1315–1338; 2 Parliamentary Debates V (1821), 203–8.

[77] 1 & 2 Geo. IV, c. 26. Convictions for offences relating to the forgery of Bank of England notes dropped from 352 in 1820 to 134 in 1821, the year when cash payments were resumed, and then to 16 in 1822 (*A Return of the Number of Persons convicted of Forgery, or passing Forged Notes and Post Bills of the Bank of England, in each Year from 1791–1829, inclusive* PP 1830 XXIII, 184).

[78] *The Morning Chronicle*, 11 Dec. 1818.

[79] *The New Times*, 10 Dec. 1818.

crucial factor in enabling Mackintosh to carry a motion in the House of Commons against the government for the appointment of a select committee to consider the criminal laws. Government ministers warned in vain of the danger of responding to a "factious and unreasonable clamour" raised out of doors, which was "not the unmixed voice of speculative benevolence".[80] Thomas Buxton referred to the forgery crisis specifically in the leading speech in favour of the motion, and the problems associated with the forgery laws provided much of the substance to his argument.[81]

When Mackintosh reported to Parliament on the committee's progress, he made explicit the importance of the forgery crisis to the committee's deliberations. He referred to the evidence that the committee had heard "respecting the crimes of shoplifting, stealing in warehouses above the value of forty shillings, and, above all, respecting the crime of forgery".[82] This evidence uniformly pointed to reluctance amongst traders to use the criminal law and a widespread desire for penal reform. Mackintosh went on to say that besides this evidence, there were "other considerations—considerations of policy of a very grave nature—which ought to induce the House to consider the amendment of the laws respecting forgery as an imperative measure".[83] He stated that the committee's recommendations with regard to forgery were founded on the principle of making the return to cash payments as acceptable to the public as possible. The aim of the recommended law reforms therefore was to restore "to the Bank, and to all connected with recent events of a financial nature, the character that has been so seriously endangered".[84] In the report this justification was reiterated and forgery was the only crime to which a special section was devoted. This section recommended that private forgeries should be punished by transportation or imprisonment and that the first offence of uttering forged bank notes should be punished by transportation. The forging of bank notes or the second offence of uttering should remain capital.[85] The recommendations were not acted upon by Parliament until 1821, when Mackintosh brought a Forgery Punishment Mitigation Bill that was defeated by a small majority.[86]

The acquittals of December 1818 did not precipitate any substantial revision of the penal laws then, but they did shift the terms of the debate over law reform. It has been argued that the main motive behind the jury interventions was to hold the Bank to account for its failure to prevent the forgery of its notes; in doing so the jurors were also concerning themselves with a concept of justice or procedural fairness. This was a crucial part of

80 1 Parliamentary Debates XXXIX (1819), 837.
81 Ibid., 807–24.
82 1 Parliamentary Debates XL (1819), 1528.
83 Ibid., 1533.
84 Ibid., 1534.
85 SC 1819, *supra* n. 1, 13–15.
86 2 Parliamentary Debates V (1821), 893–971, 999–1001, 1099–114.

the argument against the old system because it took hold in the courtroom itself. The proceedings appeared unfair: the Bank was a highly visible symbol of elite power that had done nothing to prevent the forgery of its notes and yet enjoyed significant advantages in the trial process. The more the printed press attacked the injustices arising out of perceived abuses of power by the elite, the stronger the reformers' case became. At the heart of their case was the fact that the revered institution of the British jury had rejected the law outright. The juries' actions and the public debate that ensued, laid the quality of justice that the Old Bailey delivered open to widespread public scrutiny. Radicals, clamouring for an end to the hated paper system, ensured that it did not get a good press.

The forgery crisis marked an unusually high point of feeling with regard to the criminal justice system. Penal reformers and radicals often referred to public outcries at the infliction of death, or the state of the law, without being able to point to any concrete evidence. The jurors' verdicts in the forgery trials spoke out of injustice directly from within the system itself. In a sense, however, they were self-condemnatory because such open subversion of the law was not accepted as being within the legitimate province of the ordinary criminal trial jury by the beginning of the nineteenth century. Defenders of the old law criticised the jurors for breaking their oaths; reformers criticised the law for putting the jurors into such an unenviable position. Both of these positions implicitly rejected the traditional discretionary role of the jury in coming to a verdict according to its own conscience. The forgery acquittals may have sprung from a radical conception of the juries' role to nullify the law to safeguard against tyranny, but their effect was to undermine its older role of modestly mitigating the severity of the law. In the ensuing decades, reform of the law of sanctions, the coming of the police and the adversarial criminal trial reduced the jury to its modern, more passive and less overtly discretionary role. Underpinning these reforms was a need, at a time when public opinion was increasingly being referred to as a legitimating authority, for justice to be seen to be done. The crisis in the forgery trials was illustrative of many of the difficulties that the authorities were likely to face if it was not.

10

The Strange Life of the English Civil Jury, 1837–1914

MICHAEL LOBBAN (LONDON)

The nineteenth century is generally seen as an age of decline for the civil jury, as questions of fact were increasingly turned into questions of law.[1] The jury's power to decide according to its own notions of justice, or from its own knowledge, became increasingly circumscribed. Thomas Erskine's notion, enshrined in Fox's Libel Act, that juries had a right to decide questions of law in giving their general verdicts in criminal libel cases, came under attack in the 1820s from authors who sought to make the broader point that juries must at all times obey the legal directions of the judge.[2] Mid-century jurors who protested to judges when they found that their findings of fact had the opposite legal results from those they intended were rebuked as being "utterly unfit" to be jurymen, in as much as they were seeking to usurp the judicial role.[3] Nor was the jury allowed to be self-informing: by the 1830s, the courts were insisting that any juror who had particular expertise had to be called as a witness before the jury could act on his opinion.[4] Control of the jury was

[1] On the general trend, see J H Baker, *An Introduction to English Legal History*, 3rd edn (London, Butterworths, 1990), 107–10; W R Cornish and G de N Clark, *Law and Society in England, 1750–1950* (London, Sweet & Maxwell, 1989), 19–21; A H Manchester, *Modern Legal History* (London, Butterworths, 1980), 88–99. For a recent study where legal rules were gradually developed from what was largely a vacuum hitherto, see K J M Smith, *Lawyers, Legislators and Theorists: Developments in English Criminal Jurisprudence, 1800–1957* (Oxford, Clarendon Press, 1998). On nineteenth-century discussions of the province of the jury, see W Forsyth, *History of Trial by Jury* (London, J W Parker, 1852), ch. 12, [T Starkie], "Of the distinction between law and fact", (1844) 1 *Law Review* 37–61; [Anon.], "Of the Functions of the Judge as distinguished from those of the jury", (1845) 2 *Law Review* 27–44.

[2] George Worthington, *An Inquiry into the Power of Juries to decide incidentally on questions of law* (London, S Sweet, R Pheney, A Maxwell and Stevens & Sons, 1825); Forsyth, *supra* n. 1, 280. See also *Sixth Report of the Criminal Law Commissioners*, PP 1841 [316] X 1, at 65–7,

[3] *Raphael* v. *The Bank of England* (1855) 17 CB 161.

[4] In *Rex* v. *Frederick Rosser* (1836) 7 C & P 648, Parke B ruled: "That general knowledge which any man can bring to the subject may be used without; but if it depends on any knowledge of the trade, the gentleman must be sworn"; while in *Manley* v. *Shaw* (1840) C. & M. 361, Tindal CJ ruled that a jury could only act on the opinion of juryman who claimed that a stamp on a bill of exchange was forged if he were sworn as a witness.

guaranteed by the power of the court to award a new trial, not merely where there had been a misdirection on a point of law, or where evidence had been wrongly admitted, but also where there had been a verdict against the evidence. Moreover, under new Rules of the Supreme Court introduced in 1875, the court, if it felt it had all the materials necessary for finally determining the question before it, could on a motion for judgment or for a new trial award any relief sought, without referring the question back to a jury.[5]

There was good reason to be suspicious of the jury. The mid-nineteenth-century press abounded with stories of the absurdities of civil jury trials. In 1875, *The Times* ran a leading article on the case of *Mallam* v. *Attree*, decided at the Gloucester assizes. The defendant was a lady who had been injured in a railway accident on the Great Western Railway, and who had been taken to a hotel in Oxford for treatment, for which the company promised to pay. The company failed to pay the bill, and the hotel duly sued the woman. The jury listened patiently to the evidence and the summing up, and after an hour found a verdict for £100—against the Great Western Railway. Grove J sent the jury back, telling them that the company was not a party to the action; and they returned some time later finding a verdict for the defendant, for £100. They were sent away again. At their third attempt, they found a verdict for £17 for the plaintiff, a small proportion of the sum claimed. The jury clearly felt that it would be fair to give the hotel something for their trouble: but, in so doing, they forgot that the lady would be saddled with the costs of the suit. As *The Times* saw it, juries were used in civil cases since it was felt that they would apply the common sense they used in their own affairs to the cases before them:

> "Unfortunately, it is too plain that Jurymen are sometimes influenced in their verdicts by sentimental considerations to which they would give no weight whatever in their ordinary relations of business."[6]

Nine years earlier, in *Hill* v. *Finney*, a man who had lost his case in the Divorce Court sued his solicitor for negligence for advising him not to enter the witness box. The jury found that Hill had no defence to the charges of cruelty or adultery levied against him, and that his defence had not been prejudiced by his not testifying. The foreman then began to talk of the damages to be awarded, but Cockburn CJ stopped him, pointing out that if the jury found for the defendant there could be no damages. The jury went back to reconsider, and returned, finding a verdict against the plaintiff, but awarding only a farthing in damages. The Chief Justice was clearly incredulous at the result:
Cockburn CJ:

> "You think that the plaintiff is entitled to a verdict, but not to damages; that he has lost his defence through the defendant's fault, but that he has suffered no loss?"

[5] RSC 1875 Order XL rule 10. See Bramwell LJ's judgment in *Hamilton* v. *Johnson & Co* (1879) LR 5 QBD 263, and the comments in (1882) 27 *Solicitor's Journal* 18.

[6] *The Times*, 14 Aug. 1875, 9d. The case was reported on 13 Aug. 1875, 11c.

The Foreman:

> "Yes; but we desire to give him another start in life; a new trial in the world, so to speak."

The *Law Times* castigated it as an absurd verdict, pointing out that the solicitor

> "is mulcted in heavy costs, because some of the jury, with more of heart than brain, wanted to do a good turn to the plaintiff on a matter not in issue before them".[7]

Occasionally, jurors persisted in their attempts to determine the law. When the self-deprecating Sir Cresswell Cresswell, judging a divorce case in 1859, gave a definition of condonation that he admitted might be wrong, a juror took it upon himself not merely to hold out against the judge's definition, but even to write to the *Daily News*, complaining of those who "set up law instead of facts as the basis of a verdict".[8] Equally alarming was the fear that juries could be corrupt in their decision making. One juror in 1862, for example, wrote to the winning defendant, asking him for a present in consideration of the verdict.[9] Less striking, but equally worrying, was the prevailing feeling that jurors were partial to their class. It was an often-repeated accusation that, where the jury was made up of shopkeepers, they invariably found for the plaintiff seeking to recover a debt. It was commonly asserted that no gentleman would succeed before a common jury if he disputed a trader's bill, while no plaintiff would succeed in an action against a justice of the peace before a special jury. Juries were famous for their hostility to railway companies; but others who also suffered prejudice, it was claimed, included lawyers, apothecaries, bill-discounters, and estate agents.[10]

Such conduct encouraged critics to attack the whole institution. In 1859, in a pamphlet entitled *The Dark Side of Trial by Jury*, Joseph Brown laid down the gauntlet, by accusing the jury "of incapacity, of ignorance, of partiality, of cumbersomeness, of barbarism".[11] Whereas doctors, lawyers, and even cobblers served apprenticeships, the jury was untrained in all forms of argument. He wrote:

> "The English seriously believe that judicial wisdom springs forth mature from every tradesman's head. This is a fit article of faith for a nation of shopkeepers".[12]

[7] (1866) 41 *Law Times* 164–5.

[8] (1859) 3 *Solicitor's Journal* 142.

[9] (1862) 7 *Solicitor's Journal* 121. The case was *Sabey* v. *Stephens* 11 Weekly Reporter 20. See also (1862) 38 *Law Times* 25.

[10] See G Stephen, *The Juryman's Guide* (London, Charles Knight, 1845), 13; (1864) 8 *Solicitor's Journal* 833, J Brown, *The Dark Side of Trial by Jury* (London, William Maxwell, 1859), 14–18. On railways, see R W Kostal, *Law and English Railway Capitalism, 1825–1875* (Oxford, Clarendon Press, 1994), 63–4, 101–4, and 283–308. For estate agents, see, e.g., (1881) 25 *Solicitor's Journal* (1881) 693. Bramwell B caused some offence in a criminal case in 1859 for suggesting that a Welsh jury might be prejudiced against an English litigant: (1859) 33 *Law Times* 50.

[11] Brown, *supra* n. 10, 7.

[12] Quoted in (1859) 33 *Law Times* 98.

Yet, if no sensible man would entrust his disputes to be resolved by one uneducated man, it made little more sense for the law to entrust it to 12 of them. Other commentators joined in the attack, pointing out that the jury system encouraged mere *nisi prius* advocacy, by the weakest barristers, who used cheap tricks to win over ignorant jurors. Unlike the judges, the jury gave no reasons for the decision, which created the risk that they decided on the wrong grounds, or even entirely by chance. Such a system might have sufficed in the unsophisticated world of the Middle Ages, it was argued, but it was plainly inadequate for the complex and commercial nineteenth century.[13] If the civil jury was seen as inefficient, it was also seen in many circles as unnecessary. The protection of the weak, which was one of the main benefits of jury trial, was not needed in civil courts, the *Law Times* argued in 1862.[14] Nine years earlier, the same journal insisted that arguments about "the confidence felt in a jury by the public", were "totally inapplicable to the case of a civil action, with which the public have nothing to do".[15]

Given this hostility to the civil jury, we may be tempted to assume that it faded into insignificance as an institution. However, it will be argued in what follows that the civil jury remained an important part of the legal landscape throughout the nineteenth century and into the twentieth. While there were attempts to reform it, these were often hesitant and halting, and met with strong defences of the institution from senior judges. Moreover, even when the possibility arose of having cases heard by judges alone, the jury continued to be in popular demand.

THE JURY AND THE REFORMERS: ATTACKS AND DEFENCES

Mid-nineteenth-century reformers who sought to reduce the role of the civil jury were largely inspired by the experience of the new county courts, created by the Act of 1846. In these courts, the use of the jury was optional, at the request of the parties, and could only be used in cases above £5. Yet, if they were to prove a model to show that the public could settle their disputes without a jury, it was not at all evident in the years before 1846, that the solution to the needs of local litigants had to be juryless courts. For, when the revival of local courts was debated, it was unclear whether the reform should aim at creating a cheaper and simpler version of the superior courts, or a consolidated and professionalised version of the courts of requests. The question was important for seeing how the jury would fit in. At first, reformers favoured the traditional, constitutional mode of settling disputes. When Peel brought in his bill to reform county courts in 1827, he sought to

[13] For these arguments, see "Trial by Jury", (1859) 7 *Law Magazine, or Quarterly Review of Jurisprudence*, new ser. 318–43. On *nisi prius* advocacy, see also Stephen, *supra* n. 10, 15.

[14] (1862) 38 *Law Times* 25.

[15] (1853) 21 *Law Times* 77.

provide for trials by jurors qualified to serve at *nisi prius*, though he wanted smaller juries (of five) and a summary power in sheriffs to order new trials.[16] When Brougham introduced his bill in April 1830, he also showed a common lawyer's attachment to the jury, saying that, whenever there was conflicting testimony, it was best to proceed with a jury of 12, giving a unanimous verdict, and wherever damages were to be assessed, or where reputation was at stake, a jury was needed.[17]

However attached these men were to the jury, they soon discovered the difficulties of adapting them to the local environment, for practically speaking, it was hard to reproduce Westminster Hall at local level.[18] Under Brougham's reintroduced bill of 1833, the jury was to be limited to six, and could be dispensed with, by consent.[19] If Brougham's unsuccessful bill, which aimed to give a wide jurisdiction over contract and tort cases, while making use of a jury, to some degree tried to mimic the style of the superior courts, the bill which passed in 1845 (and paved the way for the 1846 Act) owed much more to the practice of the courts of requests, where small debts were generally recovered by commissioners without the help of juries.[20] The hastily passed Act of 1845, which allowed the crown by order in council to alter the size and jurisdiction of up to 390 existing local courts, enacted that the judge should act alone on law and fact in all cases not within the jurisdiction of the court before the Act passed, and whenever there were not enough commissioners present.[21] "Here", spluttered the *Legal Observer*, "is an abolition of the trial by jury with a vengeance!"[22] The hurried and botched Act of 1845 was

[16] *Substance of the Speech delivered by the Right Hon. Robert Peel in the House of Commons on the 20th of June 1827 in moving for leave to bring in a bill for the better recovery of small debts together with a copy of the bill, as amended in committee* (London, 1827). Similarly, the *Report from the Select Committee on the Recovery of Small Debts* in 1823 stated (PP 1823 (386) IV, 4) "a great objection to departing from the tried and constitutional mode of trial by jury, so far as to give to the same person the decision of both the law and the fact, in actions to the amount of fifteen or even ten pounds."

[17] *Parliamentary Debates*, new ser. vol. 24, col. 263.

[18] For instance, as Peel pointed out, if a unanimous decision of 12 jurors was required, challenges to jurors would have to be allowed, which Brougham did not want. *Parliamentary Debates*, new ser. vol. 24, col. 281.

[19] See 5 *Legal Observer* (1833) 453. For opposition to this, see *Hansard*, 3rd ser. vol. 18, col. 1286, vol. 19, col. 324.

[20] B Boothby, *Local Courts not the remedy for defects of the law: with suggestions of a plan for adapting the superior courts of common law at Westminster, the circuit courts of assize and the sessions of the peace to the increased demands of the country, arising from its extended population and commerce* (London, Saunders and Benning, 1844), 6, condemned the expansion of courts of request as bringing "the monstrous innovation of an abolition of trial by jury in many cases". Some statutes allowed juries to be used, at the discretion of the court, but still allowed their verdicts to be disregarded: see letter from "Z" in (1844) 29 *Legal Observer* 148.

[21] 8 & 9 Vict.. c. 127, s. 11.

[22] (1845) 30 *Legal Observer* 332.

replaced in the following year by a measure based on earlier proposals, brought in 1839 and 1841.[23]

The move towards judge-only trials in expanded local jurisdictions was clearly not to every lawyer's taste. For at the same time that moves were being made to set up local courts with reduced juries, those in the legal profession who were sceptical about county courts sought to reform the procedure of the superior courts, to make juries more accessible to small litigants. In particular, as an alternative, they looked to the procedure established by the Law Amendment Act of 1833, which allowed judges to refer actions under £20 to be tried before a sheriff's jury.[24] In the late 1830s, there were attempts made to extend the jurisdiction of the sheriff.[25] The importance of the measure for our purposes is the centrality of the jury in this measure, as the body that existed to determine damages (as indeed it did on writs of inquiry before the sheriff, when a judgement had gone by default in the superior courts).[26] Yet, however keen conservative lawyers were on this system, it was clearly not going to rival the expanding courts of requests, for, by 1838, there had been only 948 cases tried under the new system.[27] Nevertheless, the attempt to provide accessible civil justice before the traditional jury remained; for, in 1843 and 1844, Jervis and Watson brought small debts bills that sought to allow cases of debt up to £5 to be taken before justices of the peace, as well as bringing in other procedural reforms—bills which were widely approved of among legal conservatives.[28]

In practice, the act of 1846 proved very popular for the recovery of small debts. It was soon evident that very few litigants in these courts opted for juries.[29] With this experience to draw on, those reformers who had been loudest in their agitation for the new county courts—notably Brougham and his acolytes in the Law Amendment Society—now sought to extend the notion of optional juries to the superior courts.[30] It was expected that, by

[23] See *Hansard*, 3rd ser. vol. 56, col. 472 and vol. 57, col. 172 (1841).

[24] 3 & 4 Will. IV, c. 42.

[25] There was a proposal in 1837 by Capt. Pechell to extend it to £50 cases: (1837) 13 *Legal Observer* 257, 273, 367. This bill was abandoned, but the following year the Solicitor-General brought another bill.

[26] The Common Law Commissioners, in their first report in 1851, proposed to allow the Master to assess damages in these cases, where it was only a matter of calculation: *First Report of her Majesty's Commissioners for Inquiring into the Process, Practice, and System of Pleading in the Superior Courts of Common Law*, PP 1851 [1389] XXII 567, at 41.

[27] *Hansard*, 3rd ser. vol. 43, col. 1246.

[28] *Hansard*, 3rd ser. vol. 72, col. 683 (13 February 1844), (1844) 27 *Legal Observer* 323, 530. The bills were not proceeded with.

[29] For contemporary comment, see (1852) 16 *Law Review* 442; (1853) 18 *Law Review* 188. The proportion of jury trials remained minute: in 1860, where 387,368 cases were determined without a jury, only 894 used a jury (0.23%). In 1880, where 614,048 were determined without a jury, only 1079 used a jury (0.17%), while in 1900, 413,171 were decided without a jury, and only 1003 with a jury (0.24%)

[30] See, e.g, (1850) 16 *Law Times* 79; (1851) 18 *Law Review* 10. It should be noted that this

making jury trial in the superior courts optional, it would wither away there, as it had in the county courts. In 1851, Brougham proposed to bring in a measure, under which a judge should try all questions of fact unless either party asked for a jury. This, John Pitt Taylor wrote to him enthusiastically, "is in accordance with one of the rules of our *fusion* code of Procedure".[31] Nevertheless, Taylor advised caution, since the Common Law Commission was about to report.[32] When the issue was not addressed in their first report in 1851, Brougham returned to the offensive, teasing Parliament with the promise of a bill, and regretting the loss of a clause in the Irish Common Law Procedure Bill of 1853 making jury trial optional.[33]

In this context, the Common Law Commissioners could hardly ignore the evidence that litigants neither needed nor wanted juries. Addressing the question in their second report in 1853, however, the commissioners defended the system of jury trial in the superior courts. They pointed out that the county courts could not be compared with the superior courts. Where in the former, "as a general rule, no cause, whether defended or undefended, is determined except upon a hearing", in the latter, 97 per cent of cases did not proceed to trial. The superior courts clearly saw more complicated and difficult matters going to trial, which, it was felt, required a jury.[34] The commissioners also pointed out that in the county courts, trial by judge alone was the rule, with jury trial the exception. The result was that litigants were reluctant to request a jury, for fear of offending the court.[35] If the evidence of the statistics seemed overwhelming proof that litigants did not want juries in county courts, there remained no shortage of commentators who found other reasons for their small use, such as the increased fees incurred in county courts when a jury was used.[36] The ability to use a jury was still seen

was not the only proposal floated by this group. Thus, the county court judge, John Herbert Koe, wrote to his friend Brougham in 1852: "Something will be have to be done about Jury Trial." His proposal was that young briefless barristers should sit as assessors, in place of the current juries. This would please the parties, who would get better fact finders (and men who often acted as arbitrators), it would give work to the junior bar, and it would keep the judges in order: J H Koe to H. Brougham, 17 Aug. 1852, UCL, Brougham MSS, MS 9740.

[31] The Equity Committee of the Law Amendment Society in 1851 reported that it wanted every disputed question to be settled in the court where it had been set down, that wherever evidence was needed which was not disputed, the judge should take it himself, and that wherever it was disputed, there should be *viva voce* evidence and the option of a jury: (1851) 18 *Law Times* 129.

[32] J P Taylor to H Brougham, 29 June 1851, UCL, Brougham MSS, MS 13156. For the Law Amendment Society's support of the option of jury trial, see (1853) 18 *Law Review* 188–91.

[33] See, e.g., *Hansard*, 3rd ser. vol. 119, col. 1130, vol. 123, col. 196; (1853) 22 *Law Times* 1.

[34] *Second Report of her Majesty's Commissioners for Inquiring into the Process, Practice, and System of Pleading in the Superior Courts of Common Law*, PP 1852–3 [1626] XL 701, at 5.

[35] See the views expressed by C R Gibson, (1853) 21 *Law Times* 89.

[36] See the letters in (1855) 25 *Law Times* 52 and (1859) 33 *Law Times* 277. Others pointed out the fact that county court juries were summoned by county court officials, and not by the under-sheriff, and that their selection was very flawed: (1864) 8 *Solicitor's Journal* 881.

as a benefit.[37] The commissioners therefore recommended that, in the superior courts, trial by jury should continue to be the rule, but that if both parties agreed, the judge alone could decide matters of fact. This became law in the Common Law Procedure Act of 1854, which also enacted that parties could be forced to go to arbitration in mere matters of account. Many reformers were deeply disappointed with the proposal, arguing instead that a jury should be dispensed with unless demanded by either party.[38] They foresaw correctly that few litigants would seek to have the facts decided by the judge. Nine years after jury trial in civil cases was made optional, the *Law Times* could therefore declare:

> "How long is the injustice of trial by jury in civil cases to be inflicted upon litigants who do not desire such a tribunal?"[39]

At the same time that the Common Law Commissioners were preserving a role for the civil jury at common law, the jury was being extended to other courts that had hitherto not used them. Neither Chancery nor the ecclesiastical courts used juries, but used paper trials, with evidence taken before examiners, before the matter came before the judge.[40] The system was notoriously imperfect; reform of the mode of taking evidence was one of the major themes of mid-century Chancery reform. One problem was that written depositions were inadequate whenever questions of the individual credibility of a witness became important—for instance, when there was contradictory testimony. In these cases, an issue would have to be directed to a jury to decide the matter. Sending issues to juries from the Chancery was a time consuming and expensive business, however, and not all judges agreed that it was necessary. In 1835, Alderson B commented in one case:

> "What is really wanted is the oral examination and cross-examination of the witnesses; and the assistance of a jury is, as it seems to me, only incidental to this important object . . .. The conscience of the Court, I should apprehend, would quite as well be satisfied by its own immediate conclusion on the evidence, as it could be mediately through the opinion of the jury; who, in cases of this description, are sometimes not altogether free from prejudice".[41]

[37] Reformers such as Pitt Taylor maintained, however, that the optional jury in the County Court was as capable as the full jury in the Superior Courts. *First Report of the Commissioners appointed to Inquire into the State of the County Courts*, PP 1854–5 XVIII [1914] 149 at 207.

[38] (1853) 21 *Law Times* 77; (1865) 40 *Law Times* 482, (1867) 42 *Law Times* 281.

[39] (1863) 38 *Law Times* 367.

[40] There was similarly no jury in bankruptcy, which had been forged out of the Chancery. This proved especially controversial, when in 1849 the Bankruptcy Consolidation Act proposed to give penal powers to the court. See, e.g., (1849) 10 *Law Review* 166.

[41] *Barnes* v. *Stuart* (1835) 1 Y. & C. 119 at 139. In *Margareson* v. *Saxton* (1835) 1 Y. & C. 525 at 532, he added: "I wish I had the power of examining witnesses in this Court. If the parties by consent will give me that power which I wish all Courts of equity had, I will examine them."

If many agreed that it was wasteful to send issues to common law courts, not all lawyers agreed with Alderson that the matter could be left to the judge alone. For instance, W A Garratt, a retired Chancery barrister, in 1837 proposed a series of reforms in Chancery that would establish "judges of circuit in equity", who would be competent to preside at jury trials.[42] A similar proposal for the establishment of a court of issues in equity was put forward in 1851 by Edward Morton.[43] No less a Chancery luminary than Sir Edward Sugden felt great unease at giving equity judges greater power to decide facts. He told the Chancery Commissioners in 1851 that "a great many of the questions of fact that come before the Court cannot be decided by anybody but a jury".[44] His view seemed to be that if oral evidence were to be heard before the judge in Chancery, in cases in which issues would otherwise be directed, there would have to be a jury.[45] The legislative compromise reached (for practical reasons) was that there would be oral examinations, but taken before the examiners.[46]

The option of a jury trial was finally introduced into the Chancery for a different purpose by Cairns's Act of 1858.[47] This Act was designed to give Chancery the power to award damages as an alternative to specific performance, and while it was felt that, in many cases, the question of damages would not be a difficult one, it was considered that it would often be expedient to have the amount of damages assessed by a jury.[48] It is curious to note that those very reformers, who sought to diminish the common law civil jury, positively welcomed it in Chancery. In 1860, hailing the first jury trial in a court of Chancery, the *Law Times* showed that it had great expectations of the then sitting Chancery Evidence Commission:

> "We cannot doubt that the result will be to lead to the general enforcement of that rational procedure by *viva voce* examination and a jury, of which the first specimen has been given this week."

42 *Suggestions for Reform in Proceedings in Chancery, particularly in respect of the Pleadings, the mode of taking evidence, and the accounts and inquiries usually directed* (London, 1837), reviewed in (1837) 14 *Legal Observer*, 281.

43 *A Letter to the Right Hon. Sir James Graham M.P. one of the Chancery Commissioners Suggesting a Solution of the Great Problem of Chancery Reform* (London, Butterworths, 1851);*A Letter on Chancery Reform; and the Mode of taking evidence on issues of fact by the establishment of an issue court*, 2nd edn (London, 1851).

44 *First Report of Her Majesty's Commissioners appointed to Inquire into the Process, Practice, and System of Pleading in the Court of Chancery*, PP 1852 [1437] XXI 1, Appendix A, 13, q. 46. However, he also said (at 10, q. 17) that it was rare for cases to come to equity "where the acts of the parties and the documents which have passed between them, are not of such a nature as to render it exceedingly difficult for them to escape from the truth."

45 He said (ibid., 9 (q. 9) in questions of *devisavit vel non*, for instance, "there is hardly any Judge who would venture to come to a conclusion satisfactory to himself upon such a question, and nothing can do but the verdict of a Jury to satisfy the parties."

46 15 & 16 Vict., c. 86, ss. 28–9.

47 21 & 22 Vict., c. 27.

48 *Third Report of Her Majesty's Commissioners appointed to inquire into the Process, Practice and System of Pleading in the Court of Chancery*, PP 1856 [2064] XXII, 4.

To underline its enthusiasm, the journal said that "reason asserts and experience proves" that jury trial "is the only procedure adapted to the discovery of truth".[49] Where critics of the Common Law Procedure Act bemoaned the fact that it made jury trial the norm, critics of Cairns's Act, such as W T S Daniel, feared that the measure would be inoperative since it was the judge, rather than the parties, who elected the mode of trial.[50]

Daniel's fears were well founded, for the judges indeed proved reluctant to use the act.[51] In spite of moves to limit the ability of Chancery to direct issues,[52] the judges continued to send issues to the assizes, including the notorious Tichborne case.[53] The judges were so conservative that H J Francis told a meeting of the Metropolitan and Provincial Law Association that "no equity judge ever tried a common law question under this statute if he could possibly help it", and that Cairns's Act was a failure on that account.[54] Part of the reason for this was practical. Just as there was no physical space for a jury in the Chancery courts, so equity lawyers and judges felt uncomfortable when dealing with juries and witnesses, and avoided it wherever they could.[55]

If Chancery men disliked the practice of using juries, then, they did not dislike the principle of sending issues to juries. Similarly, other non-common law courts adopted the jury. The inability of the ecclesiastical courts to hear *viva voce* evidence or direct issues to a jury had long been commented on. The Real Property Commission set up by Peel, which recommended that testamentary questions should be handled in Chancery since that court could direct issues, condemned the ecclesiastical courts, since "no one of them has power or machinery to try questions of fact by means of a Jury".[56] The Ecclesiastical Courts Commissioners sitting at the same time sought to retain the ecclesiastical jurisdiction over testamentary matters, but in their report of

[49] (1860) 34 *Law Times* 189. The same journal had earlier hailed the introduction of juries into Chancery as the first step towards the fusion of law and equity.

[50] (1858) 32 *Law Times* 57, 141. (1858) 3 *Solicitor's Journal* 21 feared it would become "a costly addition to, instead of a substitute for, the old-fashioned way of settling the dispute".

[51] In May 1859, Kindersley refused an application for a jury trial, on the ground that the Court would only direct a jury to be summoned where previously an issue to common law would have been granted. (1859) 3 *Solicitor's Journal* 501 commented that, if this view were to be followed, the much-vaunted legal revolution would turn out to be a nullity. See also ibid., 582–3. In the first three years of the act, it was only used twice: (1862) 7 *Solicitor's Journal* 2.

[52] Notably in 25 & 26 Vict., c. 42. In *Young* v. *Fernie* 12 WR 221 (a patent case), the court discussing the act said that it would henceforth be the exception to direct an issue.

[53] This was because it involved questions of land, excluded by the 1862 Act. The court was told by Locook Webb that Chancery could have disposed of the case in a month: (1871) 52 *Law Times* 130.

[54] (1866) 10 *Solicitor's Journal* 207.

[55] (1862) 38 *Law Times* 45. On the cramped conditions, see (1864) 8 *Solicitor's Journal* 217.

[56] *Fourth Report of the Commissioners on the Law of Real Property*, PP 1833 (226) XXII 1, at 63, 82.

[57] (1844) 3 *Law Times* 62.

1832 agreed on the right to a jury if the parties desired it. Similarly, Dr John Nicholl's bill of 1844 to reform the ecclesiastical courts made provision for jury trials.[57] By the mid 1850s, it was clear that a wholly new probate court would be required, with equitable powers and with the power to use a jury;[58] and when the new court was set up in 1857, it did give the option of jury trials. Similarly, the option of a jury was introduced in the new Divorce Court set up in the same year, and, while some lawyers were unhappy at leaving matters of divorce to a jury,[59] Sir Cresswell Cresswell said that it was "his practice always to lean to the allowing of trial by Jury".[60]

It can therefore be seen that, in the decades before fusion, there was a strong defence of the common law method of fact finding, as represented by the jury. As we shall now see, defences of the jury system continued to be made in the last quarter of the nineteenth century, after the Judicature Acts had fused the courts of law and equity. Many of the arguments found in the 1850s on both sides were rehearsed once more after the passing of the legislation. Joseph Brown returned to the attack in 1874, criticising the long Tichborne case. Why, he asked, use a panel of laymen to try such a long and complex case:

> "when we have got an expert Judge at hand, trained and paid for the work, who would do it much better, and in half the time."[61]

In September 1882, he repeated his objections to the Social Science Association, observing that the attempt made in the Judicature Acts to assimilate the common law and Chancery modes of trial had "conspicuously failed". Wise Chancery judges, he commented, never used juries; and wise litigants preferred the arbitration of experts to the unlearned juror.[62] In 1890, another debate was provoked in the columns of *The Times* by a letter from the barrister Arthur Jelf, giving a point-by-point argument as to why juries were flawed. Jelf felt that judges were far preferable because they explained themselves more clearly than juries, and could be appealed from. In addition, he said:

> "[T]rial by jury in the complicated problems of mixed law and fact which arise in the present day puts an undue strain upon the ingenuity of the Judge in disentangling the points on which the opinion of the jury ought to be taken."[63]

[58] (1853) 18 *Law Review* 323.

[59] (1859) 33 *Law Times* 95.

[60] Fitzroy Kelly to H Brougham, 4 July 1862, UCL, Brougham MSS, MS 18473. Cresswell was responding to Brougham's proposed Legitimacy and Marriage Bill, which sought to extend the right to jury trial to questions of the legitimacy of marriage, as well as those of divorce.

[61] Quoted in (1874) 56 *Law Times* 411.

[62] (1882) 74 *Law Times* 3. This argument was contentious: 17 years earlier, the same journal had argued against courts of arbitration, preferring to improve the jury: (1865) 41 *Law Times* 42.

[63] *The Times*, 29 July 1890, 4c. In 1901, S L Holland argued that a jury was unnecessary

If many of these arguments seemed hard to oppose, there was no shortage of eminent defenders of the *ancien régime*. They came to the fore, even when reformers proposed a cautious advance on the changes of 1854. For instance, when the Judicature Commissioners (who nevertheless described jury trial as "the great distinctive feature of the Common Law")[64] envisaged a system where the plaintiff could choose the mode of trial, whether by Judge, by a Jury or by a Referee, subject to the defendant's right to ask for a different mode, the profession—and even those often sceptical about jury trial—reacted with caution. The *Solicitor's Journal*, for instance, maintained that there was a need to allow either party to require a jury trial where there was any question of disputed fact or unliquidated damage. This, it said, was better than both the existing common law rule and the

> "rule now prevailing in Chancery, which practically comes to this, that a jury will be refused unless the judge desires its assistance to cut some knot which he feels himself unable to untie".[65]

In the event, the opposition of the common law judges, led by Chief Justice Cockburn, undermined the High Court of Justice Bill of 1870, which sought to implement the proposals of the Commission. For our purposes, what is important to note is Cockburn's concern at the prospect of the disappearance of jury trials.[66]

The late nineteenth century saw a variety of defenders of the jury system. George Denman told the Commons in 1872 that, if cases were tried in the superior courts without juries, suitors would soon attempt to discover the views of particular judges on certain kinds of cases, and they would resort to "all sorts of jobbery" to get the case heard by a judge who held views similar to their own. The *Saturday Review* added that if the subject no longer needed protection from the crown, he still needed it from railway companies.[67] Others pointed out that the function of a trial was not merely to persuade a judge that justice had been done, but also to persuade the wider public. For this a jury was essential.[68] Sir William Erle added his approval of the jury, saying that a jury was much more likely to come to a right decision than was a judge, even in a civil case.[69] In the 1880s, with the Lord Chancellor's Procedure Committee considering changes, J F Stephen wrote in the *Nineteenth Century* defending jury trial as "the really popular and

since, in contract cases, it was the judge who construed the contract, while in negligence cases, he determined the level of liability: "Trial by Jury at nisi prius", (1901) 17 *LQR* 171.

[64] *Judicature Commission: First Report of the Commissioners*, PP 1868–9 XXV [4130] 1, 6.

[65] (1870) 14 *Solicitor's Journal* 568.

[66] See Sir Alexander Cockburn's letter to the Lord Chancellor, printed in *The Times* 23 May 1870, 13a and his pamphlet, *Our Judicial System* (London, William Ridgway, 1870).

[67] (1872) 33 *Saturday Review* 242–3.

[68] (1874) 56 *Law Times* 410.

[69] Quoted in T W Erle, *The Jury Laws and their Amendment* (London, Stevens and Sons, 1882), 147–8.

impressive part of the administration of justice".[70] Stephen criticised the "one-judge system" proposed, fearing for the dignity of trial judges were the civil jury abolished. A raft of defences of jury trial similarly met Jelf's 1890 letter. Shackleton Hallett's defence of the jury involved attacking the judges, some of whom, he said, were

> "either ignorant or incapable of grasping the most elementary principles of the system of law and justice which they have to administer."[71]

The most prominent defence of jury trials came from the county court judge MacKenzie Chalmers, first in an anonymous letter to *The Times*, and subsequently in an article in the *Law Quarterly Review*.[72] Chalmers made the point that, when a jury was divided, and no conclusion was reached, it was because the case was not proven, and having a new trial with more evidence was the best solution. He added that juries, who were not compelled to give reasons, or to follow a consistent line of precedents, as judges were, could always arrive at the justice of the case. In his view, juries who made the right decision on the basis of common sense were better than judges making new law. Chalmers was worried about the development of law, after fusion. In particular, he abhorred the confounding of questions of law and fact that had been encouraged by the abolition of the common law system of pleading. The result, he said, was to make law like equity, "that curious conglomeration of technicality tempered by uncertainty", as he called it. For Chalmers, if the judge decided facts as well as law, the only way to prevent the principles of law from degenerating was to codify.[73] Chalmers felt that the jury was particularly suited for deciding matters such as fraud. Had *Peek* v. *Derry* been decided before a jury, he said, the case would never have gone to the House of Lords, and Parliament would not have had to pass the Directors Liability Act of 1890.[74] This pointed defence of the powers of the jury was especially notable, coming as it did from a county court judge.[75]

These defences meant that the changes to jury trial would be permissive only. The major change came with the new Rules of the Supreme Court of 1883, based on the Procedure Committee's report of 1881. That committee wanted to make trial by judge alone the prime mode of trial, though allowing

[70] Quoted in (1881) 25 *Solicitor's Journal* 214.

[71] *The Times*, 28 Aug. 1890, 5f. See also the letters of 29 Aug. 1890, 9e & 9f.

[72] *The Times*, 30 Aug. 1890, 7f; M Chalmers, "Trial by Jury in Civil Cases", (1891) 7 *LQR* 15.

[73] Chalmers, *supra* n. 72, 21. Chalmers was not the only one to express such worries. In 1872, the *Saturday Review* commented that if judges were to try law and fact, many more cases would have to be reported: (1872) 33 *Saturday Review* 243.

[74] *The Times*, 30 Aug. 1890, 7f. As a correspondent pointed out, the parties in this case were happy to have the matter decided by a jury, while the same issue did indeed come before a jury in another case (*Smissen* v. *Derry*): *The Times* 2 Sept. 1890, 4f.

[75] See also his remarks in M Chalmers, "The County Court System", (1897) 3 *LQR* 11.

trial by jury on application from either side if the case could conveniently be so tried, and allowing jury trial as of right where reputation was at issue.[76] When the new rules came into operation, there was a great outcry against a supposed abolition of jury trial, but the *Solicitor's Journal* pointed out that the right to jury trial was in effect unaffected by the changes. It argued:

> "The real and very rational intention was, doubtless to let business come, *as of course*, before judges without juries, leaving to the parties, in every case where they had it before, the right to a jury trial *if they desired it*, and requiring only that they should *express that desire*".[77]

This rule was to remain in place until 1918: clearly the rationalist reformers had failed to dislodge those who preferred the traditional system.

LITIGANTS' CHOICES AND THE JURY

The fate of the civil jury was now in the hands of the litigants, who had to seek them, if they wanted jury trial. Given this new *régime*, reformers were confident that this form of trial would soon disappear, and events seemed to support this view. By January 1885, the *Solicitor's Journal* noted a sudden fall in the proportion of jury trials since 1883, and declared:

> "Trial by jury does not seem to hold a very high place in the estimation of suitors of the present day."[78]

The decline in jury trials that they observed was studied in greater detail in a seminal article published over 60 years ago by R M Jackson. He showed that the proportion of jury trials remained high, though gradually declining, in the Queen's Bench Division throughout the 1870s, fell sharply between 1883 and 1887 to roughly 50%, and then remained stable until the end of the First World War, when it fell sharply once more. Jackson commented that the "restrictive Rules of 1883 [. . .] came into force when jury-trial was declining." Surveying the statutory changes to the availability of jury trial in the period from 1883 to 1933, he concluded:

> "It appears that the predilections of litigants and their advisers, and the opinions and influences of the judges, have brought about the changes; statutes merely accentuated changes that were already taking place."[79]

[76] For the committee's report on this, see (1881) 25 *Solicitor's Journal* 913. The proposals became Rules 2 and 3 of Order XXXVI of the Rules of the Supreme Court of 1883.

[77] (1883) 27 *Solicitor's Journal* 705. See also the view of Lord Herschell on *British South Africa Co. v. Companhia de Moçambique* [1893] AC 602, quoted in R M Jackson, "The Incidence of Jury Trial during the Past Century", (1937) 1 *Modern LR* (1937) 132 at 140.

[78] (1885) 29 *Solicitor's Journal* 177. This seemed to fulfil its prediction (in (1884) 28 *Solicitor's Journal* 493) that "the effect of the new rules will be to a very great extent to supersede trial by jury in civil cases."

[79] Jackson, *supra* n. 77, 142.

It is worth revisiting some of the material he discussed, to assess how popular jury trials were with civil litigants in the later Victorian and Edwardian eras. In what follows, we will examine how frequent civil jury trials were, why were they used, and when. It will be seen, first, that civil jury trials remained far from numerically insignificant, even when set against the number of criminal trials. Secondly, it will be argued that the sudden decline in the use of civil juries after 1883 reflects the fact that certain cases unsuited to juries were then referred systematically to judges alone. The apparent fall in the use of the jury after 1883 does not therefore represent a lack of public confidence in the civil jury as an institution.

How frequent were civil jury trials when compared with criminal ones? Statistically, by far the largest number of juries were called together to attend coroners' inquests. In 1880, for instance, there were 26,588 coroners' juries. By 1890, the figure had risen to 32,027, and in 1900, to 37,076. Ten years later, in 1910, it stood at 35,417.[80] The number of criminal trials, using juries, at assizes and quarter sessions, was also high, though the late nineteenth century saw a decline: 14,770 trials in 1880, 11,974 in 1890, 8238 in 1900, and 10,764 in 1910. How do civil juries compare? In 1900, there were 3281 civil jury cases in England and Wales, including superior courts, county courts, the other surviving local courts and inquiries under the Lands Clauses Consolidation Act.[81] In 1910, the number of civil trials before juries was 2,576.[82] The figures were probably similar in previous decades.[83] Even at the turn of the century, then, it cannot be said that the civil jury was trivial: in 1900, civil juries accounted for some 23 per cent of all jury trials in England and Wales, while in 1910 they accounted for some 19 per cent of such trials.

Such a grand total does not, however, compare like with like. A more important measure of comparison, given the jury's ideological importance, is to compare the use of juries before superior court judges. As can be seen from Table 1, the proportion of juries who sat before superior court judges in civil cases remained far from insignificant: in 1876, one third of juries

[80] These figures, and the ones on which all the discussion in this section is based, are all taken from the Civil and Criminal Judicial Statistics.

[81] Of these, 1,489 were before superior court judges at Westminster or at *nisi prius*, 83 were in the Divorce Court, 49 in the Court of Probate, 1,003 before county court judges, 65 in borough and manor courts, 129 in the Salford Court of Record, 306 before the Lord Mayor's Court and 157 before sheriffs on inquiries.

[82] Of these, 1,303 were before superior court judges at Westminster or at *nisi prius*, 69 were in the Divorce Court, 23 in the Court of Probate, 712 before county court judges, 70 in borough and manor courts, 44 in the Salford Court of Record, 274 before the Lord Mayor's Court and 81 before sheriffs on inquiries.

[83] I estimate that in 1880, there were in the region of 3,585 civil jury trials and in 1890 some 3,362. This is estimating the proportion of jury trials on circuit after 1883 to be two thirds, and counting all the cases in the Salford Hundred Court and the Lord Mayor's court as being tried with juries.

before these judges were civil ones, a proportion nearly matched in 1913. While there was a significant drop in the proportion of civil jury trials after 1883, this reflected an increase in criminal trials in the 1880s, as much as a drop in civil cases (see Figure 1: Jury Trials before Superior Court Judges, 1876–1913).[84]

Table 1 The Proportion of Criminal and Civil Juries before Superior Court Judges

	1876	1886	1896	1906	1913
Criminal	66%	82%	72%	74%	69%
Civil	34%	18%	28%	26%	31%

If we turn to metropolitan cases, seen in Table 2, comparing jury trials in the Queen's Bench Division with the Central Criminal Court, we find the proportion of civil cases is much higher, being roughly half both at the beginning and end of the period. The figure is even more striking if we take into account juries sitting in divorce and probate cases, as well as those in the Queen's Bench Division. Although, as can be seen from Figure 2 (Jury Trials before Superior Court Judges in the Metropolis, 1876–1913), the proportion of civil cases fell after 1880, due in part to a fall in civil jury cases after the new rules of 1883, and in part to an increase in crime, the number of civil cases stabilised thereafter, while the number of criminal cases fell.

Table 2 The Proportion of Metropolitan Juries before Superior Court Judges sitting in civil cases.

	1876	1886	1896	1906	1913
Civil, excl. Divorce & Probate	49%	29%	43%	39%	51%
Civil, incl. Divorce & Probate	51.5%	32%	48%	45.5%	54.5%

Outside London, as Table 3 and Figure 3 (Jury trials at Assize and *Nisi Prius*, 1876–1913) show, the proportion of civil to criminal juries before superior court judges was clearly smaller. This is not surprising, given that civil litigants were more likely to seek to bring their cases to London, while criminal trials were held in the location of the crime. However, they were not negligible. As in London, the proportion of civil cases fell in the 1880s, but thereafter remained constant.

[84] There are no official figures for the number of jury trials in *nisi prius* cases before 1894. I have based my calculations on the estimate that between 1883 and 1894, two thirds of cases on circuit would have been heard before a jury.

Table 3 The Proportion of Criminal and Civil Juries at Assize and Nisi Prius

	1876	1886	1896	1906	1913
Criminal	76%	89%	85%	85%	86.5%
Civil	24%	11%	15%	15%	13.5%

The conclusion to be drawn is that we must not dismiss the civil jury as numerically insignificant.

We are left with the question of when the civil jury was used, and for what purposes, particularly after 1883, when (as Jackson showed) the proportion of civil cases using a jury suddenly fell. To answer these questions, we need to look in more detail at the figures. It is clear that as the century went on, an increasing amount of civil litigation was drawn to the metropolis. As can be seen from Figure 4 (Civil Trials before Superior Court Judges, 1876–1913), while the volume of trials on circuit hovered consistently in the last quarter of the nineteenth century around 800 trials, declining slightly in the early twentieth, there was a slow, if uneven, growth in litigation in London, to double that number, even reaching 2,185 civil cases in one year of unusually high litigation, 1898.[85] At the same time, although there are some variations, Figure 5 (Civil Jury Trials before Superior Court Judges at Westminster and at *Nisi Prius*, 1876–1913) shows that the gap which emerged in the number of trials heard in London and on circuit was not entirely mirrored in the gap in the number of jury trials. While roughly 65 per cent of civil cases were heard in London by the last decade of the nineteenth century and first decade of the twentieth, an average of 55 per cent of civil juries sat in London.[86]

Table 4 The Proportion of civil trials heard in London, and the proportion of civil jury trials in London

	1876	1886	1896	1906	1913
Proportion of civil cases heard in London	54%	61%	67.5%	65%	73%
Proportion of jury cases heard in London	52.6%	53%	55.5%	55.5%	68%

[85] These figures look at the Queen's Bench Division, excluding Divorce and Probate cases. However, they include non-jury as well as jury cases.

[86] The figure in the table for 1913 is deceptive as it is an unusual year. By contrast in 1912, the proportion of civil cases heard in London was 65% and the proportion of civil jury trials heard in London was 57%.

Jury trials on circuit remained disproportionately important. In the metropolitan areas, the number of judge-only trials began to equal the number of jury trials from 1883, a proportion which (as Jackson showed) remained largely constant until the end of the First World War, save for a boom in judge-only trials in the mid 1890s (see Figure 6: London and Middlesex Trials, 1876–1913). By contrast, the proportion of jury trials on circuit was much higher: on average, even in the mid-1890s, two thirds of circuit trials were by jury (see Figure 7: Nisi Prius Jury trials, 1894–1913).

Why was jury trial apparently more popular in the country? Given the poor reputation of the agricultural juror,[87] one might have expected proportionally fewer jury trials in the provinces. An answer to this question may be found in looking at the nature of cases brought in the different courts. Taking the figures for the period from 1860 to 1913, looking at all trials, with or without a jury, it is evident that the metropolitan case load was consistently more weighted to contractual cases than was found on circuit.[88] We can see from Table 5 and Figure 8 (London and Middlesex Civil Trials, 1860–1913) that throughout our period, in London and Middlesex, more than half of the cases brought were contractual, while the proportion usually ranged between 55 per cent and 50 per cent. Roughly a quarter concerned torts.

Table 5 London & Middlesex Trials

Year	Contract	Tort	Other
1860	59%	27%	14%
1870	57%	21%	22%
1880	56%	27%	17%
1890	50%	35%	15%
1900	62%	24%	14%
1910	55%	31%	14%

By contrast, on circuit (as seen in Table 6 and Figure 9: Circuit Trials 1860–1913), the number of contract cases was usually less than half, while one third of cases were consistently tort ones, a proportion which rose in the latter half of the period surveyed, to account for more than half the cases

[87] As Joseph Brown ((1882) 74 *Law Times* 4) put it: "Those who have practised at the assizes and sessions know how totally unfit the country juries are to solve any litigated question which goes beyond the ordinary routine of their every-day life."

[88] I have included under contractual matters actions on promissory notes, bonds, actions on the common counts, breaches of warranty, calls on shares, insurance and wrongful dismissal cases and actions for rent. Under torts, I include personal injury cases, negligence claims, trespass, seduction, defamation, malicious prosecution, false imprisonment, assault, fraudulent representations, nuisance and conspiracy. "Other" cases include replevin, trover and detinue, ejectment, copyright cases, breach of promise of marriage.

brought. These were the kinds of cases, of course, where juries were still expected to find damages, in a way that they were not in many kinds of contract cases, where the matter was one largely of calculation.

Table 6: Circuit Trials

Year	Contract	Tort	Other
1860	45%	32%	23%
1870	45%	32%	23%
1880	50%	29%	21%
1890	40%	41%	19%
1900	45%	39%	17%
1910	36%	52%	12%

It may thus be suggested that one of the effects of the new rules of 1883 was simply to channel away cases where a jury's verdict did not help: contract cases where either there were no contentious facts at issue, or where the facts were too complicated for a jury to grasp, and cases where the jury's power to determine the issue and damages was limited. This appears to be confirmed by the trend found in Figure 10 (London and Middlesex Civil Trials, 1876–1913), which shows a very close correlation after 1883 between the number of judge-only cases, and the number of contractual cases. Similarly, Figure 11 (London and Middlesex Civil Trials, 1876–1913) shows a similar correlation between non-contract trials and the use of the jury. While we cannot argue that judges heard all contractual cases, the trend seems strongly to suggest a link in the number of contractual cases, and the number of judge-only trials. In this context, of course, we should note the establishment of the Commercial Court in 1895, where a specialist judge presided over complex commercial cases which were felt to be inappropriate for a jury.

A second observation may be made on the Rules of 1883. Looking at the figures for London, seen in Figure 12 (Special and Common Juries in London and Middlesex, 1876–1913) it is evident that the number of special juries remained largely constant throughout the 1880s and early 1890s. There is however a sharp decline in the number of common juries after 1883, followed by a stable trend, when there were marginally more common juries used than special juries. It may therefore be conjectured that the major effect of the new Rules of 1883 was largely to stop the routine use of common juries in matters where they were not needed, notably in liquidated damages cases, while special juries remained popular.[89] The special jury was felt to be

[89] The civil judicial statistics after 1876 only record the breakdown of special and common juries in London and Middlesex, while the figures for the circuit were only collected from 1894 onwards. The latter figures show a similar trend for the circuit as for the metropolitan areas,

better educated and more capable than the inferior common jury.[90] The special jury, to be sure, also gave opportunities for a vexatious litigant to drive up costs and delay the cause. However, the scope for such action diminished after 1852 on circuit and after 1870 in London.[91] In any event, the possibility of having a judge to decide the case was not sufficiently alluring to undermine the special jury, and in 1913, the Report of the Departmental Committee on Juries observed that it had "become far too much a matter of course to insist on a right to a jury in every case".[92] The committee was particularly critical of the fact that there was an unrestricted right to call for a special jury, and that parties did so when it was not really needed.

It can therefore be argued that in cases where damages were not simply a matter for calculation, and especially in tort cases, the demand for jury trials remained high. Judges may have been reducing the discretion of juries by developing new rules of law, but there was a strong defence of the jury's right to determine the damages it desired, particularly in tort,[93] where, in any case, legal doctrine was less developed than in contract.[94]

with slightly more common than special jurors. It may be conjectured that the statistics for the earlier period were probably not dissimilar to the London ones. Thus, at the Bristol assizes (spring and summer) in 1880, there were 30 cases, of which 8 (26.6%) were special jury ones. In the following year, there were again 30 cases, 7 (23.3%) of which were by special jury. In Winchester in 1881, 9 out of 27 (33%) cases were with a special jury (figures taken from PRO, ASSI 30/3). By comparison, in 1880, 29% of cases were heard by special jury in London and Middlesex. Similarly, at the summer assizes of 1877 on the Northern Circuit, 33% of the 204 cases set down sought special juries, at a time when 33% of cases in London went before special juries (figures from PRO, ASSI 54/4: Northern Circuit: Associate's Minute Book). Of course, the relative use of special juries varied from town to town.

90 *Report of the Departmental Committee appointed to inquire into and report upon the Law and Practice with regard to the Constitution, qualifications, selection, summoning, etc., of Juries* (1913) Cd 6817 XXX 403, 34. For a general discussion, see J Oldham, "Special Juries in England: Nineteenth Century Usage and Reform", (1987) 8 *JLH* 148 and *supra* ch. 8.

91 The opportunities for delay were greatest where the panel was struck in the old style, as practised in London before 1870 and on circuit until 1852, and which was available exceptionally thereafter. Under this procedure, the party seeking a special jury had to obtain a rule of court, which was followed by two meetings with the sheriff and the opposite attorney to select the jury. A further opportunity for delay came when the jurors had to be summoned, for if the attorney left his notification to the sheriff late, and not all the jurors appeared, he could have the case postponed. This procedure also raised the suspicion that attorneys might influence the composition of the jury. Regarding costs, each special juror was paid a guinea, which was made part of the general costs if the judge felt the case was suitable for such a trial. Since the costs were paid at the end of the suit, this procedure was useful for litigants hoping to force a settlement.

92 *Departmental Committee*, *supra* n. 90, 31.

93 See, e.g., (1858) 32 *Law Times* 109, commenting on *Fatcher* v. *Hinder*: "A very mischievous, and we believe a very illegal, disposition has shown itself lately on the bench to review the assessment of damages in cases where such assessment is wholly a matter for the discretion of the jury."

94 Even here, however, commentators defended the jury's right to find fact, disapproving of the attempt by judges to turn questions, such as the intention of parties to contract, into legal questions. See the comments on the House of Lords' decision in *Slattery* v. *Dublin, Wicklow and Wexford Railway Company*, in *The Times* 6 Aug. 1878, 7e.

IDEOLOGY OR PRACTICE: THE FUNCTION OF THE JURY

What was the purpose of trial by jury? Was it to provide a service which litigants required, or was it aimed at fulfilling a wider constitutional function, of educating the citizen, possibly at the expense of the suitor? Looking at the constitutional defences, one might be inclined to assume the latter, for one of the main arguments in favour of maintaining civil juries was Tocqueville's argument, quoted by William Forsyth, that

> "[i]t clothes every citizen with a kind of magisterial office; it makes all feel that they have duties to fulfil towards society, and that they take a part in its government"

and that it educated the public.[95] Looking, however, at the actual level of jury participation, it can be seen that, in practice, such an argument was deceptive. A Parliamentary return of 1855 stated that there were just under one million people on the county and borough jury lists. To put that into perspective, there were just over one million voters in the counties and boroughs of England and Wales on the eve of the reform act of 1867.[96] Voters went to the polls in general elections on average once every four and one-quarter years in Victoria's reign. How often did jurors serve? According to William Henry Palmer, the under-sheriff of Kent, speaking in 1850, jurors were selected from throughout the county in turn, serving about once every five years.[97] Similarly, in 1867, Charles James Abbott, the under-sheriff of Surrey, said that the 25,000 common jurors in his county only had to serve on average once every three years. In the same year, the secondary of the City of London stated that it took two and three quarter years to get through the City common jury list.[98] Such an interval would make jury service as common as voting.[99]

Taking into account the various kinds of jury service men were liable to, not only at the assizes and quarter sessions, but also in coroners' courts, local courts (such as Liverpool's active Court of Passage), county courts and courts assessing compensation in an age when the expansion of

[95] *Democracy in America*, found quoted in Forsyth, *supra* n. 1, 416.

[96] The exact figure for jurors is 937,551: PP 1854–5 (134) XLIII 843. The figure for voters is 1,054,297, taken from J Parry, *The Rise and Fall of Liberal Government in Victorian Britain*, (New Haven, Yale University Press, 1993), 335. It had risen from c. 700,000 in 1833.

[97] *First Report of the Common Law Commissioners*, *supra* n. 26, Appendix F, 122, q. 239 (evidence of W H Palmer).

[98] *Report from the Select Committee on Special and Common Juries*, PP 1867 (425) IX, 45, 36.

[99] J F Burton, under sheriff of Lincolnshire, said in 1870 that 180 common jurors were summoned to the assizes, but in addition, 384, 416 and 416 jurors were summoned for the quarter sessions in the three divisions of the county, making a total of 1306 common jurors per annum, out of 10,782 qualified to serve. Their service came once every seven and a half years: *Report from the Select Committee on the Juries Bill*, PP 1870 (306) VI 61, 39, qq. 974–9.

municipal services frequently interfered with private property, it would appear that qualified jurors were much in demand.[100] Much of this service was at a relatively mundane level, however, and neither required the highest intellect, nor offered much chance to educate.[101] Service at the assizes, before the superior court judges, was much smaller. The practice in summoning common juries for the assizes was to have a panel of between 48 and 72 jurors to try all the cases.[102] For special juries, until 1852, the practice was to summon a different special jury panel for each case;[103] but under the Common Law Procedure Act, outside London, one special jury panel was used for all cases, as with common juries. How many jurors served? In 1852, 673 common and special jurors were summoned for the assizes in Kent, and 699 in Surrey. In addition, there were 203 and 215 grand jurors summoned in each county.[104] This was an unusually high tally, largely thanks to the large number of special jurors called; and in the following year Kent summoned only 318 common and special jurors, and Surrey 245. That year Kent also summoned 193 grand jurors and Surrey 218. Thus, in a high year, less than 1,000 were called for jury service at the assizes in each of these counties, and in an average year, half that number. To put this in perspective, in 1853, there were 10,056 on Kent's jury list and 16,800 on Surrey's. In an average year, then, the chance of being summoned to an assize jury was about one in 20 in Kent, and one in 36 in Surrey. Given the small proportion of civil suits, the chances of hearing a civil case were much smaller.

[100] Joseph Rayner, the town clerk of Liverpool (a town with a population of half a million), explained in 1870 (ibid., 8) that there were 43,212 on the Liverpool burgess roll, compared with 37,080 voters. Of these, he considered only 15,000 fit to be called to serve on juries. He pointed out that each year, 184 and 640 common jurors were summoned to the quarter sessions, 336 jurors were summoned to the Court of Passage, 384 were summoned to the County Court (of whom only 130 served). In addition, "two or three" juries sat a week for compensation cases, and 2304 sat on coroners' inquests. 3594 jurors served during the year for borough purposes, making an average service of once every four years. In addition, however, jurors from Liverpool were also summoned for county purposes.

[101] Joseph Rayner said (ibid., 8, qq. 168–9) that "county court service, and service on compensation juries, might be disregarded, for it is never more than a service of a few hours"; and while coroners' inquests took longer, people from the lower class of jurors, but from the locality, were generally selected to serve on them.

[102] In some counties, such as Kent, there were two lists on one panel, with one list serving for the first half of the assizes and another for the second half. *First Report of the Common Law Commissioners, supra* n. 26, Appendix F, 122, q. 246 (evidence of W H Palmer).

[103] Under this system, the attorneys from each side in a case attended before the sheriff, who drew 48 names from the ballot box. At a later meeting, both sides struck out 12 names, leaving 24 summoned for the cause. The names were then put back in the ballot box, from which the special jurors for the next case were selected.

[104] Figure taken from PP 1854–5 (134) XLIII 843, supplemented by a return for the Home circuit in PRO, ASSI 39/19. The figures for these two counties were unusually high: on the Home Circuit, 2005 common and special jurors were summoned, along with 859 grand jurors. No other county in England or Wales summoned as many jurors in 1852.

What of London, where more than half the cases were heard? There were of course many more superior court sittings in the metropolis than a county jury could see. In London and Middlesex, there were sittings both in term, and after term, in all three courts.[105] For the Westminster sittings 60 common jurymen were summoned into each court from Middlesex.[106] These common jurymen were summoned for up to eight weeks at a time, hearing a large succession of cases. Less than 1,500 common jurors were summoned in each year to try the Middlesex common jury cases, and not more than 1,000 special jurors.[107] This was from a jury list (in 1853) of 37,756. The chances of hearing a civil suit in Middlesex before the superior court judges, none the less, were higher than in the provinces, there being a one in 15 chance. It was in the City of London where the chances of service were highest. The number of cases heard in the City was not much less than in Middlesex. In 1865, for instance, there were 662 common jury cases in Middlesex, and 383 in London; and London had a larger special jury case load than did Middlesex, 190 against 111.[108] While the special jury pool was larger in London than Middlesex (4,100 against 1,000), the number of available common jurors was, however, much smaller, there being only 5,000 in London.[109] Statistically, there was perhaps a one in eight chance of qualified jurors serving on a common jury in London.

The number of men who served on juries before superior court judges was therefore quite limited: it was hardly a democratic institution. It must also be borne in mind that a great deal of discretion was exercised by town clerks and under-sheriffs in summoning jurors. For example, Frederick Deacon, whose firm acted as under-sheriffs of Lancashire, stated in 1867 that there were 40,000 available on the jury list for the county. However, half of these were never used: "We consider them not competent; we strike out all those who are called mechanics, journeymen, and beersellers." There was thus an effective pool of 20,000 for the 3,160 summoned each year to the assizes and quarter sessions, making an average service there once every six years. But in fact the system was more exclusive still, for, as he put it:

> "The way in which we work the Juries is this; we select what we consider the best kind of men for the assizes, and that answers very well; the next best men we select for the sessions, and I believe they are all sufficiently intelligent jurors."[110]

[105] In term, there were three sittings for Middlesex in the Queen's Bench, and one for London, two for Middlesex and two for London in the Common Pleas, and three for Middlesex and two for London in the Exchequer. See J Paterson, H Macnamara and W Marshall, *The New Practice of the Common Law* (London, Law Times Office, 1856), 23–4.

[106] *Select Committee, supra* n. 98, 26 (evidence of William Burchell).

[107] According to figures in PP 1854 (447) LIII.507, 1274 special jurors were summoned for Westminster cases in 1853. In 1867, T W Erle pointed out that only about 1,000 of the special jurors on the list were alive and resident: *Select Committee, supra* n. 98, 1.

[108] PP 1867–8 (60) LVII 243.

[109] *Select Committee, supra* n. 98, 36 (evidence of G W G Potter).

[110] *Select Committee, supra* n. 99, 13, q. 311.

Joseph Rayner, town clerk of Liverpool, said that in his town, the clerk of the peace and the deputy registrar "know how to choose a good jury".[111]

Moreover, jury service was particularly focused where special juries were used. The pool of such jurors liable for service on circuit was small: in Surrey, for instance, there were just over 900 special jurors on the list. Twice yearly 48 were summoned to the assizes to hear the special jury cases, and according to Abbott in 1867, "we have not summoned anybody, except by accident, more than once during the last 13 years".[112] In the metropolitan areas, however, special jury service was much more frequent, and more troublesome. The chances of being called for special jury service in London were very high. In 1865, there were 190 special jury trials in London, and 111 in Middlesex, which accounted for 22.3 per cent of the civil suits heard in the superior courts in London and Westminster, and 11.7 per cent of all civil trials in the superior courts. In the City, there were some 4,100 special jurors available in London, and in Middlesex there were 1,000. Prior to 1870, the statistical chances of a special juror being required for a case were very high indeed, since at that time a fresh panel was summoned for every case. The system abolished outside the metropolis in 1852 was deliberately retained in London and Westminster, because it was argued that London jurors would find it far more inconvenient to be kept from their businesses for a week or a fortnight at a stretch than to be called case by case.[113] In the event, these jurors found themselves repeatedly called. At this time, a special juror's statistical chance of being called was better than evens in the City, and almost three to one in Middlesex. A very small pool indeed heard one tenth of all civil cases. Though the introduction of a special jury panel reduced the chances of being called (while extending the period for which a juror was called), special jury service in metropolitan areas remained heavy.[114] Elite jurors were clearly much in demand, especially in London. George Potter, the Secondary of the City of London, observed in 1867 that:

> "The jurymen generally sought after, are those about Fenchurch-street, Mark-lane, Mincing-lane, and all that locality. They possess great mercantile knowledge, and a great number of cases in London are mercantile cases."[115]

[111] Ibid., 9, q. 192.

[112] *Select Committee, supra* n. 98, 43. Statistically, the chances of being summoned in any year were just over one in nine: Abbott's figure reflects a turnover of special jurors over time, as new men qualified and older men died.

[113] *First Report of the Common Law Commissioners, supra* n. 26, 43.

[114] This is something that continued. According to Sir John Macdonnell, in 1913 there were 18,180 special jurors in the metropolitan districts, of whom 7,666 (42%) were summoned to court. *Departmental Committee, supra* n. 90, 19.

[115] *Select Committee, supra* n. 98, 38, q 782. Those summoning jurors did work on a street-by-street basis: as *The Times*, 25 Sept. 1888, 9e said: "When the returning officer visits Mark-lane he carries off half the corn factors. When he makes a raid on Mincing-lane the produce market is depleted of brokers."

The elite focus of jury service may help to explain why it was so frequently asserted in this period that the burden of jury service was increasing, at a time when the statistics do not bear this out.[116]

The constitutional defence of trial by jury—that it brought the nation into the administration of justice, and that it taught the arts of citizenship—was hence rather misleading. If jury service overall extended no farther than the franchise in mid-century, as the franchise widened in 1867 and 1884, and the use of juries fell, it fell behind.[117] Moreover, the average English juror was far more likely to learn his law from a justice of the peace in quarter sessions, hearing a petty criminal case, than from a superior court judge: yet, it was in this area particularly that the mid nineteenth-century saw the growth of summary trials. The Rolls-Royce justice in the civil cases in the superior courts required a higher class of jurors, men who did not need educating. When in 1913, Sir John Macdonnell defended jury trial, by arguing that "the administration of justice should be kept in close touch with the public" and that jury trial had been so reduced it was not safe to go further,[118] he was in effect asking for an elite, educated watchdog for the highest cases. At a time of political reform, legal reformers in fact showed little inclination to broaden the social composition of the jury.

This can be seen in the reaction to demands from the working classes for access to the jury. Throughout the later nineteenth century, there were calls from trade unionists for working men to be put on juries, a call taken up in the 1870s by Gathorne Hardy in Parliament.[119] According to the Trades Union Congress, the qualification for jury service should be the same as the franchise qualification.[120] The campaign, however, did not get far. One practical obstacle to be overcome was the problem that poor men could usually not afford the time away from work. There were many who argued that the gap in remuneration between common jurors and special jurors was inequitable, and that jurors should be paid. Against this, it was argued that to pay jurors adequately would run the risk of creating professional jurymen.[121] In the event, the provisions in Enfield's Act in 1870 for the remuneration of jurors proved unworkable, and had to be repealed within a year.[122]

[116] The impression that reformers held that jury service was increasing, and proving a particular burden to jurors, is not echoed by the statistics for civil jury trials in this era. In 1867, William Burchell asserted that "the business of Westminster Hall is certainly twice as great as it was a few years ago": *Select Committee*, *supra* n. 98, 28, q. 549. This was not true: in 1851, there were 1,073 trials in the superior courts at Westminster, compared with 1,173 in 1860, 1,347 in 1865 and 1,204 in 1870.

[117] In 1872, *The Times* (15 May, 9b) commented that it had been estimated that only 1% of the population had ever sat on a jury.

[118] *Departmental Committee*, *supra* n. 90, 159, q. 4581.

[119] *The Times*, 10 Apr. 1873, 11f, 10 May 1873, 7f.

[120] *The Times*, 8 Nov. 1878, 8d.

[121] *The Times*, 17 Sept. 1878, 7b.

[122] 34 & 35 Vict., c. 2.

Besides this practical problem, the campaigners for working class jurymen encountered more ideological objections from middle class commentators. In January 1876, *The Observer* even suggested that bitter workers wanted to swamp juries.[123] Edward W Cox similarly wrote in October 1878 that:

> "[I]f the qualifications were lowered swarms of the unfit would be admitted, and it would be impossible to invest in any officer the determination of intellectual competency."[124]

Rather than widening access to juries, reformers therefore tended to favour raising the barrier.[125] In 1853, the Common Law Commissioners favoured raising the qualification of jurors, at least in the country areas.[126] The issue was discussed again in the mid-1860s by Alexander Pulling, who chaired a committee of the Law Amendment Society on juries. He also testified before Lord Enfield's select committee on juries in the House of Commons in 1867. Pulling argued that Peel's consolidating act of 1825, which qualified all £10 freeholders and £20 leaseholders, had debased the ordinary jury. If the old standard of jury qualification were still observed (by which he meant the qualifications set in legislation of 1415 and 1585), a juryman's proper qualification would be £150 per annum landed property, or personal property of £1500 in value. He argued that one reason why special juries were so popular was because common juries were so bad, and he argued for a £100 qualification.[127] Like many others, he argued that the best way to spread jury service more equally was not to make the jury more popular, but to remove the exemptions which allowed clergymen, army officers, lawyers and even inland revenue officials to escape service.[128]

Bills were introduced in 1869 and 1870 that sought to raise the jury qualification to the occupation of property with a rateable value of £30, or £50 in towns with populations above 20,000. This question was referred to another

[123] This was disclaimed by Henry Crompton, who was then leading the campaign. *The Times*, 17 Jan. 1876, 4f, 22 Jan. 1876, 4f, 27 Jan. 1876, 11d.

[124] *The Times*, 5 Oct. 1878, 8b.

[125] Thus, (1850) 16 *Law Times* 224, argued that jury qualification should be raised to exclude all who were unfit, while all the educated classes should be included. If this were done, it said, the distinction between common and special jurors could be ended.

[126] *Second Report of the Common Law Commissioners*, *supra* n. 34, 6. A proposal was put into the Common Law Procedure Bill, but dropped in face of anxieties that it might create difficulties in finding enough common jurors: *Hansard*, 3rd ser. vol. 134, col. 874 (1854).

[127] A Pulling, "Proposal for Amending the Laws Affecting Juries and Jurymen", (1865) 40 *Law Times* 112; *Select Committee*, *supra* n. 98, 12, 17, qq. 289–93, 317. Agreeing with Pulling's elitist view of the jury, Erle, *supra* n. 69, iv-v, observed in 1882 that "the degenerate form of jury has now prevailed for just so long, that people to-day, knowing of nothing better, mistake it for what it essentially is not, that is to say, the jury approved and adopted by our forefathers, which was an assemblage of *selected* men, of a substantial condition, such as that of special jurors of the present date."

[128] It may be noted that T W Erle said that since the jury was useful for popular education, ministers of religion should be on the jury panel. This implied that the ministers would then teach what they had learned to their flocks: *The Times*, 28 Feb. 1873, 4d.

select committee. While many were in favour of increasing the qualification of jurors (particularly in those cities and boroughs where jury qualification was given to all those on the burgess roll, which had been greatly swelled by the 1867 Reform Act), a sizeable proportion also argued that making the threshold too high would seriously reduce the pool of jurors, so that, in some areas, there would simply not be enough jurors to do the work. The question of raising the jury qualification was mooted again in 1873, but given the difficulties of changing the system, the qualifications set in 1825 for common jurors remained in place into the twentieth century. Nevertheless, it was clear that in practice, the good jury was required more for the benefit of the suitor, than for the benefit of the citizen.

IMPROVING THE JURY

From the mid-1860s, in the age of the Judicature Acts, reformers turned their attention to improving the jury system, but not to abolishing it. In this decade, it became increasingly clear that the Rolls-Royce system was not working. What concerned men most was the composition and summoning of the jury. Reformers now had three aims. First, they wanted to widen the pool of capable jurors, and relieve the burden on a small number, especially of special jurors. Secondly, they sought to remove bad men from the jury. Thirdly, they aimed to raise the level of the common jury, in particular by introducing a system of composite juries, which would mix together special and common jurors. The reformers' minds were focused particularly on problems arising in London.

The heavy burden on the small number of men qualified for special jury service in the metropolis led to many complaints in the press. It was not uncommon for men to be summoned up to eight times for a single session, and to have this occur three to four times a year.[129] Few disagreed with the *Pall Mall Gazette*'s comment in 1865 that:

> "The London special juryman undoubtedly is, next to the costermonger's jack-ass, the worst used animal within the bills of mortality."[130]

The matter was taken up by T W Erle, the Associate of the Court of Common Pleas, in a pamphlet published in 1865, which had already been sent, in manuscript form, to the Home Secretary, who passed a copy on to the Chief Justice.[131] Erle in particular pointed to the evils of summoning a separate special jury for each case, in place of having a panel. He also wanted a more careful revision of the list of those liable to serve on special

[129] See, e.g., (1866) 41 *Law Times* 594; *Select Committee*, *supra* n. 98, qq. 813 ff.

[130] *The Times*, 9 Dec. 1865, 10f.

[131] T W Erle, *On the Present System of Summoning Special Juries in London and Middlesex* (London, 1865). The copy and correspondence is in PRO, HO 45/7788.

juries, and the adoption of arrangements to make service on juries fall more equally on those liable to it. The pamphlet clearly caught the attention of the government.[132]

The issue took on greater urgency in February 1867, when on the opening day of the *nisi prius* sittings in Queen's Bench, every special jury case ready for trial had to be postponed for want of jurors. In an outburst that would be widely reported, the presiding judge, Shee, exclaimed "it is manifest that our jury system has broken down; it is an utter failure".[133] He then asked John Coleridge, an MP practising in the court, whether legislation could not be brought to solve the problem caused by the nature of the jury lists. The principal difficulty was that there were too few special jurors qualified, largely because many of those who should have been on the jury list escaped being put on it.[134] It was constantly asserted that the system of summoning jurors was rife with corruption, and that greasing the right palm would invariably result in the man's name being omitted from the jury list.[135] This placed an undue burden on those who were on the lists; and their response in many cases was to evade service, preferring to pay a fine rather than attend.[136] The result was that in only roughly a quarter of cases was there a full special jury, the rest having between two and four talesmen,[137] who were not qualified for special jury service. Erle stated in his pamphlet that the more important a case was, the less likely it was that a full special jury would be obtained, since men knew they would be kept away from their business for long periods. The system fell into more disrepute in 1867, when the Court of Aldermen discovered that one Charles Mayhew, who had formerly been a clerk in the Tower Ward office with access to the jury list, ran a lucrative business in getting men excused from jury service. In return for paying Mayhew a guinea a year, any man not wanting to serve in the city could send him the summons, and he would swear a false affidavit to get him excused.[138] Non-attendance by

[132] Collier, the Solicitor-General, agreed that legislation should be passed in London to make the practice of summoning jurors the same as that practised in the country; and that there should be an inquiry into the preparation of the special jury lists: R P Collier to Sir George Grey, 23 May 1865, PRO HO 45/7788.

[133] *The Times*, 2 Feb. 1867, 10f.

[134] Pulling estimated that if the Middlesex lists were properly made out, there would be 15,000 on the list. Burchell hoped an improved system would put 6–8000 on the list: *Select Committee*, *supra* n. 98, 17, q. 343, 27, q. 529.

[135] Ibid., 55, q. 1137 (evidence of Henry Pollock, Associate of the Court of Exchequer).

[136] This was policy which even Erle (ibid., 8, q. 173) conceded was the logical thing for special jurors to do: "I think that at present, owing to the long waiting at the court, and the uncertainty, and the numerous summonses, it is much the best policy for a merchant to keep away from the courts, and run his chance of a fine."

[137] Ibid., 7, q. 160.

[138] Mayhew was apprehended, and put on trial at the Old Bailey, but died before the case came to court. His assistant, Richard Davis, was convicted, however: (1867) 42 *Law Times* 286. For another case of corrupt officials, see *The Times*, 23 May 1873, 10e.

special jurors was clearly a problem that judges wanted to solve;[139] but, given the particular problems of London special jurors, it was hard to be too strict, and many of those who were fined were able to have their fines remitted.

The main difficulty came from the vague definition of the qualification of the special juror, as an "esquire, merchant or banker", since these descriptions were very vague. As Erle put it, "practically any juror can get himself placed upon the list of common or special jurors as he likes".[140] Busy men of affairs who wanted to avoid jury service told the overseer that they were gentlemen, and were left off the special jury, and put on the common jury panel, where their chances of service were much smaller. In this way, stock-brokers, ship-owners, and colonial brokers were routinely left off. Those who were coal merchants or potato merchants were included, however, and they were among the same faces who (according to Erle) kept appearing on special juries. They were the so-called guinea pigs, who courted jury service for the fee they got per case.[141]

The problem was to some degree addressed by the Act of 1870, which put a rating qualification for special jury service alongside the traditional status qualification. Besides merchants, bankers and esquires, those in residential property assessed at over £100 a year in towns and at over £50 in the country were qualified as special jurors, as well as occupiers of premises (other than farms) assessed at over £100 per annum. This change increased the pool of special jurors significantly.[142] However, Enfield's Act of 1870 only changed the law as to special jurors' qualifications, and left unaddressed the question of the slovenly and haphazard preparation of the jury lists by overseers. This meant that jury service continued to fall unequally. As early as 1872, the matter was raised again in Parliament by Lopes, and a bill to reform jury law more widely, prepared by Erle, was introduced by Coleridge. The bill sought to codify the law of juries anew, and was thus ambitious and extensive, appropriately enough for an age of judicature reform. However, it contained many controversial elements, which failed to secure support on the three occasions it was brought.

[139] In March 1877, A D Coleridge, clerk of assizes on the Midland Circuit, wrote to the under-sheriffs of the counties on the circuit: "[T]hat in consequence of the laxity of attendance of Special Jurors in several counties, their Lordships will scrupulously examine all written excuses, and that any Doctor giving a Medical Cert. must attend the Assizes in person in order to answer any questions as to the inability of Special Jurors to appear in obedience to the summons." In the following year, Hawkins J rejected a doctor's certificate on the basis that the doctor did not examine the patient on the day he was due to be a juror: PRO, ASSI 15/6, f. 69, 122–5.

[140] *Select Committee*, *supra* n. 98, 1, q. 6. See also evidence of William Burchell, at 27 qq. 521–5.

[141] Ibid., 10, qq. 247–8, 261.

[142] In 1913, there were 18,180 special jurors in the county of London and Middlesex: *Departmental Committee*, *supra* n. 90, 19 (figures of Sir John Macdonnell).

Perhaps the least controversial reform proposed was the practical one of jury qualification. The reformers aimed to abandon the qualification formula of banker, merchant and esquire, left in place by the Act of 1870, to extend the qualification to lodgers and tenants of highly rated properties, and to add representatives of public trading companies to the list of special jurors. They also sought to revise the system of calling jurors, to ensure that selection would be by rota, not by the discretion of the under-sheriff. Equally, they wanted to reduce the exemptions from service, in order to increase the size of the pool of special jurors, without diluting its quality. Each proposal, however, faced opposition from traditionalists, who feared that the proposed changes would lower rather than raise the standard of the jury. Many felt that since special jurors should be chosen for intellect and character rather than simple rating, the old qualifications should be retained. Similarly, it was argued that if an alphabetical or rota system were used, it would dilute the quality of the jury. William Burchell wrote to the press in May and June 1872, arguing that since the 1870 Act qualified publicans, discretion was still needed in summoning jurors, to ensure that the bad men were omitted. For good measure, he added that he would find the proposed reforms to the drawing of the jury lists unworkable.[143] Others agreed that the introduction of a rating qualification reduced the quality of the special jurors. In 1873, Sir John Karslake commented that it was no longer the case that a London special jury was capable of knowing the details of business transactions. He said that since men were now chosen for their rating rather than their rank, there were no longer "real" merchants at the London sittings, but only shopkeepers.[144] In fact, this argument was slightly disingenuous, for the old system of allowing men to be qualified as "merchants" brought those very shopkeepers into the system.[145]

In the event, the attempt to reform the way that jury lists were drawn failed in 1873, largely for financial reasons, rather than ones of principle.[146] This failure to carry the proposed reforms undermined the attempts to ensure that the special jury would remain of high quality. Economic changes, particularly in the city, were changing the nature of jurors there. The growth of joint stock companies, whose directors lived in the suburbs, increasingly removed the highest class from special jury service, which was now carried out by more mundane traders.[147] Moreover, the method of summoning jurors in the

[143] *The Times*, 19 May 1872, 12f, 11 June, 6f.

[144] (1873) 17 *Solicitor's Journal* 498.

[145] One of the reasons why Erle and Coleridge wanted to use a rating or rental qualification only was to ensure that men of lower intelligence would not get onto City of London special juries: Erle, *supra* n. 69, 73–6.

[146] The bill failed when parliament agreed that overseers should be paid, but could not agree on whether they should be paid out of local or central taxation: *The Times*, 23 Apr. 1874, 9b.

[147] *The Times*, 23 Apr. 1874, 9b. The problem was discussed again by the Departmental Committee in 1913.

City was haphazard. Since summonses were issued on foot, men were called street by street. Given the concentration of trades in the city, this meant that the entire business of an area could be paralysed during the sittings. If the special jury was from Farringdon Without or from Cripplegate Without, areas largely dominated by retailers, its quality was likely to be much lower than a common jury taken from Aldgate.[148] Confidence in the London mercantile special jury thus diminished, and it was recognised that these juries could not be relied on to guide on mercantile customs.[149] After the opening of the Royal Courts of Justice in the Strand, there was a campaign by the Bar Council and the Incorporated Law Society to confine the London list to purely mercantile cases, a matter taken up with the Lord Chancellor by Erle. In Erle's view, if this were done, the list of city jurors would have to be reformed to get only men of mercantile expertise on it.[150]

There was a rearguard action fought by some magistrates, who wanted to keep the special jury pure. For a number of years after 1870, different benches of magistrates in Middlesex disagreed on the interpretation of the Act of that year, with the Kensington bench of justices arguing that the provision respecting the qualification by occupation of premises did not apply in towns. This interpretation would have excluded publicans. Nevertheless, when the question was submitted to the law officers in 1886, they took the view that the reading of the Kensington bench was not the correct one.[151] By 1913, almost one in four of London's special jurors were publicans. Witnesses to the Departmental Committee on juries in 1913 commented on the low quality of special jurors now, and the report itself noted that special jurors had declined in quality in London, though common jurors had improved.[152]

The proposed reforms of the 1870s included more controversial matters than the formation of jury lists, however, all of which aroused strong opposition. Presuming that the special jurors would continue to be an elite group, the reformers aimed, first, to reduce the size of the jury,[153] secondly, to ensure that every jury contained a man of the higher class, and thirdly, to remove the need for unanimity in juries. The proposal to reduce the size of

[148] Erle, *supra* n. 69, 78; letter from J Tayler, *The Times* 21 Sept. 1888, 4b.

[149] (1884) 28 *Solicitor's Journal* 493.

[150] *The Times*, 28 Sept. 1888, 10c.

[151] London Metropolitan Archives, MR/F/Misc/Box 159.

[152] E C Coles-Webb, chief clerk to the sheriff of the county of London, pointed out in 1913 that 22% of the 13,000 special jurors in the county of London were publicans: *Departmental Committee*, *supra* n. 90, 29–30, esp. qq. 935–7.

[153] Though Enfield's Act of 1870 did not address this (though his committee had recommended that Parliament turn its attention to it), A W Young (who brought with him experience of civil juries of 4 in Australia), proposed in 1870 that a bill should be brought to reduce the number of jurors: *Hansard*, 3rd ser. vol. 200, col. 1415 (1870). The idea was hardly new. E W Cox in letters to Lord Campbell in 1851 had suggested that with a better qualified juryman, it would be safe to reduce the number to seven or even five: (1851) 18 *Law Times* 10.

the jury was purely pragmatic, aimed at lessening the burden of serving on a jury.[154] Erle contended that it was safe to do. First, changes in the law of evidence (such as allowing parties to testify) and procedure (such as allowing speeches by counsel for prisoners) made juries' jobs much easier than they had been in the past. Secondly, it was no longer the case that juries needed safety in numbers, to protect themselves from intimidating judges. Thirdly, he argued, in special jury cases, in only a quarter of cases was there a full jury: and where a tales was prayed, it was generally from the generous feeling of counsel that some poor common jurors should hit the one guinea jackpot. If there were two special jurors on each panel, he would be happy to see a jury of eight.[155] In fact, Coleridge's bill proposed a jury of seven.

The proposal for reduced jury numbers failed, however, for it faced the determined opposition of the common law judges and many in the profession.[156] The *Solicitor's Journal* pointed out that one reason why juries were so little used in county courts was because there were only five on the jury. It argued that, if the anomalous jury system worked, it was only thanks to the safety of numbers, concluding:

> "The verdicts of juries are generally given by two or three men of ability and character, who lead the others."[157]

Men like Erle of course saw the creation of composite juries as a solution to this problem. In theory (and in law) special jurors were qualified for common jury service, and no legislation was needed to get them onto these juries, even if under-sheriffs needed reminding that special jurors were liable. In practice, however, they were kept on separate lists, and not called for common jury service.[158] However, the proposal to create composite juries was controversial, and was removed from the 1872 bill by the select committee which felt that it would be invidious to have men of different classes on the same jury, with one paid a guinea and another a shilling.[159]

The proposal to remove unanimity proved equally contentious. This proposal had a long provenance among reformers, dating from 1831, when the Common Law Commissioners attacked the requirement for unanimity in civil suits.[160] The ancient common law system that required unanimity, but which forced juries to agree by locking them up without fire or food, seemed barbaric to many reformers. In 1839, Cecil Fane urged Brougham

[154] *The Times*, 28 Feb. 1873, 4d, reprinted in Erle, *supra* n. 69, 119–34.

[155] Erle, *supra* n. 69, 124–5.

[156] They met in April 1873, agreeing that the number of jurors should stay at 12, and that unanimity should still be required: *The Times*, 28 Apr. 1873, 13e.

[157] (1872) 16 *Solicitor's Journal* 301–2.

[158] Those who were called often expressed their irritation at being called away from their business for petty cases. See, e.g., T Williams to A D Coleridge, 29 Jan. 1884, PRO, ASSI 15/6.

[159] See (1873) 17 *Solicitor's Journal* 687.

[160] They proposed that the jury should be kept in deliberation for12 hours, after which a majority of nine should be allowed.

to take the matter up in his motion on the administration of law in Ireland. He wrote:

> "If it is right to starve Jurymen why should not a slow Chancellor, like Lord Eldon, be denied his bottle of Port &c till he had given Judgement in all cases heard, but not decided. What's sauce for the goose is sauce for the gander."[161]

Others agreed that it was anomalous that juries had to be united while judges were not required to be unanimous. At the same time, some reformers argued that disagreements were bound to occur now that juries were more intelligent than they had been in the past. It was also said that in civil suits, where there were balanced rights on both sides, it was unrealistic to expect complete unanimity.[162] Throughout the mid-century, there was widespread discussion of the need for reform in this area.[163] Not all agreed, however, that the unanimity requirement should be abolished. Indeed, even reformers within the legal profession were divided on the issue. In 1858, a committee of the Law Amendment Society considered the question (after Serjeant Woolrych had spoken to them defending it) and came to the conclusion that it was essential in criminal cases. The committee and the society remained divided on whether to retain unanimity in civil cases.[164] If the general trend in the press was to attack unanimity in civil suits, no less a reformer than Erle told *The Times* that he supported unanimity, particularly if the number of jurors was reduced.[165]

Given this disagreement, earlier attempts at reform had foundered as rival law lords had put forward counter proposals. The Common Law Commissioners in 1853 favoured unanimity, but agreed that the ancient method of starving the jury into agreement should be abolished. They suggested that after 12 hours, jurors who disagreed should be discharged, rather than being coerced to make a judgement.[166] The Common Law Procedure Bill was accordingly introduced on these lines, but while it was passing through the Lords, Campbell proposed that the idea proposed in 1831 should be substituted, that after 12 hours a majority verdict would be taken. Though not entirely convinced, Cranworth, the Lord Chancellor, agreed. The proposal, however, was fiercely opposed in the Lords by St Leonards and in the Commons by those concerned that the notion of allowing majority verdicts in civil cases would involve its introduction in criminal

[161] Fane to Brougham, 4 Aug. 1839, UCL, Brougham MSS, MS 32014. Brougham, in his proposed jury law reforms, did seek to remove the unanimity requirement. See *Hansard*, 3rd ser. vol. 133, col. 1154 (1854).

[162] See (1859) 33 *Law Times* 26, (1862) 38 *Law Times* 25, 222, 559, *The Times*, 1 Sept. 1863, 11d.

[163] See, e.g., the exchange in 1859 between Bramwell and a juryman: (1859) 34 *Law Times* 145.

[164] (1859) 7 *Law Magazine and Law Review* 388.

[165] Erle, *supra* n. 69, 125.

[166] *Second Report of the Common Law Commissioners*, *supra* n. 34, 8.

ones.[167] The result was preservation of the status quo, with juries being required to be unanimous, and being starved into unanimity.

Yet, it was soon evident that this rule led in jury verdicts to the very kind of messy compromise that made nonsense of the law. Things came to a head in *Smith* v. *Great Northern Railway* in 1858, when a passenger sued the railway company for negligence, because of the serious injuries he had sustained on a very stormy night, when a station master had failed to put up a caution signal. After two hours, the jury found for the plaintiff, but awarded only a farthing damages. Campbell told them that this was insufficient for a serious injury, and sent them back. Two hours later, they were still disagreed, so he sent them away all night, at the end of which they were still disagreed.[168] Campbell discharged them, but resolved to bring in a bill to allow majority verdicts. His bill failed, however, after it was subjected to a stinging attack by Lyndhurst, who said that the bill aimed to alter "one of the most important and fundamental laws of the kingdom".[169] The arguments against removing unanimity were that juries would simply decide on a verdict by casting lots, rather than by discussing the issue, and that they would fall under the influence of the presiding judge. In Lyndhurst's view, disagreement was rare, and where it occurred, it was for good reason.[170] Given this opposition, which was supported by pamphlets by experienced lawyers such as George Rochfort Clarke,[171] the bill failed.

If the question of abolishing unanimity in juries was controversial by itself, when (in the bill of 1872) it was placed alongside reducing the size of the jury, and extended to criminal trials, save for murder, felony and treason, it became explosive. Under Coleridge's bill, while there would normally be a jury of seven, the trial could proceed with five if there were not enough jurors available. *The Times* commented:

> "Now if five Jurors, who need not even be unanimous, are to send a man to penal servitude for life, the time will have come to talk as little as possible of a British Jury as the Palladium of English liberty."[172]

When the bill was reintroduced in 1874, the proposal for a smaller jury was limited to civil juries. Given the lack of agreement on the issue, the clause was withdrawn, while a large majority voted in favour of retaining the unanimity requirement.[173]

[167] *Hansard*, 3rd ser. vol. 133, cols. 787 ff (1854), vol. 134, cols. 877ff (1854), vol. 135, cols. 1505 ff (1854).

[168] *The Times*, 18 Dec. 1858, 8c, 21 Dec. 1858, 8e, (1858) 32 *Law Times* 158.

[169] *Hansard*, 3rd ser. vol 153, col. 1018 (1859).

[170] He pointed out that *Smith* v. *Great Northern Railway Company* was only one of ten cases arising from this accident, five of which had seen juries divided. Lord Chelmsford LC also commented on the difficulties of that litigation: *Hansard*, 3rd ser. vol. 153, col. 1028 (1859).

[171] G R Clarke, *Unanimity in Trial by Jury Defended* (London, Stevens and Norton, 1859).

[172] *The Times*, 18 Feb. 1873, 9a, 24 Feb. 1873, 9b.

[173] *The Times* 15 May 1874, 9b, 22 May 1874, 8a.

THE JURY PRESERVED

Thus, Coleridge's great attempt to reform the law of juries in the 1870s failed. Despite widespread criticism of the practical working of the civil jury, the institution was vigorously defended with all its imperfections, even when incremental reforms were proposed. The reformers were seen as iconoclasts, attacking a cherished institution. Thus, in 1873, *Punch* carried a cartoon showing Coleridge and the Lord Chancellor, Selborne, attempting to steal the palladium of British liberty.[174] Juries remained secure in their place in the civil justice system, in spite of the salvos of numerous opponents. Up to the outbreak of the First World War, there were repeated criticisms of the use of juries in civil cases, and occasional attempts at reform. Various minor pieces of legislation were passed in the last years of the nineteenth century and early years of the twentieth, which sought to make improvements in various areas.[175] Nonetheless, after Coleridge's failed legislation, there was no major inquiry into the jury system in civil cases again until the 1913 Departmental Committee. This committee noted that there had been "a decided failure to keep pace with changing conditions",[176] and devoted much attention to possible improvement of the administrative means by which jurors were summoned. It commented, however, that:

> "[W]e have nowhere met with any traces of a feeling that an ordinary jury of to-day is not as a rule a competent tribunal."

If complex commercial transactions were baffling to jurymen, it was to be remembered that such cases almost invariably went before the Commercial Court, where the judge sat alone.[177] While the committee considered there might usefully be some restriction on the right to a civil jury, it concluded that:

> "[N]o sweeping change is practicable or desirable at the present day, and that no acceptance would be found for any proposal entirely to abolish the traditional right to trial by jury even in purely civil cases."[178]

It was proposed, however, that trial by jury should only be available as of right where both sides requested it, or where questions of personal character were at stake. In other cases, it should be for the judge to decide.

174 It was accompanied by a satirical ditty: (1873) 64 *Punch* 88.

175 The Special Juries Act of 1898 (61 & 62 Vict., c. 6) and the County Common Juries Act of 1910 (10 Edw. VII & 1 Geo. V, c. 17) amended the law relating to the number of special and common jurors to be summoned on a panel. The Juries Detention Act 1897 (60 & 61 Vict., c. 18) allowed the jury to be separated before reaching a verdict in cases of felony other than murder or treason, while the Assizes and Quarter Sessions Act of 1908 (8 Edw. VII, c. 41) allowed the attendance of jurors at sessions be dispensed with if there was no business.

176 *Departmental Committee*, *supra* n. 90, 25.

177 Ibid., 28–9.

178 Ibid., 31.

STEALING THE "PALLADIUM,"

OR, ULYSSES AND DIOMED IN THE NINETEENTH CENTURY.

In fact, change was postponed until 1918, when the Juries Act was passed, enacting that all cases in the High Court, save those involving questions of character, should be before a judge alone, unless the judge saw fit to order a jury.[179] As Jackson showed, this change was a wartime response to the shortage of available jurors, and was repealed in 1925, when litigants again chose to use juries.[180]

[179] This was re-enacted in the Administration of Juries Act of 1920.

[180] Jackson, *supra* n. 77. As he shows, the right to jury trial was once more restricted by the 1933 Administration of Justice (Miscellaneous Provisions) Act, which was followed by a sharp fall in the proportion of jury trials.

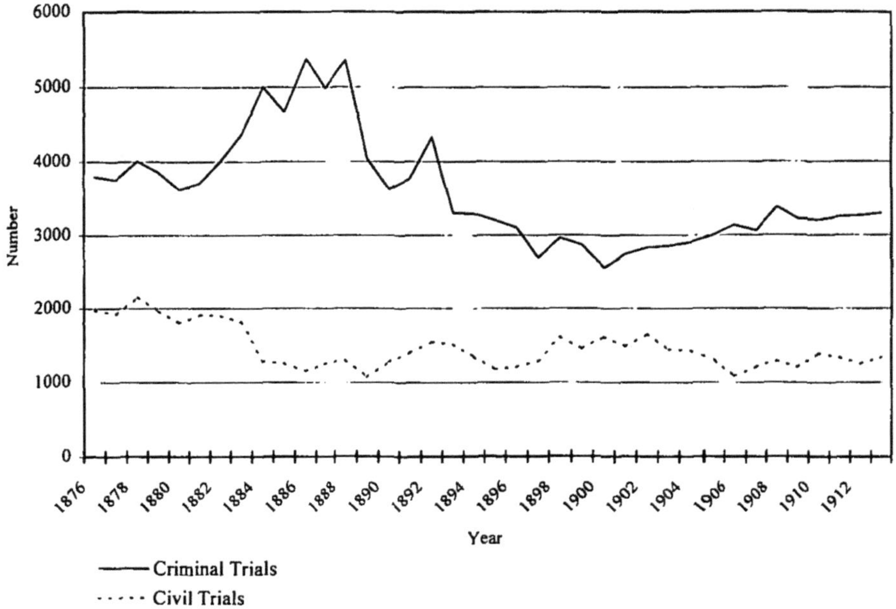

Figure 1 Jury trials before Superior Court Judges, 1876–1913

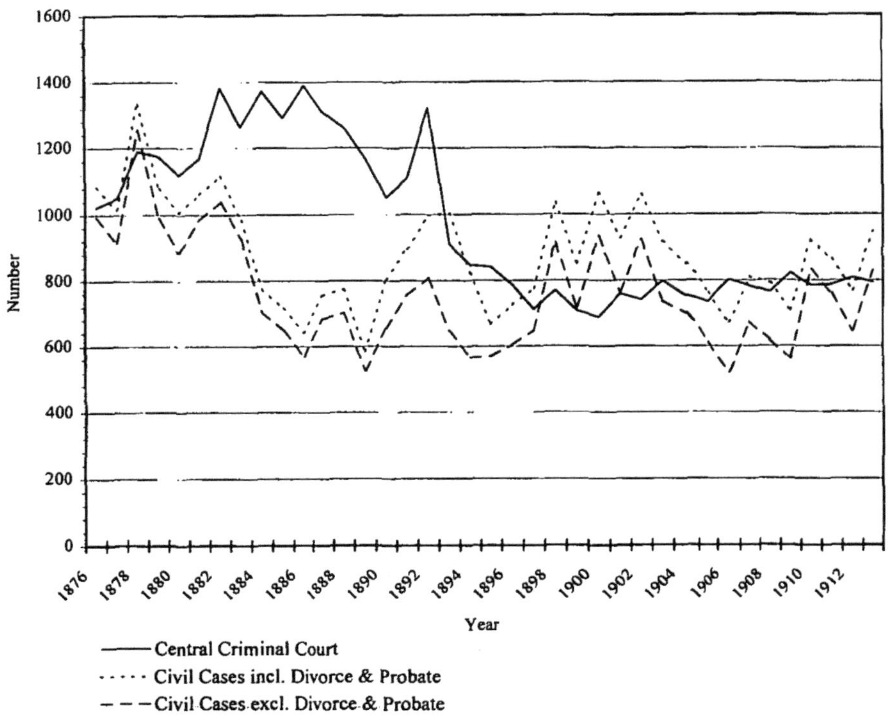

Figure 2 Jury trials before Superior Court Judges in the Metropolis, 1876–1913

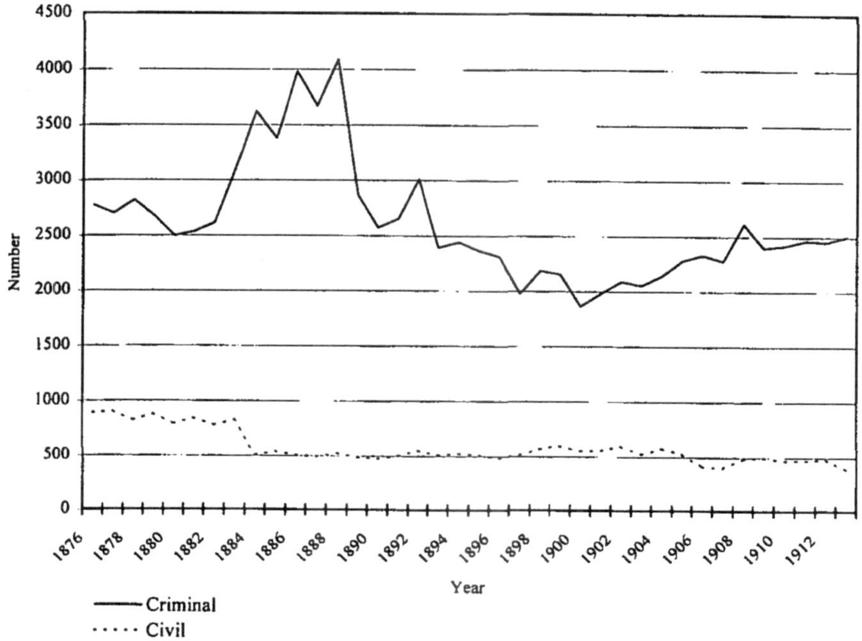

Figure 3 Jury trials at Assize and *Nisi Prius*, 1876–1913

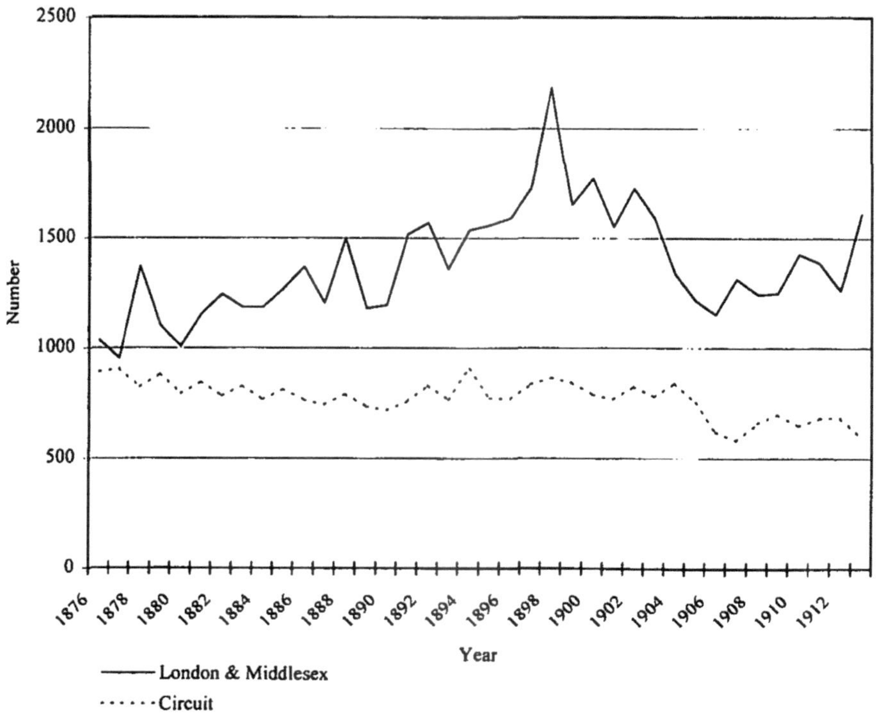

Figure 4 Civil trials before Superior Court Judges, 1876–1913

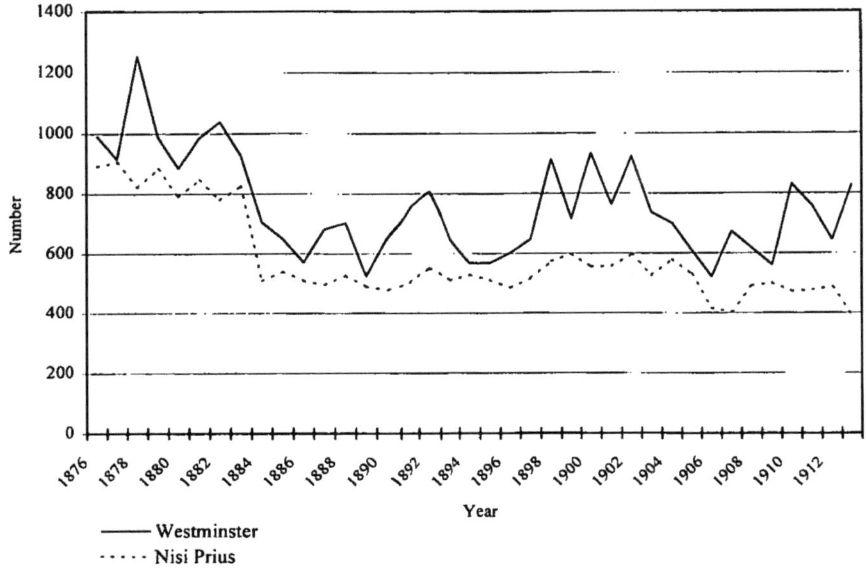

Figure 5 Civil jury trials before Superior Court Judges at Westminster and at *Nisi Prius*, 1876–1913

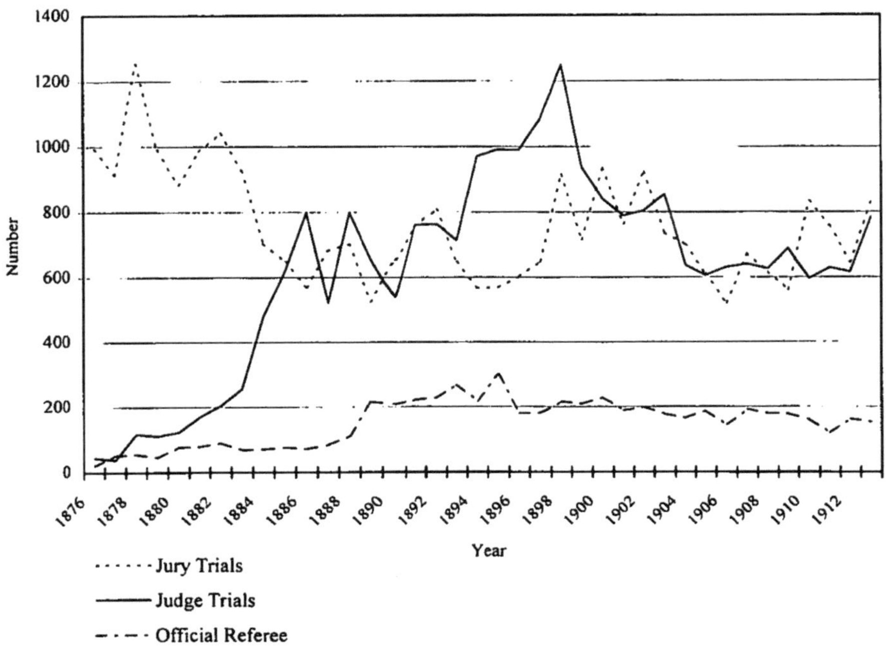

Figure 6 London and Middlesex trials, 1876–1913

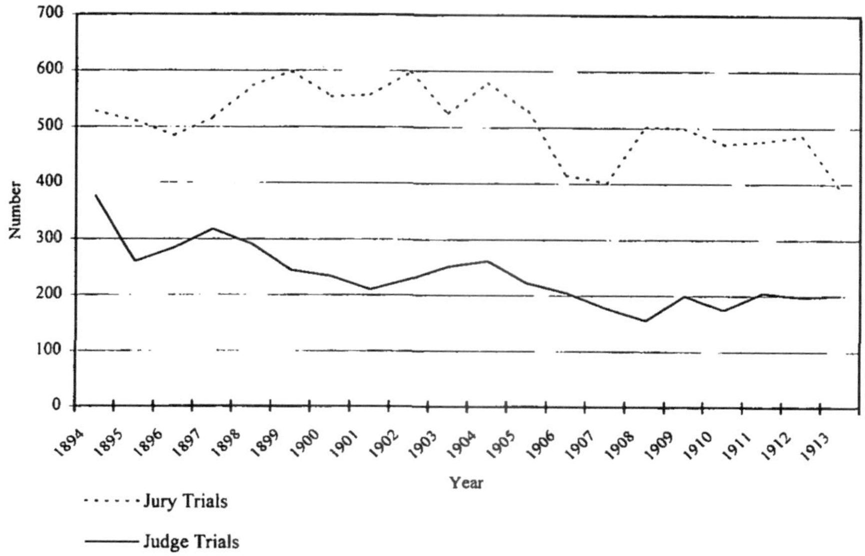

Figure 7 *Nisi Prius* jury trials, 1894–1913

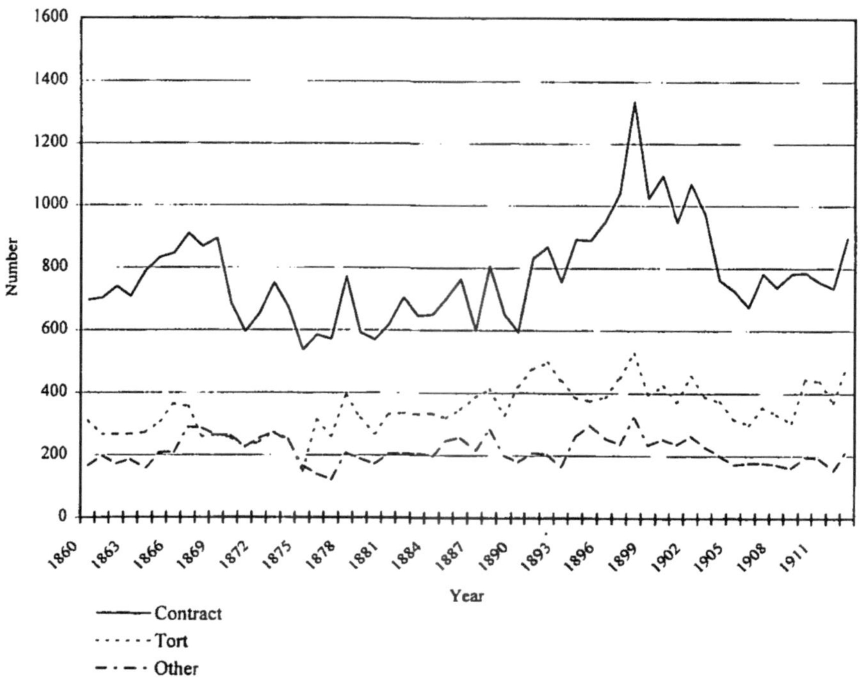

Figure 8 London and Middlesex Civil trials, 1860–1913

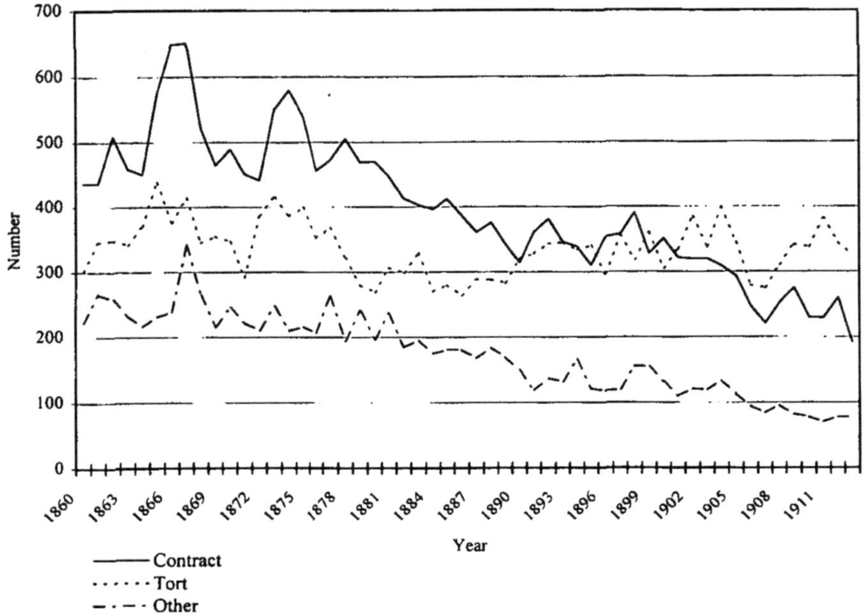

Figure 9 Circuit trials, 1860–1913

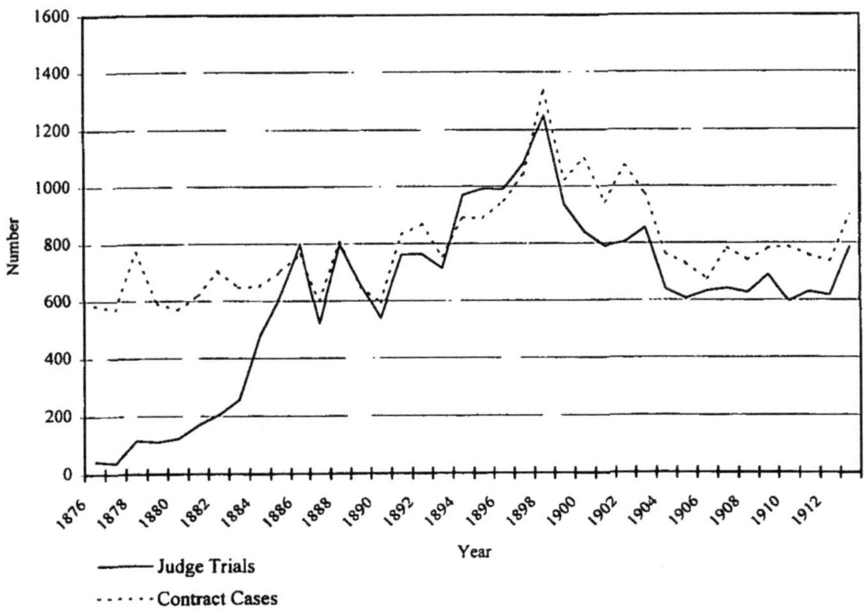

Figure 10 London and Middlesex Civil trials, 1876–1913

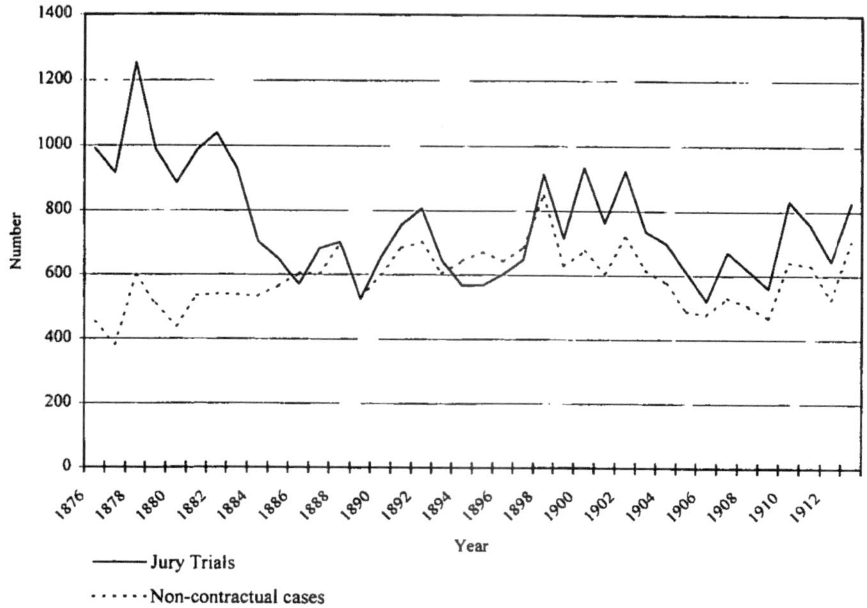

Figure 11 London and Middlesex Civil trials, 1876–1913

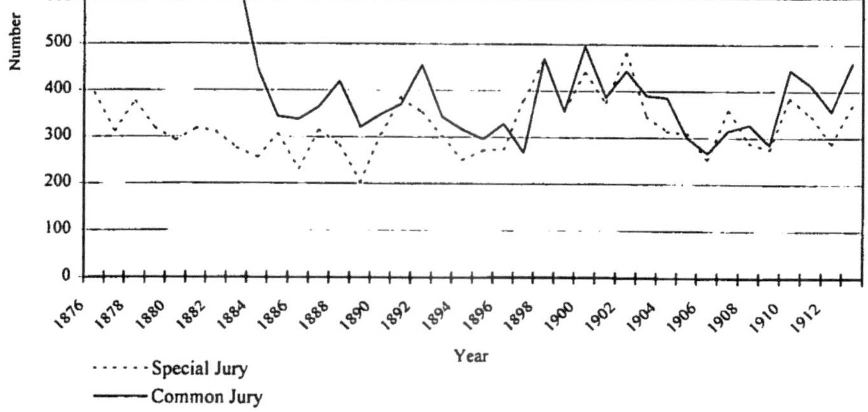

Figure 12 Special and Common juries in London and Middlesex, 1876–1913

11

The Fate of the Civil Jury in Late Victorian England: Malicious Prosecution as a Test Case

JOSHUA GETZLER (OXFORD)*

The history of the criminal law in Victorian England can be portrayed as a struggle between judge and jury over who can best assess the moral culpability of the defendant. Judges mistrusted the instincts of the jury, especially in the more lurid cases;[1] but the ancient principle that life and liberty should depend on the verdict of one's peers remained unchallenged. This essay turns attention to the history of the civil jury, asking how the common lawyers of nineteenth-century England regarded the influence of the lay jury on litigations in property, contract and tort, where fortunes rather than liberty were at stake. The short answer is that the courts all but eliminated the jury from civil trials; but the survivals are instructive, and help explain the motivations for the eviction of the civil jury from the courtroom in the first place.

The decline of the civil jury trial in Victorian England may be regarded as interesting in itself; it may also serve as an object lesson for modern law reformers. Today the constitutionally entrenched jury trial in the United States consumes an average of $14,000 per trial in public costs, and has helped create a notably Byzantine law of civil wrongs.[2] The new Russian

* Reprinted, with minor revisions, from K O'Donovan and G R Rubin (eds), *Human Rights and Legal History: Essays in Honour of Brian Simpson* (Oxford, University Press, 2000), 205–24, with the kind permission of the editors and Oxford University Press. © K O'Donovan and G R Rubin. For helpful discussion and assistance the author would like to thank Roderick Bagshaw, Gerald Fridman, Daniel Klerman, Martin Matthews and the audience at the July 1999 British Legal History Conference in Edinburgh.

[1] A W B Simpson, *Cannibalism and the Common Law* (Chicago, University of Chicago Press, 1984; reprinted Harmondsworth, Penguin, 1986 and London, Hambledon Press, 1994), esp. ch. 9.

[2] J G Fleming, *The American Tort Process* (Oxford, University Press, 1988), 101–39; D W Robertson, "An American Perspective", in B S Markesinis and S F Deakin, *Tort Law*, 4th edn (Oxford, University Press, 1999), 203–37. For the history of attempts to control the American civil jury see A W Scott, "Trial By Jury and the Reform of Civil Procedure", (1918) 31 *Harvard LR* 669; Note, "The Changing Role of the Jury in the Nineteenth Century", (1964) 74 *Yale LJ* 170.

Commonwealth attempted to institute wide access to jury trial in the mid-1990s, but abandoned the experiment when it was found that the jury consumed one quarter of the entire justice budget.[3] Do these modern experiences indicate that the late-Victorian exclusion of the jury was well founded? The costs of mounting a jury trial in a civil law system is another important theme.

THE DETHRONEMENT OF THE JURY BY JUDICIALISING OF DECISION-MAKING

The evolution of English private law has been told before as the story of a long decline in jury power, matched by the rise of the judge who comes to control nearly all significant aspects of the civil trial process. According to this model, there first comes the redefinition of adjudication as the matching of fact to fine-spun doctrinal rules, presumptions and precedents, rather than the refining of relevant fact to put to the jury.[4] Forsyth and Thayer, the great Victorian historians of evidence and procedure, demonstrated how procedural devices such as demurrers to evidence, special verdicts and colourable pleading, combined to squeeze out jury discretion as expressed through the general verdict.[5] Judges thereby enlarged their powers to define and ascribe liability and to fix the level of remedy. Trial issues became issues of law not fact.

The emasculation or diminution of the civil jury was then followed in the second stage by its elimination. A series of court reforms from the mid-nineteenth century, led by the legislature, created a discretion or power to remove the jury almost entirely from the civil trial process. By 1933 it had become sensible to eliminate juries almost entirely because their functions had been denuded.[6]

The dominance of the jury in criminal trials remains, and indeed is enshrined as a foundation of the legal polity. This is because of a perception that findings of wicked conduct occasioning state punishment should be

[3] See further S Holmes and C Sunstein, *The Cost of Rights: Why Liberty Depends on Taxes* (New York, Norton, 1999), 24–8.

[4] Cf. S F C Milsom, "Law and Fact in Legal Development", in idem, *Studies in the History of the Common Law* (London, Hambledon Press, 1985), 171–89; idem, *Historical Foundations of the Common Law*, 2nd edn (London, Butterworths, 1981; hereafter *Historial Foundations*), 296–300, 413–24.

[5] W Forsyth, *History of Trial By Jury* (London, Parker and Son, 1852), 168–91, 259–98; J B Thayer, *A Preliminary Treatise on Evidence at the Common Law* (London, Sweet & Maxwell, 1898) 183–262; J B Thayer, "'Law and Fact' in Jury Trials", (1890) 4 *Harvard LR* 147.

[6] P Devlin, *Trial By Jury* (London, Stevens, 1956 and 1966), 130–3. There are now only some two dozen civil trials with jury in England and Wales per year: M Zander, *Cases and Materials on the English Legal System*, 7th edn (London, Butterworths, 1996), 376–83.

inflicted only through the operation of peer or lay justice.[7] Elsewhere, pockets of strong jury control remain only in those tortious areas with stronger moralistic resonance—as where it is an element of the action itself that the defendant must be found guilty of having had a malicious or wicked state of mind when inflicting the injury. The chief examples are defamation, fraud and abuse of legal process, including false imprisonment and malicious prosecution.[8] In each of these spheres a lay, communal judgment is sought to legitimise the possibility of severe legal and moral sanctioning of the defendant, even though there is no criminal dimension of state punishment.

Controversy in recent years has focused on explaining why the civil jury was diminished outside the areas of crime and some of the intentional torts. In the 1970s, it was powerfully suggested (for example, by Nelson, Gilmore, Horwitz and Atiyah) that the jury was dethroned by elitist judges for ideological reasons.[9] According to this neo-realist interpretation, Victorian judges and jurists looked askance at the jury as a suspect *locus* of populist moral economy and reactionary economic paternalism. Judges could be shown to be influenced by philosophical radicalism and political economy, inclining them to believe in market competition and the natural selection of the economically fit. The argument runs that judges were therefore determined to stamp out the antiquated commercial morality represented by the jury, especially in contract and tort actions. For juries to decide civil law liabilities and so regulate market competition made as much sense to efficiency-minded judges as the old assizes fixing the price of bread. Ideology dictated that the civil jury had to be cut down. Thus did the political economy of the law vanquish the moral economy of the jury.[10]

The ideological explanation equating juries with pre-capitalist nostalgia, and judicial doctrine with free market theory, has attracted detailed and sometimes devastating empirical criticism. Brian Simpson's "line by line refutation" of Horwitz's history of modern contract is justly celebrated.[11] Can anything be saved, then, of the striking theory that juries were eliminated

[7] A doctrine undermined by strict liability regulatory offences—see A S Ashworth, *Principles of Criminal Law*, 3rd edn (Oxford, University Press, 1999), 159–76; A S Ashworth, "Is the Criminal Law a Lost Cause?", (2000) 116 *LQR* 225.

[8] Supreme Court Act 1981, s. 69(1).

[9] W Nelson, *The Americanization of the Common Law* (Cambridge, Harvard University Press, 1975), 165–74; G Gilmore, *The Death of Contract* (Columbus, Ohio State University Press, 1974; 2nd edn with R K L Collins, 1995), 98–100; M J Horwitz, *The Transformation of American Law 1780–1860* (Cambridge, Mass. Harvard University Press, 1977), 28–9, 84–5, 141–3, 155–9; P S Atiyah, *The Rise and Fall of Freedom of Contract* (Oxford, University Press, 1979), 47–9, 210–11, 390–4.

[10] Cf. W S Malone, "The Formative Era of Contributory Negligence", (1946) 41 *Illinois LR* (Northwestern University), 151 at 155–69.

[11] A W B Simpson, "The Horwitz Thesis and the History of Contracts", in idem, *Legal Theory and Legal History. Essays on the Common Law* (London, Hambledon Press, 1987), 203–72; cf. idem, "Innovation in Nineteenth Century Contract Law", ibid., 171–202; J L Barton, "The Enforcement of Hard Bargains", (1987) 103 *LQR* 118.

from the English civil trial in pursuit of market efficiency? An alternative interpretation is to stress a drive to efficiency not in the type of results sought by courts, but rather in their internal procedures of law making. The judges were not seeking to govern the real, producer economy of competitive markets by issuing rational legal rules, but rather were trying to enhance the legal process itself, as a system to enforce the transactions and protect the interests of litigants. Judges and jurists looked askance at the jury because of its high costs in time and money, and also for the imprecision, uncertainty, irrationality and lack of intelligence perceived to infect lay decisions. A jury-based system could not develop precise rules enabling disputes to be determined by actors prospectively without resort to court. By contrast, a judge-based system, stating reasons for assessing fact and developing rulings through repetitive and consistent decision, could provide such hortatory guidance.[12] Juries were therefore targeted, not because they supported a counter-capitalist ideology, but because they could not successfully reason or purpose at all.

The Common Law Commissioners of 1852–1853 may have been expressing the opinion of many judges when they reported to Parliament on the perceived inadequacies of the civil jury:

> "[W]e are not at all blind to the fact that in many instances juries are not so constituted as to ensure such an average amount of intelligence as might be desired . . . in the agricultural districts the common juries are sometimes composed of a class of persons whose intelligence by no means qualifies them for the due discharge of judicial functions. Such persons, unaccustomed to severe intellectual exercise or to protracted thought . . . sometimes pronounce verdicts which bring the institution of juries into disrespect."[13]

Driven by sentiments such as these, judges sought to replace the breadth of jury discretion with more and more elaborate adjectival and substantive law. In 1854 and 1873 statutes permitted reference of matters of account and then "matters requiring prolonged examination of documents or accounts or any scientific or local investigation" to a curial referee.

It was not until 1883, however, that formal rules permitted judges to exclude the jury from civil trials at discretion, wherever matters were formerly dealt with in Chancery or Admiralty without the assistance of a jury, or in matters where a jury could not conveniently make investigation.[14] Even

12 O W Holmes, *The Common Law* ed. by M De Howe (Cambridge, Belknap Press, 1963; 1st edn, Boston, Little, Brown, 1881), 89–92, 98–103; cf. E Thayer, "Judicial Legislation", (1891) 5 *Harvard LR* 172; A L Green, *Judge and Jury* (Kansas City, Vernon, 1930), 268–79.

13 *Second Report of Her Majesty's Commissioners for Inquiring into the Process, Practice, and System of Pleading in the Superior Courts of Common Law*, PP 1852–3 [1626] XL at 701, 708, found quoted in Atiyah, *supra* n. 9, 390.

14 Rules of the Supreme Court (1883) Order XXXVI, Rule 26; P Devlin, "Jury Trial of Complex Cases: English Practice at the Time of the Seventh Amendment", (1980) 80 *Columbia LR* 43 at 95–9. The reform was entrenched by later legislation; see *infra*, text accompanying notes 17–18.

after that important reform, common lawyers could still assail the unintelligent and unguided populism of jury trial. Dicey, for example, wrote a celebrated attack in 1885:

> "Trial by jury is open to much criticism . . . the habit of submitting difficult problems of fact to twelve men of not more than average education and intelligence will in the near future be considered an absurdity as patent as ordeal by battle . . . Juries are often biased against the Government. A technical question is referred for decision, from persons who know something about the subject, and are impartial, to persons who are both ignorant and prejudiced."[15]

Dicey cannot be accepted as a representative common lawyer; his belief in a technocratic rule of law administered by elites was, at base, an anti-collectivist crusade more than an analytical jurisprudential theory. But the ideology of expertise propounded by Dicey cannot entirely be quarantined from the common-law thought of his time.[16]

What was the practical impact of all this anti-jury sentiment? Jackson has estimated that until the 1883 procedural reform, 90 per cent of common-law civil trials were heard before juries; after the reform, the proportion dipped to 50 per cent and then continued to decline. The Juries Acts of 1918–1933 finally decreed that civil trials be conducted without juries unless ordered by the court.[17] Civil jury trials became the exception rather than the rule.[18] Before these reforms, however, and throughout the formative period of the common law of the eighteenth and nineteenth centuries, juries sat on almost all common-law civil hearings;[19] and judges strove to find methods to hem the jury in and curb its decisional power.

In trials dealing with complex and technical matters the judge might deem the lay jury incompetent to assess the evidence and constitute the

[15] A V Dicey, *An Introduction to the Study of the Law of the Constitution* (1st edn, London, Macmillan, 1885; 10th edn, 1959), 394, 398. Dicey also preferred the judge-made law of the professional courts to the legislation of an untutored and shortsighted Parliament: see A V Dicey, *Lectures on the Relation Between Law and Public Opinion in England During the Nineteenth Century*, (2nd edn, London, Macmillan, 1914; 1st edn, 1905), 361–98.

[16] R A Cosgrove, *The Rule of Law: Albert Venn Dicey, Victorian Jurist* (London, Macmillan, 1980). Dicey was more elitist in life than death; he is buried amongst modest Oxford townsfolk and artisans, in St Sepulchre's Cemetery within the site of Lucy's Ironworks, a little north of the University Press in Jericho, Oxford.

[17] The discretion is now stated in Supreme Court Act 1981, s. 69(1), (3) and (4).

[18] W R Cornish, *The Jury* (London, Allen Lane, 1968), 210–42; Devlin, *supra* n. 6, 130–3; R M Jackson, "The Incidence of Jury Trial During the Past Century", (1937) 1 *Modern LR* 132, at 138–43. Jackson's findings must now be reviewed in light of new statistical findings by Michael Lobban suggesting a more gradual decline, "The Strange Life of the Victorian Civil Jury in England", ch. 10 *supra*. Reasons for the resilience of jury trials on the criminal side are anatomised in A A S Zuckerman, *The Principles of Criminal Evidence* (Oxford, Clarendon Press, 1989), 29–46.

[19] Juries never sat in Chancery suits unless the court remitted a factual question for jury trial: see Devlin, *supra* n. 14.

court itself as the fact-finder.[20] But the jury role could be diminished by more subtle means than exclusion. The chief method employed was to engage in more and more judicial fact-finding, in the guise of testing the propriety of pleadings—and then applying formal legal doctrine to the established facts. Juries were thereby reduced to deciding narrow questions of fact as determined by the judges, with a seemingly automatic legal result following from the factual findings. Once the judges could decide which narrow factual questions for the jury were relevant by means of fine-grained legal tests, they, the judges, had won control of the adjudicative process.

There were important exceptions to this general trend, notably the use of special juries to advise the court on some specific area of expertise and so help the court determine which business norms and practices to absorb into legal principle, whether as evidential presumptions subject to rebuttal, or as definite legal rules. The best known instance was Lord Mansfield's liberal use of special juries of merchants to help develop new doctrines of insurance, bills of exchange, promissory notes and other areas of commercial law.[21] However, the traditional use of the special jury, with its valued non-legal expertise, did not contradict the wider swing away from the ideal of the untutored citizen jury as a sure fount of justice.[22]

In order to apply the more elaborate and discriminating judicial tests to fact in the course of determining rights, modern courts were required to sit as tribunals of fact, rather than allow the pleading process to narrow the facts in issue down to a stylized point. English law reports after the 1830s show a marked shift in presentation, as the detailed facts of cases slide away from the pleading statements and counsels' arguments, and resurface in the judicial summation of evidence within elaborate reserved judgments. Courts are now sifting through evidence of the parties' conduct to discover who had acted, at which times, with which state of knowledge. For example, in the important 1839 case of *Arkwright* v. *Gell* dealing with natural property rights, Chief Baron Abinger began his discussion of the case by observing:

> "A special case was reserved on the trial, for the opinion of the Court, stating a great number of documents and facts, upon which the Court are not merely to give their judgment on matters of law, but to take the office of the jury, by determining whether any and what inferences of fact ought to be drawn from the facts

[20] Ibid., 65–95; cf. M Arnold, "A Historical Inquiry into the Right to Trial by Jury in Complex Civil Litigation", (1980) 128 *Pennsylvania LR* 829 at 840–6. The inherent discretion was codified by nineteenth-century legislation culminating in the Supreme Court Act 1981, s. 69.

[21] See J C Oldham, "Special Juries in England: Nineteenth Century Usage and Reform", (1987) 8 *JLH* 148; *idem*, *The Mansfield Manuscripts and the Growth of English Law in the Eighteenth Century*, 2 vols. (Chapel Hill, University of North Carolina Press, 1992), vol. 1, 82–99.

[22] J C Oldham, "The Origins of the Special Jury", (1983) 50 *University of Chicago LR* 137.

> stated. This course leads to one great inconvenience, as it tends to confound the rule of law with an inference of fact only, which inference may have been varied by a very slight circumstance."[23]

This was a special case where the judges formally sat in the office of a fact-finding jury. But the judges' experience of adjudication was not dissimilar where a standard jury did participate. Chief Baron Abinger revealed a growing sense that the courts had bitten off more than they could chew in the field of fact-finding and evidence. Intense pressures on court time, with the heightened litigation of a burgeoning industrial and commercial economy, soon demanded a different style of adjudication and definition of rights.[24]

One solution to this problem was to preserve the common law's concepts of action and intention as the basis of rights, but to simplify them by objectifying the operative intention or consent—what Holmes in *The Common Law* called the "external standard".[25] The final simplification of the law was to allow external standards to predominate over actual intents, agreements, or mind-states of the parties in defining civil rights and duties. The devil only knows the mind of a party; the modern lawyer does not even care to guess, but is interested only in behaviour. This shift allows adjudication to proceed in a more peremptory or summary mode, directly enforcing broad, discretionary policy standards; and in tandem, discouraging parties from litigating chiefly on the basis of instance-specific, detailed factual pleading. Atiyah and Gilmore made much of such trends in nineteenth-century contract doctrine, with Gilmore observing:

> "At the height of the classical period it seemed that it was hardly possible to phrase any contract issue other than as a question of law."[26]

The result of this shift in pleading and proof was a new type of equity in the common law—particular justice and *aequum et bonum* achieved not through fact discretions, but through the working-up of every factual nuance of a case into a discriminating point of law. The Judicature Acts marked a further change by arming the common law with extended interlocutory powers, enabling courts to process still more fact into law. As a result, special pleading no longer served to reduce the wash of significant

[23] (1839) 5 M. & W. 227 at 227–8, 151 ER 87 at 97 (Ex). A similar complaint against conversion of factual inference to *ratio* is articulated in *Harris* v. *Great Western Railway Company* (1876) 1 QBD 515 at 521–3 per Mellor J; at 529–34 per Blackburn J.

[24] Cf. Atiyah, *supra* n. 9, 390–1.

[25] "Objectification" of consent in English legal history is perhaps the leading theme of Holmes, *supra* n. 12; see M De W Howe, "Introduction", ibid., xx-xxvii; H L A Hart, "Diamonds and String: Holmes and the Common Law", in idem, *Essays in Jurisprudence and Philosophy* (Oxford, University Press, 1983), 278, 279–83; M J Horwitz, "The Legacy of 1776 in Legal and Economic Thought", (1976) 19 *Journal of Law and Economics* 621 at 626–628.

[26] Gilmore, *supra* n. 9, 99; Atiyah, *supra* n. 9, 388–90, 405–8.

evidence going into the courtroom. But the Judicature Acts did not initiate these changes; the common-law courts were reaching for a peculiarly doctrinal style of equity long before 1873.[27]

Occasionally this process was noted and decried by the common lawyers. An example was Mackenzie Chalmers who, despite his position as the leading draftsman of codifying commercial legislation of his time, was also a strong partisan of jury trial.[28] In a speech given to the Oxford Law Club in November 1890, Chalmers pointed out that the elimination of the jury had rendered common-law judgments indistinguishable from those of Chancery. By this he meant the use of fine-spun tests sensitive to every nuance of fact attempting to construct legal rules as a set of finely tuned moral standards. Chalmers advocated maintaining the civil jury, it seems, on the grounds that a little intuitive and irrational decision-making by the jury on the edge of bright-line legal rules would help protect those rules from fragmenting.[29] In other words, the Aristotelian equity of the jury protected the common law from the natural-law equity of the Chancery. However, thoughtful pro-jury voices such as Chalmers' were seldom heard in the chorus of anti-jury lawyers of the post-Judicature Act period.

COUNTERSTREAMS TO JURY ABOLITION

It is always useful to look for counterstreams to the orthodoxy: exceptions that probe the edge of a rule. For example, *Rylands* v. *Fletcher* attracts the historian as a new burst of strict liability in a swelling sea of Victorian fault liability.[30] If we look in the right places, evidence emerges that many Victorian judges apart from Chalmers were ambivalent about hastening the death of the jury, and often tried to reverse the decline of the jury in civil trials. This proclivity to favour jury power was not necessarily driven by trust in lay justice; but rather by a perception that a strong jury role was necessary in order to maintain respect for legality and to protect the Bench from accusations of

[27] Cf. M S Arnold, "Law and Fact in the Medieval Jury Trial: Out of Sight, Out of Mind", (1974) 18 *AJLH* 267; Milsom, "Law and Fact in Legal Development", *supra* n. 4, 171–89; J Getzler, "Patterns of Fusion", in P B H Birks (ed.), *The Classification of Obligations* (Oxford, University Press, 1997), 157, 170–90.

[28] See A W B Simpson (ed.), *Biographical Dictionary of the Common Law* (London, Butterworths, 1984), 107–8.

[29] M D Chalmers, "Trial by Jury in Civil Cases", (1891) 7 *LQR* 15.

[30] A W B Simpson, "Legal Liability for Bursting Reservoirs: The Historical Context of *Rylands* v. *Fletcher*", (1984) 13 *Journal of Legal Studies* 209, revised and reprinted as "Bursting Reservoirs and Victorian Tort Law: *Rylands and Horrocks* v. *Fletcher* (1868)", in *idem*, *Leading Cases in the Common Law* (Oxford, University Press, 1995; hereafter *Leading Cases*), 195–226; C Dalton, Losing History: Tort Liability in the Nineteenth Century and the Case of *Rylands* v *Fletcher*, (Unpublished MS, 1987).

moral bias or political ambition.[31] With appropriate mutation we may adapt to the Victorian era Maitland's comments on the thirteenth century:

> "The once popular doctrine which represents the justices as encroaching on the province that belonged to the jurors will not commend itself to students of the . . . century. Neither jurors nor justices had any wish to decide dubious questions."[32]

In the sixteenth century, Sir Thomas More is recorded as complaining that the judges' fear of decisional power was the chief preserver of the inefficient common-law jury system and, what is more, the chief bar to a rational fusion of law and equity with an inquisitorial method of taking evidence. More, as Chancellor, asked that the law courts should exercise their discretion to "mitigate and reform the rigour of the law". But the judges refused, as More later recounted, because "they may by the verdict of the jury cast off all quarrels from themselves upon them, which they account their chief defence".[33]

As the common law developed in later centuries, lively debate continued over the division of the role of judge and jury in civil trials in areas including: the definition of tortious negligence liability;[34] the method for construing terms of documents in contract;[35] the fixing of damages rules in tort and especially in contract, as the action on the case gave damages for loss at large, rather than for a liquidated sum;[36] the finding of reputation-harming statements in defamation;[37] and, finally, the method for determining the ingredients of liability for false imprisonment and malicious prosecution.

[31] Compare the American regard for the civil jury as a constitutionally entrenched institution of the common law: see J C Oldham, "Reconsidering the Seventh Amendment Right to Jury Trial in Light of English Trial Practice of the Late Eighteenth Century", in K O'Donovan and G R Rubin (eds), *Human Rights and Legal History* (Oxford, University Press, 2000), 225–53.

[32] Pollock and Maitland, vol. 1, 631.

[33] W Roper, *The Lyfe of Sir Thomas More*, ed. by E V Hitchcock (London, Oxford University Press 1935), 44–5, found cited in T F T Plucknett, *A Concise History of the Common Law*, 5th edn (London, Butterworths, 1956), 687–8. See further J Guy, *The Public Career of Sir Thomas More* (Brighton, Harvester, 1980); J H Baker, "The Common Lawyers and the Chancery: 1616", in idem, *The Legal Profession and the Common Law. Historical Essays* (London, Hambledon Press, 1986), 205; Getzler, *supra* n. 27, 175–7.

[34] Thayer, *supra* n. 5, 209–10, 241–53; Milsom, *Historical Foundations*, *supra* n. 4, 296–300, 392–400.

[35] *Bartlett* v. *Smith* (1843) 11 M. & W. 483, 152 ER 895 (Ex); *Lewis* v. *Marshall* (1844) 7 Man. & Gra. 743, 135 ER 293 (CP); *Hutchison* v. *Bowker* (1839) 5 M. & W. 535, 151 ER 227 (Ex.); 9 LJ Ex. 24; *Neilson* v. *Herford* (1841) 8 M. & W. 806, 151 ER 1266; J B Thayer, *A Selection of Cases on Evidence at the Common Law*, rev. edn by J M Maguire (Cambridge, Mass. Harvard University Press, 1925), 92–128.

[36] G T Washington, "Damages in Contract at Common Law", (1931) 47 *LQR* 345 & (1932) 48 *LQR* 90; R H Helmholz, "Damages in Actions for Slander at Common Law", (1987) 103 *LQR* 624; R Danzig, "*Hadley* v. *Baxendale*: A Study in the Industrialization of the Law", (1975) 4 *Journal of Legal Studies* 249.

[37] Forsyth, *supra* n. 5, 268–82; R H Helmholz and T A Green, *Juries, Libel and Justice: The Role of English Juries in Seventeenth- and Eighteenth-Century Trials for Libel and Slander* (Los Angeles, Clark Library, 1984); P Mitchell, "Malice in Defamation", (1998) 114 *LQR* 639.

Malicious prosecution is perhaps the least studied of all these. Yet it was a highly significant arena of debate over jury power, regularly attracting the attention of the Exchequer Chamber and the House of Lords in the classical Victorian age. It is an interesting test case for the issue of civil jury jurisdiction, because the appellate courts shifted decisional power uneasily back and forth from judge to jury, and along the way raised many arguments about the role of the jury in modern civil law process. The rest of this chapter describes the role of the jury in actions for malicious prosecution, and from this material looks to extract some general ideas about the role of civil juries.

MALICIOUS PROSECUTION

The action for malicious prosecution is descended from action on the case for conspiracy to abuse legal process.[38] As a tort action it is peculiar in that it requires a *mens rea*, namely malice (a subjective test); and also the *actus reus* of the launching of an unsuccessful criminal prosecution where there was no reasonable and probable cause appearing to the prosecution to justify such an action, either before or during the running of the trial. This last ingredient amounts to a mixed subjective/objective test, similar to that for modern provocation: what would a reasonable man, in the place and context of the actor, have done in the circumstances? A prosecution brought with malicious motive but with reasonable cause was not actionable; a reasonable law-enforcing citizen could well hate the defendant and wish him harm at the same time as bringing a justified prosecution against him. A wholly unreasonable failed prosecution brought without proven malice was not actionable; but extreme lack of reasonable cause could ground a jury finding of malice without more.[39] Outside criminal prosecutions, there were a small number of cases where a failed civil action could result in a tort claim for abuse of process along similar lines, for example, by maliciously proceeding against a foe in bankruptcy.[40]

The combined *indicia* of liability for abuse of process produced an action that was more than usually difficult to define and apply. Judges disliked the action and greatly resented the jury discretions infecting the process, fearing

[38] P H Winfield, *The History of Conspiracy and Abuse of Legal Procedure* (Cambridge, University Press, 1921), chs. 2 & 5.

[39] *Turner* v. *Ambler* (1847) 10 QB 252, 116 ER 98; see also *Hailes* v. *Marks* (1861) 7 H. & N. 56, 158 ER 391 (Ex.); *Johnson* v. *Emerson* (1871) LR 6 Ex. 329; *Shrosbery* v. *Osmoston* (1877) 37 LT 793 (Ex); *Hicks* v. *Faulkner* (1881–2) 8 QBD 167.

[40] *Grainger* v. *Hill* (1838) 4 Bing. NC. 212, 132 ER 769; *Johnson* v. *Emerson* (1871) LR 6 Ex. 329; *Quartz Hill Consolidated Gold Mining Company* v. *Eyre* (1883) 11 QBD 674 (CA); *Cox* v. *English, Scottish, and Australian Bank Ltd* [1905] AC 168 (PC); J F Clerk and W H B Lindsell, *The Law of Torts*, 2nd edn (London, Sweet & Maxwell, 1896), 566, 574–6; J W Salmond, *The Law of Torts*, 1st edn (London, Stevens and Haynes, 1907), 455–68.

that juries would find for plaintiffs freshly acquitted of the initial charge, and thus open up a vexatious avenue of revenge against unsuccessful defendants merely striving to advance their own interests by law. In 1599, for example, a court decried the propensity of "lay gents" of the jury to find for plaintiffs in such actions.[41]

Many judgments hostile to the existence of the malicious prosecution jurisdiction have been made across the centuries, but two stand out. In the great case of *Sutton* v. *Johnstone* in 1786,[42] Lord Mansfield held *obiter* that malicious prosecution ought not to be brought in any case in the wake of an unsuccessfully prosecuted court martial. The civil action ought not to be available to control military jurisdiction because of the need for stern professional discipline in the armed forces, especially during combat. No rule of law squeamishness about the military here; rather the opposite:

> "The salvation of this country depends on the discipline of the fleet; without discipline they would be a rabble, dangerous only to their friends, and harmless to the enemy. Commanders, in a day of battle, must act upon delicate suspicions; upon the evidence of their own eye; they must give desperate commands; they must require instantaneous obedience. In case of a general misbehaviour, they may be forced to suspend several officers, and put others in their places. A military tribunal is capable of feeling all these circumstances, and understanding that the first, second and third part of a soldier is obedience. But what condition will a commander be in, if, upon exercising his authority, he is liable to be tried by a common law judicature? If this action is admitted, every acquittal before a court martial will produce one."[43]

These high policy considerations might be thought to be confined to cases of "national security". But Lord Mansfield held that the final decision as to reasonable and probable cause in all criminal prosecutions, not just courts martial, was reserved to the judge as "a question of law".[44] The courts feared an endless regress of actions following a failed prosecution; to permit a fight over the propriety of that earlier prosecution seemed to create a reverse jeopardy where the accuser was punished. One controlling mechanism was to state that the court would not release all the files of the original criminal trial to the aggrieved defendant, to prevent him or her from commencing a malicious prosecution action in its wake—a device especially resorted to where the court regarded the defendant as unrespectable or unworthy.[45]

[41] *Pain* v. *Rochester* (1599) Cro. Eliz. 871, 78 ER 1096 & 1097.

[42] *Sutton* v. *Johnstone* (1786) 1 TR 492, 99 ER 1215 (Ex. Ch., affd . HL).

[43] Ibid., 549, 1246.

[44] Ibid. at 545, 1244. To like effect: *Busst* v. *Gibbons* (1861) 30 LJ Ex 76.

[45] See D Hay, "Controlling the English Prosecutor", (1983) 21 *Osgoode Hall LJ* 165; D Hay, "Prosecution and Power: Malicious Prosecution in the English Courts, 1750–1850", in D Hay and F Snyder, *Policing and Prosecution in Britain 1750–1850* (Oxford, Clarendon Press, 1989), 343–95.

Our second leading case, that of *Abrath* v. *North Eastern Railway Company*, was decided a century after Lord Mansfield's time, in 1883.[46] In *Abrath* a railway company prosecuted a doctor for conspiracy to defraud by collaborating with an accident victim to exaggerate the injuries suffered in a railway accident in order thus to increase the compensation due. The doctor was acquitted of the charge, but lost his own subsequent action for malicious prosecution. *Abrath* is a modern *locus classicus* for the doctrine, superseded only in 1962.[47] In *Abrath*, Lord Bramwell, like Lord Mansfield before him, put the objection to malicious prosecution actions in terms of the dangers of jury discretion irrationally favouring the plaintiff. He stated that bodies corporate ought generally to be immune to the action for this very reason:

> "[E]very one, or every counsel and solicitor listening to me, knows that the only reason why a railway company is selected for an action of this sort is that a jury would be more likely to give a verdict against a company than against an individual. Everybody knows it; and perhaps there is a sort of hope of confusion; it is said 'the man was innocent; somebody ought to be punished for it; here is a railway company; there was an improper motive;' and so there is a jumble; the case gets before a jury, and a railway company is exactly the party to have damages awarded against it. If ever there was a necessity for protecting persons it is in an action for malicious prosecution, and for two reasons. First of all a prosecutor is a very useful person to the community. We have something in the nature of a public prosecutor, but everybody knows that the greater number of prosecutions in this country are undertaken not by the state but by private persons, or, as in this case, corporations."[48]

Lord Bramwell was prepared to go still further and condemn the existence of the doctrine itself:

> "One may venture to quote Bentham even upon this matter. He said that laws would be of very little use if there were no informers, and that it is necessary for the benefit of the public that people when they prosecute, and prosecute duly, should be protected. And there is an additional reason. A man brings an action for a malicious prosecution; he gives evidence which shews or goes to shew that he is innocent. You may tell the jury over and over again that this is not the question, but they never or very rarely can be got to understand it. They think that it is not right that a man should be prosecuted when he is innocent, and in the end they pay him for it. It is, therefore, all-important that these actions should not be

[46] (1883) 11 QBD 79 (QB); 11 QBD 440 (CA); 11 App. Cas. 247 (HL).

[47] See *Glinski* v. *McIver* [1962] AC 726 (HL) per Lords Denning and Devlin. The more recent House of Lords decision in *Martin* v. *Watson* [1996] AC 74 is confined to the question of when a defendant is responsible for launching the initial unsuccessful prosecution and does not investigate the meanings of malice and reasonable cause.

[48] *Abrath* v. *North East Railway Company* (1886) 11 App. Cas. 247 at 252. Note that in modern times at least, the action was also available against a public prosecutor, e.g. a policeman: *Glinski* v. *McIver* [1962] AC 726 (HL); R Clayton and H Tomlinson, *Civil Actions Against the Police* (London, Sweet & Maxwell, 1992), ch. 8.

permitted to be brought against persons or bodies or others who are not properly liable in respect of them."[49]

It is worth noting that Lord Selborne LC felt compelled to give a second impromptu speech immediately upon hearing Bramwell's, where he made clear that Bramwell's judgment, whilst deserving the usual high respect, was to be regarded by the lower courts as the *obiter dicta* of a solitary judge.[50] We cannot dismiss Lord Bramwell's speech in *Abrath*, however, solely as the maverick view of a violent partisan of railway companies and of economic development generally. Bramwell could hand down decisions hostile to monopoly capital as well as curbing pro-plaintiff juries;[51] and judges with different political commitments and prejudices to Bramwell's also questioned the justifications for sustaining the malicious prosecution action and the extent of the jury's role in the action.[52]

If the judges were wary of the malicious prosecution action, they were not happy to abolish or scale back the action either. The privilege to bring a criminal prosecution or serious civil action against another person was not to be exercised irresponsibly, without let, for the impact on the reputation, credit and peace of innocent defendants could be devastating. So the judges continuously spoke of a balance to be struck between due private prosecution of wrongdoing, and safeguarding the innocent from harassment through abuse of legal process.[53] This was an emergent example of the Diceyan model of control of public powers and functions by the technique of private writs. The malicious prosecution action was (and still is) available against officers of the police—though a good defence is that the police and prosecutorial bureaucracy relied in good faith on information collected from informers and witnesses.[54]

The Victorian courts continuously revised and restated the elements of the malicious prosecution action, with hundreds of actions and dozens of appellate hearings taking place across the nineteenth century. Judges were wont to complain when faced with a malicious prosecution case that the law was so difficult and indeterminate that mis-trial through mis-statement of the relevant law, or inaccurate charging of the jury was almost inevitable.[55]

49 *Abrath* v. *North East Railway Company* (1886) 11 App. Cas. 247 at 252.

50 Ibid., 256.

51 Compare Lord Bramwell's judgment in *Dynen* v. *Leach* (1857) 26 LJ Ex 221 at 223 with that in *Osborn* v. *Gillett* (1873) LR Ex 88 at 94–6.

52 See *Panton* v. *Williams* (1841) 2 QB 170, 114 ER 66 (QB & Ex. Ch.); SC 1 G. & D. 504; 10 LJ Ex. 545 per Tindal CJ; *Shrosbery* v. *Osmoston* (1877) 37 LT 793 (Ex); *Allen* v. *Flood* [1898] AC 1 at 125 per Lord Herschell, at 172 per Lord Davey (HL); F Pollock, *The Law of Torts*, (6th edn. London, Stevens and Sons, 1901; 9th edn., 1912), 324–8.

53 See e.g. *Broad* v. *Ham* (1839) 5 Bing. (NC) 722 at 727, 132 ER 1278 at 1280 per Erskine J (CP); *Haddrick* v. *Heslop* (1848) 12 QB 267, 116 ER 869 per Lord Denman CJ.

54 *Glinski* v. *McIver* [1962] AC 726 (HL); *Martin* v. *Watson* [1996] 1 AC 74 (HL).

55 See e.g. Bowen LJ in *Abrath* v. *North East Railway Company* (1883) 11 QBD 440 at 455 (CA).

The chief problem was to decide the respective roles of judge and jury, first in evaluating the presence or absence of malicious motive, and secondly in assessing reasonable and probable cause. The lack of a reasonable basis for the decision to prosecute could factually imply malice, but need not do so. The presence of malice, however, could not of itself imply lack of reasonable basis, since many reasonable private prosecutions would be actuated in part by a motive of harming or punishing the defendant through process of law.[56] Malice as a legally disqualifying factor was therefore ultimately defined with perfect circularity as a motive that the law did not like.

Sir Herbert Stephen wrote an entire book on this convoluted subject in 1888, claiming in the preface that he had been provoked to write in part by the implications of the decision in *Abrath*. Stephen claimed that, despite all formal doctrinal postures by the judges, the two key mental *indicia* of malice and reasonable cause were entirely within the purview of the jury as issues of fact. The jury's role was to find malice allied to facts that would not support reasonable and probable cause for bringing a prosecution; the judge was then compelled to draw the factual (but not legal) inference that there was a lack of reasonable and probable cause. Hence the judge tended to ratify the jury's basic factual finding as a matter of course.[57]

It was indeed rare for trial judges to overturn initial jury findings in the spheres of malice and reasonable cause. Most appeals went to misdirection, with disappointed litigants claiming that the judge had arrogated too much or too little power to the jury. In one appeal after another the higher judges expressed their dislike of the judicial role as a fact-trier in this area, but attempted no thorough reform. Some light is thrown on this issue by the 1868–70 case of *Lister* v. *Perryman*, where the House of Lords were prepared to concede that the judge of a malicious prosecution action was acting as a trier of pure fact and not law, and could not look to any precedents to help him decide the presence of reasonable and probable cause, nor attempt to confine jury discretion with tests screening the evidence.[58] In that case Lister, a local magnate, caused Perryman, a farmer's son, to be imprisoned and prosecuted for felony, accusing him of stealing his favourite rifle. On the way to the police station Lister himself beat up Perryman, who was later acquitted of the felony. The bruised and unfortunate Perryman then in turn sued Lister for false imprisonment and malicious prosecution without reasonable cause. The factual matter to be tested was whether Lister had been reasonable to rely solely on the hearsay of a servant reporting another's hearsay informing on Perryman. Chief

[56] *Ravenga* v. *Mackintosh* (1824) 2 B. & C. 693, 107 ER 541 (KB); *Hicks* v. *Faulkner* (1878) 8 QBD 167.

[57] See e. g. *Rowlands* v. *Samuel* (1847) 11 QB 39 at 41 n., 116 ER 389 at 390 per Denman CJ; H Stephen, *The Law Relating to Actions for Malicious Prosecution* (London, Stevens and Sons, 1888), v-vi, 28–84, giving an exhaustive treatment of the authorities.

[58] *Lister* v. *Perryman* (1868) LR 3 Ex. 197 (Ex. and Ex. Ch.); (1870) LR 4 HL 535 (HL).

Baron Kelly tried the action and held that as a matter of law there would be no reasonable cause if the jury found as a point of fact that Lister had relied on hearsay alone.

Lister sought review of the trial judge's instructions to the jury as an over-direction. The Court of Exchequer, reviewing the trial, split two-two. Barons Pigott and Bramwell held that there could be no automatic rule excluding a hearsay basis for private prosecution. In Bramwell's words:

> "[I]t is a question of fact for the jury, whether the channels of information were such that the information they conveyed might be reasonably relied upon. Consequently I think there was in this case a misdirection, and that there should be a new trial."[59]

This cogent judgment was trumped by Chief Baron Kelly himself, who sat on the tribunal reviewing his own trial directions and (unsurprisingly) decided that he had been right all along. He stated, in effect, that judges should vigorously control juries and set policy lines in this field:

> "I agree that we should pronounce no decision which could tend to prevent or impede a firm but honest attempt to obtain justice by one who believes himself to be aggrieved; but on the other hand, I feel that our fellow-subjects are entitled to our protection against the imprisonment of their persons, and the disgrace which necessarily attends a charge of felony, where the accuser has no other ground to act upon than that somebody has told him that he has been told by somebody else of something which may be capable of explanation upon inquiry, though, unexplained, it may be calculated to create suspicion."[60]

Baron Channell concurred with the chief baron, giving an equally divided court; and as was customary a *puisne* justice (Pigott B) withdrew his contrary judgment in order to give precedence to the chief justice's opinion. It is worth noting that Chief Baron Kelly had been the successful lead counsel in the important hearing of *Panton* v. *Williams* in Exchequer Chamber in 1841, where an anti-jury judge, Chief Justice Tindal, had insisted that the judge, as a question of law, should tell the jury what factual findings would support a reasonable prosecution, and what would exclude a malicious one. Chief Justice Tindal based that decision on Lord Mansfield's anti-jury speech in *Sutton* v. *Johnstone*.[61]

If matters had rested there, then abuse of process litigation would probably have been subjected in future cases to tight judicial control. But fortunately for legal history, our litigant Lister was not to be defeated so easily, and he took his defence up to a heavyweight Court of Exchequer Chamber. He lost. Mr Justice Byles delivered the briefest of judgments for his brothers Justices Blackburn, Keating, Montague Smith and Lush:

[59] *Lister* v. *Perryman* (1868) LR 3 Ex. 197 at 202.
[60] Ibid, 205.
[61] *Panton* v. *Williams* (1841) 2 QB 170, 114 ER 66 (QB, Ex. Ch.).

> "Where there is a ready and obvious method of ascertaining the truth, and the opportunity of so doing is neglected by the defendant . . . we think the absence of inquiry is an element in determining the difficult question of the presence or absence of reasonable and probable cause. What its weight may be must depend on the circumstances of each particular case, but we cannot say that . . . [Kelly CB] . . . was wrong in saying that the failure to obtain information from [a witness] would prevent the existence of reasonable and probable cause."[62]

Lister fought on to the House of Lords.

The surprise of the litigation was the forceful decision of the Law Lords overturning all three of the lower courts, and affirming the sovereignty of the jury on the question of reasonable cause. Lord Chelmsford stated that in this area the judge had to take the verdict of the jury on questions of fact and then ratify it or not as a question of fact; the judge could not attempt to state his conclusion as a matter of law without provoking a mis-trial. It was an anomalous case of a factual verdict taking place in two steps, divided between judge and jury. Lord Westbury stated that the judge must be careful to decide reasonable cause as a matter of factual, not legal inference, which Chief Baron Kelly had failed to do. Lord Westbury went on to state:

> "I regret, therefore, to find the law to be, that it is an inference to be drawn by the Judge, and not by the jury. *I think it ought to be the other way* [emphasis supplied]. I cannot agree with the Judges in the Exchequer Chamber, for they lay down an abstract proposition . . .. It is impossible to lay down a general rule, and that proposition of the Court of Exchequer Chamber might in future lead to great inconveniences."[63]

Lord Colonsay gave the truly fascinating speech. He also stated that reasonable cause ought to be a jury issue. The learned Scottish lord felt that the English lawyers had got this whole area badly wrong, partly because of the backwardness of their criminal law system:

> "I . . . find . . . myself placed in what is to me the somewhat novel position of having to deal with the question of want of reasonable and probable cause as a question of law for the Court, and not a question of fact for the jury. I have frequently had to deal with cases of this kind in the other end of the island; but there this question of want of reasonable and probable cause is treated as an inference in fact to be deduced by the jury from the whole of the circumstances of the case, in like manner as the question of malice is left to the jury."[64]

He then held that a Scottish jury could fittingly have found for either plaintiff or defendant in the present case on the question of probable cause; this would be a factual finding impervious to curial control save for patent irrationality:

62 *Lister* v. *Perryman* (1868) LR 3 Ex. 197 at 208.
63 *Lister* v. *Perryman* (1870) LR 4 HL 535 at 538.
64 Ibid., 538–9.

"But in England it is settled law that this is a matter for the Court to deal with. The Court deals with it as an inference to be drawn by the Court from the facts, but whether an inference of law or an inference of fact does not, I think, appear from the reports. I do not see clearly whether it is called an inference of law merely because it is left to the Court, or whether it is left to the Court because it is really an inference of law."[65]

The doctrine according this decision to the court rather than the jury was firmly established by Lord Mansfield in *Sutton* v. *Johnstone*,

"Probably . . . from anxiety to protect parties from being oppressed or harassed in consequence of having caused arrests or prosecutions in the fair pursuit of their legitimate interests, or as a matter of duty, in a country where parties injured have not the aid of a public prosecutor to do these things for them."

Lord Colonsay then asked which rules and principles of law existed to guide the court's inquiry: "I did not find that there were any".[66] The authorities dictated that there was properly to be no authoritative guidance, but rather that

"[I]t is a mere question of opinion, depending entirely on the view which the Judge may happen to take of the circumstances of each particular case."

The only extant guiding doctrine was that of Chief Justice Tindal in *Panton* v. *Williams*, which held that the judge must decide how a "reasonable and discreet person would have acted".[67] Lord Colonsay indicated that this was inherently a question suitable for a jury; and if a judge was fated to decide it, he must think as a juryman if he could, not as a lawyer.[68]

Lister v. *Perryman* demonstrated that the division of roles between judge and jury in deciding abuse of legal process was essentially contested territory; and further that at least some of the higher judges favoured a strong or predominant jury role.[69] The majority of the Lords in the later case of *Abrath* were finally content to leave the issue as a question of fact for the sole decision of the jury, monitored only for due weight of evidence by the judge. In a series of appellate decisions that followed, elaborate criteria by which the trial judge could weight the evidence for the jury were supplied;[70]

[65] Ibid. at 539.

[66] Ibid.

[67] *Panton* v. *Williams* (1841) 2 QB 170, 114 ER 66 (Ex. Ch., rev. QB); SC 1 G. & D. 504; 10 LJ Ex. 545.

[68] *Lister* v. *Perryman* (1870) LR 4 HL 535 at 539–40.

[69] H Smith, *Addison On Torts*, 7th edn (London, Stevens and Sons, 1893), 222–9; Clerk and Lindsell, *supra* n. 40 at 564–74; Forsyth, *supra* n. 5 at 284–9; D B Dobbs, "Belief and Doubt in Malicious Prosecution", (1979) 21 *Arizona Law* 607; G H L Fridman, "Compensation of the Innocent", (1963) 26 *Modern LR* 481 at 481–95. For the nineteenth-century American debate see Lawyers' Reports Annotated (LRA, NS), (Rochester, New York, Lawyers' Cooperative Publishing Company), vol. 56 (1915 D) at 72–80.

[70] *Hicks* v. *Faulkner* (1881–2) 8 QBD 167; *Brown* v. *Hawkes* (1891) 2 QBD 718 (CA); *Cox* v. *English, Scottish, and Australian Bank Ltd* [1905] AC 168 (PC); *Herniman* v. *Smith* [1938] AC 305 (HL); *Glinski* v. *McIver* [1962] AC 726 (HL).

by this time, however, such controls of the jury were common enough in mainstream criminal law.[71]

MALICE, PRIVILEGE AND INTENT REVISITED

When doctrine cannot speak clearly, this may be a warning that the policy foundations of the laws in question are not agreed or well understood. It may be concluded that the issues clouding clear judgment in the area of abuse of process went much deeper than the intractable law-fact, judge-jury split. The issues reached into the heart of tort policies in the late-Victorian age.

Here we might look to a grand debate that has run for more than a century in the Anglo-American common-law tradition, concerning the relationship between actionable tort damage and the absolute nature of common-law rights and privileges. The issue is whether rights at common law may be used according to the untrammelled will of the rights-holder, for any motive whatsoever—whether that motive be wholesome and well-intentioned, or immoral and anti-social. At common law (but not in equity) one can generally "abuse" one's substantive property and contract rights through malicious exercise. For example, a property owner may build a "spite fence", or block a view, or cause degradation of water supply to a neighbour, all for motives other than exploiting his own land, such as a desire to harm another for spite, or to subject that other to intense pressure regarding some other interest. *Bradford* v. *Pickles*[72] and *Keeble* v. *Hickeringill*[73] are classic examples of this phenomenon.[74] Likewise, in contract, one can exercise one's rights to hurt another, independent of one's desire to make profit—as with strikes, lockouts and other forms of monopolistic competition, as in the celebrated decisions in *Allen* v. *Flood*[75] and the *Mogul Steamship* case.[76]

Judges and jurists at the turn of the century were fascinated by the general problem of whether intentional infliction of harm invalidated or delegitimated the exercise of rights; for example, a good portion of the fourth

[71] The United States law of malicious prosecution by contrast tends to allocate assessment of reasonable cause entirely to the judge: see S Weiner, "The Civil Jury Trial and the Law-Fact Distinction", (1966) 54 *California LR* 1867 at 1876–94; J W Wade, "On Frivolous Litigation: A Study of Tort Liability and Procedural Sanctions", (1986) 14 *Hofstra LR* 433; W P Keeton et al, *Prosser and Keeton on the Law of Torts*, 5th edn (St Paul, West Publishing Company, 1984), 882.

[72] [1895] AC 587 (HL).

[73] (1707) Holt KB 14 at 17, 19, 90, 90 ER 906 at 907, 908 (one of many extant reports).

[74]. See the elucidation of these last two cases by A W B Simpson in, respectively, *Victorian Law and the Industrial Spirit* (London, Selden Society, 1995); and "The Timeless Principles of the Common Law: *Keeble* v. *Hickeringill* (1707)", in idem, *Leading Cases, supra* n. 30, 45–75.

[75] [1898] AC 1 (HL).

[76] *Mogul Steamship Company Ltd.* v. *McGregor, Gow & Company* [1892] AC 25 (HL).

lecture on tort in Holmes's *The Common Law* of 1881 addresses this issue.[77] Holmes there approved of the English judiciary's conclusion that there was properly no doctrine of abuse of rights in the common law. In this view, to moralise about the exercise of vested legal rights through manipulating discretionary legal remedies was to be resisted as a pre-modern throwback. But, by 1894, in Holmes's important essay "Privilege, Malice, and Intent", the author was himself doubting this theory.[78] He accepted that where one person intentionally damages another through exercise of an undoubted right, the court must perforce balance between two contending right-holders, and the law ought not necessarily permit one right-holder wilfully to injure the holdings of another, at least without a good justification. Typically the justifications for such legal side taking were based on communal expediency, such as to prevent strangulation of markets by unfair competition and monopolism, or to redistribute economic power to the vulnerable.

It has been suggested that Holmes's 1894 theory of utilitarian justification for harms provided the genesis of an articulate legal realism in the United States—that is, a theory of law that is suspicious of the capacity of formal doctrine to provide meaningful or definite answers, and a concomitant favouring of discretionary balancing tests and overt social engineering.[79] Certainly the United States bench accepted Holmes's theory that intentional infliction of harm was a *prima facie* tort that needed some utilitarian policy justification to escape liability; to that extent some version of realism was entrenched in American law.[80] It was an irony that the Supreme Court tended to reject the liberal justifications for competitive harms propounded by Holmes and did not follow him in allowing trade unions the right to strike and so injure their employers' businesses in order to bargain for wages in the industrial market place.[81]

The English courts in the great case of *Allen* v. *Flood* decided against adopting the *prima facie* tort doctrine.[82] Despite campaigns by moralising

[77] Holmes, *supra* n. 12, 104–29.

[78] O W Holmes, "Privilege, Malice, and Intent", (1894) 8 *Harvard LR* 1.

[79] P J Kelley, "A Critical Analysis of Holmes's Theory of Torts", (1983) 61 *Washington University LQ* 681; K J Vandevelde, "A History of Prima Facie Tort: The Origins of a General Theory of Intentional Tort", (1990) 19 *Hofstra LR* 447 at 471–6, 495–7; and M J Horwitz, *The Transformation of American Law 1870–1960: The Crisis of Legal Orthodoxy* (New York, Oxford University Press, 1992), 123–42.

[80] J B Ames, "How Far an Act May be a Tort Because of the Wrongful Motive of the Actor", (1905) 18 *Harvard LR* 411; F V Harper, "Malicious Prosecution, False Imprisonment and Defamation", (1937) 15 *Texas LR* 157; American Law Institute, *Restatement of Torts 2d*, 1977 (St Paul, ALI Publishers, 1979) at §870, comments a-c, e; M A Kotler, "Motivation And Tort Law: Acting For Economic Gain As A Suspect Motive", (1988) 41 *Vanderbilt LR* 63; K J Vandevelde, "The Modern Prima Facie Tort Doctrine", (1990–1) 79 *Kentucky LJ* 519.

[81] Vandevelde, *supra* n. 79, 476–95.

[82] [1898] AC 1.

jurists such as Devlin, Fleming and Finnis in the twentieth century,[83] the doctrine of *Allen* v. *Flood* still commands adherents.[84] What is less often noticed is that the majority of the judges sitting on *Allen* v. *Flood* wanted to attach liability to intentional abuse of contract rights to cause harm and so adopt the Holmesian *prima facie* tort theory. It was a narrow liberal majority in the Lords that rejected the idea, precisely because they mistrusted the jury, especially the prejudices that middle-class juries might bring against insurgent trades unions. This much may be collected from the leading speech by Lord Herschell, who stated:

> "I can imagine no greater danger to the community than that a jury should be at liberty to impose the penalty of paying damages for acts which are otherwise lawful, because they choose, without any legal definition of the term, to say that they are malicious. No one would know what his rights were. The result would be to put all our actions at the mercy of a particular tribunal whose view of their propriety might differ from our own. However malice may be defined, if motive be an ingredient of it, my sense of the danger would not be diminished."[85]

In other words, it was a desire to restrain the class power of the jury as much as belief in the amorality of positive legal rights that led to the rejection of the abuse of rights doctrine in England.[86] But much extant common law—such as malicious prosecution itself—could not easily be fitted into this newly stated, positivist doctrine, as Holmes himself conceded.[87]

It was a bothersome contradiction to hold that, in some areas of life, persons were free to abuse their substantive rights and maliciously or intentionally do down their fellows; yet, in other cases, to enjoin persons from abusing their adjectival rights and mulct them for unsuccessfully invoking the courts to vindicate their interests. The pain of this contradiction was lessened by pushing the test of malicious prosecution and abuse of interests away from the judges and into the sphere of jury discretion. We can see now why English judges, forced to balance between the right to prosecute and the right not to be legally harassed, might tend to favour an enlarged jury sphere

[83] P Devlin, *Samples of Lawmaking* (London, Oxford University Press, 1962), 11–13; J G Fleming, *The Law of Torts*, 9th edn (Sydney, Law Book Company, 1998), at 471–3, 751–3; J Finnis, "Intention in Tort Law", in D G Owen (ed.), *Philosophical Foundations of Tort Law* (Oxford, University Press, 1995), 229, 237–42; and see also G H L Fridman, "Malice in the Law of Torts", (1958) 21 *Modern LR* 484; G H L Fridman, "Malice in the English Law of Nuisance", (1954) 40 *Virginia LR* 583; J D Heydon, *Economic Torts*, 2nd edn (London, Sweet & Maxwell, 1978), 128–30; Markesinis and Deakin, *supra* n. 2, 466–70.

[84] T Weir, *Economic Torts* (Oxford, Clarendon Press, 1997); H Carty, "Intentional Violation of Economic Interests: The Limits of Common Law Liability", (1988) 104 *LQR* 250; for alternative views: D Howarth, "Is There a Future For the Intentional Torts?", in Birks (ed.), *supra* n. 27, 233; R Bagshaw, "Inducing Breach of Contract", in J Horder (ed.), *Oxford Essays in Jurisprudence, Fourth Series* (Oxford, University Press, 2000), 131.

[85] [1898] AC 1 at 118.

[86] See further L H Hoffmann, "*Rookes* v. *Barnard*", (1965) 81 *LQR* 116.

[87] Holmes, *supra* n 12, 112–3; Vandevelde, *supra* n. 79, 457–62.

to try malicious prosecution. Let the jury decide and give no reasons; no light is shed and the contradiction is dimmed.

There were other areas of sharply contentious public policy where judges might seek to evade clear decisional power, either by the technique of enhancing the jurisdiction of the jury, or by constituting the judges themselves as triers of fact, sheltering behind rationally empty tests of reasonableness and interest-balancing. The modern theory (or circular non-theory) of negligence is a prime example.[88] It was rare for explicit tests of social utility to be invented as the Americans did; realism did not suit the English legal mind with its devotion to the sharp separation of law and politics. For these good legal and political reasons, the Victorian judges were not always hostile to civil jury power; indeed, to avoid spelling out the political implications of their work they were often happy to become civil juries themselves.

[88] Cf. Weiner, *supra* n. 71, 1876–94.

Index

www.ingramcontent.com/pod-product-compliance
Ingram Content Group UK Ltd.
Pitfield, Milton Keynes, MK11 3LW, UK
UKHW020832290926
15470UKWH00009B/1858/J

9 781841 133256